The Designbook for Building Partnerships

School, Home, and Community

Mary Ann Blank

Cheryl Kershaw

scarecrow education

The Scarecrow Press, Inc.
A Scarecrow Education Book
Lanham, Maryland, and London
2001
Originally published 1998
Technomic Publishing Co., Inc.
Lancaster, Pennsylvania

SCARECROW PRESS, INC.
A Scarecrow Education Book

Published in the United States of America
by Scarecrow Press, Inc.
4720 Boston Way, Lanham, Maryland 20706
www.scarecroweducation.com

4 Pleydell Gardens, Folkestone
Kent CT20 2DN, England

Copyright © 2001 by Mary Ann Blank, Cheryl Kershaw
Originally published in 1998 by Technomic Publishing Co., Inc.

All rights reserved. No part of this publication may be reproduced, stored in a retrieval system, or transmitted in any form or by any means, electronic, mechanical, recording, or otherwise, without the prior permission of the publisher.

The Technomic edition of this book was catalogued as follows by the Library of Congress:
Main entry under title:
  The Designbook for Building Partnerships: School, Home, and Community

A Technomic Publishing Company book
Bibliography: p. 415
Includes index: p. 423

Library of Congress Catalog Card No. 97-62016
ISBN 978-1-5667-6619-7
Reprinted by Scarecrow Education

™ The paper used in this publication meets the minimum requirements of American National Standard for Information Sciences—Permanence of Paper for Printed Library Materials, ANSI/NISO Z39.48-1992. Manufactured in the United States of America.

Table of Contents

Acknowledgements xi

Introduction and Background..1
   Important Features 1
   Research Support for Parent Involvement 3
   Assumptions About School, Family, and Community Partnerships 5
   Challenges and Barriers to Parental Involvement 7
   Essential Components for Effective Partnerships 11
   How to Use the *Designbook* 16

Design 1: Gathering Perceptions and Collaborating on Results..........................17
   Plan 1.1 Strategies for Gaining Input from Parents and Community Members 22
      Tool 1.1.1 *Building Community–Strengthening Partnerships: Parent Survey* 25
      Tool 1.1.2 *Building Community–Strengthening Partnerships: Community Survey* 28
      Tool 1.1.3 *Guidelines for Gathering Perceptions from "Hard to Reach" Parents* 30
      Tool 1.1.4 *Building Community–Strengthening Partnerships: Parent Survey Tally Sheet* 31
      Tool 1.1.5 *Building Community–Strengthening Partnerships: Community Survey Tally Sheet* 36
   Plan 1.2 Collaborating Productively: Using Effective Decision Making and Problem Solving Process 39
      Tool 1.2.1 *When Should We Collaborate?* 42
      Tool 1.2.2 *Facilitating Collaboration* 43
      Tool 1.2.3 *Facilitator's "Lesson" Plan for Collaboration* 44
      Tool 1.2.4 *Pitfalls to Avoid in Effective Collaboration* 47
      Tool 1.2.5a *Guidelines for Collaboration or "Rules We Live By"* 49
      Tool 1.2.5b *Rules We Live By–Name Tent* 51
      Tool 1.2.6 *Brainstorming* 52

Tool 1.2.7   Challenge (or Opportunity) Identification   53
Tool 1.2.8   Prioritizing   54
Tool 1.2.9   Decision Making   56
Tool 1.2.10   The PMI (Plus-Minus-Interesting) Strategy for Making Decisions   58
Tool 1.2.11   Dimensions of Learning: Decision Making Process   59
Tool 1.2.12   Consensus Decision Making   60
Tool 1.2.13   Problem Solving   61
Tool 1.2.14   Problem Understanding   62
Tool 1.2.15   Problem Solving Worksheet   63
Tool 1.2.16   Thinking About . . . Risk Taking & Creative Thinking   64
Tool 1.2.17   Creative Problem Solving: IWWMW In What Ways Might We . . .   65
Tool 1.2.18   Starburst   67
Tool 1.2.19   Data-based Problem Solving Action Research   68
*Tool 1.2.20   Reflection on Our Collaborative Decision Making or
               Problem Solving   69*

Design 2: Creating a School Environment for Learning..................................71
  Plan 2.1 Creating a Welcoming Atmosphere   76
   Tool 2.1.1   Positive Beginnings   79
   Tool 2.1.2   Putting Our Best Foot Forward   81
   Tool 2.1.3   What School and Student Successes Should Be Highlighted and How?   83
   Tool 2.1.4   Making the School Accessible for Parents With . . .   84
   Tool 2.1.5a   Parents as Greeters   85
   Tool 2.1.5b   Students as Greeters   86
   Tool 2.1.6a   Friendliness Audit   87
   Tool 2.1.6b   Friendliness Audit   88

  Plan 2.2 Establishing a Climate of Cooperation and Acceptance   89
   Tool 2.2.1a   Primary Student School Climate Questionnaire   92
   Tool 2.2.1a   Primary Student School Questionnaire Tally Sheet   93
   Tool 2.2.1b   Elementary Student School Climate Questionnaire   94
   Tool 2.2.1b   Elementary Student School Climate Questionnaire Tally Sheet   95
   Tool 2.2.1c   Student Classroom Questionnaire   96
   Tool 2.2.1c   Student Classroom Questionnaire Tally Sheet   97
   Tool 2.2.2   Parent Classroom Questionnaire   98
   Tool 2.2.2   Parent Classroom Questionnaire Tally Sheet   99
   Tool 2.2.3a   Student Classroom Questionnaire Results   100
   Tool 2.2.3b   Parent Classroom Questionnaire Results   101
   Tool 2.2.4a   Appreciating and Celebrating Diversity   102
   Tool 2.2.4b   Visual   103
   Tool 2.2.4c   Reflections on Diversity   104
   Tool 2.2.4d   Appreciating and Celebrating Diversity   105
   Tool 2.2.4e   Appreciating and Celebrating Diversity: What We Can Do   106
   *Tool 2.2.5   Guidelines for Promoting Trust and Respect Throughout the
                 School Community   107*
   *Tool 2.2.6   Faculty Reflection: Promoting Trust and Respect Throughout the
                 School Community   109*
   Tool 2.2.7   Promoting Positive Social Behaviors: Building Character   110

Tool 2.2.8   Successful Practices for Promoting Positive Social Behaviors   111
Tool 2.2.9   Educators' Guidelines for Helping Parents Reinforce Social
             Behaviors at Home   114
Tool 2.2.10 Letter to Parents   115

Plan 2.3 Ensuring a Safe and Secure Climate for Learning   116
    Tool 2.3.1   Strategies for Collaborating With Parents on Discipline   119
    Tool 2.3.2   Student Discipline Contract   122
    Tool 2.3.3   Assessing Progress Worksheet   123
    Tool 2.3.4   Working With Parents to Resolve Conflicts   124
    Tool 2.3.5   Strategies for Managing Conflicts   125
    Tool 2.3.6   A Process for Working With Parents to Help Students
                 Resolve Conflicts or Solve Problems   126
    Tool 2.3.7   Guidelines for Resolving Conflicts Positively and Productively   127
    Tool 2.3.8   "Win-Win" Confrontation Strategies   131
    Tool 2.3.9   Developing a School Climate That Reduces the Impact of
                 Negative Peer Pressure   132
    Tool 2.3.10 Developing Home Atmospheres That Reduce the Impact of
                 Negative Peer Pressure   134
    Tool 2.3.11 Visuals   136
    Tool 2.3.12 Violence Prevention: Questions for Self-Reflection   139
    Tool 2.3.13 Faculty School Climate Worksheet   140

Design 3: Communicating Effectively 141
Plan 3.1 Understanding and Overcoming Barriers to Effective Communication   146
    Tool 3.1.1   Recognizing Our Perceptual Filters   150
    Tool 3.1.2   The Ladder of Inference   151
    Tool 3.1.3   Skit: Climbing the Ladder of Inference   152
    Tool 3.1.4   Promoting Dialogue   154
    Tool 3.1.5   Improving Interpersonal Communication Skills   155
    Tool 3.1.6   Understanding Differences and Appreciating Diversity   156

Plan 3.2 Keeping Parents and Faculty "In the Know"   158
    Tool 3.2.1   Checklist for Written Communications   161
    Tool 3.2.2   Communication Specs   163
    Tool 3.2.3   Communication Web   169
    Tool 3.2.4   Parent Communication Form   172
    Tool 3.2.5   Communication Extras   173

Plan 3.3 Making the Most of Parent-Teacher Conferences   174
    Tool 3.3.1   Our School's Parent-Teacher Conferences: How Effective Are They?
                 (Educator's Reflection)   176
    Tool 3.3.2   Our School's Parent-Teacher Conferences: How Effective Are They?
                 (Parents' Reflection)   178
    Tool 3.3.3   Initial Letter from Educator to Parent to Schedule a
                 Parent-Teacher Conference   180
    Tool 3.3.4   Follow-up Letter from Educator Notifying Parent of
                 Conference Time   181
    Tool 3.3.5   Details for Successful Parent-Teacher Conferences   182

*Tool 3.3.6   Checklist for Verbal Communications Especially for
             Parent-Teacher Conferences   183*
Tool 3.3.7   Preparing for the Conference: Teacher Worksheet   185
Tool 3.3.8   Comments for Parents to Share with the Child After the Conference   187
Tool 3.3.9   Follow-up Note or Phone Call to Parent(s)   188
Tool 3.3.10 Student-led Conferences: A Positive Alternative   189
Tool 3.3.11 Preparing for a "Challenging" Conference with Parent(s)   190

Plan 3.4 Moving Beyond Report Cards in Communicating Student Progress   192
Tool 3.4.1   Using Parent Focus Groups To Improve Reporting Practices   196
*Tool 3.4.2   Faculty Discussion Guide for Describing the Current Grading and
             Reporting System   197*
*Tool 3.4.3   Faculty Discussion Guide for Assessing the Current Grading
             and Reporting System   198*
Tool 3.4.4   Designing Alternative Report Cards   199
Tool 3.4.5   Reverse/Interactive Report Card   202

Plan 3.5 Promoting Positive Public Perceptions   203
Tool 3.5.1   Communicating School Pride   206
Tool 3.5.2   Getting the Word Out. So—What's So Great About This School?   207
Tool 3.5.3   Students as Ambassadors to the Community   208
Tool 3.5.4   Media Support For Education. Ten for the Future: A Model   209

Design 4: Promoting Supportive Relationships..**211**
Plan 4.1 Reaching Out   216
Tool 4.1.1   Current Practices to Reach Out To Families   218
Tool 4.1.2   How Effective Are Our Practices to Reach Out to Families?   219
Tool 4.1.3   Getting Acquainted   220
Tool 4.1.4   Making the Most of Informal Events   224
Tool 4.1.5   Making the Most of Formal Events: Open House   226
Tool 4.1.6   Making the Most of Events: Performances   228
Tool 4.1.7   Making the Most of Formal Events: Holiday Celebrations   229
Tool 4.1.8   Traditions That Encourage Parent Participation   230
Tool 4.1.9   Going "Above and Beyond" Tactics   232
Tool 4.1.10 Evaluating Formal Events   233

Plan 4.2 Making Connections: *Really* Getting to Know One Another   234
Tool 4.2.1   Parent Information and Interest Inventory   237
Tool 4.2.2   Parent Information Chart   239
Tool 4.2.3   Parent Visits with the Principal   240
Tool 4.2.4   Home Visits   241
Tool 4.2.5   Hosting a Retreat   245
Tool 4.2.6   Guidelines for Creating a Parent Center   248
*Tool 4.2.7a Assuring "Smooth Transitions" to New Schools or
             School Levels   250*
Tool 4.2.7b Transitions: Helping Parents Help Their Child   252
Tool 4.2.7c Transitions: Helping Parents Help Their Child   253
Tool 4.2.7d Ideas for Helping Parents and Students Make Smooth Transitions   254

Plan 4.3 Developing and Maintaining Relationships   256
   Tool 4.3.1   *Parent Networking Strategies   259*
   Tool 4.3.2   *Guidelines for Connecting Parents and Families with*
                  Agencies and Services   261
   Tool 4.3.3a *What Educators and Business Leaders Can Do to*
                  Promote Effective Partnerships   262
   Tool 4.3.3b *Criteria for Successful School and Business Partnerships   263*
   Tool 4.3.4   *School and Business Partnerships: One School System's Ideas for*
                  What Each Can Provide   264
   Tool 4.3.5   *Strategies for Making the School The Hub of the Community   265*
   Tool 4.3.6   *Guidelines for Supporting Members of The School*
                  Community During a Crisis   267
   Tool 4.3.7   *Recognizing and Celebrating Accomplishments   268*

Design 5: Developing Shared Expectations.................................273
Plan 5.1 Understanding Current Needs: Collect, Portray, and Analyze Data   278
   Tool 5.1.1   *Data Collection, Portrayal, and Analysis Results in . . .   281*
   Tool 5.1.2   *Steps in Developing A Database   282*
   Tool 5.1.3   *Potential Data Sources   283*
   Tool 5.1.4   *Data Portrayal: Longitudinal and Disaggregated   284*
   Tool 5.1.5   *Identifying Significant Findings from the Data   285*
   Tool 5.1.6   *Future Trends That Will Shape Our Lives and Our Schools   286*

Plan 5.2 Establish a Vision for the Future   287
   Tool 5.2.1   *How do a Vision and Mission Contribute to a School?   290*
   Tool 5.2.2   *One School's Vision and Missions   291*
   Tool 5.2.3   *PreVision Activities to Identify Important Beliefs and Values   292*
   Tool 5.2.4   *Setting the Stage for Establishing a Vision   293*
   Tool 5.2.5   *Criteria for a Good Vision and Vision Setting Process   295*
   Tool 5.2.6   *Sharing the Vision   296*
   Tool 5.2.7   *Our Vision is Our Shared Responsibility at_____   297*
   Tool 5.2.8   *Aligning Actions and Decisions with Vision   298*

Plan 5.3 Moving the Vision to Action Through Collaborative Long Range Planning   300
   Tool 5.3.1   *Moving the Vision to Action Through Collaborative*
                  Long Range Planning   304
   Tool 5.3.2   *Capitalizing on Strengths and Finding Ways Around Obstacles   305*
   Tool 5.3.3   *Vision   306*
   Tool 5.3.4   *Finding New Alternatives   307*
   Tool 5.3.5   *Planning Guide   308*
   Tool 5.3.6   *Reflection on the Planning Process   309*

Plan 5.4 Reinforcing Learning Expectations   311
   Tool 5.4.1   *Expectation Discussion Guide   313*
   Tool 5.4.2   *Developing a "Can Do" Attitude   314*
   Tool 5.4.3   *Checklist: Are We A "Can Do" School?   315*
   Tool 5.4.4   *Collaborative Goal Setting for Student Growth   317*
   Tool 5.4.5   *Student Goal Setting Worksheet   320*
   Tool 5.4.6   *Reflecting about Possible Goals   322*

Tool 5.4.7   Parent Observation Form   323
Tool 5.4.8   Parent Report Card   324
Tool 5.4.9   Reflecting on Expectations Our Children Hold for Themselves   325
Tool 5.4.10   Being Positive Role Models for Children   326

Design 6: Involving Others Productively 327

Plan 6.1 Increasing Opportunities for Parent and Community Involvement   332
Tool 6.1.1   Here They Come — Ready or Not!   334
Tool 6.1.2   Worksheet for Identifying Possible Roles   335
Tool 6.1.3   Range of Involvement Roles   336
Tool 6.1.4   Involvement Opportunities   337
Tool 6.1.5   Opportunities for Student Involvement   338

Plan 6.2 Maximizing the Potential of Volunteers   339
Tool 6.2.1   Discovering Barriers to Involvement   342
Tool 6.2.2   Barriers To Successful Volunteer Programs and Strategies to Overcome the Barriers   344
Tool 6.2.3   Volunteer Coordinator's Responsibilities   346
Tool 6.2.4   Parent Talent Book   347
Tool 6.2.5   Recruiting Poster   348
Tool 6.2.6a   Educator Need Form   349
Tool 6.2.6b   Parent/Community Member Volunteer Form   350
Tool 6.2.7   Orientation and Training Agenda   351
Tool 6.2.8   Volunteer Contract   352
Tool 6.2.9   Quality Control Measures for the Volunteer Program   353
Tool 6.2.10a Educator Formative Evaluation of the Volunteer Program   354
Tool 6.2.10b Volunteer Formative Evaluation of the Volunteer Program   355
Tool 6.2.10c Educator Summative Evaluation of the Volunteer Program   356
Tool 6.2.10d Volunteer Summative Evaluation of the Volunteer Program   357
Tool 6.2.11   Ways to Recognize Volunteers and Show Appreciation   358

Plan 6.3 Working as a Team   359
Tool 6.3.1   Determining Team Membership   362
Tool 6.3.2   Team Worksheet   363
Tool 6.3.3   Productive Team Behaviors   364
Tool 6.3.4   Potential Roles for Team Members   365
Tool 6.3.5   Guidelines for Productive Meetings: Working Smarter, Not Harder   366
Tool 6.3.6   Succeeding at TEAMWORK   368
Tool 6.3.7   Team Building Strategies: Developmental Activities for Teams   370
Tool 6.3.8a   Teamwork Assessment: Team Member Reflection   372
Tool 6.3.8b   Teamwork Assessment: Team Reflection   373
Tool 6.3.9   Interaction Chart   374

Design 7: Supporting Teaching and Learning 375

Plan 7.1 Engaging Parental and Community Support for Learning   381
Tool 7.1.1   Invitation to a Classroom Visit   383
Tool 7.1.2   A Visitor to Learner-Centered Classrooms   384
Tool 7.1.3   The Value of Cooperative Learning   385

    Tool 7.1.4   Strategies for Involving Individuals and Groups in the Private or Public Sector   387

Plan 7.2 Supporting Learning at Home   389
    Tool 7.2.1   Discussion Guide to Developing a Schoolwide Homework Policy   391
    Tool 7.2.2   Homework   393
    Tool 7.2.3   Student Study Habits Assessment   395
    Tool 7.2.4   Additional Learning Support   397
    Tool 7.2.5   George Washington Elementary School's   399
    Tool 7.2.6   Developing Lifelong Learners   400

Plan 7.3 Promoting Lifelong Learning—"You're Never Too Old to Learn!"   402
    Tool 7.3.1   Topics of Interest to Parenting Adults   406
    Tool 7.3.2   Options for Identifying Adult Learner Needs and Interests   407
    Tool 7.3.3   Suggestions for Facilitating Adult Learning   409
    Tool 7.3.4   Lesson Plan for Adult Learning Sessions   410
    Tool 7.3.5   Meeting Learner Needs Preassessment and Postassessment   412
    Tool 7.3.6   Participant Evaluations of Learning Session   413

Bibliography   415

Index   423

Acknowledgements

As is true in any collaborative effort, many others contributed to the *Designbook* in a variety of ways. We are truly thankful for their assistance. Most of all, we thank our husbands, Kermit and George. Their encouragement and willingness to "go the extra mile" in keeping our families functioning smoothly allowed us to pursue this challenge. We appreciate our valued friends and colleagues who gave us many of the ideas we have included in the book. We especially want to thank Vicki Andrews, an elementary principal, for reviewing our early drafts and providing encouragement and suggestions. We also want to acknowledge those who willingly participated with us as "guinea pigs" in many of the collaborative activities included in the *Designbook*. Finally, we gratefully acknowledge the opportunities given to us by our mentors, Drs. Jerry and Elner Bellon. They have provided us with invaluable experiences in some of the very best schools in the nation. Without their guidance and mentoring, the *Designbook* might still be just another good idea.

Introduction and Background

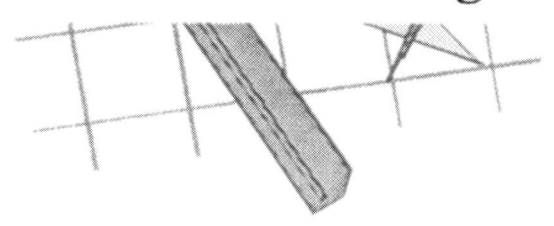

The *Designbook for Building Partnerships: School, Home, and Community* is a guide and a comprehensive summary of innovative ideas for building collaborative school cultures. Its purpose is to provide educators with information and processes to use in creating mutually beneficial partnerships with parenting adults and other members of the school community. The focus extends well beyond the typical attempts at parent involvement to the more significant goal of promoting true collaborative partnerships. The organization of the *Designbook* ensures systematic attention to the essential components of productive partnerships by making each a focus of a chapter, called a *Design*. The research-based components are: gathering perceptions about the school, creating a school environment for learning, communicating effectively, promoting supportive relationships, developing shared expectations, involving others productively, and supporting teaching and learning. Not only are these components of partnerships, they are essential attributes of highly effective schools. Engaging in the processes outlined in the various *Designs* will allow educators to develop their own unique plans for enhancing educator-parent-community member partnerships--specific to the needs and desires of those within the school community.

Important Features

The *Designbook* features the following unique characteristics:

▼ *A parent survey is the book's organizing center.* A survey is provided as a means for educators to gather parent perceptions and to identify needs. Each *Design*, or chapter, also includes a faculty "reflection" to allow educators to compare their perceptions with those of the parents. A survey for community members is also provided and addresses the same components.

▼ *The book is organized according to Designs, Plans, and Tools.* While the survey is valuable in itself, the major benefit of the *Designbook* is the guidance it provides to educators as they address needs it identifies. Each component addressed by the survey is a chapter in the book, called a *Design*. Each *Design* provides a detailed description of the component, a rationale for its importance to the partnership, guidelines for developing it to its "ideal state," and specific responsibilities of educators and parents. *Plans* and *Tools* are provided for each *Design* to guide collaborative efforts. These *Plans* and *Tools* are a compilation of strategies, activities, guidelines, real-world scenarios, checklists, reproducible forms, and supplementary information gathered from an extensive research and experience data base. Each *Tool* was included because it met important criteria of worth, feasibility, and impact and because it represents what is considered to be "best practice." It is not suggested that each *Plan* and *Tool* be used, but rather that educators consider them as options as they develop their own unique designs.

▼ *Shared responsibilities are a priority.* The "Shared Responsibilities" section of each *Design* illustrates the joint obligations that are critical for each of the components of effective partnerships. These responsibilities provide direction for collaborating productively for the collective good.

▼ *Partnership plans can be tailored to each school.* The survey allows a school to assess the current state ("what is") and then to pursue numerous options in designing unique plans for involvement ("what ought to be"). *Designs, Plans,* and *Tools* are available to guide collaborative efforts, but have been developed in a way that promotes their adaptation to each individual context.

▼ *Research is translated into practice. Plans* and *Tools* encourage a high degree of interaction and collaboration. They are "user-friendly" applications of the research on parent involvement, effective parenting, and the quality of school life.

▼ *Specific procedures and considerations are provided for each Design. Designs* and *Plans* provide guidelines, cautions, and processes, rather then recipes. Educators are encouraged to adapt the suggested procedures and processes to their own needs.

▼ *Real-world examples illustrate successful practices.* The book is filled with hundreds of strategies, ideas, and scenarios that have been shared by many effective schools across the country. They have been incorporated into *Tools* that can be used to implement each *Design* or *Plan*.

▼ *Reproducible pages are provided to facilitate the use of the Designbook. Designs, Plans,* and *Tools* can be used "as is" or as a model for adaptation.

The *Designbook* developed out of our work with educators and parents at all school levels on school improvement and renewal efforts. Regardless of the particular focus of our work or the section of the country, our conversations with educators quickly turn to their distress over the lack of parent support and its impact on their overall effectiveness. Educators express this dilemma in many different ways, but it adds up to a great deal of exasperation, pessimism, and indecision about how to improve the situation. In working with parents (and being parents ourselves), we know of the frustrations on the other side as well. From either perspective, the major challenge appears to be in identifying how to work together most productively and finding the most appropriate ways to engage each other in the process. While the challenges are significant, we have seen that in most situations they can be successfully overcome.

In addition to our experiences in the field, much of our research for the past thirteen years has been on the Quality of School Life (QSL). We have worked with over sixty schools in six states on analyzing the school's culture and using the information that is generated to guide school improvement efforts. The QSL process involves gathering and comparing the perceptions of all groups within the school community: teachers, students, parents, support personnel, and administrators. From our QSL experiences, we have gained insight into the conditions within schools that are important to parents and those areas that generate feelings of satisfaction or distress. A great deal of our consulting efforts have also been directed toward assisting school personnel in addressing the findings of the QSL studies. The *Designbook* is a refinement and extension of our QSL work.

The *Designbook* is our attempt to combine what we have learned from our experiences in schools and our knowledge of relevant research on parent involvement, school improvement, and learning organizations. The *Designbook* is not a recipe or a quick fix approach and does not promote random, sporadic improvement efforts. Instead, it is a "we're in this together for the long haul" approach that involves a great deal of professional and parental input and shared decision making. The resulting partnerships can generate a high level of commitment and ownership as educators and parents work together to build a sense of community and shared responsibility within schools.

The *Designbook* is about building partnerships. We see partnerships as mutually beneficial relationships. They are interdependent, meaningful connections among individuals and groups. These relationships and connections are critical to developing a sense of community and shared responsibility within our schools. According to John Gardner (1989), distinguished professor and noted authority on leadership, "where community exists it confers upon its members identity, a sense of belonging, and a measure of security" (p. 73). He has provided for us a vision of what vital, healthy school communities can be. He says that "Most Americans who endorse the idea of community today have in mind communities that strive to exemplify the best of contemporary values, communities that are inclusive, that balance individual freedom and group obligation, that foster the release of human possibilities, that invite participation and the sharing of leadership tasks" (p.75). Gardner believes, as we do, that schools can become communities in the best sense of the word. They do not have to be "simply geographical locations where young people spend a certain number of allotted hours performing required activities" (p.75). They can be a force that acknowledges differing perspectives, pulls individuals and groups together, and energizes them to reach for common ground.

We have found that partnerships can be the foundation for building true communities. When they are well designed, regularly nurtured, and systematically maintained, they can foster deep and lasting relationships. We have seen that educators and parents respond willingly and often eagerly when opportunities for involvement are based on sharing of important perspectives and addressing common interests or concerns.

Research Support for Parent Involvement

From the volumes of research, there is no doubt about the benefits of parent involvement on the academic, personal, and social development of children. The importance of parent involvement in helping children in the educational experience has long been recognized. The term "parent involvement" was first used to denote the practice of increasing parents' participation and planning in schools as a part of Project Head Start in the 1960's (Ziegler & Styfco, 1993). Since that time, there have been numerous studies that document the specific effects of parent involvement, the conditions that promote it, and suggested activities and guidelines.

Conclusions overwhelmingly point to parent involvement as a key to optimal student achievement. Studies consistently show that when parents are involved and demonstrate a desire for their children to succeed in school, students perform better academically (Jesse, 1996; Kaplan 1992; Cutright, 1990; Cotton & Wikelund, 1989). The more intense the involvement, the greater the effects. This is especially true during the early years of schooling. According to Cotton & Wikelund (1989), "the earlier in a child's educational process parent involvement begins, the more powerful the effects will be" (p.3). Educators have long known of the critical role of the home and family environment in determining a child's success in school. Researchers assert that parents are the one continuous force in the education of their children from infancy to adulthood. Although much of the research has focused on young children, additional studies show that parent involvement remains very beneficial in promoting positive achievement and affective outcomes with older students. While there are many valid reasons for the increased challenges of maintaining a high level of parent involvement in middle and high schools (e.g., larger schools farther from home, sophisticated curriculum, multiple teachers, and students' developing sense of independence and separation from home), these challenges can be overcome or minimized when educators and parents join forces. Studies have also documented the important contributions of parents of disadvantaged and minority students. These parents can and do make significant differences when they are involved, but they are often under represented in schools (Comer, 1984). A strong conclusion that cuts across studies of students of all ages, ability levels, and socioeconomic backgrounds is that "all types of parent involvement work and work well" (Cotton & Wikelund, 1989, p.4). It appears that some, even minimal, involvement is better than none.

Parent involvement is also linked to other beneficial outcomes. Improved student attitudes toward peers, school, and particular subjects; improved social behavior; enhanced self-concept; improved classroom behavior; increased time spent on homework; higher expectations for one's future; increased motivation; and reduced absenteeism and retention rates have been identified as results of parents taking an active role in their child's education (Henderson & Berla, 1994; Cotton & Wikelund, 1989). Educators themselves experience benefits when parent involvement is strong. The better the rapport with parents, the greater the support with learning expectations, activities, and projects (Cotton & Wikelund, 1989). Likewise, when parents are involved, their self-concept is generally enhanced when they realize their contributions are valued and their efforts are making a difference.

Educators and parents alike perceive a need for greater parent involvement. Teachers ranked "strengthening parents' roles in their children's learning" as the issue that should receive the highest priority in public education policy over the next few years (Jesse, 1996; U.S. Department of Education, 1994; Louis Harris & Associates, 1993). In addition, a 1993 Metropolitan Life survey of teachers concluded that U.S. schools could be greatly improved if parents were encouraged to be more visible in their children's education (Jesse, 1996). Like educators, parents express their desire to be more active in schools and in their child's education. In *Strong Families, Strong Schools* (1994), it was reported that 40% of parents across the country believe that they are not devoting enough time to their children's education (Finney, 1993). According to *Reaching All Families,* a publication of the U.S. Department of Education, "parents, regardless of their background, want guidance from schools on ways to help their children learn better. Thus parents look to schools for help even if they do not or cannot make the first contact themselves" (Moles, 1996, p. 1).

Students have also expressed their desire for more parent involvement. It was recently reported that 72% of students aged 10-13 said they would like to talk to their parents more about their schoolwork. In addition, 48% of older adolescents (aged 14-17) agreed with their position (U.S. Department of Education, 1994; National Commission on Children, 1991). In today's world students have an increasing need for stability in their at-home experiences. Having a parenting adult take an interest in their learning and providing the needed encouragement and support are crucial to the child's developing to his or her full potential.

In addition to those most directly affected by schooling, voices from the business sector support the need for greater parent participation in their child's education. Researchers have determined that nearly ninety percent of company executives perceive a lack of parent involvement as the biggest obstacle to school reform (U.S. Department of Education, 1994; Perry, 1993). The business sector needs potential workers who have developed positive attitudes about lifelong learning, have strong self-concepts, are critical and creative thinkers, and have become self-regulated learners and workers. They have found that employees who possess these traits and who have the attitude and desire to learn can successfully benefit from any additional training they receive on the job. These are outcomes that educators and parents, working together, are more likely to achieve than if it were just "left to the teachers."

Schools as organizations also are positively affected when parents are more actively engaged. Epstein (1987) reports that parents are an essential element in effective schools--and they must be involved in a variety of ways. Schools that are able to design opportunities that mobilize the talents and energy of parents and community members are using their available resources to their fullest potential.

Unfortunately, there is a tremendous discrepancy between "what is" and "what ought to be" when it comes to parent involvement. Its importance and lack of uniform effectiveness made it a targeted national goal (U.S. Department of Education: Goals 2000). According to Hamby (in Kaplan, 1992), "Although they have cooperated with each other on some tasks, the home and school have traditionally gone about their business with no more than a nodding acquaintance of each other's roles. Given the magnitude of youth problems in modern society, however, this situation must change if progress is to be made. Home-school collaboration is the key to unlocking the doors to future success for young people in today's complex world" (p. 58). The goal of the *Designbook* is to enhance existing parent involvement efforts and to encourage new ones to promote this critical collaboration.

Assumptions About School, Family, and Community Partnerships

Several important assumptions underlie strong partnerships. We believe that partnerships designed to reflect these assumptions will have a greater potential for success. Therefore, it is important to consider them in developing new partnerships or enhancing existing ones.

▼ *True communities and strong partnerships are highly desirable for both parents and educators.* Parents want their children to be in good schools and educators want to provide those schools (Jesse, 1996). There is a felt need on both sides. When the focus of the partnership remains on what is best for children, the collaboration can result in the best possible environment for learning. While positively impacting students, the partners are also enhancing their own feelings of belonging, trust, and respect as they carry out their shared responsibilities.

▼ *For the partnership to be strong, there must be a commitment on both sides and a willingness to fully understand the diversity of perspectives within the school community.* Productive partnerships do not tolerate finger pointing and blame. Members learn from one another and develop shared expectations. They realize that no one person has all the answers, but that the solutions to the challenges of the school community can be found within the members of the community. By working together, they can design creative and feasible solutions to problems that initially seem intractable. An important and stimulating synergy develops when committed individuals collaborate to achieve a common goal.

▼ *Leadership is critical to strong partnerships.* Educators should provide leadership by initiating partnership activities and maintaining control over them. Schools cannot wait for parents to come to them. Educators are the professionals; parents are the supporters. Educators have an understanding of what it takes to be a fully functioning community and can reach out to others in providing the essential conditions. Educators are not the only ones responsible for maintaining an appropriate learning environment, but they are the leaders in seeing that it is done. Parents also have responsibilities, but they are not the ones in charge. Strong building level leadership is also critical to initiating partnerships and sustaining the momentum as they develop.

▼ *The success of school efforts at developing parent partnerships rests on effective planning, monitoring progress, and celebrating results.* It will not happen without plans. Educators must ensure continuity in parent involvement partnerships--making a commitment and ensuring follow through. Strong partnerships evolve out of a planned approach, clear policies, visibility, and recognition for the program and parents' involvement.

▼ *Diversity and inclusiveness in partnerships are highly prized.* The goal of partnerships is to encourage all parents, care givers, extended family members, and community members to be supportive of children and education. Partnerships actively invite *all* to be involved to the extent possible. Potential members have their own unique talents, resources, and energy to bring to the collaboration. A major task in building partnerships is to identify significant ways to capitalize on the diverse interests and talents throughout the school community.

▼ *For parent involvement partnerships to be successful, there should be numerous connections and a range of opportunities rather than single, isolated activities or events.* They should address the needs of the hard-to-reach, disadvantaged, and single working parents as well as those who are typically active supporters. In order to use all available resources (individuals, agencies, businesses, etc.) to the fullest, the opportunities need to extend beyond the walls of the school building. If the efforts are successful, the result is a community wide support system for the children.

▼ *All contributions to the partnerships are valued equally.* Studies of individual families show that what the family does is more important to student success than any other variable. This is true whether the family is rich or poor, whether the parents completed high school or not, or whether the child is in preschool or in the upper grades (U.S. Department of Education 1994). In all school communities, the number of nontraditional families is increasing. Alternative family structures can be effective and should be recognized as such (Jesse, 1996).

▼ *Strong partnerships should build the capacity of all individuals involved.* There may be initial personal risks, but partners who maintain a positive attitude and a willingness to learn will ultimately feel more capable and confident. As they acquire new knowledge, skills, and attitudes, they improve their ability to function independently and to contribute productively to the partnership. As a result, they also experience increased feelings of efficacy. Partnership activities should not be seen as additional burdens on educators, but as opportunities for all to learn and grow to be the best they can be.

▼ *Barriers to building strong partnerships should be recognized and acknowledged.* Issues of turf, territory, and blurred roles and responsibilities should be dealt with at the outset. It is important to maintain the focus on turning obstacles into opportunities--or at least to finding ways around them. In fully functioning partnerships, strategies are developed to overcome these obstacles as partners strengthen their abilities to communicate, make decisions, and resolve problems. Their continual search for common ground results in a workable, two-way support system. When the barriers are not acknowledged and addressed, there is no chance of overcoming them and building the types of partnerships that can enhance the educational experiences of their children.

▼ *Partnerships will be designed in different ways for each school depending on the specific needs and desires of those within the school community.* As Jesse (1996) reports, "there is no one best way for schools to effectively engage parents in the achievement of their children. Each school and its community will have to develop, test and refine their own strategies" (p.3). Each partnership will be unique, but will also exhibit certain commonalities that exist in all effective programs.

Challenges and Barriers to Parental Involvement

Numerous research studies have identified the most common barriers to productive parent involvement and strong partnerships. Among the most often cited are:

▼ *Perceptions that the school environment is not supportive of parents.* There are parents who report that they do not feel welcome at their child's school. Some view educators with suspicion and distrust. For those who have previously had bad experiences with schools or educators (even during their own school years), anything associated with school may be intimidating. Those whose initial contacts with educators during a school year are not perceived as productive are far less likely to try a second time. Furthermore, school personnel sometimes contribute to the problem without realizing it. If they do not make an effort to "go out of their way" to help parents feel welcome or do not communicate frequently with them, parents often feel that their input and involvement is not valued. If their communications or interactions with parents relate primarily to problems or concerns, parents feel that they focus only on the negatives of their child's behavior or performance rather than the positives (Liontos, 1992). If they do not assure that the school is "family friendly," the public's perception of the school as a barrier to parent involvement is reinforced (Moore, 1991).

▼ *Logistic, cultural, and language barriers.* The "distance between parents and teachers" is a challenge to parent involvement. This distance could be due to physical, cultural or language, class, gender, or psychological situations that emphasize the separation of home and school (Henderson & Berla, 1994). Logistically, parents' work sites and schedules make school meetings difficult to attend. Several researchers suggest that race, economic, and class differences can make the gap even greater (Rigsby, Reynolds, & Wang, 1995; Moore 1991; Chavkin & Williams, 1989). According to Moles (1996), this must not be mistaken by educators to mean that these parents are disinterested in their child's education, despite the fact that they may not be easily involved. To make matters worse, it is difficult for educators and parents alike to overcome ethnocentrism (the tendency to regard one's own culture, ethnic group, or nation as better or more correct than others). This lack of understanding of other cultures may lead to false stereotyping, misunderstanding, and lack of appreciation (Rigsby, Reynolds, & Wang, 1995; Claremont Graduate School, 1993). This barrier also impacts students' social and academic success. Students encounter more adjustment problems at school when there are inconsistencies between their school and home contexts.

▼ *Time and lack of other resources.* The lack of time and money are major barriers to parent involvement (Liontos, 1992). Many parents reluctantly admit that they do not have enough time to focus on their child(ren)'s education. Teachers have difficulty finding more minutes in the day to plan activities to encourage greater parent participation. While both groups indicate a desire and a need for more involvement, they also know that they have only so much time and energy. Both are forced to make decisions about how to spend this limited resource wisely--where they will make the most difference. At the same time, many schools are faced with decreasing financial resources which may curtail their parent involvement efforts. Limited family incomes and resources are another factor. At a very basic level, many families have difficulty with transportation and child care (Henderson & Berla, 1994). Without adequate resources, they also have restricted access to libraries, cultural institutions, and recreation which adversely impacts their participation in some parent involvement activities (U. S. Department of Education, 1994).

▼ *Uncertainty about what to do.* Anxieties and feelings of inadequacy are common to both educators and parents. Many parents express uncertainty about their own importance and seem to lack a healthy level of self-worth when it comes to interacting with school personnel (Liontos, 1992). Parents in this category are shy and embarrassed by their lack of "know how" and feel uncomfortable expressing a need for help. Other parents suggest that they would be willing to spend more time on activities with their children if teachers gave them more guidance. They would also be more willing to volunteer if they were given more meaningful work that utilized their talents or abilities. At the same time, teachers also need guidance since few have had any formal preparation or training in how to involve parents productively. According to Moore (1991), they may be falsely guided by limited views of parent involvement. Their own experiences or training may have led them to define parent involvement as sending in forms and appearing at "Open House" and parent conferences. Some teachers also express doubt about being able to work effectively with at-risk students and their parents.

▼ *Pessimistic expectations about what can be accomplished.* Negative beliefs, perceptions, and attitudes of teachers, administrators, and parents about the value of parent involvement is a major barrier. There are "mistaken beliefs" on both sides. Some educators perceive parents to be disinterested and apathetic and many of them can cite example after example to substantiate their beliefs. Repeatedly trying to reach parents who do not return notes or telephone calls and rescheduling meetings missed by parents are just two of many frequently mentioned complaints. Others believe that encouraging parent involvement is too time consuming and is one more responsibility added onto an already demanding workload. At the same time, some parents add credibility to these beliefs. Some do not even respond to teachers' requests for help. Many say that they are willing to help, but then fall short of their commitment. Some are also guilty of promoting negative expectations by exhibiting "leave it to the school" or "it's the teacher's job" attitudes (Liontos, 1992).

▼ *Lack of mutual understanding.* When parents experience being "talked at, but not really listened to," hearing primarily negative reports about their children, or learning about problems when it is too late to do anything constructive about them, they interpret the teacher's actions in a variety of ways. Some view the teachers as disinterested, uncaring, or unwilling to take the time to really understand the obstacles the child or family faces. Others feel that the teachers do not value the information they have about their children or do not think that parents really know what is best for their children. In many cases, well meaning educators are unaware of the impact that their words or actions (sometimes inactions) are having on their "receivers." Many parents also realize that they do not know "what is going on" at school and desire more reliable and frequent information, especially when they typically hear only one side of the story from their children. Understanding is also hampered when either parents or educators do not feel that they can be open and honest in sharing their perceptions. Parents are sometimes reluctant to contact teachers with concerns or complaints. They fear being labeled as meddlesome and do not want their actions to make matters worse for their child. Educators in the parenting role are also careful not to intimidate their child's teacher with their own knowledge or expertise. Many parents also fear that sharing important information may reveal personal problems at home or their inadequate parenting skills. Some equate their child's failure with their own shortcomings as parents and, therefore, avoid situations where problems or failures are discussed. At the same time, educators fear overstepping their boundaries and are afraid of creating an adversarial relationship with parents by sharing true concerns or suspicions. They are reluctant to tell parents anything that may be interpreted as an affront to their parenting skills. They are even more unwilling to say too much if they feel that parents are putting too much pressure on their children. They will avoid making an important suggestion if they feel that it may only add to the pressure or may cause the parent to overreact and escalate the situation.

▼ *Personality differences.* Parents and educators are people with their own unique styles and ways of relating to others. Unfortunately, there are some parents and educators, hopefully very few, who are simply not "joys" to work with. Irritating personal characteristics, lack of interpersonal skills, unpleasant attitudes, aggressiveness, and defensiveness can be descriptors of either group. When they exist, they are impediments to developing supportive relationships.

▼ *Decreasing parent involvement as students approach adolescence.* As students advance to the middle and high school levels, parent involvement typically decreases. Teachers have so many students on their rolls that maintaining personal relationships with all of their parents is unrealistic. Parents sometimes feel overwhelmed and intimidated at having to get to know five or six teachers each year. It is especially difficult for some parents to face a teacher conference with all of the teachers at one time. This is a real challenge for secondary schools. Students are becoming increasingly more independent at a time when parents are less likely to be involved. This creates a gap that is not healthy for students, parents, or teachers. As students transition from elementary to middle school it is especially important to get their parents involved and to sustain their interest and involvement. The challenge is to find appropriate ways to engage them so they can feel they are contributing positively to their child's success.

▼ *Unclear expectations about parent involvement.* Schools have been accused of taking a passive role and not providing needed guidance to promote parental involvement (Liontos, 1992). This has been attributed to a lack of planning and unclear policies and guidelines. At the same time, confusion about the roles and responsibilities of teachers and concerns about "territory" and "turf" compound the problem.

▼ *Unfulfilled responsibilities leading to resentment.* Some families are not fulfilling their basic parenting responsibilities. According to Epstein (1987), the basic obligations of parents are to provide food, clothing and shelter; to ensure health and safety; to provide child rearing and home training; to provide school supplies and support for homework; and to build home conditions for learning. Educators feel helpless when students come from dysfunctional home environments where parents do not assure that they have the basic prerequisites for learning. On the other hand, some parents feel that educators are not doing their part. Families that are struggling to exist, those trapped at Maslow's survival level, often feel that school personnel are not doing all they can to link them with family assistance programs or to help them fulfill their parenting obligations (Epstein, 1987).

The *Designbook* is an attempt to find ways around these barriers. There is a tremendous need in schools to translate obstacles into opportunities, to identify strategies to address the challenges, and to find common ground between educators and parents. Once common ground is established, both "partners" soon become aware that many of the identified barriers may be real, but others are only imagined. There are ways to deal with the real barriers once the perceived ones are out of the way.

Essential Components for Effective Partnerships

Partnerships enhance a sense of belonging and commitment throughout the school community. As school personnel focus on developing partnerships, they are actually strengthening and mobilizing their school communities. We understand that today's communities are not like those of old. They are different, but no less valuable. Unlike traditional communities that have generations of history and continuity, contemporary communities must continually strive to fully develop their shared culture. As Gardner (1989) points out, strong contemporary communities have many desirable qualities that contribute positively to partnership activities. Many communities are heterogeneous, pluralistic, and inclusive. They embrace the challenges of constant change and threats from the outside world. They attempt to generate feelings of wholeness rather than segmentation, to form networks of responsibility, and to generate shared values and commitment to the community. Building strong communities in today's world requires much more effort than it did in the past. It requires a plan that places it as a priority.

The *Designbook* will assist schools in developing partnerships or enhancing those that already exist. It recognizes that each school's plan to achieve this goal will be unique, based upon the unique needs of the community it serves. It incorporates research based plans, guidelines, and strategies to achieve the school's desired outcomes. They are incorporated into each chapter, or *Design*. The research supporting each of the *Designs* illustrates how critical each is in creating effective, rewarding, and lasting partnerships as well as a sense of community.

Design 1: Gathering Perceptions and Collaborating on Results

The "given" in any school community is that people have diverse beliefs, perceptions, and life experiences. Educators have a real need to know what these beliefs and perceptions are. Numerous studies have shown that parental perceptions are not necessarily what educators think they are (Jesse, 1996). Educators cannot rely on intuition or faulty data collection. Nor should they only listen to a few vocal parents and assume they represent the majority. They need a systematic way to gather important perceptions of those served by the school. This is not a one time process, either. We all know that communities change, people change, and needs change. It is important, therefore, to periodically reassess perceptions. When gathering perceptions of stakeholders is a priority, educators are sending the message that the input of parents and community members is valued and are promoting ownership in the partnership. As Lindle (1989) reminds us, parents appreciate educators who take the time to find out about their perspectives.

Jesse (1996) states that "what is needed is a framework for understanding [these] varying perspectives" (p. 1). We propose that the major components necessary for successful parent partnerships, those included in the *Designbook,* will serve effectively as such a framework.

Assessing perceptions is the first step. Collaborating with members of the school community to celebrate strengths and identify challenges is the second step. This is a far different approach than designing a parent involvement program that simply may or may not reflect the needs and concerns of the parents they are trying to attract. When there is purpose and structure to their collaboration, a stronger sense of community and unity of purpose can develop.

Design 2: Maintaining a School Environment Supportive of Learning

Educators and parents alike want safe, disciplined learning environments for every child. Research has shown that in order to promote academic growth and social, emotional and motivational development, students must have orderly, disciplined school environments. Wang, Haertel, and Walberg (1993) reinforce the importance of quality classroom instruction in a positive climate by documenting that it has nearly as great an impact on student learning as does student aptitude.

Students also need supportive, accommodating environments at home. Educators can encourage and guide parents in providing that kind of environment, but only if the parents are willing to work with them. Educators can begin by creating a climate that welcomes, invites, and encourages -- one that is comfortable, accepting, and helps to overcome threats and negative feelings. Once educators get parents through their doors, there are many ways they can be "hooked" into staying (or, at least, visiting more often).

Educators also realize that life in almost any community today poses many physical and emotional threats to the safety and security of our children. Reports of neglect, abuse, abandonment, and violence are part of daily life. Of particular concern is violence, especially in our inner cities. It is a cause of stress for youth, parents, and educators (Garbarino, Dubraw, Kostelny, & Pardo, 1992). It has been reported that 20% of our youth have been threatened with a gun and 12% have had gunfire directed at them (Hammond & Yung, 1993). Educators know all too well that when students are at Maslow's survival level, they cannot learn or motivate themselves to reach their potential. It is essential, therefore, to ensure that school is a "safe haven" where students feel a sense of order, security, comfort, and belonging. This requires vigilance against the threats of violence, vandalism, crime, and drugs. It also calls for strong partnerships with parents, community members, and community organizations.

Design 3: Communicating Effectively

The need to develop effective and multiple means for communication between educators and parents is highlighted in virtually every report, research study, or article on parent involvement. Ames, Khoju, and Watkins (1993) report that when parents feel that they are receiving frequent and positive messages from teachers, they tend to get more involved in their children's education than their peers who do not perceive that they are receiving such communication. Parents want to know about their student's progress and successes and what is going on at school--and will find out one way or another. If not through the school's communications, they gather it from their own observations, comments from children (which is often one-sided), rumors, talking with other parents, or listening to neighbors or friends. Schools that innundate parents with information through assignment sheets, agendas, written communication, conferences, and meetings are giving parents what they need to know to be able to be effective partners in their child's education.

Many potential problems can also be avoided if members of the school community feel free to openly communicate with one another. Frequent face-to-face communication fosters an information sharing network that is critical to fully functioning partnerships. Open lines of communication also help to break down "we-they" barriers since everyone has an opportunity for input (Gardner, 1989).

Design 4: Promoting Supportive Relationships

Educators and parents both believe in the power of positive relationships in building and maintaining strong school communities. Their beliefs are supported by the major findings of a massive study, *Voices From the Inside* (Claremont Graduate School, 1993). The study emphasizes that schooling is actually a series of relationships (students-students, teachers-teachers, teachers-parents, teachers-students, administrators-teachers, administrators-parents, administrators-students, etc.) and that these relationships are critical to student achievement. At the same time, this study found that "no group inside the schools felt adequately respected, connected, or affirmed" (p.19). It is clear that until strong relationships built on mutual respect and a sense of belonging are a priority, all efforts at promoting parent involvement and partnerships will fall short. The "personal, caring touch" educators add to communications, open invitations to the school and classroom, reaching out to uninvolved families, informal and regular contact, and willingness to be open to parents' ideas and suggestions are all actions that build these types of relationships. Yet they will not happen unless educators are willing to reach out to parents as partners.

For Gardner (1989), healthy, vital communities have a "spirit of mutuality and cooperation" marked by caring, trust, and teamwork (p.78). Diversity is respected and cooperation, compromise, and consensus-building are widely shared pursuits. He cautions that partnerships should "protect and give a measure of autonomy to the individual" and feels that partnerships should have a sense of wholeness, but also support and value diversity (p.76).

Design 5: Developing Shared Expectations

Members of a partnership should form "networks of responsibility" to set goals and work together on the most pressing challenges (Gardner, 1989, p.76). As they work together to achieve common goals, they develop shared norms and values as well as a sense of commitment. As Gardner (1989) tells us, "A healthy community affirms itself and builds morale and motivation through ceremonies and celebrations that honor the symbols of shared identity and enable members to rededicate themselves" (p.77). Proven parent involvement strategies reported in research are engaging parents in mutual goal setting and in assessing school policies, practices, and rituals (Schuur, 1992). They are also based upon identifying key demographics of the parent population so everyone has a clear picture of who the school community represents, being aware of the major issues and concerns of stakeholders, and using this information to identify and build upon commonalities.

When parents realize that the partnerships are focused on improving student achievement, they are more willing to exert the energy and effort that is required to assure that expectations are realized. Parents actually have more influence on student achievement than they realize. According to the U.S. Department of Education (1994), the factors over which parents exercise authority--student absenteeism, variety of reading materials in the home, and television watching--explain nearly 90% of the difference in eighth-grade mathematics test scores across 37 states and the District of Columbia on the National Assessment of Educational Progress (NAEP). In this analysis, controllable home factors account for almost all the differences in average student achievement. Additional international comparisons highlight the exceptional academic success of students from Asian countries, which may be attributed to the priority their families place on education (U.S. Department of Education, 1994). Without generalizing these studies to the total population, it does seem that parents' influence significantly affects student achievement. This underscores the need to work closely with parents as partners in developing expectations for their children and in monitoring their progress.

Design 6: Involving Others Productively

In Gardner's (1989) definition of community, there is a balance between collective action and individual responsibility. There must be a shared commitment to working together on common tasks, sharing everyone's talent, energy and resources. When members engage in collaboration, sharing, and supportive actions, everyone wins. At the same time, individuals should be free to become involved to the degree they desire. While all segments of the community are encouraged to participate, some will be more active than others. A good community is one that will "find a productive balance between individuality and group obligation" (p.79).

In theory, this may sound far too optimistic; in reality, all things are possible. According to an ABC Nightly News (2/13/97) Solutions segment, it is possible to gain 100% participation from parents. One school required each parent to sign a Parent Contract, an agreement between parents and school personnel, as they enrolled their children at the school. Educators pledged to do everything they could to help the children succeed. Parents committed to being as involved as possible in the educational experiences of their children. Both groups lived up to their pledges. Parents gave up lunch hours, took personal leave days, and made many other sacrifices to be a part of their child's school experience. The contract was "binding" because the children would not allow their parents to ignore it. While this may seem like a "pie-in-the-sky dream" to some, it is a reality at Pine Ridge Elementary in Stone Mountain, Georgia.

This is just one example of many to illustrate how creatively many schools are approaching the challenge of increasing the level of parent involvement. Most schools realize that they need to expand what it means to be a volunteer beyond traditional boundaries and are offering parents and community members multiple ways of participating (Vandergrift & Greene, 1992). Realizing the differences in parents' willingness, ability, and time available to participate, parent involvement is taking many forms from high to low visibility and high to low activity. The options provided also vary according to the ages of the children served. Many of the parent involvement activities for younger children are not relevant or useful for older students and vice versa. For example, parents of secondary students should be very involved in designing students' post secondary academic and vocational plans which is not yet a need for parents of elementary students.

One of the more controversial areas related to parental involvement is decision making. In some situations, parents have not been given adequate input into decisions that affect their children and have begun to assert control over schools to see that the needs of their students are met (Kaplan, 1992). Although some parents want to have a voice in managing schools, many educators have concerns about their experience or capabilities to make sound decisions that reflect the total perspective, rather than their child's best interests (Cotton & Wikelund, 1989). While the research in this area is not extensive, studies do not show a conclusive link between parental involvement in school governance and student achievement. However, Comer (1984) suggests that achievement, motivation, and self-concept are all positively affected when parents of children from low income, at-risk families are involved on planning or management teams. Furthermore, parents' inclusion in decision making processes does remove mistaken assumptions of both parties about each others' motives, attitudes, intentions, and abilities. It also breaks down barriers and can open the door for other types of involvement (Cotton & Wikelund, 1989).

Design 7: Supporting Teaching and Learning

Parents are the first teachers of their children and continue to be the primary influence throughout their youth. They are the experts on the child and teachers are the experts on learning. Their views on the value of education greatly impact their child's attitude toward school (Sanders, 1990). It is obvious, then, that their involvement in their child's learning process is critical. The research on parent involvement strongly suggests that the most effective forms of involvement are those which "engage parents in working directly with their children on learning activities in the home" (Cotton & Wikelund, 1989, p.2). Reading aloud to children is the single most important activity for promoting eventual success in school (Anderson et al., 1985). When parents realize that reading achievement is more dependent on learning activities in the home than is math or science, they are more likely to find time in their busy schedules for reading with their children (U. S. Department of Education, 1994). Impressive results in student achievement are also gained when parents assume a more active role in providing encouragement, arranging for appropriate study time and space, modeling desired behaviors, monitoring homework, and actively tutoring.

Effective teaching and learning is really the primary goal of partnerships and has reciprocal benefits. Educators can assist parents in providing a language rich home environment and supporting their child's learning (Lindle, 1989). Parents can help educators understand how their child learns most effectively and can support their instruction at home. As each helps the other, the child benefits. It is essential, however, that educators help parents understand "innovative" approaches that are being used to improve instruction and assessment. Best practices in today's classrooms may differ from what parents experienced. For parents to be willing and able to support these innovations, educators must take the time to explain their reasons for selecting them. Parents want to know what these new approaches are, why they have been selected, and how they will benefit the child. With this information in hand, they are less likely to be influenced by uninformed or biased parents or community members who oppose their use.

An important secondary goal for strong partnerships is increasing the knowledge, skills, and abilities of parents and community members. As they grow, their children will benefit as well. So will our schools. For example, many adults are unaware of the new research on the brain's development. This research strongly underscores the need to "turn on" receptors in a very young child's brain (e.g., language, music, movement, shapes) to prepare the brain for later learning. While it may be too late for some parents to apply this research to their school-aged children, it may make a difference for their future children and our future students. This research and other "parenting skills" information are important to parents who are faced with the increasingly difficult challenge of raising children. Furthermore, our society has begun to realize that lifelong learning is both a desired approach and necessary strategy for survival in today's world. Adults who find themselves in new circumstances and work situations often have a need for continued learning. Through continued educational experiences, they gain increased confidence in their ability to learn and become open to new ideas. In the process, they become even better role models, resources, and advocates for students and education.

How To Use the *Designbook*

The *Designbook* will help educators as they develop specific designs and plans for successful parent involvement. It's research based *Designs, Plans,* and *Tools* will provide direction for any school contemplating ways to create or strengthen parent participation, relationships, and involvement. Taken as a whole, it provides the foundation for building a highly effective and responsive school and lasting partnerships throughout the school community.

It will be helpful for the reader to look first at the *Building Community Parent Survey* (Tool 1.1.1) before proceeding to other *Designs*. The survey will highlight important conditions that should be addressed in any school community. If the survey is used to gather perceptions, it will provide rich "baseline data" regarding current practices. If not, it illustrates the conditions that the *Designbook* addresses. If a survey is not possible, *Design 1* also provides additional strategies for understanding the needs and desires of parents and community members. The reader is also encouraged to preview Plan 1.2 (Collaborating on Results). The guidelines and processes provided in that plan can be used when attending to all other *Designs*.

The authors feel that beginning the design process by gathering perceptions is the ideal approach. It allows schools to identify and celebrate their successes as well as their challenges. It is important to take advantage of the opportunity to celebrate successes, make them public, and build on them. Then target areas that parents, community members, and educators perceive as needing improvement and refer to the appropriate *Designs*. Select the most appropriate *Plans* and *Tools* to achieve your purposes. They are intended to build on each other and to be used as appropriate to fit the special circumstances within each school. None is intended to be a solution in itself. Use "as is" or adapt the *Designs, Plans,* and *Tools* as vehicles to build the partnerships your school values.

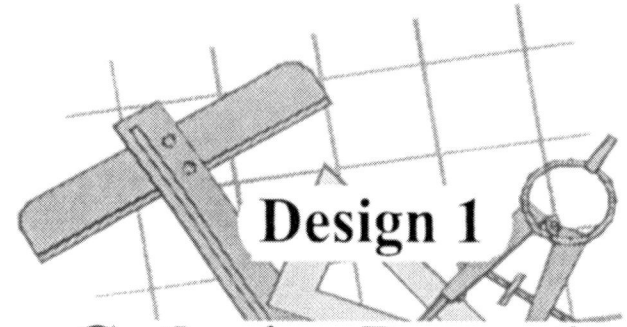

Design 1
Gathering Perceptions And Collaborating on Results

Gathering Perceptions is . . .
- finding answers to the question, "I wonder how parents and community members feel about...?"
- gaining opinions of parents and community members in a systematic, formal way.
- involving stakeholders in assessing significant school-related conditions.
- soliciting perceptions of others through surveys, questionnaires, interviews, and focus groups.

Collaborating on Results is . . .
- a way to focus individuals' interests and perspectives on what is best for *all* students.
- encouraging stakeholder input in making decisions and solving problems of mutual interest.
- a means to strengthen partnerships between educators, parents, and community members.

Although educators and parents both want to create the best possible learning environments for children, they often have differing views about how this should be accomplished. Educators rely primarily on research or best practices they have gained from conferences, workshops, and visits to other schools. They also use input from parents, generally those involved in parent-teacher organizations or the few who volunteer on a regular basis. Parents rely mainly on their own past experiences as students, what they hear from older children or other parents, and what they learn from the media. The result from these traditional, hit or miss methods of data gathering is a failure to communicate.

Polling interested stakeholders can give educators needed information about the school's effectiveness and ability to maintain partnerships. Carefully constructed surveys, interviews, and other means to gather the perceptions are relatively inexpensive tools that have tremendous potential for opening lines of communication. They give parents and community members a voice in school affairs, provide direction, and serve as a catalyst for constructive collaborating and problem solving.

When educators and parents make a concerted effort to understand each other's perspectives, they are then well positioned to collaborate effectively about important issues. Their collaboration can result in more cooperation, active involvement, and feelings of ownership. Perhaps the greatest benefit of collaboration is the improvement in the school's planning process. Creative and successful solutions emerge when committed individuals are engaged in resolving seemingly overwhelming challenges. The synergy that evolves heightens their energy and commitment to bringing about a better future for the school and all within. Furthermore, many potential conflicts can be avoided or resolved constructively.

What we hear from ...

EDUCATORS

"I wonder what the parents think about the school in general. I know what my parents think about my classroom because I ask them every year in a questionnaire."
(Middle school teacher)

"Collaboration with parents sounds great, but I don't want parents thinking that they can run the school."
(Middle school principal)

"Our community just isn't as supportive of our schools as we would like. We have not been able to figure out why."
(Superintendent)

"Every time we have meetings with parents they seem to last forever. They go on and on about the same topics. We've heard enough--let's get moving!"
(Elementary teacher)

PARENTS

"How do they know what parents think about _____? They haven't asked us."
(Parent of high school student)

"I enjoyed filling out the survey the school sent. It gave me an opportunity to say some things I'd been wanting to say."
(Parent of elementary student)

"When I was asked to be a member of a focus group, I didn't feel that it was something I wanted to do. I thought it would be a waste of my time. I went anyway and it turned out to be a very worthwhile experience. I think some good things will result from our ideas."
(Parent of middle school student)

STUDENTS

"If they really want to make this school better, they should ask us. We know." (7th grader)

"It was fun to be a part of the discipline policy task force. I was surprised that I was asked. I'm not the student council president."
(High school junior)

"Being in a meeting with teachers, principals, and parents is a little scary. I really didn't have a chance to say some of the things I wanted to say."
(High school sophomore)

"I don't know why they asked me. I guess I was the 'token' student on the committee."
(High school senior)

Shared Responsibilities

In effective partnerships, *both* educators and parents, families, guardians, or caregivers take responsibility for collaborating effectively with one another. The following diagram illustrates the responsibilities that are unique to each group and those that both groups share.

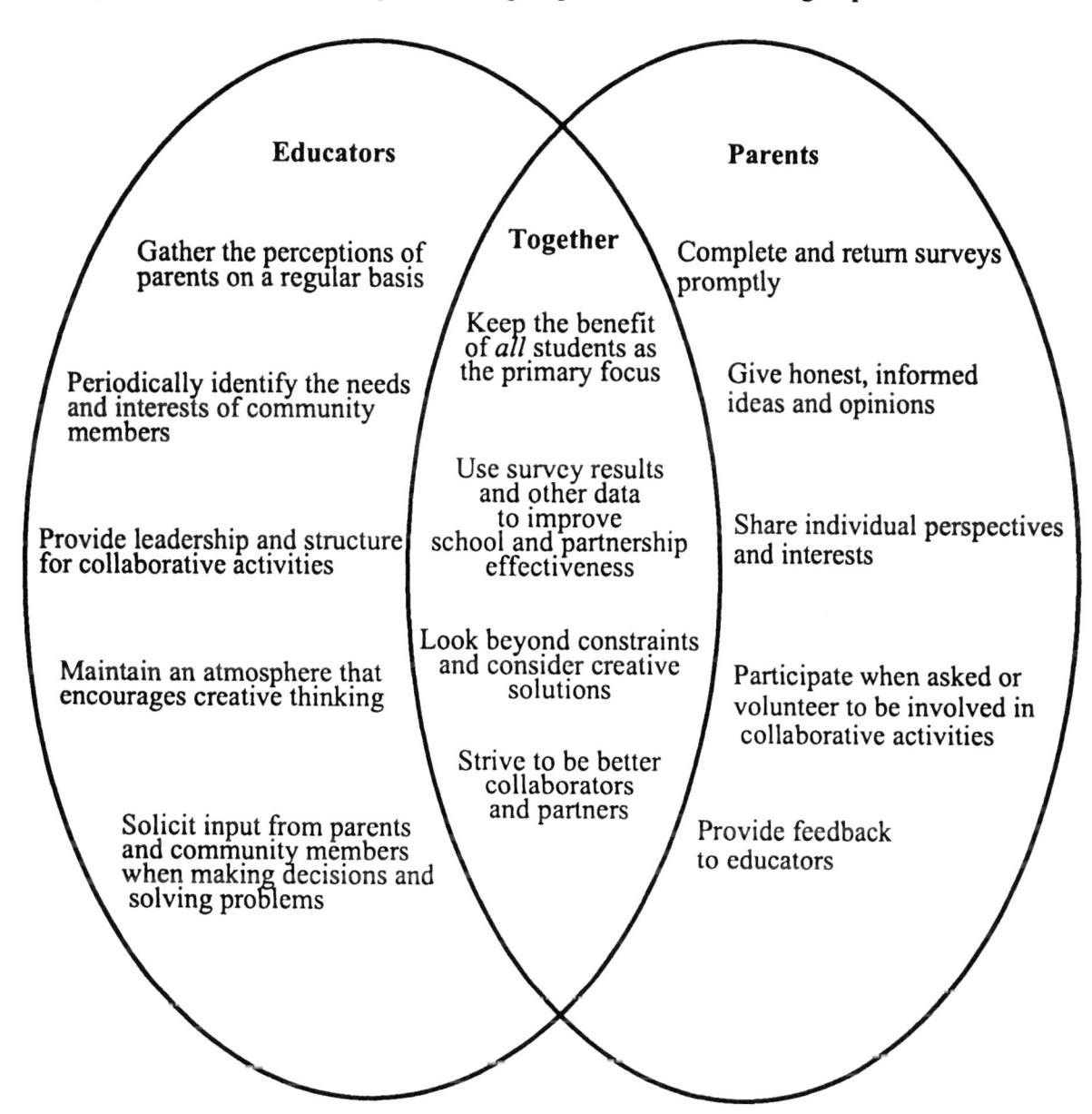

Educators
- Gather the perceptions of parents on a regular basis
- Periodically identify the needs and interests of community members
- Provide leadership and structure for collaborative activities
- Maintain an atmosphere that encourages creative thinking
- Solicit input from parents and community members when making decisions and solving problems

Together
- Keep the benefit of *all* students as the primary focus
- Use survey results and other data to improve school and partnership effectiveness
- Look beyond constraints and consider creative solutions
- Strive to be better collaborators and partners

Parents
- Complete and return surveys promptly
- Give honest, informed ideas and opinions
- Share individual perspectives and interests
- Participate when asked or volunteer to be involved in collaborative activities
- Provide feedback to educators

If families are to be involved as true partners in their children's education, it is important to provide on-going opportunities to hear their concerns and comments as well as providing them information.

Moles, 1996

Plans and Tools
for carrying out our responsibilities in gathering perceptions and collaborating on results

Plan 1.1. Strategies for Gaining Input from Parents and Community Members

This plan provides strategies for gaining input from parents and community members. Included are sample surveys entitled *Building Community--Strengthening Partnerships*. One is for parents and the other for community members. Guidelines are presented for conducting the surveys which include suggestions for reaching "hard to reach" parents. Processes for analyzing the surveys and reporting their results are also included.

Plan 1.2. Collaborating Productively

The primary intent of this plan is to provide suggestions for facilitators to use when engaging others in collaborating on survey results. Within this plan are numerous structures to promote constructive decision making and problem solving. These strategies can be applied to a number of situations and can be used with faculty or parent groups alone or with a combined faculty-parent group. Many of these *Plans* and *Tools* will also be helpful in working with other *Designs*.

Educator Reflection
Gathering Perceptions and Collaborating on Results

How effective are we as a faculty in gathering the perceptions of parents and community members? Are we involving them in the best possible ways in collaborating on the results? Take a few minutes to consider how frequently the following events or opportunities take place at your school. Put an "X" in the box that most closely reflects your perception.

Often   Sometimes   Rarely

1. We give parents adequate opportunities to express their opinions about important school issues.

2. We solicit the perceptions of community members and other interested stakeholders.

3. We are proactive rather than reactive in identifying the current needs and interests of parents and community members.

4. When we do gather perceptions, we make sure that we have heard from all groups within our school community.

5. Once we know the perceptions of others, we are responsive in taking action to improve less than desirable conditions.

6. We involve interested stakeholders in establishing priorities and developing plans for the targeted conditions.

7. We have clear guidelines for collaborating with parents and other interested stakeholders.

8. Collaborative activities are well organized and structured to make the best use of everyone's time and energy.

9. We use effective processes for making decisions and solving problems.

10. We are able to move beyond constraints and obstacles to identify creative and potentially effective solutions.

11. The results of collaborative activities (decisions, solutions, actions) are generally perceived to be valuable and effective.

12. We as a faculty are growing in our ability to collaborate productively with others.

Plan 1.1
Strategies for Gaining Input
from Parents and Community Members

Developing an overall strategy for gathering perceptions is the key to keeping the faculty in tune with the needs and desires of the school community. The benefits are twofold. It keeps educators informed while assuring parents and community members that their input is valued. Unfortunately, systematically gathering perceptions is not a common practice in many schools. It is often an unfortunate situation that sparks the need to gather perceptions. In such cases schools are taking a reactive approach, finding out what stakeholders feel after the fact, rather than a proactive approach that might have prevented the unfortunate situation in the first place.

Before the decision is made to move ahead, several important preliminary questions need to be answered. First, what is the purpose for gathering perceptions? The discussion should focus on why the opinions are desired and how the information will be used. Second, is this the right time to be asking for opinions? A regular interval of time (possibly every 3 years) allows educators to stay up-to-date without overburdening the stakeholders with surveys and/or meetings. If the school has not been engaged in this practice on a periodic basis, then it would be a very appropriate time to get started. Third, what is the best means for gathering the desired information? Conducting surveys or questionnaires, holding focus sessions, or interviewing stakeholders by telephone or in face-to-face arrangements are all viable options. Many schools feel a survey is the most feasible of the opinions since it can involve a large numbers of parents and community members.

Once these questions have been answered and the decision has been made to incorporate gathering perceptions into the school's long range planning efforts, it is time to develop a plan to make it happen. The following steps have been designed to assist schools in developing an effective strategy that will produce meaningful and useful information.

- Decide on the survey instrument to be used or develop one of your own. A sample survey for parents is provided as Tool 1.1.1 and one for community members as Tool 1.1.2. These surveys are ready for use. The surveys are titled *Building Community--Strengthening Partnerships* and are designed to gather perceptions of parents and community members about significant conditions within the school. They can also be used as is or as a starting point for educators who want to tailor a survey to their specific school context. Experience has shown that a comprehensive survey like one of these should address the concerns of stakeholders if it is to provide relevant information for school improvement.

- Add a comment page to the survey. This will allow respondents to share specific perceptions about what they identify as strengths or challenges and to add any

information that they have not had an opportunity to relate by completing the it
the survey. Tailor the comment page to the particular needs of the school, but inc&
questions such as the following *as a minimum.*

> *What I like best about this school is . . .*
> *The most important change I could suggest for this school is . . .*
> *The only comment I would like to add is . . .*

- Include a cover letter and an envelope with the survey. Use the cover letter to explain the purpose of the survey, the guarantee of confidentiality, how and when to return the survey to the school, and incentives being used to guarantee the survey's completion. The cover letter also allows school personnel to thank respondents for taking their time to help the school continue to improve its programs and services. Providing directions for sealing the survey in the envelope and placing it in a box in the school office assures confidentiality of responses.

- Decide how many individuals should be involved in the survey. Determine if it is necessary or feasible to reach all members of a group or if a sample would be adequate. For example, sending a survey to all 1,100 families of a large high school may be too costly. According to statisticians, a stratified random sample of one-third to one-half of the families (distributed to represent gender, ethnicity, grade levels, and students' ability levels) would provide information that should be considered representative of the views of the total population. If a sample is selected, be sure to explain the sampling plan to the faculty and to the parent-teacher organization.

- Identify strategies to ensure an adequate number of respondents and appropriate representation of all subgroups of parents and community members. Parents and community members are typically the most challenging groups in terms of returning surveys. See Tool 1.1.3 for guidelines for encouraging their participation and response, including those who are typically hard to reach.

- If different groups will be completing the survey, decide how to identify each one. This could be done by color coding or placing an identifying number on each survey (e.g., "1" or yellow paper for neighborhood parents; "2" or green paper for parents of children who are bused in to the school). It could also be desirable to analyze survey results by grade levels. Whatever the categories, procedures for keeping the surveys separate need to be identified prior to initiating the process.

- Develop procedures for guaranteeing confidentiality. Respondents will be more open and honest if they are assured that their opinions will not be shared with others and that no specific comments will be attributed to them. They can complete the survey anonymously and seal it in a plain envelope to return to the school. They also need to know who will complete the survey analysis and when the results will be made available.

- If school personnel decide to develop their own survey, it is important to pilot it as a trial run. Select a small group of typical respondents and ask them to complete the survey. It could be that this group will provide suggestions about how to make the instructions or items clearer. They may also suggest items that may have been overlooked.

- Set up an appropriate time frame for conducting the surveys, interviews, or focus groups and for analyzing their results. Identify dates for distributing the surveys and for their return. Consider the following in establishing a schedule:
    - The first few months of a school year are generally not a good time to gather perceptions. Parents new to the school need enough time to become familiar with the school and to form their own opinions about it. Late fall or just after the first of the year are ideal times.
    - Surveys, like other items, tend to be misplaced when received on Fridays, over the weekend, or just before holidays. It is better to initiate them early in the week.
    - Allow people enough time to complete the surveys, but do not give them so much time that they put them aside and forget about them. Sending them out one week and asking to have them back the next week allows enough, but not too much, time for them to respond.

- Tally the survey results. See Tools 1.1.4 and 1.1.5 for Tally Sheets for the parent and community survey. Responses to items on the survey itself simply need to be counted and tabulated. Responses to interviews or comments from focus groups should be analyzed for themes and patterns. This is more time consuming, but it provides a wealth of specific information. Using the open-ended questions on the surveys as an example, identify the various themes or topics addressed in each respondent's comments. Write them down and keep a tally of the times that theme is mentioned by others. Patterns will soon emerge. Only write down specific comments if they are particularly well stated and could be used as quotes to convey a theme mentioned by a large number of respondents. There is one important caution to keep in mind in tallying results. Some people are succinct in their comments and others are more verbose. For those that fill a page with their comments, be sure to only count the themes or topics they mention one time--or else they will be given more than their fair share of emphasis just because they repeat themselves.

- Present survey results. Present the responses in a form that is easy to understand. Use charts, tables, or graphs if possible. It may be helpful to involve parents and community members in identifying the most appropriate ways to share and use the information. It is also important to report the findings to all groups that participated. Meetings, letters, or newsletters are appropriate means for communicating this information.

Other Possibilities . . .

Building Community -- Strengthening Partnerships
Parent Survey

Tool 1.1.1

Please take a few minutes to respond to our parent survey. Your responses will help us in identifying and celebrating our strengths and in selecting areas that can be improved to make our school the best place for your child and all children to learn. To ensure your confidentiality, we ask that you not put your name or any personal information on the survey. Respond to each of the following items. **Mark only one response as "Strongly Agree," "Agree," "Disagree," "Strongly Disagree," or "Do Not Know."**

	Strongly Agree	Agree	Disagree	Strongly Disagree	Do Not Know

School Environment

1. As a parent, I feel welcome in this school. ○ ○ ○ ○ ○
2. This school is child- and family-centered. ○ ○ ○ ○ ○
3. My child is appreciated for his or her unique talents, challenges, and potential. ○ ○ ○ ○ ○
4. Children and families from different backgrounds are welcomed and appreciated. ○ ○ ○ ○ ○
5. The school provides a clean, attractive, and enjoyable setting for learning. ○ ○ ○ ○ ○
6. At school, my child is physically and emotionally safe. ○ ○ ○ ○ ○
7. School personnel work with students and parents to develop appropriate social behaviors. ○ ○ ○ ○ ○
8. Discipline policies are reasonable and are administered fairly. ○ ○ ○ ○ ○
9. The school building and grounds are available for use by parents and community members. ○ ○ ○ ○ ○
10. The school offers programs designed for parents and community members. ○ ○ ○ ○ ○
11. The school's daily and yearly schedules meet my needs and those of my children. ○ ○ ○ ○ ○
12. The school building is adequate for the numbers of students. ○ ○ ○ ○ ○
13. My child has safe transportation to and from school. ○ ○ ○ ○ ○
14. The school cafeteria food and environment are pleasing to children. ○ ○ ○ ○ ○
15. The school provides the materials, supplies, and equipment my child needs. ○ ○ ○ ○ ○

Communication

16. School personnel are willing to listen to my concerns. ○ ○ ○ ○ ○
17. School personnel respect my opinion and try to understand my point of view. ○ ○ ○ ○ ○
18. I am provided with clear and timely information about programs, policies, and rules. ○ ○ ○ ○ ○
19. I am always informed about school events. ○ ○ ○ ○ ○
20. School personnel communicate often with me (newsletters, notes, calls, recorded messages, etc.). ○ ○ ○ ○ ○

Tool 1.1.1

	Strongly Agree	Agree	Disagree	Strongly Disagree	Do Not Know
21. I am contacted about my child's problems and/or accomplishments.	O	O	O	O	O
22. Conferences and report cards provide the information I need about my child's progress.	O	O	O	O	O
23. School personnel use the media to make the public aware of student and school successes.	O	O	O	O	O

Relationships

	SA	A	D	SD	DK
24. School personnel make efforts to get to know me as a parent.	O	O	O	O	O
25. I am satisfied with the relationships I have with school personnel.	O	O	O	O	O
26. School personnel provide opportunities for me to get to know other parents.	O	O	O	O	O
27. Relationships throughout the school community are based upon trust and respect.	O	O	O	O	O
28. Teachers and other school personnel treat me and my child with kindness and understanding.	O	O	O	O	O
29. School personnel and parents are supportive of one another.	O	O	O	O	O
30. Students at this school treat each other well.	O	O	O	O	O
31. My child is developing positive friendships at school.	O	O	O	O	O
32. School personnel recognize my child's accomplishments and contributions.	O	O	O	O	O
33. When our family has a problem or concern, someone at school is willing to help.	O	O	O	O	O
34. School personnel work with me in obtaining special services or assistance for my child.	O	O	O	O	O

Expectations

	SA	A	D	SD	DK
35. The school's vision and mission are appropriate for our students.	O	O	O	O	O
36. The school's vision or mission was developed with parent input.	O	O	O	O	O
37. Parents are included in developing plans/activities to achieve the school's goals.	O	O	O	O	O
38. As a parent, I can share my opinions about issues that are important to me.	O	O	O	O	O
39. My child has appropriate opportunities to express opinions about important student issues.	O	O	O	O	O
40. Everyone in the school expects success and exhibits a can do attitude.	O	O	O	O	O
41. School personnel are positive role models for my child.	O	O	O	O	O
42. Building level leadership provides needed direction for the school.	O	O	O	O	O
43. My child is held to reasonable and challenging expectations for learning and behavior.	O	O	O	O	O
44. My child is encouraged to work to his or her ability.	O	O	O	O	O

Tool 1.1.1

	Strongly Agree	Agree	Disagree	Strongly Disagree	Do Not Know

Involvement

45. I have been given opportunities and encouragement to become involved in school activities. ○ ○ ○ ○ ○
46. I am as involved in school activities as I want to be or am able to be. ○ ○ ○ ○ ○
47. I am as involved in my child's education as I want to be or am able to be. ○ ○ ○ ○ ○
48. I am encouraged to make suggestions about school issues that are important to me. ○ ○ ○ ○ ○
49. Opportunities for parent involvement are well organized and worth the parents' time. ○ ○ ○ ○ ○
50. School personnel recognize and appreciate my contributions as a parent. ○ ○ ○ ○ ○
51. My child is encouraged to become involved in school activities. ○ ○ ○ ○ ○
52. My child is as involved in school activities as he or she wants to be. ○ ○ ○ ○ ○

Teaching and Learning

53. My child finds class work and homework interesting and useful. ○ ○ ○ ○ ○
54. My child is given opportunities to develop his or her talents, interests, and leadership abilities. ○ ○ ○ ○ ○
55. School personnel make an effort to develop my child's confidence and self-esteem. ○ ○ ○ ○ ○
56. My child is helped to become a more organized, responsible, and self-disciplined student. ○ ○ ○ ○ ○
57. Teachers provide clear directions and assistance when needed. ○ ○ ○ ○ ○
58. The grades my child receives appropriately reflect his or her effort. ○ ○ ○ ○ ○
59. My child experiences instruction that is innovative and includes the latest technology. ○ ○ ○ ○ ○
60. My child is given opportunities to develop skills that are necessary for success in life (problem solving, decision making, and conflict resolution, etc.). ○ ○ ○ ○ ○
61. Classroom instruction emphasizes appropriate academic, social, and civic learning. ○ ○ ○ ○ ○
62. My child's class size is small enough for teachers to have time for each student. ○ ○ ○ ○ ○
63. Teachers hold appropriate expectations for my child's behavior and academic growth. ○ ○ ○ ○ ○
64. School personnel provide learning opportunities on topics of interest to parents. ○ ○ ○ ○ ○

In General,

65. My child looks forward to coming to school. ○ ○ ○ ○ ○
66. This is the best school for my child. ○ ○ ○ ○ ○
67. There is a feeling of school pride throughout the school community. ○ ○ ○ ○ ○

Building Community -- Strengthening Partnerships
Community Survey

Tool 1.1.2

Please take a few minutes to respond to our survey. Your responses will help us in identifying and celebrating our strengths and in selecting areas that can be improved to make our school the best place for our community's children. To ensure your confidentiality, we ask that you not put your name or any personal information on the survey. Respond to each of the following items. Mark only one response as "Strongly Agree," "Agree," "Disagree," "Strongly Disagree," or "Do Not Know" (if you have not had an opportunity to form an opinion). Add any additional comments on the back of the survey.

	Strongly Agree	Agree	Disagree	Strongly Disagree	Do Not Know
School Environment					
1. When attending school-sponsored events such as athletic events, plays, concerts, school personnel and students make me feel welcome.	○	○	○	○	○
2. Community members from different backgrounds are welcomed and appreciated.	○	○	○	○	○
3. Students represent the school well when they are involved in community activities.	○	○	○	○	○
4. The school building and grounds are available for use by community members.	○	○	○	○	○
5. The school building and grounds are attractive and well maintained.	○	○	○	○	○
6. The school building and grounds are adequate for the number of students.	○	○	○	○	○
Communication					
7. Whenever I have had a school-related question or concern, school personnel have responded.	○	○	○	○	○
8. I am informed about school events that may be of interest to me.	○	○	○	○	○
9. School personnel communicate with community members in a variety of ways (e.g., notes, newsletters, calls, recorded messages, signs).	○	○	○	○	○
10. School personnel use the media to make the public aware of student and school successes.	○	○	○	○	○
11. As a community member, I can share my opinions about issues that are important to me.	○	○	○	○	○
Relationships					
12. School personnel make an effort to get to know me.	○	○	○	○	○
13. Students are recognized for their accomplishments in the community as well as at school.	○	○	○	○	○
14. School personnel appreciate and recognize my contributions.	○	○	○	○	○

	Strongly Agree	Agree	Disagree	Strongly Agree	Do Not Know
Expectations					
15. I know what the school's vision and mission are and feel they are appropriate.	○	○	○	○	○
16. The school's vision or mission reflect community input.	○	○	○	○	○
17. Community members are included in developing plans/activities to achieve school goals.	○	○	○	○	○
18. School personnel appear to be positive role models for children.	○	○	○	○	○
19. Students are held to reasonable and challenging expectations for learning and behavior.	○	○	○	○	○
20. The school's fund raising activities seem appropriate.	○	○	○	○	○
Involvement					
21. School personnel value the involvement of parents and community members.	○	○	○	○	○
22. I have been made aware of opportunities to become involved in school activities (e.g., as a volunteer in the classroom, as a committee member).	○	○	○	○	○
23. Opportunities for involvement are well organized and worth community members' time.	○	○	○	○	○
24. I am as involved in school activities as I want to be or am able to be.	○	○	○	○	○
Teaching and Learning					
25. Former students seem well prepared for personal, social, and civic responsibilities.	○	○	○	○	○
26. Former students have learned skills that are necessary for success in life (e.g., problem solving, decision making, conflict resolution, and communication).	○	○	○	○	○
27. Former students have the necessary skills to compete successfully in the workforce.	○	○	○	○	○
28. The school offers programs of interest to community members.	○	○	○	○	○
In General,					
29. There is a great deal of school pride in the community.	○	○	○	○	○
30. This school is known throughout the community as a good school.	○	○	○	○	○
31. For the level of financial support community members are asked to make, this school is a good investment.	○	○	○	○	○

Thank you for your willingness to help us make our school the best it can be!

Tool 1.1.2

Guidelines for Gathering Perceptions from "Hard to Reach" Parents

Tool 1.1.3

- ▼ Develop survey forms in all the target languages of parents and community members. Enlist the assistance of language teachers and community members who can help with the translation. A suggestion from one school that had over 29 different languages represented in their population was to convene potential respondents in separate groups (by ethnic group). Because many of the parents may be intimidated or reluctant, this school found it much more comfortable for the groups to meet, have the survey read orally, and allow participants time to complete their responses. For them, this approach was very satisfying and offered opportunities for questions and clarification. Making the extra effort also helped to build relationships.

- ▼ Consider the readability level of the survey. If the literacy level of the participants is low, the strategy described above may again be a good structure. Avoid using difficult words or educational terms that make the questions more difficult to comprehend.

- ▼ The personal touch is critical in gaining access to hard to reach parents. When parents are asked to participate in a survey because their opinion is important and needed, there is a much better chance that they will comply. A call from teacher, parent coordinator, principal, or counselor who has a relationship with a parent also encourages participation. Each "homeroom" should identify strategies to reach those parents whose opinions they might otherwise not hear.

- ▼ Consider holding meetings away from school in more familiar settings for parents and community members. If parents will not come to the school, go to them. Meetings can beheld in local churches or community centers. At one school, teacher and parent volunteers set up a table at a grocery store and asked parents and community members to fill out a survey before they began shopping.

- ▼ If a specific school function, like the spring festival, typically draws large numbers of parents, capitalize on their presence. Make it easy for parents to fill out a survey before they leave.

- ▼ Offer incentives for completing the survey. Some schools have enlisted the help of local fast food franchises to offer a coupon for respondents who returned their surveys. Students are often given prizes such as a logo item or candy bar for assuring that their parents complete the survey. Other schools have secured prizes to be awarded to selected respondents (e.g., from each homeroom or from the room with the highest completion rate).

- ▼ Another alternative could be to use the survey items as telephone interview questions. The caution is that some potential respondents may be hesitant to give their opinions over the phone to someone with whom they may or may not have a positive relationship.

Building Community -- Strengthening Partnerships
Parent Survey Tally Sheet

Tool 1.1.4

School Environment	Strongly Agree	Agree	Disagree	Strongly Disagree	Do Not Know
1. I feel welcome					
2. The school is child- and family-centered					
3. My child is appreciated					
4. Different backgrounds are welcomed/appreciated					
5. The school is lean, attractive, and enjoyable					
6. My child is physically and emotionally safe					
7. School personnel work with students/parents					
8. Discipline policies are reasonable/fair					
9. School building and grounds are available					
10. Programs provided for parents/community members					
11. Daily and yearly schedules meet our needs					
12. The school building is adequate					
13. Transportation to and from school is safe					
14. School cafeteria food and environment are pleasing					
15. Materials, supplies, and equipment are adequate					

Parent Survey Tally Sheet (Page 2)

Tool 1.1.4

	Strongly Agree	Agree	Disagree	Strongly Disagree	Do Not Know
Communication					
16. School personnel are willing to listen.					
17. School personnel respect my opinion.					
18. I receive clear and timely information.					
19. I am kept informed about school events.					
20. School personnel communicate often with me.					
21. I am contacted about my child.					
22. Conferences and report cards meet my needs.					
23. School personnel use the media.					
Relationships					
24. School personnel make efforts to get to know me.					
25. I am satisfied with the relationships I have.					
26. School personnel help me to get to know others.					
27. Relationships are based upon trust and respect.					
28. My child is treated with kindness and understanding.					
29. School personnel are supportive of one another.					

Parent Survey Tally Sheet (Page 3)

Tool 1.1.4

	Strongly Agree	Agree	Disagree	Strongly Disagree	Do Not Know
30. Students at this school treat each other well.					
31. My child is developing positive friendships.					
32. Educators recognize child's accomplishments.					
33. Someone will listen to problems or concerns.					
34. Educators work with me in obtaining special services.					

Expectations

35. The vision and mission are appropriate.					
36. Vision/mission was developed with parent input.					
37. Parents are included in developing plans/activities.					
38. I can share my opinions on important issues.					
39. My child can express opinions.					
40. Everyone expects success/can do attitude.					
41. School personnel are positive role models.					
42. Building leaders provide needed direction.					
43. Teachers hold challenging expectations for my child.					
44. My child is encouraged to work to his or her ability.					

Tool 1.1.4

Parent Survey Tally Sheet (Page 4)

	Strongly Agree	Agree	Disagree	Strongly Disagree	Do Not Know
Involvement					
45. I have opportunities/encouragement for involvement					
46. I am as involved in school activities as I want to be					
47. I am as involved in my child's education as I want to be					
48. I am encouraged to make suggestions					
49. Parent involvement activities are organized/worth time					
50. Educators recognize/appreciate my contributions					
51. My child is encouraged to become involved					
52. My child is as involved as he or she wants to be.					
Teaching and Learning					
53. Class work/homework are interesting and useful.					
54. My child is developing talents, interests, etc.					
55. Educators develop my child's self esteem					
56. My child is becoming organized, responsible, etc.					
57. Teachers provide clear directions and assistance					
58. My child's grades appropriately reflect his/her effort.					
59. Instruction is innovative/uses latest technology.					

Tool 1.1.4

Parent Survey Tally Sheet (Page 5)

	Strongly Agree	Agree	Disagree	Strongly Disagree	Do Not Know
60. My child is developing skills for success in life.					
61. Instruction is appropriate (academic, social, civic).					
62. Class size is small enough.					
63. Appropriate expectations for behavior/academics.					
64. Learning opportunities are provided for parents.					

In General

	Strongly Agree	Agree	Disagree	Strongly Disagree	Do Not Know
65. My child looks forward to coming to school.					
66. This is the best school for my child.					
67. There is a feeling of school pride in the community.					

Notes

Tool 1.1.5

Building Community -- Strengthening Partnerships
Community Survey Tally Sheet

	Strongly Agree	Agree	Disagree	Strongly Disagree	Do Not Know
School Environment					
1. School personnel/students make me feel welcome					
2. Different backgrounds are welcomed/appreciated					
3. Students represent the school well in community					
4. School building and grounds are available for use					
5. School building and grounds are attractive					
6. School building and grounds are adequate					
Communication					
7. School personnel have responded to questions					
8. I am informed about school events					
9. School personnel communicate in variety of ways					
10. School personnel use media					
11. I can share my opinions					

Community Survey Tally Sheet (Page 2)

Tool 1.1.5

	Strongly Agree	Agree	Disagree	Strongly Disagree	Do Not Know

Relationships

12. School personnel make an effort to get to know me
13. Students are recognized for accomplishments
14. My contributions are appreciated and recognized

Expectations

15. I know the school's vision and mission
16. Vision/mission developed with community input
17. Community members help with planning/activities
18. School personnel seem to be positive role models
19. Reasonable/challenging expectations held for students
20. School's fund raising activities seem appropriate

Involvement

21. School personnel value community involvement
22. I am aware of opportunities for involvement
23. Involvement opportunities are well organized
24. I am as involved as I want to be

37

Tool 1.1.5

Community Survey Tally Sheet (Page 3)

	Strongly Agree	Agree	Disagree	Strongly Disagree	Do Not Know
Teaching and Learning					
25. Former students prepared personally, socially, etc.					
26. Former students have skills for success in life					
27. Former students can compete in workforce					
28. School offers programs of interest to community					
In General					
29. Great deal of school pride in the community					
30. This school is known as a good school					
31. This school is a good investment					

Notes

Plan 1.2
Collaborating Productively:
Using Effective Decision Making and Problem Solving Processes

Strong partnerships between parents and educators develop when collaborative efforts are structured to promote cooperation, active involvement, and ownership. Collaboration that produces these results most often involves complex, perplexing, and unique situations of importance to all of the participants. Analyzing the results of the *Building Community-Strengthening Partnerships Survey* is a good example of such a situation. It is a task that has the potential for impacting the school in a significant way. Each particpant's contribution to the task will make a difference. It also requires interpretation and time for deliberation, discussion, and reflection. Given specific guidelines to follow, the collaborators generally produce more creative and potentially successful outcomes than one person working independently could have generated. The idea that two heads are better than one becomes a reality when true collaboration exists.

When collaborative processes are to be used, it is important to clearly delineate the responsibility and authority of the group before it begins collaborating. Will the group serve in an advisory capacity and primarily provide input to decision makers? Will it be expected to suggest solutions that will be acted upon by the person with the ultimate authority? Will it have full power to make decisions within clearly established parameters? There is nothing more frustrating for a group than to put time and effort into solving a problem only to have their solutions ignored or to be told, after the fact, that their solutions cannot be implemented for one reason or another. Treated in this manner, they would view this and any future collaborative efforts as counterproductive.

It is also important to structure collaborative activities. There are many appropriate structures and the key is to match the structure with the task. To achieve the desired partnerships that are the focus of the *Designbook,* providing structures for decision making and problem solving are particularly important. While these processes are often blurred into one, there are some important differences and some helpful variations that may facilitate collaboration as schools work with information generated through discussions, focus groups, interviews, or surveys. Review the following processes and use the most appropriate ones to structure your collaborative efforts.

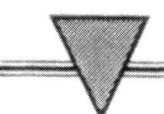

- Develop a plan of action. Productive collaboration doesn't just happen. It takes a well-prepared and workable plan that attends to the affective needs of the participants as well as the task requirements and time constraints. Begin by deciding whether or not the task requires a collaborative approach. Tool 1.2.1 provides considerations for making the decision.

- Identify a facilitator (or facilitators) to guide the development and implementation of the plan. Tool 1.2.2 provides guidelines for those who facilitate collaborative sessions. Tool 1.2.3 is a lesson plan for promoting productive collaboration. It is recommended that the facilitator(s) preview all the *Tools* in this *Plan* before making final decisions about session activities.

- Since collaboration involves individuals working together, organize the collaborative sessions in a way that assures the best possible representation and outcomes. Many schools use focus sessions as their vehicles for collaboration. Focus sessions are an organized gathering with an important purpose that is usually centered on one issue or task. Three important decisions have to be made when planning focus sessions. First, who should be included in the collaborative group? Should faculty, parent, or community members be involved? Should students be included? While middle and high school students are often overlooked as potential group members, they offer a unique perspective that can enhance the collaborative process. Perhaps the major consideration for group composition is the sensitivity of the topic. Is it one that is open to student, parent, or community involvement? Not all issues are or should be. It is also crucial to ensure that the group reflects the composition of the entire school in terms of gender, ethnicity, grade levels, student groups (i.e., athletics, gifted, special needs, at risk) and includes representatives from all groups important to the identified issue or activity. Second, how should the group(s) be structured? Should they meet separately or together with representatives from each of the stakeholder groups. Could they begin by meeting separately and then combine forces at a later date? The third major decision involves the size of the group. The size can range from very small (fewer than 10) to very large (more than 100). If the total group is large, be sure to break it down into manageable sized teams before beginning (6 to 8 team members is ideal).

- For a rather tongue-in-cheek look at situations in which decision making and problem solving do not work, see Tool 1.2.4. These Pitfalls to Avoid would make a humorous and useful introduction to collaboration.

- Provide clear guidelines for participation in collaborative activities. As people who may or may not know each other come together to work through some often difficult issues, having clear and agreed upon rules for participation can prevent unforeseen problems and obstacles. As the group is convened, let them propose rules they can agree to follow. See Tool 1.2.5 a for an example of *Rules We Live By* which have been adopted by a number of schools. Tool 1.2.5 b is provided as an example of a name tent that keeps the *Rules We Live By* visible during all collaborative sessions.

- Select the most appropriate processes for the task. Three standard collaborative processes are brainstorming, identifying problems or challenges, and prioritizing. When it is important to identify what is known about a particular topic, brainstorming is a good technique to use. See Tool 1.2.6 for a summary of the brainstorming process. Tool 1.2.7 provides some strategies for identifying problem areas or challenges. Included in the Tool is a description of a discrepancy analysis process that is helpful in determining the extent to which the challenge area is impacting desired school outcomes. Prioritizing is also an extremely useful process. In education as in other areas, our needs far exceed our ability and resources. Prioritizing helps us focus our limited resources while providing all participants input into the direction of collaborative activities. See Tool 1.2.8 for a suggested prioritizing strategy.

- Decide on appropriate models to guide decision making and problem solving. It may be helpful to develop operational definitions of the processes since there are some important differences that should be considered. Tools 1.2.9 through 1.2.15 provide several variations of these processes that are well suited to specific purposes. Each is research based and provides clearly delineated steps to follow.

- Maintain a focus on thinking creatively. Why do schools or organizations have to continue to operate in "traditional" ways? Why do they hold onto traditions when it is obvious that new ways of doing business may be far better? Encourage creative thinking and innovative solution finding. Tools 1.2.16 through 1.2.19 provide a variety of approaches for viewing problems and solutions in creative ways.

- Evaluate the effectiveness of the collaborative processes that were used and identify refinements that will make them work better in the future. Develop measures to evaluate the quality of decision making or problem solving efforts. Appointing a process observer and/or using self-assessments are two ways to assure that attention is paid to improving collaborative efforts. By focusing on improvement, the group is also strengthening the skills and competence of its members. See Tool 1.2.20 for ways to analyze collaborative processes. While the focus is generally on the quality of the end product (the decision or solution), the quality of the interactions and the relationships that are developed in the process may ultimately be the most important outcome.

When Should We Collaborate?

Tool 1.2.1

It all depends . . .
on the situation.

Collaborative processes work best when . . .
- they focus on situations of mutual interest to all participants.
- the situations are complex, perplexing, and/or unique.
- the situations require an interpretation of policy.
- there is time for deliberation and reflection.
- participants have information and/or expertise to contribute.

Individual approaches work best when . . .
- the situation is a simple, recurring one that could easily be remedied by the person in charge.
- simple solutions or decisions would not be enhanced by multiple perspectives.
- the situation clearly falls within the parameters of established policy.
- a potentially dangerous situation exists or there is no time for collaboration. In this situation, the authority figure needs to make a quick decision.
- the individual has all the necessary expertise and information.

When collaborative processes are used, be sure that . . .
- the right people are involved. There are some issues that are appropriate for parent involvement and some that are not.
- the decision question or problem has been clearly defined.
- the responsibility and authority of the group is clearly identified before beginning.
- the person in charge is committed to follow through with recommendations, decisions, or solutions the group is permitted to make.

> **Be creative in finding time to collaborate.**

Facilitating Collaboration

Tool 1.2.2

What is collaboration?
American Heritage Dictionary defines collaboration as "working together, especially in a joint intellectual effort." Translated into practical terms, it is sharing perspectives on issues of mutual interest or concern to lead to improved future actions.

What are the goals of collaboration?

- to cooperate in accomplishing a significant task
- to promote growth and maintain future orientation
- to communicate effectively
- to gain new insights, understandings, and appreciations--to construct meaning together
- to generate a quality product--identifying and maintaining quality standards
- to improve skills in collaboration

What are some important suggestions for facilitators?

- Refer to Tools in other *Designs* for additional suggestions and considerations. The Table of Contents will be helpful in identifying Plans and Tools that may be especially appropriate.

- Use your professional judgment in structuring your sessions to address the needs of the participants and the goals to be achieved. The following lesson plan leaves room for adding in your own creative touch. Incorporate your own successful practices. Most importantly, make collaboration fun and stimulating. It should be perceived by participants as a rewarding experience, not a chore. Work with building leaders to identify themes, slogans, incentives, treats, and refreshments that send the message that the time educators are devoting to collaboration is appreciated and valued.

- Plan, implement, seek feedback from participants, reflect, analyze, and improve. Keep a focus on growth and renewal. As the school is improving, continue to enhance your own skills in the process.

Tool 1.2.3
Facilitator's "Lesson" Plan for Collaboration

Make decisions about grouping participants. Large groups are effective for some activities, but small groups are preferable when participants are to think about an issue, brainstorm, or identify strategies. These groups can be designated in a variety of ways. If it is important to mix participants across grade levels or stakeholder groups, it may be preferable to make this decision prior to the meeting. Name tents or seating charts help participants find their designated groups. If group size, but not representation, is critical, groups can be determined as participants enter the room. Name tags, candy, or other markers can be used to identify group members. Place a matching name tag or piece of paper at the table designated for each group. If groups are to be randomly selected, simply count off during the meeting and designate a place where each group will meet or allow them to work at tables where they chose to sit.

Have participants fill in name tents or name tags. See Tool 1.2.5 for an example of a name tent that keeps the Rules We Live By visible for the participants and the name for the facilitators.

Welcome participants and put them at ease. Let them know that they were asked to be involved because of their expertise and stake in the situation. Tell them that they will be working hard, but having fun at the same time. Encourage them to kick back from their hectic daily routines to think about what is best for children. Jokes, cartoons, or other ice breaker activities enhance any introductory remarks. Those that illustrate the differing perspectives of educators, parents, and community members are particularly effective in introducing the concept of collaboration.

Communicate the purpose, goals, and objectives of the session. If there are to be several sessions, let participants know where this session fits in the sequence, what has previously been accomplished, and what types of sessions should follow. Most importantly, assure them that the total plan of action has not been predetermined--that they will be involved in determining the next steps. Encourage participants to ask questions or to make comments and address their issues before proceeding.

Establish expectations for how the group members will work together. Communicate and discuss the Rules We Live By (Tool 1.2.5a) or guidelines for participation. Introduce participants or have them introduce themselves (to the total group or within their smaller group). Be sure they all know why they are involved or why they were chosen. Tool 1.2.5b is a name tent that could be used to help with learning names and remembering the guidelines.

Communicate the time frame for this session and other sessions. Explain what has been planned for breaks, refreshments, or other necessary concerns. Establish a cue or signal that means it is time to come back together.

Tool 1.2.3

Designate roles for members of the small groups. As with cooperative learning for students, roles for adult participants help everyone know how they can contribute most effectively. Participants can designate members for the roles or the facilitator can identify them. If the selection is left to the facilitator, make creative decisions. For example, the recorder could be the member of the group who drove the farthest to attend this session, has the birthday closest to the meeting date, or has been on the most recent vacation. Be as creative as possible about assigning the initial role. The remaining roles can be assigned in a similar manner or by saying, "to the recorder's left." Consider the following participant roles and select or adapt them according to the task and the number in each group. If the groups are relatively large, there can be several encouragers.

Recorder
Writes down all ideas and contributions
(Everyone helps with spelling!)

Facilitator
Monitors adherence to the Rules We Live By

Summarizer
Ensures that everyone understands the task
and periodically
reviews what is being discussed

Reporter
Posts the group's product and share with the total group

Runner
Acquires needed supplies

Encourager(s)
Ensures that everyone has the opportunity to participate actively
(Each group member does not have to contribute, but should
be assured of the opportunity if they desire.)

Clarify the role of the session facilitator. This person is responsible for structuring and coordinating decision making and problem solving processes and obtaining needed information, materials, and supplies. The facilitator may provide process input, but should be an objective bystander who maintains a neutral position on the issue. The facilitator should also assure that no one participant lectures the group or dominates the session at the expense of others. Finally, it is the facilitator(s) who should pace the activities. Be sensitive to timing. Groups can't always come to the best solution when time is pressing, so adjustments may need to be made during a session about how much can be covered and what should be postponed until a later date.

Tool 1.2.3

Initiate the collaborative activities. Preview all Tools before deciding on the most appropriate ones. Once the selections have been made, provide clear instructions for the task(s) and opportunities for clarification. Communicate approximate time frames and remind the group about the signal to be used for stopping their discussion at important points. Distribute, or have runners obtain, necessary materials and supplies.

Be sure to have all the materials on hand that will be needed to facilitate all of the activities. Consider the following as basic necessities:
- post-a-notes for clustering ideas (This allows group members to move ideas from the "do as soon as possible" list to the "parking lot" where they will remain until a later time--and not get lost.)
- butcher paper or large tablet paper (Those with adhesive are easier to hang.)
- markers (Different colors can be used for different groups or segments.)
- masking tape
- adhesive spray
- handouts (Enough for each individual or for every two-encourages interaction.)
- transparencies, transparency markers, overhead, and screen (Remember to include blank transparencies.)
- a timer, bell, music, or other creative way to signal stopping points
- candy, door prizes, or other treats to designate groups or provide incentives

Take a few minutes at the end of each session to debrief the collaborative efforts. Ask how effectively participants carried out their roles and how they feel about the quality of ideas generated, the time provided for discussion, or their interactions. Ask them to reflect as a group before sharing one or two ideas with the total group. The facilitator(s) should record the groups' reflections. After the meeting, the facilitator(s) should add their own reflections to the groups to use in planning for future meetings.

Identify next steps. This can be done with the total group or with a smaller planning team that represents the various stakeholder groups, grade levels, or subject areas. Write the plan for future sessions so that the ideas will not be lost or forgotten.

Pitfalls to Avoid
in Effective Collaboration

Tool 1.2.4

Do We Exhibit Any of These Characteristics?

Ostrich Syndrome
Keep your head in the sand and remain unaware of any signs of trouble.
"Things are going great, why mess with it?"

Blue Smoke
Talk the issue to death so there isn't enough time or energy to do anything about it.
"We always talk in circles and never decide on anything."

Fear of Risk Taking
The unknown is often worse than what is known. The general feeling is that it may be riskier to change than not to change, especially if group members are not sure that leaders will support them as they embark upon new challenges.
"Why change? We may not be doing it perfectly, but at least we know what we're dealing with."

Stymied by Too Many Priorities
Waging too many battles at one time consumes resources and energy that could be more productively channeled into one front that would make a real difference.
"It's really hard to tell what's important around here."

Defeatist Attitude
Many participants need efficacy retraining. They need to develop the belief and confidence that they have the power to bring about productive change.
"Why bother? Nothing ever changes anyway."

Passive Aggressive Behaviors
In public, participants give their commitment to an initiative, but in private they are unsupportive and even actively sabotage it.
"I don't think it's a good idea, but I wasn't going to say anything against something the principal is for."

Wait and See
The negative effects of previous unsuccessful school improvement efforts often keep people from actively embracing new attempts. Many participants maintain a "this too shall pass" attitude.
"What's the 'hot topic' for this year?"

Fear of Failure and Ambiguity
Participants are hesitant to move because every detail has not been thought out perfectly. For collaboration to be genuine, the exact path is not certain and the specific details cannot be worked out in advance.
"Why don't they just tell us what to do next?"

Not Taking Full Responsibility
Inaction often occurs because participants are focusing on situations over which they have no control rather than on the ones they do. Rather than realigning their thinking and taking responsibility for those areas they can control, they justify their inaction.
"We could do it if we had . . . (different kids, better parent support)."

Yeah-Buts*
Potentially productive ideas countered with reasons they might not work.
"Yeah, we thought about doing that, but---we tried that once and it didn't work."
"Yeah, that's okay in theory, but in the real world that won't work."

Real or Perceived Constraints
Sometimes the barriers to solutions are not actual obstacles, but are believed to be-- or rumored to be--obstacles.
"Central Office would never let us to that."

Jumping to Solutions
School problems and issues are often complex. It is critical to examine the problem from all perspectives and to develop a full understanding of its components before attempting to solve it. Restraining impulsiveness and avoiding quick fixes are necessary if thoughtful, responsible, and reflective approaches are to be taken.
"We don't have enough time to think about all these issues. Isn't there some program that we can buy to do this?"

If we are encountering these pitfalls in our efforts to collaborate, what should we do to eliminate them?
What could we do to prevent them in the first place?

Thanks to Dr. Bob Eaker, Dean of the College of Education,
Middle Tennessee State University, Murfreesboro, Tennessee.

Guidelines for Collaboration
or
"Rules We Live By"

Tool 1.2.5a

It is extremely helpful to establish behavioral expectations early so everyone is clear about how they are to engage in collaboration. It is also helpful to communicate overtly rather than just assume that everyone knows how to collaborate effectively. As all good teachers know, it is far easier to be proactive in developing positive norms of participation rather than reactive in continually responding to misbehavior. Expectations can be identified in a participatory manner with individuals responding to the question, "If we are to collaborate and work together successfully, what guidelines for our behavior can we all commit to following?" Expectations can also be established by proposing the following Rules We Live By, providing clarification, and asking the participants for changes, additions, or deletions. Some may feel that using the term, rules, may be a bit strong and choose to use guidelines instead. The following "Rules We Live By" have been used successfully with a number of groups. Use them as is or adapt them to reflect the group's agreed upon guidelines. The name tent can be printed on heavy card stock paper that stands by itself providing a place for names and for a gentle reminder of commitments.

Align thinking with what is best for *all* our students
Another way to communicate this is to align our thinking with our vision. The idea is to maintain the focus on the greater good for as many of our students as possible. For this to happen, all participants must be willing to examine the issue from all perspectives, not just their own.

Maintain an open minded attitude
Participants should be willing to accept some degree of ambiguity and uncertainty. For some issues, the obvious right path is not readily apparent and sometimes the end result cannot be predicted. The collaborative process works best when participants can engage in creative thinking and remain open to the ideas of others.

Share your perspective and your ideas
Since the group is composed of individuals with differing backgrounds and experiences, each individual should act as an advocate for those they represent. One major goal of collaboration is to capitalize on the diversity within the group. Participants should be willing to make suggestions and contributions that may move the group forward.

Participate actively--this is not a spectator sport
Participants should be willing to invest energy, expertise, and effort to making the collaboration productive. It is important individuals reflect on their own positions and attempt to understand those of others by paraphrasing and probing.

Tool 1.2.5a

Resist impulsivity--avoid jumping to solutions

Participants should be sure that the problem is fully understood from all perspectives before they engage in identifying solutions. The interconnections of the situation should be explored before taking action. It is also important to remain alert to what is not known and develop strategies to find additional information and opinions.

Be precise without personalizing

Participants need to provide accurate and detailed information related to the issues, not to individuals associated with the issue. Finger pointing frequently results in negative feelings and breaks down the collaborative process. The intent of the Rules We Live By is to ensure a no blame approach to solving problems.

Build on the positives of "What Is"..
Add the creative possibilities of "What Ought To Be"

The idea is to maintain currently effective strategies while considering new ones to enhance current practices. While collaboration focuses on striving to attain the desired state, it also involves managing and manipulating the realities of the current situation.

Say "We should" or "We need"
rather than "They should" or "They need"

The subtle message is that we exert some control over the context and our situation. We are in this together and should feel a sense of shared responsibility and ownership.

Tool 1.2.5b

My Name is

Rules We Live By

We will think about what is best for *all* students.

We will maintain an open minded attitude.

We will participate actively. This is not a spectator sport.

We will avoid jumping to conclusions until problems are fully understood.

We will deal with the issues, not personalities.

We will build on the positives of "What is" and add the creative possibilities of "What Ought to Be."

We will *always* think "We should" rather than "They should."

Brainstorming

Tool 1.2.6

Purpose:
The general purpose of brainstorming is to generate as many ideas about a particular topic as possible in a short period of time (approximately 5 to 10 or 15 minutes). The quantity of ideas is the goal, not the quality. While quality is important, it will be addressed later when the ideas gathered through brainstorming are being assessed. In brainstorming sessions all suggestions must be accepted and written down. It is permissible to question a suggestion when the meaning is not clear, but not to evaluate or discuss it. While there may be a need for some elaboration to clarify a contribution, there should be no extended lectures.

Structure:
Form participants into small groups, no larger than 6 to 8 members. (Participants tend to break off into smaller groups when they cannot see or hear each other easily.) Group membership could be assigned or voluntary. Either way, it is important that they reflect the diversity within the larger, total group. Encourage participants to take advantage of the opportunity to work with others they do not normally have time to get to know. Select a facilitator for each group. Assign one prior to the session (especially if there is a need for any preparation for the session) or let the groups choose their own. Review the role of the facilitator so everyone is aware of procedures to be followed. The facilitator is to accept all contributions made by any group member and add it to the developing list. At the same time, the facilitator will be encouraging participation and discouraging discussion to pace the session and keep the group focused on the task. Establish rules for participation. The following work well, but adapt them as needed.

Fast
Pace should be rapid trying to identify as many possibilities as possible.

Focused
Any idea or suggestion as long as it relates to the topic is fine.

Fun
It is okay to verge on the ridiculous in order to spark some really good ideas.

Fruitful
Build on each others ideas--one good suggestion may lead to many more.

Materials:
- Several sheets of oversized butcher paper at each station. Large rolls of white paper can be cut to the desired size and are more economical than pads of oversized paper.
- Several different colors of magic markers at each station.
- Tape to display the finished products on the wall.

Challenge (or Opportunity) Identification

Tool 1.2.7

Refer to "Taking Stock" (Tool 5.3.1)

If the Building Community--Strengthening Partnerships survey is used, areas of dissatisfaction identified by parents or community members will be indicators of challenge areas. In addition, within overall categories that have a fairly high level of satisfaction, there may be some specific areas that are not as well satisfied as educators would like. These specific areas could also be challenges for the school.

If educator reflections (accompanying each design) are used, there will be certain areas that are identified as areas for growth. These reflections include some items not addressed in the parent and community member surveys, but are significant concerns for schools that wish to remain effective and responsive to the needs of the school community.

If focus group meetings are used, themes or patterns from their discussions will reflect both strengths and challenges perceived by various stakeholder groups. Those areas identified as challenges by several focus groups should be addressed.

If a longitudinal data base is updated and reviewed annually, the trends and patterns seen in the data will be indicators of challenge areas. A comprehensive and current data base provides objective information that can guide decisions about challenges. (See Tool 5.1.2 for steps in developing a data base.)

If surveys or focus groups have not been used, an informal discrepancy analysis can be used to identify challenge areas. Without actual perceptual (survey or focus group) data or a comprehensive data base about student performance, the analysis relies primarily on best estimates of current and desired performance. A discrepancy analysis begins by identifying the actual situation ("what is") and the desired future state ("what ought to be"). These can be equated to a numerical scale. While the assessment of "what is" relies primarily on judgment, the "what ought to be" should also incorporate standards, national and state norms, research, and professional literature. The analysis occurs when participants systematically compare the current state with the desired future state. The discrepancies between the two states identify specific "gaps" which become the school's challenges.

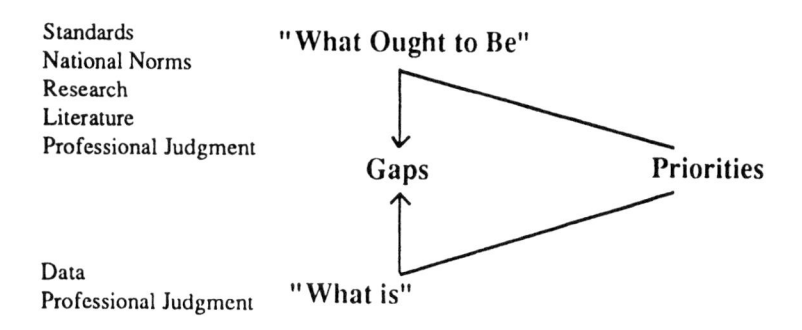

```
Standards              "What Ought to Be"
National Norms
Research
Literature                    │
Professional Judgment         ▼
                           Gaps ─────────── Priorities
                              ▲
Data                          │
Professional Judgment   "What is"
```

Prioritizing

Tool 1.2.8

Purpose:
The purpose of prioritizing is to identify an order of importance, a ranking according to urgency, or a list of areas that are more deserving of attention than others. Prioritizing is a way to rate items to establish precedence. The prioritizing process described here is a way to have small groups identify priorities, then to engage individuals in identifying their preferences.

Use in working with survey results:
After thoroughly examining and analyzing survey results, prioritizing can be used to focus improvement efforts on the most important challenge areas. Begin by looking at the major categories on the survey. Which were least satisfied for large numbers of respondents? If one or more are clearly in greater need of attention than others, begin the prioritizing process with them. Next, look at the specific items within these categories. Again, some should stand out more than others as problem areas. Looking across the total survey, there may be some specific topics that also need attention that are not included in the major categories. Include them if the group feels they are important. Once the topics have been identified, start looking for similarities that might link several together in a new cluster. Participants often note the interrelated nature of the challenges and are generally able to identify general categories or subcategories they feel are the most significant. For example, with the *Building Community--Strengthening Partnerships* survey, communication is frequently identified as a challenge area. Within this category there are several subcategories that might also be identified as challenges: within school communications, school to home communications, or public relations via media. Once the information has been regrouped into subcategories the group agrees upon, the facilitator should guide the discussion toward identifying which should be targeted as priorities.

Structure:
- Generate a collective list of suggested priorities by asking each small group to identify their top three to five priorities and to write them on a large piece of paper. After the small groups have finished this task, ask them share their priorities with the total group. As they share, they generally explain why their selections were considered more important than other areas. If there is available wall space, hang the lists for all participants to see.
- Combine all the suggested priorities into one list. Depending on the number of groups involved, a combined list of possibly eight to twelve priorities may result. Be sure that the list identifies categories and subcategories rather than specific activities or suggested actions. Post the combined list of suggested priorities and briefly review each of them. It is important to define what is included in each category. The participants need to develop a general understanding of the proposed challenge areas. If there is time, each potential priority could have an "advocate" speak for it.
- Allow several minutes for each participant to vote for their top three priorities. While the group has had the opportunity for discussion about priorities, this step allows each individual the chance to identify the challenges that are personally important and to have a voice in the direction of improvement efforts. This strategy also helps promote

Tool 1.2.8

ownership in the process and commitment to the results. Give each participant three cards (index cards or small pieces of scrap paper will do). Have them label the cards by writing "1" on the first card, "3" on the second card, and "5" on the third card. Ask each participant to select their top three priorities and to write a priority on each of the cards. The "5" card will represent their top priority, "3" will be their second priority, and "1" will be the third.
- Gather the individual cards and tally them. The priorities will be those with the highest numbers. There are usually natural break points among items on the total list which once again highlight what is most important to the total group. The example provided below illustrates the results of one school's prioritizing process.
- Report the total verbally and in writing to the total group. Share totals as well as the number of "5s," "3s," and "1s" that were assigned to each item. This may clarify the difference in two similar scores and helps the group see how everyone rated the priorities.

Materials:
- Butcher paper
- Markers
- Three index cards or small pieces of scrap paper for each participant
- Pencils or pens for each participant

_____ **Intermediate School**

PRIORITIES
(5/13/97)

Communication	74	(13-5s/3-3s)
Relationships	42	(3-5s/9-3s)
Involvement	22	(2-5s/4-3s)
Teaching/Learning	16	(2-5s/2-3s)
School Pride & Reputation	13	(2-5s/1-3)
Student Responsibility	9	(3-3s)

Decision Making

Tool 1.2.9

What is Decision Making?
It is the process of choosing one alternative from several possibilities based upon how well the alternatives fulfill specific criteria. It can be applied to academic, personal, and social situations and is especially useful when the most appealing alternative is not readily apparent. The process forces the decision maker to engage in high level analysis and to assign priorities to outcomes. There are several models for decision making which include both narrative and numerical processes.

Answers the questions ...
- "What is the best way to _____?"
- "Which of these is the most suitable way to _____?"
- "Which is the best course of action?"

Considerations ...
- Is the decision to be made an appropriate one for a collaborative effort? It is important to determine if this decision:
    - should be arrived at through a collaborative process--or is a clear cut one that simply requires a quick "yes" or "no."
    - is significant enough to warrant the time and effort collaboration requires.
    - is one that those involved have the expertise (and information) to make.
    - is one that the group has the responsibility and the authority to decide.
    - is one that group members want to be involved in.

- Most importantly, deal with any of the parameters listed above before entering into a collaborative decision making process.

Steps ...
- Formulate a decision question. Phrase it in a way that reflects the decision that will ultimately be made. For example, "What is the best incentive plan to encourage student attendance?" is more appropriate than "Deciding on an incentive plan."
- Identify the choices or alternatives for consideration. Identify as many viable options possible. Some investigation may need to take place to determine if all options are viable or if all good options have been identified before the actual decision making process is begun.
- Identify all criteria that are important to a good decision. The criteria selected will ultimately determine the outcome of the decision. As an example, think of the times that your faculty has been asked to make a decision about how to allocate limited funds. Has the decision been based upon frivolous criteria or on important criteria such as the impact on the greatest number of students? When participants feel that they have established the most important criteria, they have greater confidence in the outcome of the decision making process.

Tool 1.2.9

- Select the most appropriate alternative. Once the options and the criteria have been identified, simply writing down the plusses and minuses of each option helps clarify the best choice. Tool 1.2.10 describes this process. The *Dimensions of Learning* (DoL) framework provides a quantifying process that allows participants to assign a numerical value to the criteria and to each criteria's fit with the various options (Marzano et al., 1992) Tool 1.2.10 illustrates the DoL decision making process.
- Reflect upon the decision that has been made by rethinking the process used in making it. Is it aligned with our vision? Is it a decision that can be carried out? Is it realistic and feasible? Will it produce positive results? Were the options the best ones that could have been considered? Were the criteria the critical ones? If a quantifying process was applied, were the importance values and the fit scores applied correctly?

Tool 1.2.10

The PMI* (Plus-Minus-Interesting) Strategy for Making Decisions

PMI is an efficient decision-making strategy that illustrates the advantages and disadvantages of an idea, proposition, or solution. It involves listing and examining interesting aspects of each alternative. Using this strategy can help prevent making judgments based solely on emotion. It also can prevent a valuable idea or interesting component from being rejected without adequate thought.

Directions:

1. Identify a proposition or alternative to be explored.

2. Divide newsprint, a blackboard, or a piece of paper into three sections. Label the sections.

P (Plus)	M (Minus)	I (Interesting)

3. Allow participants three to five minutes to individually consider advantages and disadvantages of the alternative. Then have them identify aspects of the alternative that have neither a positive or negative value, but are interesting to consider. This individual thinking will enhance involvement and reduce impulsivity.

4. Have each person contribute what they considered related to the alternative. Make a list compiling everyone's ideas.

5. Carefully examine the lists to make decisions and judgments.

* Source unknown

Dimensions of Learning
Decision Making Process

Tool 1.2.11

Dimensions of Learning, a framework for developing higher level thinking skills, provides a numerical decision making process that can be applied to any situation (Marzano et al., 1992). The following is a summary of the DoL decision making process and a grid that makes it easy to use with students or parent and community groups.

Process:
- Identify a decision you wish to make and write it down.
- Identify the different choices or options to be considered.
- Identify the criteria you consider important to a good decision.
- Assign each criterion an "importance score"
  (very important = 3; moderately important = 2; least important = 1).
- Determine the extent to which each choice possesses each criterion (0 through 3).
- Multiply the "criterion scores" by the "choice" scores.
- Determine which choices have the highest total points.
- Think about the decision that was made. Was it the best one? If not, what affected it? Should the options be reconsidered? Could better criteria be selected?

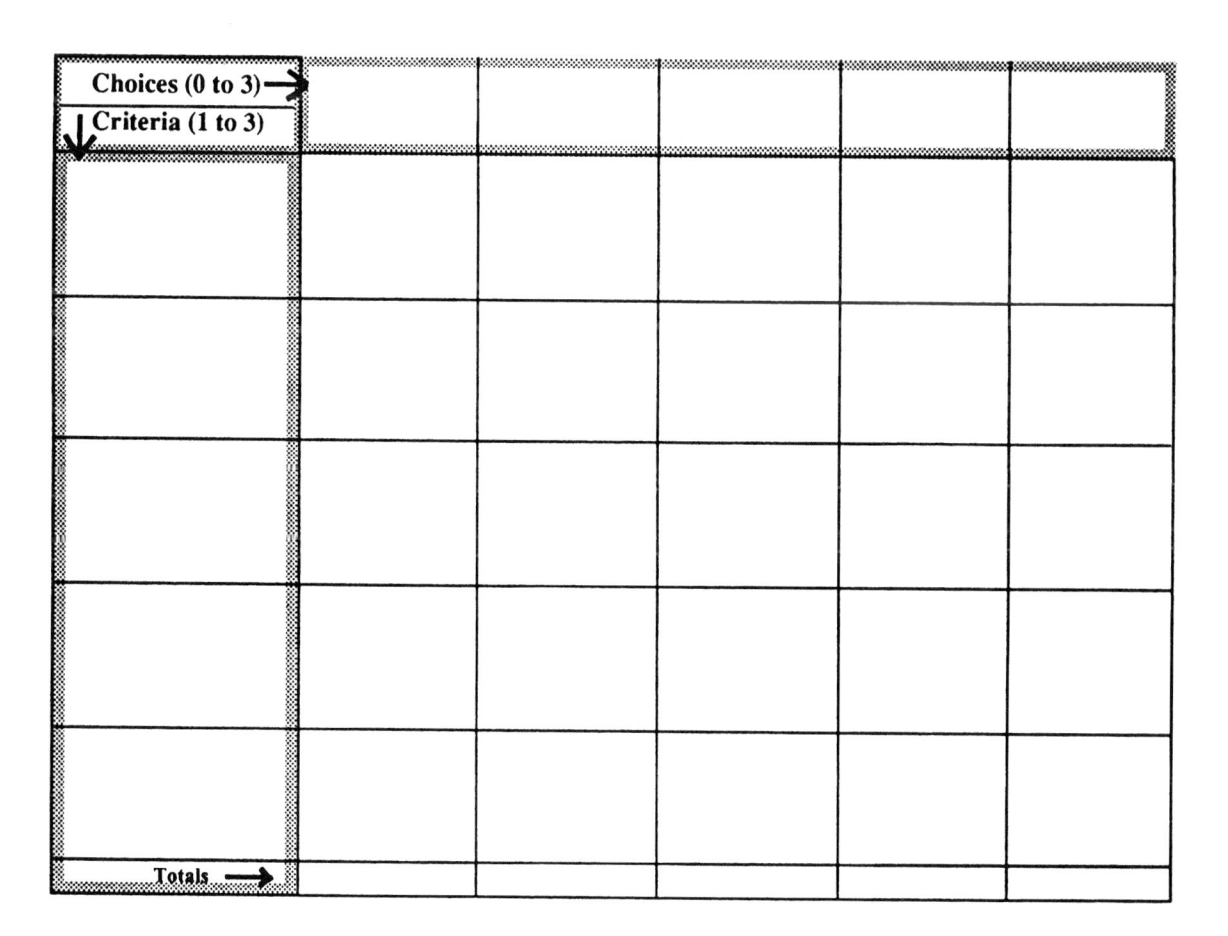

Choices (0 to 3) → ↓ Criteria (1 to 3)					
Totals →					

Consensus Decision Making

Consensus means general agreement and concord. Consensus occurs when every participant has been heard from and no one believes that the decision violates his or her convictions. It is not necessary that every participant totally agrees with the decision or feels that it is the best one. Complete agreement is not the goal, but when all participants feel that they can support the group's decision, consensus has been reached. It is not a win-lose situation since each person should be in agreement with at least part of the proposal. At some point in the decision making process, it may be helpful to test the waters and determine where everyone stands on a particular issue. This may be early in the process or the final step in making the decision. Verbal or card processes provide a structure for reaching consensus. A show of hands or voting, commonly used strategies in group settings, do not result in consensus.

Verbal Process

Each participant should present his or her position on the issue logically and concisely, but with enough elaboration to ensure understanding. It is acceptable for others to ask for clarification, but not to elicit an argument. Divergent views are valued because the different perspectives promote better decisions. Allow adequate time to talk through the decision. Some suggest proposing a time limit before beginning which can be extended with the groups' permission.

Card Process

Give participants a small index card or a piece of scrap paper and ask them to share their current position. A variation is to use hands with participants showing the appropriate number of fingers. Use the following scale and have each participant put a number on their card that best reflects his or her position. The cards can be collected and shared anonymously with the total group or each person can explain his or her position.

- 5 = I'm whole heartedly in favor of it. No reservations what-so-ever.
- 4 = It sounds like a potentially good idea to me, but it needs more discussion.
- 3 = I basically like it, but there are some components that I do not agree with and want to change.
- 2 = I'm basically opposed to it, but I can't think of anything better. I will not block it.
- 1 = I'm opposed to it, but here's my idea.
- 0 = I cannot agree to any part of the proposal nor any alternative.

Problem Solving

Tool 1.2.13

Problem solving is the process of achieving a goal, and more specifically, a goal that is usually blocked by some obstacle or limiting condition (Marzano et al., 1992). Everyone is challenged to solving life's unstructured problem tasks. These unstructured tasks are complex: the goal is not readily apparent (who's goal? one goal or several?), the constraints are not clear (real or perceived?), and there are many possible solutions and ways to solve the problem.

Answers the questions . . .
- "How will I overcome this obstacle?"
- "How will I reach my goal but still meet these conditions?"

Steps:
- Specify a goal. What is hoped to be accomplished?
- Identify the constraints or limiting conditions. What is getting in the way of achieving the goal? What are the givens in the situation?
- Identify alternative ways to solve the problem. Look to the possible problem solving strategies. Select one or several of the most promising ones that best fit the problem.
- Select a solution and try it out. It may be that the solution itself is fairly complex or would require several steps. Make a plan as to how best to implement the solution.
- Evaluate the effectiveness of the solution. The most obvious questions to answer are: Did the solution accomplish the goal satisfactorily? Did the solution adequately accommodate the constraints? Is the solution one that is consistent with our vision? Is the solution feasible and realistic in terms of resources?

Considerations:
- Designate the length of the trial period. Identify a date for reviewing the effects of the trail solution.
- Prior to implementing a solution, decide how its success will be determined. What will be the indicators of success? How will we know they have been met? What data or information will need to be collected and how? This may seem like a laborious process, but disagreements and hurt feelings can be avoided if these steps are followed. The evaluation of the solution will be made based on data rather than intuition or feelings.

Problem Solving Strategies
Visualize it
Draw a picture
Perform it (act it out)
Build a model or mock up
Draw a flow chart or directional graph
Use systematic trial and error (guess & try)
Think it out-talk it out
Research it
Postpone it (put aside the confusing part and deal with it later)

Tool 1.2.14

Problem Understanding

Look at the problem from several points of view. Identify four stakeholder groups and assign one to each of the arrows. Think about how each group would view or describe the problem and write down key points on the lines provided. It may become evident that more information about various stakeholder groups needs to be acquired.

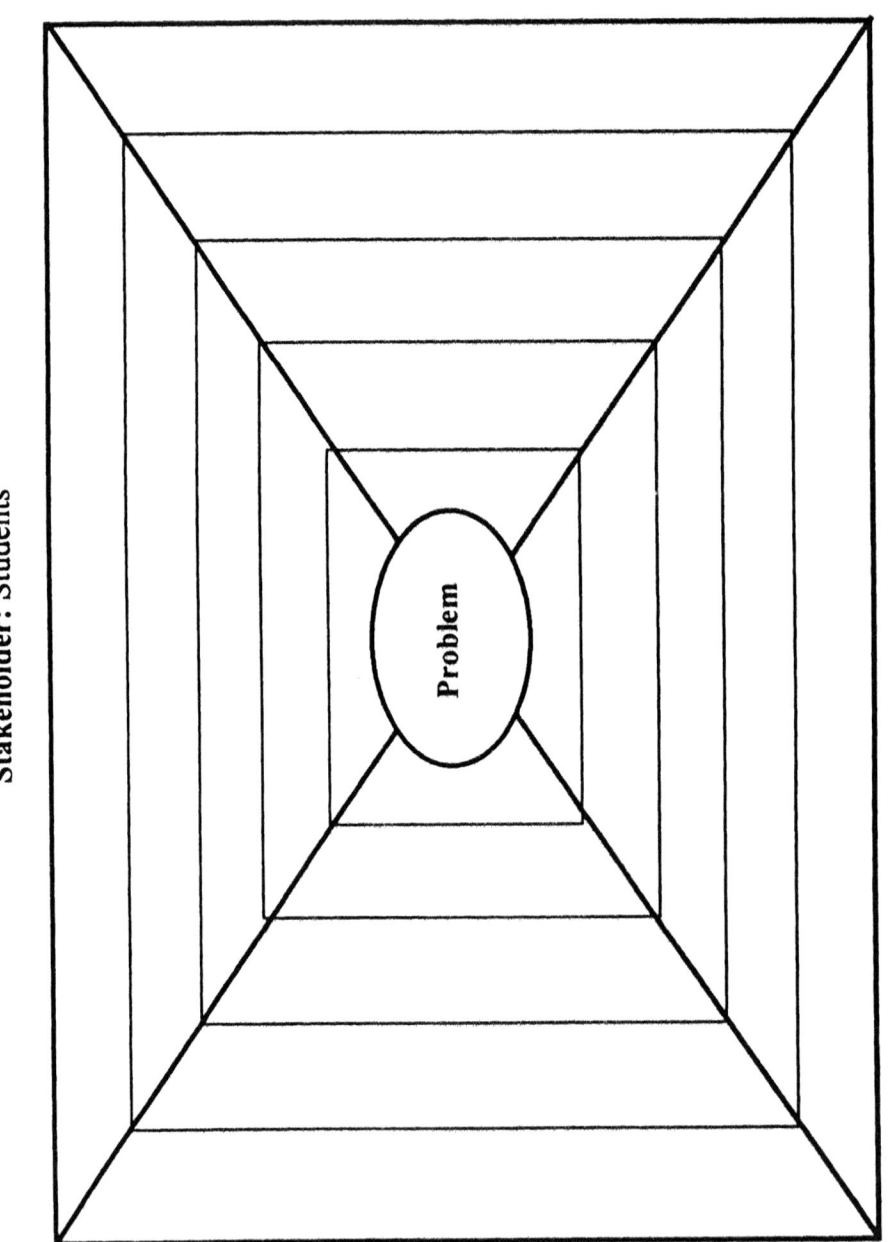

Stakeholder: Educators

Stakeholder: Students

Stakeholder: Parents and Families

Stakeholder: Community Members

Problem

Problem Solving Worksheet

Problem

Goal

Limits or Constraints

Possible Solutions

My Choice

Tool 1.2.15

Tool 1.2.16

Thinking about...
Risk Taking & Creative Thinking

Taking risks is...

- the only way to cope successfully with this world of change. Personal and professional risk taking is becoming part of our day to day lives.

- taking intelligent risks. Most people are comfortable with a 60-90% chance of success. Above 90% really not a risk and below 60% is foolish.

- going beyond the predictable into the unknown. We leave our comfort zone and enter ambiguous territory.

- part of almost everything we do. When all the danger is eliminated, so are opportunities.

- ready-aim-fire. After study, discussion, and small trials, there comes a time when you just have to do it.

- ready-fire-aim. Michael Fullan (1994) suggests that sometimes it is better to take the risk of firing a less than perfect shot to initiate important change.

- learning from our failures. The old adage, "The only person who doesn't make mistakes is the one who doesn't do anything worthwhile" holds true for risk taking. Mistakes and failures often provide the best learning experiences.

- usually not accomplished successfully by individuals working alone. Working as a member of a team increases the potential of taking intelligent risks.

- only going to happen when individuals feel safe and secure. We have to know that others encourage and support our risk taking and will help us if the need arises.

- the only way to move beyond the status quo. It is the basis for every invention or discovery and our hope for a better future.

One way to determine the amount of risk involved is to describe the most optimistic and the most pessimistic scenarios. It could be that the worst possible outcome is one that cannot be chanced and the idea should be rejected or revised significantly.

Creative Problem Solving: IWWMW
In What Ways Might We...

Tool 1.2.17

The **IWWMW** strategy works very well with large groups and does not require long periods of time. It is an adaptation of the brainstorming process that involves all participants in thinking rapidly on a focused topic to generate creative possibilities.

▼ Divide the large group into small groups of 6 to 8 participants. This can be by grade level, subject area, team, random, or simply grouping people where they chose to sit.

▼ Identify the goal with an **I W W M W** Statement.

I W W M W ...
(In What Ways Might We ...)

or an alternative ...

IWWMI ...
(In What Ways Might I ...)

▼ Acknowledge facilitating (strengths/opportunities) and limiting (obstacles) conditions within the problem situation.

▼ Begin the group brainstorming. All ideas should be accepted and written down. Use butcher paper so the writing can be large enough for everyone to see. The facilitator should present the rules for participation. The key behaviors are:

Speed
Fast-paced is the idea. Quantity is the goal.

Suspend Judgment
Do not evaluate as you go!

Silly
Be as ridiculous as you want. It may spark some real possibility.

Synergy
Build on the ideas of others.

▼ After a designated period of time (maybe 5-8 minutes), stop the brainstorming process. Ask each group to share one of their good solutions. This step, which is called *Cross Pollination*, sparks everyone's thinking with a few good ideas. It may also provide a direction for thinking about the topic that group members have not considered.

▼ Resume the creative thinking process. After another designated period of time (another 5-8 minutes), stop again. This time instruct participants to *Think in Reverse*. They are to provide solutions or suggestions that would create the worst possible result--or do the exact opposite of what is desired. Allow another 5 to 8 minutes to generate this separate list. This may appear to be a silly step, but it is really a most productive one. The participants will find that some of the worst solutions are the very ones currently being used and that they actually contributed to the problem in the first place. Hopefully, within these worst solutions there are some positive answers.

▼ Allow the group to continue the IWWMW-- for about 5 to 8 minutes. At this point, have each group identify 2 or 3 solutions they feel have the most potential for success. Share those with the total group.

Within a one hour session, hundreds of creative possibilities can be generated, negative actions (past and future) can be identified so that they can be addressed or avoided, and decisions can be made about the most promising potential solutions. Not only is this an effective process, it is engaging and fun!

Used with permission of Dr. Richard Villa, President, Bayridge Educational Consortium

Tool 1.2.18

Starburst

Starburst is a creative thinking technique that allows groups to gain a better understanding of an issue by asking questions. The goal is for the group to come to a different perspective about an issue as the result of posing questions and thinking collectively to answer them.

Steps:
- Identify facilitators prior to the activity and orient them to their role. Their job would be to write all questions down as fast as possible (as legibly as possible), encourage all members to participate, and to pace the activity so that no extended debates occur about the questions as they are being generated and so that more thoughtful discussion occurs when formulating answers.
- In a fast paced session, ask as many questions (from significant to silly) about the topic as possible.
- After all questions have been asked and recorded, have the group identify the two or three most important ones to answer.

Considerations:
- The groups could either be mixed with representatives from each population in one group (about 6 to 8 members in size) or there could be three homogeneous groups with each population separate. Either option could work well.

Data-based Problem Solving
Action Research

Tool 1.2.19

Action research involves teachers as researchers in studying what they are currently doing (Education Update, 1995). It is a disciplined approach to problem solving that encouragers insiders to analyze current practices in order to make the best possible decisions about how to improve. It moves beyond the prevalent tendency to base actions on intuition and hunches. Instead, it results in actions based upon data, analysis, and thorough consideration. It also reduces the urge to take action without stopping to gather adequate information.

Why Action Research?
Action research is an appealing approach for many reasons. It can be a collaborative venture capitalizing on the energy and expertise of many individuals within the school community. It addresses significant problems within the environment and is therefore a proactive, positive approach. Constructive changes within the school can result from action research. It allows individuals to address issues in an objective, impersonal, and unbiased way. The data are a springboard for discussion and the participants draw their own conclusions.

Steps:
- Formulation of a problem question. Identify a particular issue or practice as the focus for the study. Then describe what is known, what is not known, what is troubling, and the important variables affecting it. For educators, it is important to identify a problem that is related to instructional areas (curriculum and assessment) that affect student learning and is one that they have control over.

- Identify the sources of data that will provide needed information about the problem area. They can be both quantitative (statistics, tallies, frequency counts) and quantitative (descriptive, perceptual). These can be existing sources (records, test results, survey responses) or potential sources that need to be created (portfolios, observational logs, journals, pre- and post-assessments). It is suggested that at least three different sources be used so that a valid representation of the problem is developed.

- Analyze the data. This involves categorizing and sorting, developing findings, identifying patterns and trends, and drawing conclusions. A complicated statistical analysis is often not required.

- Report the results. This could range from an informal oral presentation to a more formal written report.

- Plan actions based on the findings and conclusions. It could be obvious as to what action to take. It could also be that additional information is needed to determine the appropriate courseof action. It may be helpful to find relevant articles and studies in the professional literature, to consult with experts, or to visit sites that are already addressing the problem area.

Reflection on Our Collaborative Decision Making or Problem Solving

Tool 1.2.20

This is to be used by an individual or group after engaging in decision making and/or problem solving activities. It is designed to reflect on the completeness, accuracy, and effectiveness of the group's collaborative efforts.

Decision Making

The extent to which I (or we) . . .	Okay	Could Do Better
• clearly defined the decision question?	_____	_____
• identified appropriate alternatives?	_____	_____
• identified significant criteria to be assessed in making the decision?	_____	_____
• accurately assessed the importance of the criteria to the decision?	_____	_____
• assessed the fit of the alternative with the criteria?	_____	_____
• selected a final alternative?	_____	_____

Problem Solving

The extent to which I (or we) . . .	Okay	Could Do Better
• clearly identified a goal?	_____	_____
• clearly and accurately identified the limiting conditions or constraints?	_____	_____
• described viable and appropriate ways of overcoming the constraints?	_____	_____
• thought creatively about possible solutions?	_____	_____
• selected an important and viable alternative or solution?	_____	_____
• tested the alternative selected to see if it would work?	_____	_____
• tried another alternative if the initial one did not work?	_____	_____

Design 2

Creating a School Environment For Learning

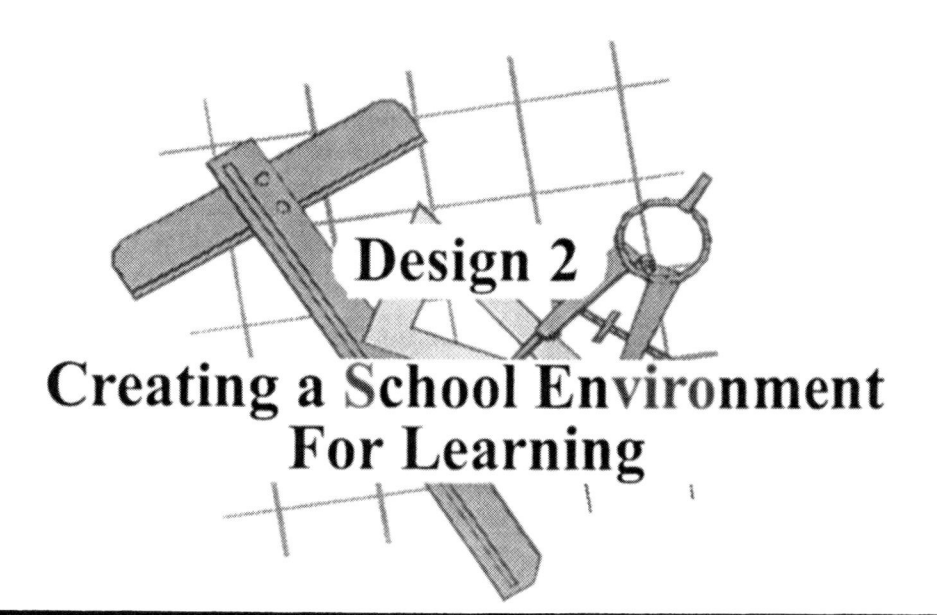

A Positive School Environment....

- creates an inviting and stimulating atmosphere in which educators, families, and community members enjoy working together to educate students.
- assures the physical and emotional well being of *all* members of the school community.
- provides an attractive, enticing setting for learning and interacting.
- is flexible enough to meet the needs of *all* members of the school community while consistently maintaining high standards and expectations.
- fosters a sense of pride in students, families, and community members.

Visitors to schools will often comment that they can sense the atmosphere of the school within the first few minutes. They see it in the way they're greeted in the office. It is reflected in the casual interactions among faculty members, students, and parents. It is illustrated by what is displayed on the walls. Researchers have documented these visitors' impressions. School environments that promote learning and positive relationships are those in which outsiders feel welcomed and valued, school personnel make an effort to put their best foot forward, the child and family consistently remain the focus of day to day business, the facility's maintenance and decor reflect the importance of pleasant surroundings, and all members of the school community feel safe and secure. These are the schools that instill pride, build confidence, and secure commitment. While these schools may not have the best facilities or resources, they have a spirit that lifts them above their obstacles. They live the philosophy of turning obstacles into opportunities and translating adversity into success. They clearly know who they are, what they value, and where they are going--and create a mythology that permeates their total environment. That's why it is so easy for visitors to perceive the quality of the school environment in such a short period of time.

Unfortunately, many schools are struggling to create such environments. They are making the best of inadequate facilities and resources; fighting problems with discipline and violence;

and dealing with student, parent, and community apathy. To make matters worse, they continue to be frustrated by lower than desirable student achievement levels. These issues are serious and will never be overcome until strategies are in place to create a positive environment for learning. As one principal found, "An atmosphere of care and casual comfort can do wonders for a school's academic standing and discipline problems" (Hean & Tin, 1996, p.70).

What we hear from ...

EDUCATORS

"I love this job. Look at this! My classroom has plenty of space, walls to display the children's work, and closets I can use to organize my supplies! With very few exceptions, my students come from homes where mom and dad will do anything to see that they learn. It was worth the pay cut to work in a school like this." (Middle School English Teacher)

"I try to make my classroom as welcoming and inviting as possible. I don't have much say in what happens beyond my classroom walls, but this is one area I can control!" (First Grade Teacher)

"Our classes are so crowded that all we can do is survive. There is no space for displaying student work or creating learning centers. Just rows of desks and chairs -- even along the side and back walls! You don't see businessmen working in this kind of setting." (High School Teacher)

PARENTS

"My child NEVER goes to the restroom at school. She says kids smoke, use drugs (especially in one of the bathrooms), and intimidate the 'straight' students. It's unhealthy. Why doesn't someone monitor this? Why should good students fear being tormented or bullied at school?" (Parent of a high school student)

"The secretary and janitor are the school's best emissaries. They make everyone glad to be at the school. I remember my first visit to the office. The janitor politely pointed the way as he was patting a child on the shoulder. The secretary, who was obviously quite busy, cheerfully answered my questions and made me feel that making an effort to ask them was really important. No wonder _____ is considered such a good school!" (Parent of an elementary student)

STUDENTS

"We wish our school could stay open all summer. For many of us, it's the best and safest place we have. I dread summer vacation. It's too violent these days. I can't even sit on my front porch any more." (High school sophomore)

"If schools realized that students are important, the schools would be better." (High school senior)

"Some of the kids are real nice and some of the teachers are, but I would like to change it. I want to have a safe school where you don't get pushed around, but where everybody is nice as they can be." (Seventh grade student)

"I think this school is a very good school. The teachers and principals run it very well. All of my teachers are willing to help me with anything - school work, home, or even friends." (Eighth grader)

Shared Responsibilities

Although educators must take the lead in creating positive school climates, both educators and parents have important roles in nuturing and maintaining them. The following diagram illustrates the responsibilities that are unique to each group and those that both groups share.

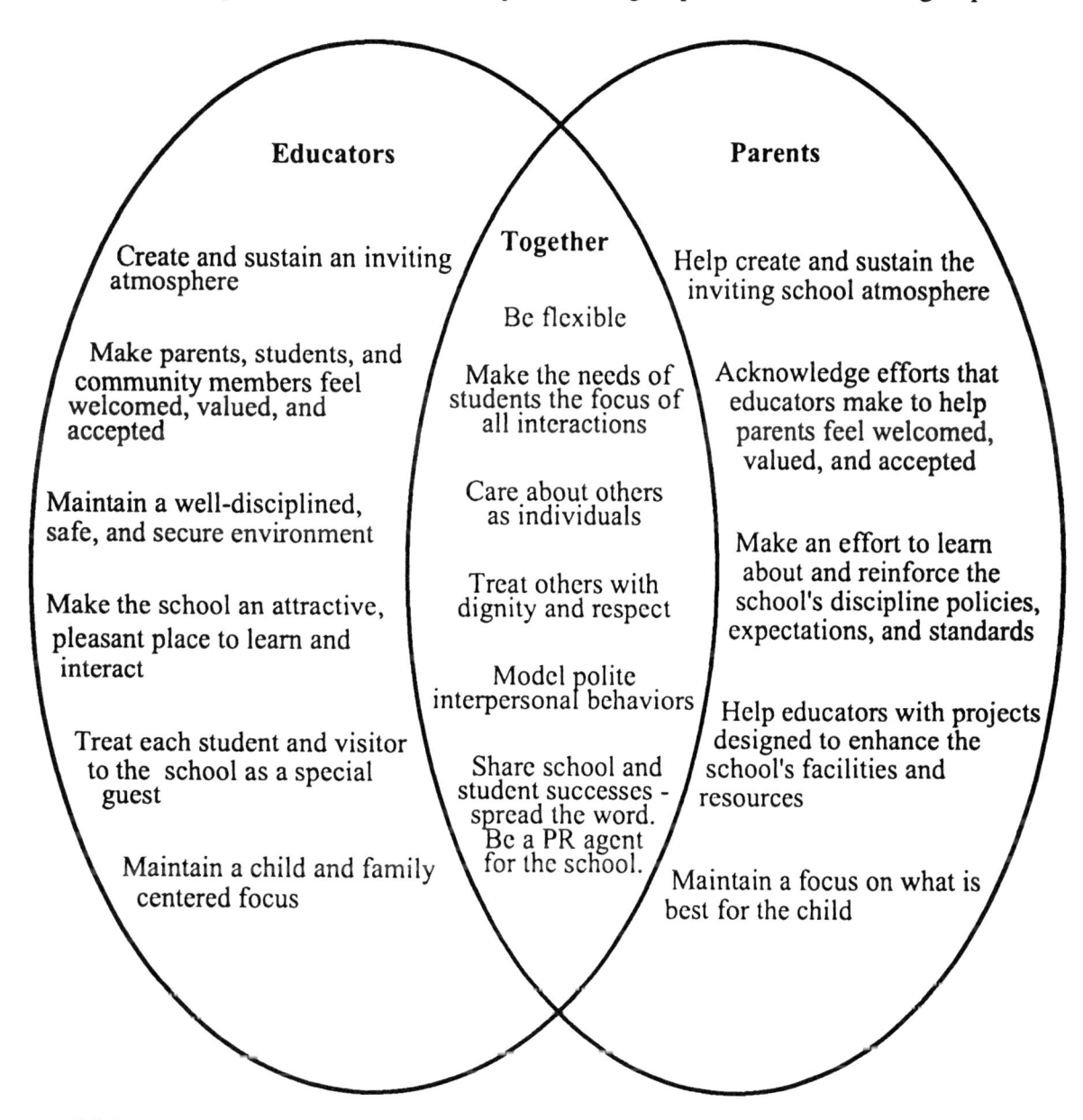

Educators
- Create and sustain an inviting atmosphere
- Make parents, students, and community members feel welcomed, valued, and accepted
- Maintain a well-disciplined, safe, and secure environment
- Make the school an attractive, pleasant place to learn and interact
- Treat each student and visitor to the school as a special guest
- Maintain a child and family centered focus

Together
- Be flexible
- Make the needs of students the focus of all interactions
- Care about others as individuals
- Treat others with dignity and respect
- Model polite interpersonal behaviors
- Share school and student successes - spread the word. Be a PR agent for the school.

Parents
- Help create and sustain the inviting school atmosphere
- Acknowledge efforts that educators make to help parents feel welcomed, valued, and accepted
- Make an effort to learn about and reinforce the school's discipline policies, expectations, and standards
- Help educators with projects designed to enhance the school's facilities and resources
- Maintain a focus on what is best for the child

There is a strong sense that physical environment, safety, and student and staff feelings about themselves are inextricably linked.

Claremont Graduate School study, Voices from the Inside, 1993, p.35

Plans and Tools
for carrying out our responsibilities in creating a school environment for learning

Plan 2.1. Creating a welcoming atmosphere

This plan guides educators in ways to greet students, parents, and community members as they are making their first impressions of the school environment. The plan includes activities for welcoming new groups of students and their families as well as individual families that are new to the school during the school year. It also provides suggestions for working with community members as they make their initial visits to the school.

Plan 2.2. Establishing a climate for cooperation and acceptance

This plan provides educators with the steps and processes needed to assess and improve the current learning climate, to develop strategies for appreciating and celebrating diversity, and to work with students in developing a positive peer culture.

Plan 2.3. Ensuring a safe and secure climate for learning

With this plan, educators will have guidelines and strategies for promoting positive social behaviors and developing proactive strategies for preventing violence.

Educator Reflection
Creating a School Environment for Learning

What type of school environment do we have? How do would our school be perceived by a visitor or a parent? What are we doing well to create and maintain a positive climate for learning? What areas should we be addressing that are currently being overlooked? Take a few minutes to reflect on the following statements. Put an "X" in the box that most closely reflects your perception.

Often   Sometimes   Rarely

1. Visitors and parents are greeted in a friendly, respectful manner.

2. Our school maintains a focus on the child and family.

3. The uniqueness of each individual is recognized, accepted, and celebrated.

4. Children and their families are accepted for who they are and do not experience prejudice due to gender, race, social class, or disabilities.

5. Faculty members make an effort to make the school as inviting, pleasant, and attractive as possible.

6. Students feel physically and emotionally safe at our school.

7. Students and parents are involved in helping to make the school environment inviting, attractive, and enjoyable.

8. Discipline policies are appropriate for creating the desired learning environment and are implemented consistently.

9. Students feel that the discipline policies are appropriate and areimplemented consistently.

10. The school is available for parent and community member use after school hours.

11. The faculty offers programs to address the needs and interests of parents and community members.

12. Educators have the materials, supplies, and equipment they need to assure student learning.

13. Programs such as food services and transportation meet the needs of students and faculty members.

Plan 2.1
Creating a Welcoming Atmosphere

When visiting a place of business (a doctor's office, a store, a restaurant), notice how you are treated when you arrive. Are you a person or a number? Are you greeted with a warm smile, a stern look, or an absent gaze? Does the receptionist or secretary look up --or just keep working? Does a request for assistance appear to be an intrusion that is keeping the receptionist from doing something that is *really important?* In answering these questions, you are forming an initial impression about the environment and your level of importance to those who are part of it. These first impressions are critical to a visitor or newcomer and often determine whether the person continues as a customer or a client.

Parents and community members are clients and schools must work as hard as any business to earn their friendship, trust, respect, and involvement. It starts with creating a positive first impression. How do visitors and parents feel about the school when they enter it the first time? What does the way they are greeted say about the school culture? Does it suggest that educators are too busy to waste time with outsiders or families? Does it indicate that family involvement is valued? Does it communicate an exciting, stimulating, and enjoyable teaching and learning environment--and that we want others to be a part of it as well?

How do successful schools accomplish such a goal? It can be as simple as a smile and a positive comment or as complex as a strategic plan to ensure successful interactions among all members of the school community. It involves taking stock of day-to-day actions, enhancing those that are creating their desired school climate, and developing others to fill gaps or voids. It requires identifying numerous ways to be friendly to others and reinforce the strengths of students and their families. It means that teaching students how to be supportive of each other, and expecting it from their interactions, is as important as academic subjects. In short, faculties that place a high priority on the school's climate model positive, caring, and supportive attitudes each and every time they interact with others. These educators know the value of taking an extra few seconds it requires to treat others in a way that instills confidence and respect.

Whatever the approach, it is critical that *all* faculty and staff realize that their attitudes and interpersonal skills contribute either positively or negatively to the school's climate. They must also recognize that the extra effort it takes to treat parents and visitors well may make the difference in how they perceive the school and its programs. The faculty's willingness to collectively put their best foot forward throughout the school year lets others know that developing partnerships to assure a positive, supportive learning environment is a priority.

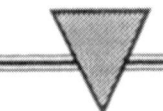

- Creating a positive first impression should be a priority for all faculty and staff during the first few weeks of each school year. Make the school, communications, and interactions as inviting as possible. Assure that parents' first visits, whether they are in the fall or later in the year, are pleasant and productive experiences. Develop ways to greet family members as they walk through the school doors--or even before they enter the building. Share highlights of the school through letters, new parent brochures, parent-to-parent visits, or home visits. Tool 2.1.1 provides ideas many educators use to ensure positive beginnings that can be nurtured into lasting partnerships.

- Throughout the year, build on the positive first impression. Develop strategies for enhancing the school climate for students, faculty, staff, parents, and visitors. Identify ways each faculty and staff member can put our best foot forward on a day-to-day basis. Tool 2.1.2 includes ideas that many schools have translated into successful practices.

- Assure that anyone who greets a parent or a visitor treats the individual as they would want to be treated. Discuss the importance of this simple principle throughout the school year, especially when the faculty and staff are feeling tired and overwhelmed--and might forget how powerful a simple greeting can be.

- As a faculty, agree upon what strengths and successes of the school should be highlighted and how they should be shared. Think beyond Open House. Although Open House has proved to be an excellent way to begin the year, it should not be the only time to introduce students, faculty, and programs and to celebrate successes. Align faculty ideas with those being developed by the parent-teacher association. Tool 2.1.3 provides an organizer for optimizing faculty and parent efforts. Which success stories or strengths could be shared by faculty and parents? What strategies for sharing these successes might be most productive? Completing an analysis such as this one might also indicate areas where too much attention is being placed and others where more is needed to achieve desired results.

- Make the school as accessible to parents and community members as possible. Through regular communication, such as the school newsletter, assure parents and community members that they are welcome to visit the school. Let them know preferred times and procedures to be followed to avoid any conflicts if they should decide to accept the offer. Also consider scheduling appointments, conferences, and parent meetings in a variety of ways to meet the needs of parents who work or have conflicts with the typical meeting times. This may even involve having more than one meeting. It doesn't matter how friendly and welcoming the atmosphere of the school is if families cannot take advantage of the opportunities educators provide. If families are a priority, educators must consider alternative ways to encourage the participation of those with work schedules, home situations, language barriers, or handicapping conditions that might prevent them from responding to invitations to the school. Try some of these ideas Tool 2.1.4 provides.

- Use parents and students as greeters at the school and at school events. The greeter concept works well for Walmart--and it can be just as powerful at school. Tools 2.15a and 2.1.5b illustrate how parents and students can effectively fulfill this role.

For parents, this is an honor and a way to be involved in a manner that fits with a parent's abilities and schedule. For students, it is a leadership opportunity that could be extended to those who are not the most popular or who do not already hold offices or leadership positions.

- Involve family and community members as PR agents for the school. Include positive and enthusiastic supporters of the school in activities that highlight the school and make invited guests realize that they are the key to building upon the school's current successes. Ask the parent group to help in sharing the strengths and successes of the school throughout the community and work with them in developing appropriate strategies. Capitalize on their strengths, talents, and careers. For example, if some parents work with the local newspaper or television station, seek their assistance with advertising strategies. They may suggest some that we as educators have not yet been considered! See Plan 3.3 for additional ideas in this area.

- Periodically assess how others perceive the faculty's efforts to create a welcoming and supportive school climate. Tools 2.1.6a and 2.1.6b provide two formats for a survey to assess the perceptions of others regarding the friendliness of the school.

Other Possibilities:

Positive Beginnings
Ideas for Communicating a Positive School Climate to New Parents

Tool 2.1.1

Welcoming Attitudes

Parents often tell us that they sense the climate of the school by the way they are treated as they enter the main office. Be sure that secretarial staff members and any teachers who greet parents in or around the office treat them as if they were a prized commodity. Let them know that educators realize that they care enough about their child to come to school. A smile, a pleasant "hello," or a quick acknowledgment can make a tremendous difference in how they perceive the school.

Welcoming Atmosphere

Many educators tell us that they make an effort to transform often sterile entrances to their buildings with plants, pictures, banners, flags, benches and other cozy furnishings to make everyone feel as comfortable at school as they would at home. This is particularly important for parents whose past experiences with school were not positive ones. In some schools, picture walls, highlighting accomplishments of students and parents, are placed in prominent places in the foyer as another way of telling parents, "You are welcome and we value what you have to offer!"

Welcoming Signs and Messages

Have you ever stopped to think about the signs that parents or visitors encounter as they enter the building? What message do they communicate? Is it the message you really intend to send to visitors? Parents who enter a building with banners like "Welcome to Our School" or "Families are Our Greatest Resource" know from the moment they enter the school doors that they are valued. Why not replace harshly phrased signs with friendlier ones. One school replaced the sign on all exterior doors that read, "All visitors must report to the office" with one that saying, "Welcome to _____. Please stop by the office to tell us that you are here. Thank you." Another redesigned a sign that said, "Visitors must not proceed beyond this point" to one that says,

```
Welcome,
Visitors!
Please Stop by the Office.

Be sure you have signed in
at the office before going
beyond this point.

We are protecting your child's
learning environment.
```

Tool 2.1.1

Welcoming Letters (From the Principal)

Write to parents in the summer to welcome them to the school. This is especially effective when families are new to the community or school level. Include important information about the opening of school: dates, times for registration, when class lists will be posted, transportation guidelines, how to contact parent-teacher organization members, and any other general information about the school. Large schools often enclose maps so parents can help their child find his or her way to class on the first day of school.

Welcoming Letters (From Individual Teachers)

Teachers often write to their new students and parents in early August to introduce themselves and to heighten students' excitement about the beginning of school. These letters set the stage for ongoing communication in nontraditional ways. In the letters, teachers can also communicate their desire to work closely with the parent and to have the parent feel free to communicate with them at any time.

Summer Tour of the Building

When students and parents are new to a community or a school, the thought of how to get around without looking lost weighs heavily on their minds. Why not eliminate this concern and, at the same time, use the opportunity to make parents and community members feel more welcomed at the school? Better yet, why not let parents and students plan and take responsibility for the project? Hosting a "Summer Tour of the Building" allows tour guides to highlight more than just the building. They can share what is unique and positive about the school, which is generally far more impressive than the building they are showing. Tell new students and parents about honors students are winning, extra activities the parent-teacher organization sponsors, special events held each year to involve parents, and how hard each faculty member works to make every child successful. (Parents want to know that their child will receive this type of treatment.). The involvement of parents and students in these tours communicates excitement about what is happening at the school and lets visitors and newcomers see possibilities for their own participation.

Get Acquainted Breakfasts

Coffee and donuts are a great way to get to know parents. While more detail is provided about ways to reach out to parents in *Design 4: Promoting Supportive Relationships*, it is worth mentioning that informal invitations to visit and become involved in the school start the year on a positive note--and food almost always makes the get togethers more enjoyable.

School Brochures

When parents walk into the school or the main office, many schools have colorful displays of brochures describing the school or specific programs. Parents who are intimidated to talk to school personnel can simply pick up a brochure to read at home. See Tool 2.1.2.

Tool 2.1.2

Putting Our Best Foot Forward
Ideas for Reinforcing a Positive School Climate Throughout the School Year

Greetings
Assure that each faculty or staff member who greets a parent does so in such a way that it communicates the importance of the child and the parent. Be sure that custodians and school secretaries realize that they may be the first or only person a parent encounters. They are just as important as faculty members in portraying the climate of the school.

Student and Parent Ambassadors
Use student and parent ambassadors to represent the school throughout the year. The key to a successful ambassador program is selecting enthusiastic, positive, and responsible candidates. Although it takes time to prepare both groups for their roles, many schools find it is worth the effort. Parents can share upcoming events on a one-to-one basis with less involved parents and can actually sell the events and the total school program by sharing highlights from previous years. Student ambassadors are often used to greet parents, to usher at parent-teacher association meetings, and to greet newcomers to the school.

Special Family Evenings
View typical obligations like parent conferences and parent open houses as opportunities to develop a "sense of belonging" between the child's family and school personnel. Plan special activities that will entice the entire family to participate. Performances are a tried and true favorite and one of the best ways to get parents to school. In some schools, the parent organization plans events for the children while parents are talking with teachers. In others, parents are encouraged to take what they have learned home to share with their children.

Hook One Family
One school uses a fishing theme to make a difference with one family each six weeks. Make special telephone calls, send invitations, or make a home visit. See if the extra effort will reap dividends. Remember that if each faculty member hooked one uninvolved parent, it would soon make a major difference.

Maximize Communication Tools
Use banners and themes to welcome families and to communicate goals for the school year. Keep a family bulletin board in the school entrance hall up-to-date with notices of upcoming events and highlights of student and parent activities and contributions. Keep informative and interesting materials available for parents to see as they enter the building. The more they know about the school and all the activities it provides, the better they will feel about what it has to offer their child.

Flyers
In many schools, the counter in the main office is filled with flyers about parent-teacher organization activities, how parents are involved in special projects, and upcoming events.

Parents who visit the school for any reason can walk away with a tremendous amount of information. This also sends the message that school personnel and parent organization leaders want parents to work with them at any time during the school year.

Grade Level, Department, or Classroom Brochures

Some schools are creating brochures for specific program areas. When family members visit the school for information, the secretary does not have to stop to recite information that is attractively printed and displayed. Instead, the time can be spent getting to know the visitor while gathering the appropriate information.

Newsletters

Nearly all schools use their newsletters to get the year off to a good start. Why not treat each newsletter as if it were the first one of the year?

Calendars

A schoolwide calendar for each month can highlight upcoming events for parent involvement and can also be a way to get parents actively involved with their child's education. Many schools send a calendar home with each child--and leave others on the counter in the office for those parents who misplace their originals.

School Slogans or Themes

Identify a short, but meaningful theme or slogan and use it to promote the school culture. When the theme is repeated often enough, people will recall it when they think about the school. Themes that reinforce the school's vision, mission, or high priority goals subtly remind parents and visitors about what is valued at the school.

Parent, Student, and Teacher Appreciation Mementos

In some schools, small illustrated signs, pictures, and poems are placed in prominent places throughout the school. In one school, a restroom by the entrance has beautifully illustrated poems about how important parents are to the success of their children. In another, the teacher's lounge has similar poems highlighting the importance of teachers and parents working together.

Name Tags

In many schools, visitors are asked to wear name tags. Why not have special name tags for parents that communicate how important they are to the school?

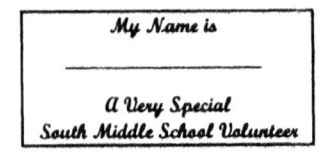

> *My Name is*
> _____
>
> *A Very Special*
> *South Middle School Volunteer*

See Other Designs

There are a wealth of ideas that can be added to these in *Design 3: Communicating Effectively* and *Design 4: Promoting Supportive Relationships*. It is in communicating and developing relationships that we have opportunities to build lasting partnerships.

What School and Student Successes Should Be Highlighted and How?

Tool 2.1.3

Faculty	Together	Parent Association
What? How?	What? How?	What? How?
What? How?	What? How?	What? How?
What? How?	What? How?	What? How?

Making the School Accessible For Parents With . . .

Tool 2.1.4

Work Schedule Conflicts
- Schedule conferences before school, after school, and in the evening on two separate days.
- Hold Saturday morning conferences--maybe in conjunction with Saturday Academies or enrichment activities.
- Ask employers of local plants and factories if a space could be provided for informal meetings with parents during their lunch hours or breaks. Provide release time for faculty members or use parent volunteers to share important information with parents and to let them know about other ways the faculty is willing to adjust for their work schedules.

Home Situation Problems
- Many parents do not attend school events because they do not have someone to care for their children when they leave. Provide child care for these parents during conferences, meetings, or other important school functions. In some schools, high school students who have had child care classes use these events as opportunities for community service.
- If families cannot come to the school, go to them. Home visits may be the only vehicle for making the school accessible to families where domestic problems, child care, or fear of the school or teachers are barriers to involvement.

Language barriers
- Use high school foreign language students to serve as translators.
- If no one in the school is able to communicate in the language, ask community members to serve as translators. Assure them that they do not have to be fluent in the language. Just making the effort lets the family members know that school personnel are trying their best to keep them involved.
- See *Design 3: Communicating Effectively* for additional Plans and Tools for overcoming language barriers.

Disabilities
- Ask parents or agency representatives who are familiar with the concerns of others with handicapping conditions to serve as ambassadors to new families. Let them share what the school is doing to meet their needs or those of their child.
- Ask the parent association to provide transportation and support for family members with handicapping conditions.
- Send families diagrams of the school highlighting handicap accessible routes to classrooms and meeting areas.
- Help families network with other families faced with handicapping conditions.

Parents as Greeters

Tool 2.1.5a

In the Office
Parent greeters can welcome family members and other visitors as they enter the office and route them to the appropriate office personnel or faculty members. At the same time, it gives the parent greeters an opportunity to share parent involvement opportunities on an informal basis.

At Special Events
Parents make wonderful greeters at music, drama, and athletic events (many are always there when their child is participating and would enjoy something to do), Open Houses, Parent Nights, and other schoolwide events. Set the stage for their success. Give them all the information, flyers, or brochures they need to be able to encourage parent participation and involvement in the school's other programs and events.

In the Entry Hall
Parent can be stationed at entry points to meet others who are accompanying their child to school or bringing materials, lunch money, and other necessities that their child forgot. This accomplishes several purposes. It relieves office personnel from taking time out to deal with minor issues. It gives parent volunteers a significant contributing role at the school. Finally, it promotes informal networking. When parents in the school community realize that a parent volunteer is at the school and available to talk with them, they are more likely to take advantage of the opportunity to ask questions or to seek information and advice they might be fearful of asking school personnel.

In the Community
Many schools have Parent Welcome Wagons or other types of networking structures to greet parents who are new to the community. Others simply ask well-informed, enthusiastic parents to visit or give new parents a telephone call to welcome them to the school community. Parents who are aware of all the programs and activities the school provides make wonderful ambassadors for the school. For more information, see *Design 4: Promoting Supportive Relationships.*

Parent Greeters Should Have:

- A desire to help others
- Outgoing, enthusiastic personalities
- Knowledge of the school and community
- Information about *all* of the schools' activities
- A willingness to make contacts in a timely manner

Students as Greeters

Tool 2.1.5b

In the Office
Many schools allow students who have demonstrated good citizenship, improved academic performance, or other accomplishments to serve as greeters for parents and visitors for a specified period of time, usually a grading period. This works best when the criteria for selection are well known and students view the opportunity as an honor.

At the Entrance to the School
Each morning as the school day begins, students could be assigned to the front of the school (by the front doors, at the curb, at busses, or where walking students enter school property) to greet classmates, teachers, family members, and visitors while opening the doors for them. This not only creates a welcoming atmosphere for those entering the building, but it also develops the social skills of the greeters.

At Special Events
Not all students are involved in music, drama, or athletics. Those who are not enjoy the chance to participate in school events by handing out brochures, ushering visitors to their seats, and greeting everyone as they enter the area. These events, along with Parent Night and other schoolwide activities, are an excellent time to involve students who may not have many opportunities to perform. Parents may come to school just to see their child in such a role.

In the Community
Assign students roles as greeters for new families in the community. Students who are new to the school and community would appreciate hearing about the school from their peers. This should be initiated as soon as a new student enrolls in the school--and could occur at any time throughout the school year. Students could be trained as greeters during the spring to be ready to greet newcomers during the summer. For more information, see *Design 4: Promoting Supportive Relationships*.

Student Greeters Should Have:

- A desire to help others
- Outgoing, enthusiastic personalities
- Knowledge of the school and community
- Information about *all* of the schools' activities
- A willingness to make contacts in a timely manner

Friendliness Audit

Tool 2.1.6a

Parents, we are very concerned about how you and your family are treated at our school. Would you take a few moments to let us know how we are doing? Please answer all items. Mark "Do not know" if you have not had experiences with any of the groups included on the audit. Please do not identify any personnel by name.

	Strongly Agree	Agree	Disagree	Strongly Disagree	Do Not Know
School personnel make family members feel welcome when they visit the school:					
1. School administrators	O	O	O	O	O
2. Office personnel	O	O	O	O	O
3. Teachers or their assistants	O	O	O	O	O
4. Custodians	O	O	O	O	O
5. Cafeteria Personnel	O	O	O	O	O
6. Security guards	O	O	O	O	O
School personnel treat family members and visitors to the school in a friendly manner:					
1. School administrators	O	O	O	O	O
2. Office personnel	O	O	O	O	O
3. Teachers or their assistants	O	O	O	O	O
4. Custodians	O	O	O	O	O
5. Cafeteria Personnel	O	O	O	O	O
6. Security guards	O	O	O	O	O
School personnel treat students in a positive and caring manner:					
1. School administrators	O	O	O	O	O
2. Office personnel	O	O	O	O	O
3. Teachers or their assistants	O	O	O	O	O
4. Custodians	O	O	O	O	O
5. Cafeteria Personnel	O	O	O	O	O
6. Security guards	O	O	O	O	O
School personnel treat each other in a positive, supportive, and caring manner.	O	O	O	O	O
Students are friendly to others they know well.	O	O	O	O	O
Most students are friendly to all of their peers.	O	O	O	O	O

Thank you for you assistance in helping us achieve one of our most important goals.

Friendliness Audit

Tool 2.1.6b

Parents, we are very concerned about how you and your family are treated at our school. Would you take a few minutes to let us know how we are doing? Fill in the appropriate circle that reflects what you have experienced as you have visited the school or met with faculty members.

	Very Well Satisfied	Well Satisfied	Poorly Satisfied	Very Poorly Satisfied	Do Not Know
I am greeted in a friendly manner when I enter the school building or attend school events.	O	O	O	O	O
Faculty members make me feel like an important part of my child's education.	O	O	O	O	O
Office personnel are helpful when I have a question or a request.	O	O	O	O	O
School administrators are willing to take time to speak to me or to answer my questions.	O	O	O	O	O
Teachers call me or send notes to let me know how my child is doing.	O	O	O	O	O
Teachers share success stories about my child as well as problems or concerns.	O	O	O	O	O
Teachers are willing to talk with me or meet with me when I request a conference.	O	O	O	O	O
Teachers make an effort to handle unique parent needs, such as language barriers and work schedules.	O	O	O	O	O
School personnel treat each other in a positive, respectful, and caring manner.	O	O	O	O	O
School personnel treat students in a positive, respectful, and caring manner.	O	O	O	O	O
Students are friendly to others they know well.	O	O	O	O	O
Students are friendly to all of their peers.	O	O	O	O	O

Thank you for your assistance in helping us achieve one of our most important goals.

Plan 2.2
Establishing a Climate of Cooperation and Acceptance

> No one is ever completely from one community. We are all active members in many communities that come already equipped with tacit rituals and rules; ways of talking, acting, valuing, being in the world.
>
> Margaret Finders, 1992, p.64

Schools that create a sense of belonging among all of their stakeholders are the ones that reap the benefits of student achievement and success, parental and community member involvement, and pride within their communities. When students feel that they are an important part of the school, they are more willing to put forth the effort to learn and to participate in school activities. When parents of all cultures and backgrounds perceive that educators value their contributions and participation, they are more likely to remain involved or to increase their level of involvement. When community members realize that school personnel prize their contributions, they are more willing to continue their support.

While most schools make an effort to create an accepting and cooperative environment, those that are most successful make it a priority. They emphasize developing a positive peer culture that includes and supports *all* students, families, and community members. They develop plans to make it happen rather than just hoping it will evolve. If this is a goal, how is your school doing? How do your students and parents feel about the success of these efforts? This Plan provides a means to reflect upon our current efforts and Tools that can be used to enhance our strengths and remedy our weaknesses.

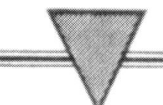

- Assess perceptions of the current school climate. Review the findings of the parent survey in *Design 1: Gathering Perceptions*. What were the general perceptions of the school climate? What areas appear to be strengths? What areas pose challenges for the school? If desired, each teacher could administer a student classroom survey to determine their students' perceptions of the social and learning climate. Tools 2.2.1a, 2.2.1b, and 2.2.1c provide sample surveys that can be used at the elementary, intermediate, and middle school or high school levels. To augment the initial parent survey, a parent version of the student classroom survey is available if the faculty wants to assess how parents' views of the social and learning climate compare to their children's views (Tool 2.2.2). Analyze the surveys (by classroom and/or by total school) to determine what students and parents perceive to be most positive and what they identify as areas of concern. Tool 2.2.3a and 2.3.3b provide pattern analysis forms that will be useful for understanding student and parent survey results.

- Discuss the survey results as a faculty. Using all of these data sources, decide as a faculty if the survey results coincide with what the faculty perceives. Consider the following questions: In what areas is there agreement? Where is the disagreement? How well are current efforts to promote cooperation and acceptance perceived? What appear to be the major concerns?

- Take Action. Celebrate the successes. We overlook this step much too often. At the same time, do not allow today's successes to become tomorrow's stumbling blocks. Develop strategies to maintain or build upon the areas perceived as strengths. *Then* address concerns. Begin by identifying strategies (both schoolwide and classroom) that are currently being used to create a climate of cooperation and acceptance. Reflect upon each and decide which are working well and which could be continued or enhanced.

- Expand the focus of planning efforts to creating a positive culture that promotes cooperation and acceptance of *all* members of the diverse school community. Appreciating and celebrating diversity is not something that can be left to chance. There are educators, students, and parents who truly appreciate, value, respect, and celebrate others for their unique abilities, talents, and cultures. However, many people are caught in the web of ethnocentrism, the tendency to regard our own ethnic group, culture, or nation as better or more correct than others. Educators have the opportunity and the responsibility for overcoming the prejudices, conflicts, and inequities that ethnocentrism fosters. Tool 2.2.4 provides a means to confront ethnocentrism and to collaboratively develop strategies for appreciating and celebrating diversity. What is generated from these activities should be the beginning of an ongoing dialogue about these differences and how faculties and partnerships can work together most effectively to achieve the best possible education for *all* children.

- Building on the synergy generated by working collaboratively to appreciate and celebrate diversity, the next critical step is to promote trust and respect throughout the school. Without this step, some educators or partners may agree on the value of accepting and cooperating with one another, but fail to translate what they value into action. It takes much more than saying "trust me" to create a climate in which trust and respect flourish and fear and doubt disappear. In fact, these words often spark feelings of skepticism in the minds of those who hear them. Unless, of course, the actions of the speaker inspire others to believe that they are sincere. This is another critical area that is neither costly nor time consuming. It does, however, require an awareness of one's actions and a commitment to doing the right thing. Tool 2.2.5 provides research based guidelines to use as conversation starters about current and desired levels of trust and respect. Adapt or add to these guidelines so they align with the faculty's beliefs. Tool 2.2.6, a self-reflection, may be helpful in initiating the conversation.

- Develop strategies for promoting positive social behaviors that will ensure a climate of cooperation and acceptance. Schools today realize the importance of social skills, cooperation, teamwork, and good character in preparing students for life and work. Educators can no longer expect students to arrive at the school's doorsteps with the ability to interact with others in a positive, supportive, and successful manner. Instead, we must overtly teach our students how to get along with each other and with adults in the school. Furthermore, national studies and major companies tell school personnel that they rank a prospective employee's ability to work collaboratively as part of a team as highly as they do outstanding grades and resumes (SCANS Report for America 2000, 1991). Educators and parents realize that students who know how to get along with their peers and to work successfully with others make better grades and have more fun during their school years. How, then, do schools develop and reinforce positive social behaviors? They teach them overtly and assist parents in reinforcing them at home. Tool 2.2.7 involves educators in identifying desired behaviors and in assessing how they are currently being taught or monitored. Tool 2.2.8 describes a variety of strategies schools are using to reinforce appropriate social behaviors. Tool 2.2.9 illustrates important guidelines for educators to follow in helping parents reinforce these behaviors at home. To help parents get started, Tool 2.2.10 is a parent letter that outlines specific actions they can take to support their child and your efforts.

Primary Student
School Climate Questionnaire

Tool 2.2.1a

1. My teacher is nice to me. _____   😊   😐   ☹️

2. My teacher helps me learn new things. ___   😊   😐   ☹️

3. My teacher answers my questions. _____   😊   😐   ☹️

4. Students in my class are nice to each other.   😊   😐   ☹️

5. I know how to behave in school. _____   😊   😐   ☹️

6. I like coming to school. _____   😊   😐   ☹️

Here is a picture of what I like best about school. . . .

Primary Student School Questionnaire Tally Sheet

Tool 2.2.1a

Item	🙂	😐	🙁
1. My teacher is nice to me.			
2. My teacher helps me learn new things.			
3. My teacher answers my questions.			
4. Students in my class are nice to each other.			
5. I know how to behave in school.			
6. I like coming to school.			
7. What students like best about school. . . .			

Elementary Student School Climate Questionnaire Tool 2.2.1b

1. My teacher is nice to me. _____ (Yes) (No) (?)

2. My teacher helps me learn new things. _____ (Yes) (No) (?)

3. My teacher answers my questions or helps me find the answers. _____ (Yes) (No) (?)

4. My teacher helps me with my problems. _____ (Yes) (No) (?)

5. Students in my class are nice to each other. _____ (Yes) (No) (?)

6. Students in my class follow the teacher's directions: (Yes) (No) (?)

7. Students in my class help each other learn. _____ (Yes) (No) (?)

8. What I am learning is interesting to me. _____ (Yes) (No) (?)

9. I know how to behave in school. _____ (Yes) (No) (?)

10. I know how to study and learn. _____ (Yes) (No) (?)

11. I can make choices about what I learn. _____ (Yes) (No) (?)

12. My teacher listens when I have a good idea. _____ (Yes) (No) (?)

13. I have friends at school. _____ (Yes) (No) (?)

14. I like coming to school. _____ (Yes) (No) (?)

What I like best about school is _____

_____

What I'd like to change about school is _____

_____

Tool 2.2.1b

Elementary Student School Climate Questionnaire Tally Sheet

Item	YES	NO	?
1. My teacher is nice to me.			
2. My teacher helps me learn new things.			
3. My teacher answers my questions/helps me find answers.			
4. My teacher helps me with my problems.			
5. Students in my class are nice to each other.			
6. Students in my class follow the teacher's directions.			
7. Students in my class help each other learn.			
8. What I am learning is interesting to me.			
9. I know how to behave in school.			
10. I know how to study and learn.			
11. I can make choices about what I learn.			
12. My teacher listens when I have a good idea.			
13. I have friends at school.			
14. I like coming to school.			
15. What I like best about school is . . .			
16. What I'd like to change about school is . . .			

Student Classroom Questionnaire

Tool 2.2.1c

Please circle the number on the following continuum that best describes your experience. Feel free to use the back of this survey to include comments or suggestions.

The atmosphere in this classroom:

is cooperative 1 – 2 – 3 – 4 – 5 is uncooperative

is encouraging 1 – 2 – 3 – 4 – 5 is discouraging

is friendly 1 – 2 – 3 – 4 – 5 is unfriendly

is warm and caring 1 – 2 – 3 – 4 – 5 is cold and hostile

lets me be myself 1 – 2 – 3 – 4 – 5 asks me to play "games"

is fair 1 – 2 – 3 – 4 – 5 is unfair

encourages me to learn 1 – 2 – 3 – 4 – 5 discourages my learning

is safe and relaxing 1 – 2 – 3 – 4 – 5 is threatening and tense

allows me input into decisions 1 – 2 – 3 – 4 – 5 does not ask for my opinions

For me, the classwork and homework:

is at the right level of difficulty 1 – 2 – 3 – 4 – 5 is too easy or too hard

is stimulating 1 – 2 – 3 – 4 – 5 is boring

is new and interesting 1 – 2 – 3 – 4 – 5 is familiar and uninteresting

is useful to me 1 – 2 – 3 – 4 – 5 is not useful to me

is challenging 1 – 2 – 3 – 4 – 5 is frustrating

My teacher:

is willing to give me extra time 1 – 2 – 3 – 4 – 5 is not willing to give me extra time

shows understanding 1 – 2 – 3 – 4 – 5 is criticizing

gives clear directions 1 – 2 – 3 – 4 – 5 does not give clear directions

uses group work to help us learn 1 – 2 – 3 – 4 – 5 does not use group work

gives me choices in what/how I learn 1 – 2 – 3 – 4 – 5 does not provide choices

tests and grades fairly 1 – 2 – 3 – 4 – 5 does not test or grade fairly

is willing to help with my problems 1 – 2 – 3 – 4 – 5 is not willing to help with my problems

recognizes my accomplishments 1 – 2 – 3 – 4 – 5 does not recognize my accomplishments

Student Classroom Questionnaire Tally Sheet

Tool 2.2.1c

	1	2	3	4	5
Atmosphere					
Cooperative/Uncooperative					
Encouraging/Discouraging					
Friendly/Unfriendly					
Warm & caring/Cold & hostile					
Be myself/Play games					
Fair/Unfair					
Encourages learning/Discourages learning					
Safe & relaxing/Threatening & tense					
Allows input/Does not ask my opinions					
Classwork/Homework					
Right level of difficulty/Too easy or hard					
Stimulating/Boring					
New & interesting/Familiar & uninteresting					
Useful to me/Not useful to me					
Challenging/Frustrating					
My Teacher					
Gives extra time/Does not give extra time					
Shows understanding/Is criticizing					
Gives clear directions/Does not give clear directions					
Uses group work to learn/Does not use group work					
Gives me choices/Does not give me choices					
Tests & grades fairly/Does not test & grade fairly					
Helps me with my problems/Does not help me					
Recognizes my accomplishments/Does not recognize					

Parent Classroom Questionnaire

Tool 2.2.2

Please circle the number on the following continuum that best describes your child's experience this year. Feel free to use the back of this survey to include comments or suggestions.

The atmosphere in my child's classroom:

is cooperative	1 — 2 — 3 — 4 — 5	is uncooperative
is encouraging	1 — 2 — 3 — 4 — 5	is discouraging
is friendly	1 — 2 — 3 — 4 — 5	is unfriendly
is warm and caring	1 — 2 — 3 — 4 — 5	is cold and hostile
encourages student individuality	1 — 2 — 3 — 4 — 5	requires students to play "games"
is fair	1 — 2 — 3 — 4 — 5	is unfair
encourages students to learn	1 — 2 — 3 — 4 — 5	discourages student learning
is safe and relaxing	1 — 2 — 3 — 4 — 5	is threatening and tense
allows students input into decisions	1 — 2 — 3 — 4 — 5	does not ask for students' opinions

For my child, the classwork and homework:

is at the right level of difficulty	1 — 2 — 3 — 4 — 5	is too easy or too hard
is stimulating	1 — 2 — 3 — 4 — 5	is boring
is new and interesting	1 — 2 — 3 — 4 — 5	is familiar and uninteresting
is useful to my child	1 — 2 — 3 — 4 — 5	is not useful to my child
is challenging	1 — 2 — 3 — 4 — 5	is frustrating

My child's teacher:

is willing to give my child extra time	1 — 2 — 3 — 4 — 5	does not give my child extra time
shows understanding	1 — 2 — 3 — 4 — 5	is criticizing
gives clear directions	1 — 2 — 3 — 4 — 5	does not give clear directions
uses group work	1 — 2 — 3 — 4 — 5	does not use group work
encourages student creativity	1 — 2 — 3 — 4 — 5	does not encourage student creativity
tests and grades fairly	1 — 2 — 3 — 4 — 5	does not test or grade fairly
helps students with their problems	1 — 2 — 3 — 4 — 5	does not help students with problems
recognizes students' accomplishments	1 — 2 — 3 — 4 — 5	does not recognize accomplishments

Parent Classroom Questionnaire Tally Sheet

Tool 2.2.2

	1	2	3	4	5
Atmosphere					
Cooperative/Uncooperative					
Encouraging/Discouraging					
Friendly/Unfriendly					
Warm & caring/Cold & hostile					
Encourages individuality/Requires student "games"					
Fair/Unfair					
Encourages learning/Discourages learning					
Safe & relaxing/Threatening & tense					
Allows input/Does not ask my opinions					
Classwork/Homework					
Right level of difficulty/Too easy or hard					
Stimulating/Boring					
New & interesting/Familiar & uninteresting					
Useful to my child/Not useful to my child					
Challenging/Frustrating					
My Child's Teacher					
Gives extra time/Does not give extra time					
Shows understanding/Is criticizing					
Gives clear directions/Does not give clear directions					
Uses group work to learn/Does not use group work					
Encourages creativity/Does not encourage creativity					
Tests & grades fairly/Does not test & grade fairly					
Helps students with problems/Does not help them					
Recognizes accomplishments/Does not recognize					

Student Classroom Questionnaire Results

Tool 2.2.3a

Areas of Greatest Satisfaction

- _____
- _____
- _____
- _____
- _____
- _____

Areas of Moderate Satisfaction

- _____
- _____
- _____
- _____
- _____
- _____

Areas of Greatest Dissatisfaction

- _____
- _____
- _____
- _____
- _____
- _____

Parent Classroom Questionnaire Results

Tool 2.2.3b

Areas of Greatest Satisfaction

- _____
- _____
- _____
- _____
- _____
- _____

Areas of Moderate Satisfaction

- _____
- _____
- _____
- _____
- _____
- _____

Areas of Greatest Dissatisfaction

- _____
- _____
- _____
- _____
- _____
- _____

Tool 2.2.4a

Appreciating and Celebrating Diversity

How Are We Doing?
Share the Johnson (1993) quote with the faculty (Tool 2.2.4b). Then ask them to complete the Reflections on Diversity self-assessment (Tool 2.2.4c) to determine how individual teachers and the faculty as a whole feel about and treat others from backgrounds different from their own. Provide an opportunity to share their perceptions in a nonthreatening manner. Do not ask for their individual reflections. This is provided for their own personal awareness and growth. Small groups could highlight what they perceive to be the faculty's strengths and challenges.

What Does it Mean to Appreciate and Celebrate Diversity?
1. In small groups of six or seven, begin by filling out the Appreciating and Celebrating Diversity T-Chart (Tool 2.2.4d). Ask each group to share their descriptions and look for common themes across the groups.
2. From the "What it is" column on the T-Chart, identify:
   - what the faculty is currently doing well, and
   - what might be considered to augment current efforts.
3. From the "What it is not" column, identify:
   - undesirable elements of the school culture that should be addressed and changed.
4. Building on these responses, brainstorm some actions that could be taken to enhance the celebration of diversity.

What Could We Be Doing to Promote the Appreciation and Celebration of Diversity?
1. Continuing with the small groups (group members could be the same or different), think of ways that faculty members (as individuals and as a group) can improve their efforts to acknowledge, appreciate, value, celebrate, and show respect for individual differences. Brainstorm (and record ideas) for a few minutes and then let each group share what it generated with the total faculty.
2. Repeat the process by focusing on what families could do to support or reinforce the faculty's efforts. Again, write ideas on butcher paper and share.
3. As a total faculty, or in combined small groups (if the faculty is too large), synthesize the two sets of responses by identifying which actions should be the exclusive responsibility of educators or families. Which overlap and should be shared by both groups?
4. Use the following Appreciating Diversity: What Can We Do form (Tool 2.2.4e) to record ideas.

What Could We Learn From Others?
1. The brainstorming process allows us to learn from others on our faculty. Build on each other's ideas and implement successful strategies immediately that match the needs of the school community.
2. At the same time, explore other ways to enhance the faculty's current approaches. Form study groups or scout groups to gather additional ideas from educational research or other schools.

Tool 2.2.4b

"Within a relationship, community,

organization, or society,

the goal is not to assimilate all groups

so that everyone is alike.

The goal is to work together

to achieve mutual goals

while recognizing cultural diversity

and learning to value and respect

fundamental differences while working

together to achieve mutual goals."

David Johnson, 1993

Reflections on Diversity

Tool 2.2.4c

Do I...					Does Our Faculty...			
Always	Often	Rarely	Never		Always	Often	Rarely	Never
—	—	—	—	Recognize, value, and respect the uniqueness of each colleague, child, parent, and community member?	—	—	—	—
—	—	—	—	Try to understand the customs and values of all of our students?	—	—	—	—
—	—	—	—	View learning about various religious, ethnic, or cultural backgrounds as an enriching experience?	—	—	—	—
—	—	—	—	Provide children with opportunities to learn about diverse cultures?	—	—	—	—
—	—	—	—	Provide parents and members of the community with opportunities to learn about diverse cultures?	—	—	—	—
—	—	—	—	Make an effort to help all students feel accepted?	—	—	—	—
—	—	—	—	Make an effort to help parents and others feel accepted?	—	—	—	—
—	—	—	—	Experience culture clashes that result from a lack of understanding about religious, ethnic, or cultural backgrounds other than my own?	—	—	—	—
—	—	—	—	Provide opportunities for parents of various religious, ethnic, or cultural backgrounds to work cooperatively on projects that will benefit all of their children?	—	—	—	—
—	—	—	—	Feel comfortable sharing personal opinions with members of different cultures?	—	—	—	—

Appreciating and Celebrating Diversity

Tool 2.2.4d

What it is	What it is not

Appreciating and Celebrating Diversity:
What We Can Do

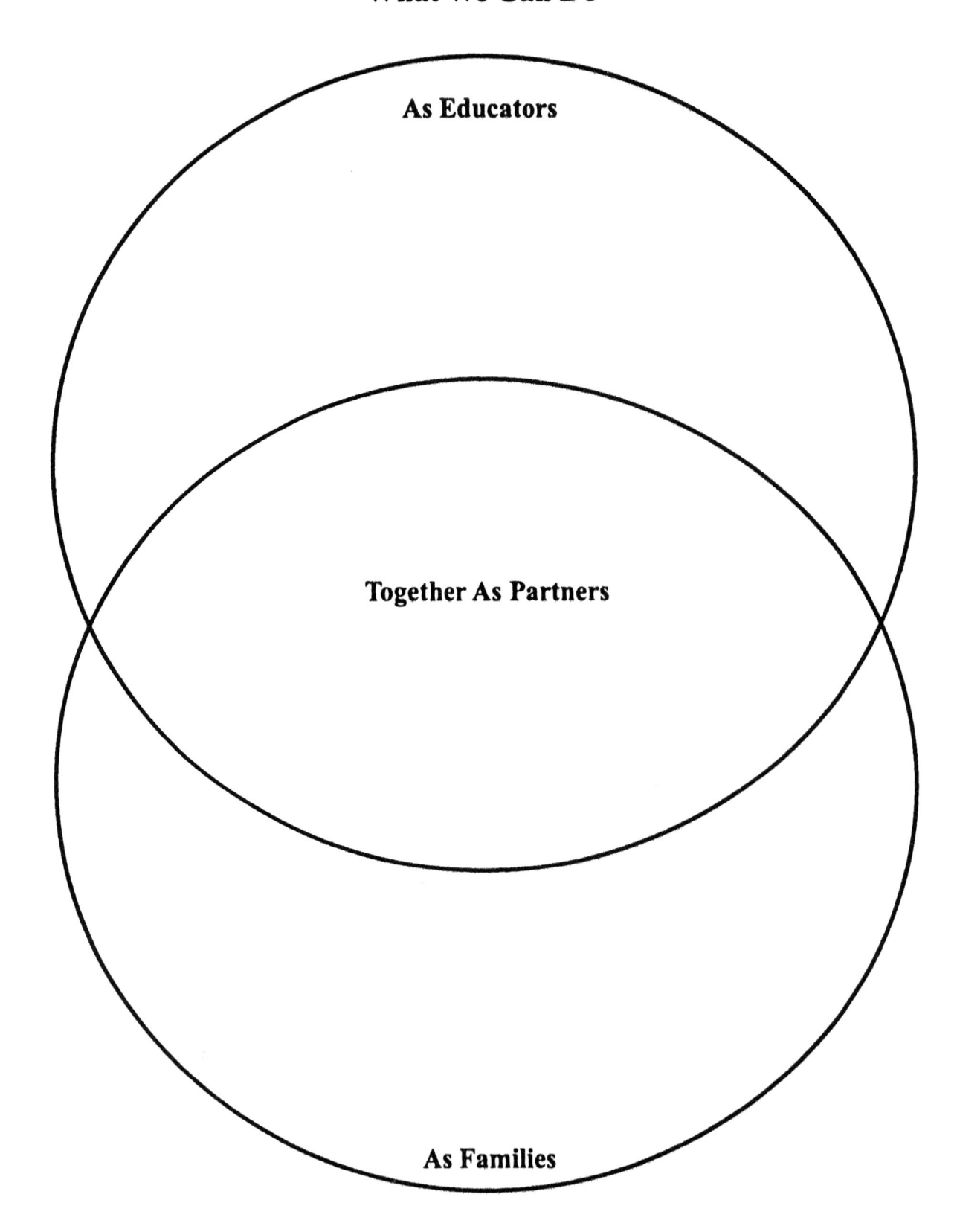

Tool 2.2.4e

As Educators

Together As Partners

As Families

Guidelines for Promoting Trust and Respect Throughout the School Community

Tool 2.2.5

▼ *Be aware that trust comes from actions, not words.* It evolves as a result of interactions among people and can change for better or worse as individuals develop their relationships. Everything we say or do in working with parents affects their level of trust for schools.

▼ *Remember that it takes time and effort to establish trusting and respectful relationships and atmospheres.* It takes a commitment to translating important school values into action over a long period of time in a variety of situations. Students, families, and community members must be able to witness this happening, directly or indirectly. While it may take years to build trust in the school, it may take only one thoughtless or careless act to destroy it.

▼ *Assume individual responsibility for being respectful and trustworthy.* This is not someone else's job. Every educator must commit to this as a goal if the school is to be successful in creating the type of atmosphere that promotes strong partnerships with families. Make it the norm throughout the school community to be accepting, supportive, open, honest, and protective of the rights and confidences of others.

▼ *Be sure that our words consistently align with our actions.* Remember the old adage, "Actions speak louder than words?" While many families do not understand educational jargon, they do know when educators say one thing and do another. In fact, the community grapevine often identifies and analyzes these inconsistencies before educators realize they have happened. Are we encouraging dependability in our relationships with families? Families and community members must know that educators will act in a consistent, predictable manner every day.

▼ *Treat families and community members as if they were favorite family members.* Be polite and courteous, listen to their comments or concerns, and help them resolve any problems they are having in a timely manner. If we cannot help them with a problem, it is better to let them know our limitations rather than to ignore the problem and create doubts about our trustworthiness.

▼ *Be sure to choose the best ways of phrasing comments to assure that family members are treated in a respectful manner.* Remember two key points. First, parents are a child's primary and most important educator. Find words that enhance this relationship; never demean it. Second, most family members are not familiar with educational terminology and may be fearful in the school setting. Select words that communicate, not intimidate.

▼ *Encourage cooperation rather than competition.* Educators who treat family members as equals and view them as partners are more successful than their colleagues who try to assume superior positions or want to win at the others' expense. Even if these educators do not win, families know that winning was their goal and are less likely to trust them as partners.

▼ *Work with parents to address a common need.* Give and take to achieve a mutual goal or take a risk with the family to help the child. Going the extra mile with a family to help their child builds both trust and respect.

▼ *Never use information given in confidence to the detriment of the child or the family.* Family members must feel safe and secure to be open and honest with educators about their children or their concerns. They are trusting educators to help them with problems they may not be willing to share with others. If educators violate their confidentiality or retaliate against the child, parents retreat to safe and secure ground and will not share further information.

Adapted from Johnson, David W. (1993). *Reaching out: Interpersonal effectiveness and self-actualization.* Needham Heights, MA: Allyn & Bacon.

Faculty Reflection: Promoting Trust and Respect Throughout the School Community

Tool 2.2.6

Do I...					Does The Faculty...			
Always	Often	Rarely	Never		Always	Often	Rarely	Never
—	—	—	—	Try to establish relationships with colleagues, students, and parents that are based upon mutual trust and respect?	—	—	—	—
—	—	—	—	Act on a day-to-day basis in ways that aligns words with actions?	—	—	—	—
—	—	—	—	Model a commitment to being trustworthy and respectful to others?	—	—	—	—
—	—	—	—	Make an effort to be consistent and dependable at all times?	—	—	—	—
—	—	—	—	Treat everyone as if they were as special as a favorite relative?	—	—	—	—
—	—	—	—	Make an effort to communicate in ways that show respect for family members' efforts and contributions?	—	—	—	—
—	—	—	—	Treat colleagues and visitors to the school in an enthusiastic and respectful manner?	—	—	—	—
—	—	—	—	Encourage cooperation with families rather than competition with them?	—	—	—	—
—	—	—	—	Work closely with parents to solve problems?	—	—	—	—
—	—	—	—	Protect the confidentialty of information shared by parents?	—	—	—	—
—	—	—	—	Avoid any statements or actions that might place a family or a child in a detrimental light or position?	—	—	—	—
—	—	—	—	Ensure that interactions with family members do not result in problems for their child?	—	—	—	—
—	—	—	—	Ensure that all interactions with family members promote their trust and respect?	—	—	—	—

Tool 2.2.7

Promoting Positive Social Behaviors: Building Character

Since each school represents a unique student and community population, it is important to make some critical decisions regarding desired social behaviors and ways to build character. First, decide what behaviors educators and parents value. Which of these behaviors are we willing to spend the time and effort to achieve? Once identified, determine what skills the students will need to exhibit them. Then, think about strategies currently in place that focus on character building and are successfully encouraging students to act in appropriate ways. Which are working well? Which are not? What are we doing as a faculty to assure that students know how to exhibit them? Use the following as a starting point for discussion. Add other behaviors and skills that are valued by faculty or parents. The challenge is to identify what behaviors are expected, determine how well they are currently being taught and monitored, and develop effective ways of working with parents to help students acquire them.

Which Desired Behaviors Are Important for Our Students?

Self-Regulated Behavior	Accepting Others
Responsibility	Caring For Others
Cooperation	Supporting Others
Respect	Goal Setting
Honesty	Learning from Failure
Accepting Others	Developing Positive Attitudes

What Skills Students Must Develop to Be Able to Exhibit the Desired Behaviors?

Dialogue	Personal Reflection
Critical Thinking	Problem Solving
Creative Thinking	Decision Making
Planning	Conflict Resolution
Restraining Impulsivity	Managing Stress

Where Are We As a Faculty in Helping Students Acquire the Desired Behaviors?

Identified Behaviors → Taught Skills → Practiced Skills → Monitored Behaviors → Reinforced Efforts → Assessed Progress → Becoming A Habit

Successful Practices for Promoting Positive Social Behaviors

Incorporate Social Skills into Curriculum and Instruction

What is not taught becomes part of a "hoped for" curriculum. If developing social skills and character are important, find ways to teach, practice, monitor, and reinforce the expected behaviors on a day to day basis. Periodically build in opportunities for students to assess their progress. Rather than spending a week on solving problems, why not develop students' ability to solve problems through what is already expected in the curriculum? Instead of working on cooperation in isolation, teachers are using a wide range of cooperative learning strategies to help students learn the expected content. By looking carefully at curriculum guides, textbooks, and other resource materials, educators are finding ways to emphasize the social skills on a day to day basis as part of what they are already doing. No time is being wasted by trying to put one more thing into an already overloaded curriculum.

Students in Leadership Roles

In some schools, upper grade students are involved in planning activities to introduce new students to the school and to help students learn the desired social behaviors. Some use technology, such as TV studios, to teach their peers how to avoid problems at school, to handle tough issues such as bullying, and to be successful at school. Other schools hold student strategy sessions with a cross-section of students to develop preventative measures or to react to problem situations. Students are also effective student mediators (helping their peers understand problem situations and work through them), peer tutors, peer mentors, and peer buddies (providing social support for students new to the school or with special needs).

Challenges

Why not challenge a class or a grade level to win the honor of "Best Social Behaviors?" This could be the class with the most commendations for desired behaviors over a designated period of time (one week? six weeks?). One middle school rewarded the class with the fewest referrals. At the same time, challenge adults in the building to issue "Social Praises" each time they note a student doing a good deed for another student or adult. Ask the parent-teacher organization or interested community members to help honor the winners.

Meetings

Psychologists have told families for years that family meetings in which children have an opportunity to have a voice in plans and decisions provide a solid foundation for their planning and decision making outside the family. Why not use class meetings in the same manner? Allowing students to have a voice in how to develop positive social skills and character building behaviors is the first step toward achieving the goal.

Incentives

While incentives are not the only method of encouraging desired behavior, they have a solid track record for motivating large numbers of students. There are several commercial programs

Tool 2.2.8

available. Many schools are also using less structured school, class, and grade level incentives. While most teachers are involving students in formulating classroom rules, some schools are extending this participation to the development of school rules and policies. Regardless of the incentive, the key is assuring that as many students as possible can achieve the awards rather than just the "top few" who consistently win them. School adopters are often willing to fund the incentives when schools develop a motivating plan.

Sharing What is Being Taught to Students with Parents

Many schools introduce social skills training to parents very carefully. This is an area where parents, if not well informed, might question why time is being taken away from the basics to teach what students should be getting at home. What many educators have found is that when parents realize what is being emphasized and why it is important to do so, they are not only pleased, but are willing to reinforce them at home. How are schools sharing this information?

Handbooks

Sharing expectations for social behaviors tells parents far more than discipline policies and procedures do. Why not emphasize positive expectations rather than dwelling on negative consequences?

Flyers

Flyers are used to describe new social skills that are being introduced or to remind parents about the social skills that are being taught and monitored. Ask parents to reinforce what is being emphasized at school. This strategy only works well when parents can and do read the flyers!

Creatively Titled Workshops

"How to Get your Child off Dead Center" was the enticement one school used to share goal setting information. "Resolving Conflicts at Home" was the hook another school used to get parents to look at the bigger issue of conflict resolution. Parents at any school level are more likely to take advantage of workshops that relate directly to their specific needs. Before establishing a schedule of workshops, find out what the parents think would be beneficial. See *Design 7: Supporting Teaching and Learning* for additional lifelong learning strategies.

Conferences

Parents want to know how to help their children through troubling development years. Why not team with another school and hold a conference for parents on topics of particular interest to them?

Tips for Parents on Local Public Television and Radio Stations

In our sound bite world, a few carefully selected words of advice repeated constantly have the impact of television commercials. The clever phrases seem to stay on our minds. Use them to sell parents on reinforcing social skills at home by giving them strategies they can easily use. Ask schools with television studios to develop the tips as part of the students' learning experience. They will learn the technological skills along with the social skills.

Tool 2.2.8

Family Counseling Nights

Many schools and social service agencies are realizing the value of making school psychologists, guidance counselors, and agency representatives available for consultation with families during the evening hours. More and more families need this type of assistance and lack the ability to secure it on their own. The flex time that school systems are providing for their personnel is paying dividends for families and the school.

Lesson Line Tips

Parents who call the Lesson Line (teachers' daily telephone messages communicating important information about topics being studied, homework assignments, special classroom events) may learn more than just their student's assignments. Ask parents to reinforce the social skills that are being emphasized in class. Lesson Line allows teachers and parents to be partners in this area without having conferences or meetings. Establish the expectation for parents at the beginning of the year that social skills tips will be shared when they are being taught or reinforced in class.

Ask Parents to Reinforce Character Development and Social Skills in their Homes

When students realize that the desired behaviors are important and expected wherever they are, they are more likely to see the benefits of developing them. Parents and educators can be effective partners in developing students' character and social skills if they communicate on a regular basis. Learning calendars, described in *Design 7: Supporting Teaching and Learning* are an easy to use way to keep parents up to date on the social skills that are being emphasized.

Encourage Risk Taking

Helping families realize that students learn from failure and that making mistakes is critical to their social development. Help them develop strategies for working with their child as they encounter difficult choices and take risks to handle them.

Tool 2.2.9

Educators' Guidelines for
Helping Parents Reinforce Social Behaviors at Home

While parents are often willing to help, they need assistance in knowing how to provide the support teachers desire. The following strategies may be helpful in working with parents:

Send notes in the students' folders, agendas, or backpacks to alert parents about particular social skills being taught or reinforced each week.

Offer suggestions to help parents reinforce the social skills at home.

Check with parents to see how the child is progressing.

Initiate dialogue. Ask parents what is working and what needs to be improved.

Allocate time for parent questions and concerns.

Look forward to parent requests for assistance. This means they are interested and trying to help.

Secure help when parents need it. This may mean linking them with counselors, social workers, or other community agencies.

Keep the focus on developing the whole child--academically, physically, and socially.

Investing time in working with parents can make a difference.

Level the playing field. Spend more time with parents who need the most help.

Look for positive outcomes.

Share and celebrate successes.

Tool 2.2.10

Parents,

We are working with our children to develop positive social skills as well as the academics. We know that you agree that our children need to be honest, caring, dependable, and responsible individuals who can work and play cooperatively with others. Here are some ideas that you could use to reinforce these behaviors at home. If we work together, we will both be more successful in preparing your child for success at school and life.

Support the development of social skills at home. Teachers will be better able to help your child if you work together as a team.

Open lines of communication with your child. Ask questions about what academic and social behaviors are expected at school.

Check your child's folder, agenda, or backpack for information about behavior and social skills that are being taught at school--and ideas you can try at home.

Initiate conversations with the teacher. Ask teachers for help or explanations when problems or concerns arise.

Ask your child questions about what he or she is learning. Talk about how social skills are also important at home and in the community. Encourage your child to practice the skills in home and community settings.

Listen to concerns your child might have about the ways he or she is being treated by others at school. Let the teacher know if problems arise.

Select ways to reinforce desired behaviors at home. Ask your child to help you develop ways to make this happen.

Keep information about social skills that teachers send home. You might want to refer to it later.

Investing time in working with teachers can make a difference.

Look for signs that your child is aware of his or her positive social behaviors--and recognize the accomplishments.

Look forward to your child's improved behavior, successful relationships with peers, and positive self-esteem.

Share and celebrate successes.

115

Plan 2.3
Ensuring a Safe and Secure Climate for Learning

Providing an environment that ensures students a physically and emotionally safe and secure learning environment is becoming increasingly difficult. The influx of drugs, gangs, and weapons into the school setting has forced school faculties and entire school systems to focus a tremendous amount of time and energy on the climate for learning. While the specific actions vary from school to school, they include reassessing behavior management expectations and systems, emphasizing expectations for appropriate social behaviors, developing violence prevention plans and policies, and experimenting with innovative strategies for conflict resolution. The following steps will provide guidance to educators as they work with students, parents, and community members to create the best possible teaching and learning environment.

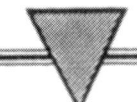

- Begin by creating guidelines for behavior that will ensure a physically and emotionally safe environment for learning. Assure that these guidelines reflect the core values of the school community. If these values (e.g., honesty, respect for others, self-control, doing one's best) have not been clarified, refer to Tool 5.2.4 to determine which values should provide the essential foundation for the school's expectations, policies, and future actions. When the values have been articulated, align them with the current expectations for student behavior. Do they adequately address both physical and psychological safety? Are there any gaps? Are there additional expectations that need to be included? If new expectations are needed, see Tool 5.4.1 for a discussion guide that will assist in the process of developing them.

- Involve students and parents in developing policies and making decisions about student behavior that will translate the expectations into practice. Tool 2.3.1 provides strategies to consider in collaborating with students and parents in planning, implementing, and reinforcing a schoolwide discipline plan. Tool 2.3.2 is a sample student, teacher, parent contract to help educators work with individual students and their parents in achieving the goals of the schoolwide plan. Tool 2.3.3 is a worksheet for educators to use to monitor the progress of the schoolwide plan. Remember that rules and policies must be adequate to provide students with the sense of comfort, order, and structure they need. However, they should not be overwhelming in number or complexity.

- While finalizing the guidelines for positive student interaction and behavior, also develop proactive strategies for handling the inevitable conflicts or crises that will arise. As Alfie Kohn (1996) reminds us, conflict is natural and learning to handle it productively is the essence of learning. Tool 2.3.4 is a pledge to share with parents that underscores the importance of working together as partners. Tool 2.3.5 will alert educators to various strategies for resolving conflicts, the most effective of which is engaging in problem solving negotiation. Tool 2.3.6 illustrates a model for problem solving and conflict resolution that parents can use in their homes to reinforce what is being taught at school. See Tools 1.2.13, 1.2.14, and 1.2.15 for additional forms and worksheets if problem solving is the approach that is selected.

- Develop guidelines for working with parents or caregivers in resolving conflicts in a manner that promotes the solution of the problem while maintaining or strengthening the adult partnerships. Tool 2.3.7 proposes sample guidelines for this purpose. They can be used as they are or can be adapted to fit each school's needs. Tool 2.3.8 contains a list of "do's" and "don'ts" for resolving conflicts in a "win-win" manner that should be considered in developing the guidelines. Keeping this information in mind should prevent educators from turning a difficult situation into an impossible one.

- Develop proactive strategies for preventing and dealing with the negative influences that today's children are encountering. As a faculty, focus on ways to enhance the school climate to assure that students feel a sense of belonging. This will reduce the likelihood that they will fulfill their affiliation needs in less productive ways. Tool 2.3.9 provides suggestions for improving the school climate by enhancing students' sense of power, self-esteem, feelings of connectedness, and security which must be reflected in the school's climate. At the same time, provide parents and community members with assistance in dealing with these negative influences. Tool 2.3.10 highlights how important it is to provide home conditions that fill the void that draws children to gangs and destructive peer relationships in the first place. It also encourages parents to take advantage of the school's efforts at developing an inclusive school climate that is resistant to negative peer pressure and the influence of gangs. With a better understanding of these negative influences, parents will be better able to handle problems that arise. Tool 2.3.11 includes key phrases and quotations that can be used as handouts, transparencies, or discussion starters for a parent meeting or workshop. Structure the dialogue to allow parents to share their current strategies and learn new ones. Share what the school is doing to address these same needs and help parents realize that no one has all the answers. When parents perceive educators as their allies in helping their children avoid potentially serious behaviors and group affiliations, they are more likely to work with them as partners. However, if When educators and parents maintain open lines of communication, increase their understanding of the temptations children are facing, and share ideas and concerns, they can present a united front in helping the child.

- In some schools, violence is becoming increasingly prevalent and problematic. If this is the case, it may be important to develop a master plan for violence prevention. Again, involve students and parents in the process. Their insights often illuminate the underlying causes for the behaviors educators are witnessing at school. Tool 2.1.12 provides questions to guide faculty reflection on current violence prevention efforts.

Tool 2.1.13 provides a worksheet to use in identifying patterns from the reflection or from faculty, parent, or community group focus sessions.

- Follow through with all policies, rules, and consequences. When students know the rules and realize that they will be punished for breaking them, they are less likely to continue to test the limits. As one psychologist once said, "Adolescents view life like a slot machine. They just keep pulling the handle hoping to hit the jackpot. When their arm gets sore, they'll give up!"

Other Possiblities...

Strategies for Collaborating With Parents on Discipline

Tool 2.3.1

Prior to any discussion about discipline, it is important that participants be knowledgeable about the current research on behavior management. There is a strong tendency to rely on our own practical knowledge and experiences, which may or may not be aligned with the research. Professional materials can be acquired, distributed, read, and discussed by participants. Another option is to have in school experts or outside consultants inform faculty and parent representatives. This is a critical step in identifying effective and ineffective approaches and gaining insights into the appropriateness of current practices. It will also highlight innovative ways to help students develop self-discipline. When participants have an opportunity to reflect on the research and their own experiences, they will better able to make informed decisions about expectations for student behavior. The following are some strategies for consideration in developing and monitoring collaborative discipline plans.

Collaborative Planning

Initial Teacher, Parent, and Student Planning

Involve representative middle and high school students, parents, and community members in collaboratively developing schoolwide rules and the school discipline policy. Separate the large group into several smaller, but still representative, groups to facilitate interaction and creative thinking. Begin by discussing what participants and others they represent value for students. Is it honesty? Caring? Positive interpersonal relationships? Following rules? Share any information that has already been generated. If the school has a mission or vision statement, use it and any any of the preliminary information that was used to develop it as a starting point for the discussion. If schoolwide rules and policies already exist, review them. If this information is not available, see *Design 5: Developing Shared Expectations* or products of this design for processes that could be used to identify these values. Once it is clear what the school community values for its students, begin thinking of how these desired outcomes are, or should be, reflected in students' behavior.

Develop a Draft of the Discipline Plan

The information in the initial planning phase should be translated into schoolwide guidelines and a draft of discipline policy. At this point, share the draft with other students, parents, and community members. The draft statement clearly communicates that the plan is not complete and that input of those asked to consider it is valued. Instead, it is at a point where input and revision are welcomed.

Small Group Parent Meetings

The draft could then be shared in small group meetings with parents. These could be arranged as grade level sessions so that parents could be given more specific examples of how the rules apply to their children. These meetings provide an opportunity for parents to ask questions and

Tool 2.3.1

to develop an understanding of the complexity of discipline issues. They also help parents become more aware of educators' efforts to prevent discipline problems and to reduce inappropriate behaviors in constructive ways. At the same time opportunities such as these encourage parent ownership of school policies and a commitment to upholding them.

Communicating the Final Version
This can be accomplished in several ways. It is usually included in the school handbook, but could also be a separate notice to parents. Be sure to include a description of the way the discipline policy was collaboratively developed with student, parent, and community member involvement. In some school districts, the discipline plan (and the description of how it was developed) is also distributed to community businesses to inform them of the school community's expectations. This is especially important for middle schools and high schools to enlist the help of the community in reinforcing school policies.

Securing Parent Commitment
Many schools include a place for the signature of a parent or a care-giving adult. With the request for the signature, there is a statement that might read, "Your signature means that you have read the discipline policy and school rules, understand them, and are willing to support them."

Strategies for Reinforcing the Plan

Student/Teacher/Parent Contracts
These contracts, specifying desired student behaviors, are especially effective ways to monitor or change inappropriate student behaviors. These contracts could be described and explained during the parent small group meetings so that parents would then be aware of their use and reinforce them at home. See Tool 2.3.2 for a sample contract.

Parent Academy Sessions
Many topics related to discipline are important ones for parent workshop sessions. Educators can help parents become more knowledgeable about what behaviors to expect at given ages or stages of development, possible reasons for misbehavior, and effective strategies for dealing with inappropriate behavior. Survey parents prior to setting up a schedule to be sure that the proposed sessions are of interest to them. See Plan 7.3 for suggestions to guide the selection and design of parent training sessions. The Tools also help educators capitalize on the knowledge that parents can contribute while setting the stage for parental networking which is a valuable outcome in itself.

Consultation with the School Counselor
Some schools are making their counselor(s) available for consultation on a scheduled basis. A monthly "Family Night" can be of benefit to parents and families who cannot otherwise obtain these important services. Counselors are generally provided flex time for their after hours sessions.

Tool 2.3.1

Parent Involvement in the Peer Resolution or Peer Mediation Programs

Parents can also take an active role in organizing and implementing peer resolution or peer mediation programs. This can be a time consuming, but effective intervention. Willing and qualified volunteers can be of great service in these efforts. Extensive training for the adults and students involved are prerequisites--as is ongoing evaluation of what is working and what could be improved.

Assessing Progress

Evaluating the discipline plan is critical to its success. Any successful evaluation is based upon several data sources. First, record student discipline referrals and determine any patterns in the numbers and types of referrals. Also track parent concerns. Have they changed? In what ways? Finally, gather the input of teachers, parents, and students including some with no discipline problems and others who have been referred to the office. Determine what the various changes indicate. Do they suggest that the plan is resulting in improved student behavior? If so, why? If not, why? If improvements are not what was expected, revisit the discipline plan and make the changes necessary to achieve the desired results. Tool 2.3.3 provides a worksheet for assessing progress that includes indicators of success that can be used as a screen to determine which changes are making a significant impact.

Student Discipline Contract

Tool 2.3.2

As a result of our conference, I agree to make the following changes in my behavior. I realize that it is my responsibility to make the changes since they represent what I want to accomplish for myself. I also know that my teacher(s) and my parent(s) are willing to help me in the process. I can tell them my problems or concerns and they have agreed to listen and to help me think of ways to handle them. I also know that we will meet on the following dates to look at my progress.

Target behaviors

_____
_____
_____
_____

Changes to be made

Student

_____
_____
_____
_____

Parent

_____
_____

Educator

_____
_____

Progress Check Dates

_____   _____
_____   _____

Signatures

Student _____   Date _____

Parent   _____   Date _____

Educator _____   Date _____

Assessing Progress Worksheet

Tool 2.3.3

Indicators of Success

▼ Discipline referrals have decreased.

▼ Parent contacts regarding discipline concerns have decreased.

▼ Educator complaints about discipline problems have decreased.

▼ Fewer students are expressing concerns about problems with peers.

▼ Parent contacts expressing appreciation for improved discipline have increased.

▼ Educator commendations for the discipline program have increased.

▼ Student comments about positive interactions with peers have increased.

Specific Areas That Have Shown Improvement
(identified from the various data sources)

1. _____
2. _____
3. _____
4. _____
5. _____

Reasons for the Successes

1. Educators attribute the improvements to:

2. Parents attribute the improvements to:

3. Students attribute the improvements to:

Next Steps

1. What should be continued?

2. What should be changed?

Working With Parents to Resolve Conflicts

Tool 2.3.4

Conflict is inevitable. While educators and parents often hold similar expectations for a child, rarely do they have the luxury of working together as a team to help a child achieve them. As a result, they often view situations quite differently. Often this results in conflicts that might be avoided and would certainly be overcome if both parties knew how to resolve them in a positive manner. Wouldn't it make our lives easier as educators or parents if we were able to share our true concerns, to express our real feelings, and to work with a partner who was not sitting in judgment? The following pledge illustrates our desired state for working through the conflicts that arise as educators and parents strive to provide the most appropriate educational environment for students:

As educators and parents, we pledge to

Work together in such a way

That our dialogue and relationship

Enable us to resolve any issues

That affect the development

Of the child.

Success in life and school

Is our common goal.

Strategies for Managing Conflicts

Tool 2.3.5

Conflict resolution can be approached in a variety of ways, depending upon the desired outcome. The following strategies are a summary of the work of Johnson and Johnson (1995) and are presented on a scale from most to least effective. Which are most typical of the approaches taken at your school? Which should be utilized more frequently if developing and sustaining partnerships are a goal?

Problem Solving Negotiations

When both the goal and the relationship are highly important, educators and parents seek solutions that ensure that the goal for the student is reached without creating lingering tensions and negative feelings. Both parties maintain their interests while focusing on the problem and finding ways to solve it. They are willing to listen to the other person's perspective and to share their own. The key to effective problem solving negotiations is to keep the focus on the problem, not the person. This process builds trust since both parties recognize their interdependence and are willing to take a risk to share their perspectives and reconcile them with the other person's views.

Smoothing

This strategy is used most frequently when the relationship is more important than the goal. It involves one person giving up his or her goal so that the relationship is maintained. Smoothing works best when both parties are committed to each other's well being. When one is determined that a specific solution is the only viable option, the other is willing to give in. Smoothing only works when both parties are willing to defer to the other equitably. It can never be achieved if one party is determined to win at the other's expense.

Win-Lose Negotiations

This strategy has the potential to destroy rather than build relationships. It occurs when either party values the goal more than the relationship. Competition rather than collaboration is the method of interaction. One party focuses on tactics that force the other to yield by making threats, imposing penalties, establishing deadlines, presenting persuasive arguments, committing oneself to unalterable positions, or making demands that far exceed what is actually acceptable.

Compromising

When both the goal and the relationship are important and neither party can seem to achieve their desired outcome, compromising is an option. It involves giving up part of one's goal to reach an agreement. By meeting on middle ground, both parties achieve part of what they originally desired. Compromising works when there is not adequate time to engage in problem-solving negotiations.

Withdrawing

When neither the goal nor the relationship are important, both parties may decide to give up on the issue. Participants are more likely to withdraw when they do not see the potential of partnerships.

A Process for Working With Parents to Help Students Resolve Conflicts or Solve Problems

Tool 2.3.6

The following process is one that works well for either conflict resolution or problem solving. Teach parents to use this process to help their children at home. Provide opportunities for them to practice the model in a hypothetical situation before asking them to use it on their own. At the same time, educators can use the same process to resolve issues that occur at school. It is important to include each step in the process. See Tool 1.2.15 for a worksheet to use in completing this process.

Identify the Problem

Describe the problem or the conflict. Focus on facts before feelings. What happened? What caused the problem? Who was involved? When and where did it happen? Why did it happen? Once the facts have been identified, share your feelings and the reasons you feel the way you do. At the same time, make an effort to understand the other person's perspective and feelings. Let the other person know that you understand how he or she feels.

Set a Goal

It is important for each person to describe what he or she wants from the resolution of the conflict or problem. Each must share their reasons for their positions. Then ask them to be sure that they understand the differences in their positions.

Identify Limits or Constraints

What may affect any decisions? Are there rules or situations that must be considered before a solution can be found? Are there any boundaries that cannot be crossed?

Identify Possible Solutions

Brainstorm possible solutions. Be creative and think "out of the box." Avoid searching for single solutions and look for those that help both parties achieve at least part of their goals.

Make a Decision on the Actions to Take

Select a solution (or possibly more) that is fair to both parties. Be sure that both parties agree with the choice.

Assess the Effectiveness of the Decision

After making the decision, look carefully at its results. Is the situation better? Has the problem or conflict continued? Has the situation worsened? If the outcomes have not been positive, go back to the "Solutions" step and rethink the best action to take.

Guidelines for Resolving Conflicts Positively and Productively

Tool 2.3.7

Remember that Resolving Conflicts Provides Opportunities to Build Open, Trusting Relationships

▼ When a conflict arises, take the opportunity to involve parents and students in resolving it. Face-to-face discussions are far more productive than telephone calls or letters. If the conflict involves the parent and the educator, set up a meeting to discuss it and to allow each participant to share his or her perspective. Let parents know how important it is for them to help resolve the issue.

Problems can be resolved much easier if teachers call parents to ask for help rather than sending letters or waiting for parent initiated calls.

▼ When educators and parents trust one another, they will share their true feelings and concerns. Where there is a lack of trust, they will only share what they consider safe information. They will not take a risk for fear of harming the child.

One parent told us, "I wish I could tell my daughters' teachers the real reasons for all of my daughter's absences. If they knew how hard we worked to keep her from cutting school, they might be able to help us. There are a couple of teachers and an assistant principal who seem to be looking for reasons to suspend her. We just want her to graduate, so we're keeping a lid on everything for six more months."

▼ Trust is the result of consistently being fair, honest, and up front with parents. It also involves safeguarding the child's and parents' best interests, maintaining confidentiality when it is assured, and always doing what we say we will do.

As one educator said, "If we say something, we mean it. If we say we will do something, we do it."

▼ Trust develops as educators model a commitment to the child and to the parent in working as a team to provide the best educational opportunities for the child.

"I was afraid to walk in the building at first. You know, I wasn't a very good student when I was in school and here I was going to talk with my son's teacher. But it was O.K. She treated me like I really was important. Even after the conference, though, I wasn't sure she really wanted to hear from me. But I called her when Sam kept asking to stay home from school. She helped me work with him and now he doesn't complain any more. She even told me that she was going to change some of the things she was doing if they bothered him. We're lucky she is his teacher. I don't want to bother her, but I know I can call her if we're having a problem."

Comment from parent of a high school senior

Tool 2.3.7

Create a Comfortable Environment for Dialogue

▼ Consider where to meet.
Would the classroom be intimidating to the parent? Would another setting, such as the school or local library or community center, be better? Does the conflict include anything in the classroom? If so, it should be the place to meet.

▼ Assure that the parent has the educator's total attention.
Avoid telephone calls or other interruptions. Assure that no other educators or students are present.

▼ Create the feeling that you and the parent are working together as colleagues in resolving the conflict.
Avoid nonverbal intimidators such as sitting across the desk or table from the parent. Keep materials and notes in clear view so the parent can see that there are no hidden agendas.

▼ Use words that reflect your desire to be open, honest, and collaborative.
Avoid using educational jargon that the parent might not understand--and the words "always" and "never." Talk to the parent as one parent would talk to another.

▼ Follow the guidelines of dialogue: listen, share your perspective, suspend judgment.
See Tool 3.1.2 for a more complete description of dialogue.

▼ Take into consideration the implications of what you are saying.
Don't say anything on the spur of the moment that you might regret later. Wait until your words reflect what you are thinking, rather than what your heart is feeling.

▼ Stand firm on values, not easy solutions.
Assure the parent that you do not believe in taking the easy way out and that you are not looking for quick fixes. Let the parent know that complex issues take time to resolve and that you are willing to work as long and as hard as is necessary to achieve the best possible solution for the child.

Take the Emotion Out of the Dialogue and Interactions

▼ Allow enough time, a cooling off period, to reduce emotions. Schedule meetings when both parties have had the opportunity to reflect on the situation, but do not wait until a small problem becomes a major one.
"When would you be able to get together to discuss the situation? It would help us if we both have time to think about all of the issues involved before we sit down to talk. Would _____ work for you?"

Tool 2.3.7

▼ Acknowledge emotions immediately.
   "I realize that this situation is upsetting. It is also frustrating for your child and for me. At this point, it is also affecting a few other students in the class."

▼ Allow the emotional party to begin the dialogue. Then listen, *really listen*. Do not interrupt, argue, minimize, or discredit the concerns being expressed. As you listen, try to understand the perspective of the parent as well as the major issues. Use paraphrasing and clarifying questions to understand what the parent is trying to say.
   "Am I hearing you say . . . ?" or "What do you see as the major issues?"

Structure the Analysis of the Conflict

▼ Break the issue or situation down into workable pieces.
   "Let me see if I understand what you are saying. First, ... Then . . . ."

▼ View the situation from all perspectives. See Tool 1.2.14 for a problem understanding worksheet.
   "It appears that from your perspective, you feel that . . ."
   "As Mikel's teacher, I have seen . . ."
   "How would you think that other students might . . ."

▼ Keep the focus on the real issue. Separate less important ones. The secondary issues are often just part of making a case. Don't spend a lot of time on something you cannot do much about.
   "Would you agree that _____ is what is really bothering Kiesha and that the other problems may be a result of it?"

▼ Prioritize the main issues.
   "If we were able to resolve one or two of these issues immediately, which would make the greatest impact on Jeremy's attitude and effort this six weeks?" or... "Of all the issues we have discussed today, which should be addressed first? We will work on all of them, but we should decide which would make the biggest difference for Jeremy and begin there."

▼ Use a conflict resolution process to reach common ground and a workable solution. See Tool 2.3.5 and 2.3.6 for a more detailed explanation of the process.
   "Can we agree that . . . ?"

▼ Determine how you can limit rules and restrictions rather than expanding them.
   "Can we decide on just one or two rules that would make a difference in the way Rosa behaves at home and at school?"

Tool 2.3.7

▼ Be sure that both parties are part of the solution. Put the ball back in the parent's court as often as possible. Make the parent part of the solution finding process.

"How can we work together more closely to be sure that what I'm trying to do in the classroom really is making a difference in Blair's attitude toward school?"

▼ Try to resolve some aspect of the conflict early. Build on the success.

"Why don't we do _____ first. We'll begin tomorrow morning when Juan comes in the door. Then, let's both be thinking of a strategy for _____. Can we talk next week to see how things are going? By then we should have a better idea if what we have decided on is the most appropriate route to take."

Follow through with the plan

▼ Set up a schedule for monitoring the plan. Keep track of progress or lack of progress in a systematic way (e.g., checklists, notes in a folder) so that you will have specific information to share with the parent at the next meeting.

"When can we talk again to be sure that our plan is working?" "Would you keep track of any changes you notice in Roberto's attitude toward school or his willingness to put forth effort on schoolwork? That will help us compare notes at our next meeting."

▼ Keep in touch with the problem rather than delegating it to someone else. While the principal, the counselor, or child and family services can and should be involved where appropriate, the teacher has the best opportunity to see that the plan is appropriate and that it is making a difference.

"I'll be watching to be sure that what we are doing at school is what we have agreed on. You can do the same at home. Let's stay in contact by telephone. I hope this will resolve the issue and we won't have to meet any more. If things do not turn out as we hope they will, we'll try another approach. Don't worry, we'll work through this together."

"Win-Win" Confrontation Strategies

Tool 2.3.8

Do	Don't
• Believe that a mutually beneficial solution can be found.	• Doubt that others can help you find an appropriate solution. Maybe you will find an even better one than you might have identified on your own.
• Diminish the threat.	• Increase anxiety levels.
• Focus on the issue.	• Focus on the people involved.
• Stick to the issue.	• Bring up unrelated issues--or past experiences to confuse the current issue.
• Remember that you are in this together.	• Be defensive or determined to win.
• Base the discussion on accurate observations and facts.	• Base the discussion on opinions or facts that have been blown out of proportion.
• Consider perspectives of others.	• Focus only on your perspective.
• Listen, clarify, and restate.	• Forget to listen while you plan what you're going to say in response.
• Agree, acknowledge, and affirm.	• Use judgmental language (good/bad; always/never).
• Probe for facts.	• Hide or ignore important information.
• Stick to "what" and "how."	• Avoid "why."
• Be open to new solutions.	• Stick only with what you have experienced in the past or with others. Give ultimatums.
• Point out strengths and benefits.	• Dwell on negatives.
• Admit your own honest errors.	• Try to hide honest errors.
• Quit if things get too hot. Try again at another time.	• Keep going when you cannot be responsible for your anger.

Tool 2.3.9

Developing a School Climate That Reduces the Impact of Negative Peer Pressure

According to Vigil (1988), gangs provide young people with a sense of power, enhanced self-esteem, feelings of connectedness, and a sense of protection. If gangs can provide this type of enticing culture, why can't schools? The focus should be on providing the same drawing cards that lure students into gangs. Educators can help students . . .

Experience a sense of power by:
- Giving students a voice in schoolwide and classroom decisions that affect them. Involve a cross-section of students from different socioeconomic levels, races, genders as well as handicapping conditions on a wide range of committees and task forces. Vary the students who are involved so that as many students as possible will have an opportunity to share their opinions at some point during each school year.
- Providing opportunities for students to assume responsibility for their own learning. This could be as simple as a choice of homework assignments or as complex as designing a portfolio that will constitute a six weeks or semester grade.
- Teaching students how to critical and creative thinkers and successful, self-regulated learners. Give them strategies that they can apply in their lives outside the classroom.
- Avoiding any behaviors or statements that make students feel powerless.

Enhance their self-esteem by:
- Finding each child's strengths and interests and build upon them.
- Letting *all* students assume leadership roles.
- Recognizing or celebrating accomplishments of *all* students, no matter how small.
- Encouraging *all* students to be the best they can be--verbally and nonverbally.
- Avoiding verbal statements or actions that might be perceived as putting a student down. Students are very sensitive and often misread a teacher's feedback. Phrase corrective feedback in as positive a manner as possible.
- Showing parents how to help their children become the best they can be. Workshops on rewarding students' behaviors, helping them handle stressful situations, and other similar topics give parents the information they need to enhance their parenting skills.

Develop feelings of connectedness and belonging by:
- Making an effort to involve more than the 10% to 20% who typically participate in nearly all school activities.
- Finding at least one activity that each child can participate in and work with parents to assure that the child participates on a regular basis.
- Using advisor/advisee, mentoring, or peer tutoring programs to maintain close contact.
- Implementing Adopt-a-student and Advisor/Advisee programs, where faculty and staff take the responsibility for greeting, remembering birthdays, checking on, and helping a small number of students sends the message that someone in the school is really interested in them.

Tool 2.3.9

- Keeping the school open after school hours for students to study, participate in athletics or other activities, and socialize. The stronger the student activities program, the more likely students will be able to take advantage of the opportunities it provides. Remember that school may be the safest place for young people to be--and for many it is the only place they can participate in wholesome activities after school hours.

Feel safe and protected by:
- Modeling caring and respectful attitudes toward others.
- Being open and honest with students and show them that it is okay to make mistakes--that mistakes and failures are part of learning and growing.
- Providing an academic environment that consistently values all cultures, races, socio-economic levels, languages, and genders. Avoid experiences that create tension for children related to any of these areas.
- Assuring fair treatment of *all* students.
- Targeting the most violent or potentially violent students and helping them deal with their anger and suppress their violent tendencies.
- Avoiding "marginalizing" students who exhibit inappropriate behavior. Marginalizing occurs when students are first targeted as misbehaving. Due to the manner with which they are treated, they become more hostile or aggressive and, as a result, more a part of the margins of the school rather than the mainstream.
- Concentrating on providing a positive and inviting school climate that values *all* children.
- Developing faculty competence with intervention strategies.
- Creating task forces to identify the causes of violence.
- Providing counseling services to students who have been involved in violent incidents.
- Remembering that surveillance measures, zero-tolerance policies, tougher discipline policies and punishments, weapon or gang hotlines, and security personnel are only part of the approach to preventing violence and gang activities. Providing an emotionally safe and secure school environment reduces the need for these interventions.

Developing Home Atmospheres That Reduce the Impact of Negative Peer Pressure

Tool 2.3.10

According to Vigil (1993), gangs provide young people with a sense of power, enhanced self-esteem, feelings of connectedness, and a sense of protection. What can families do to fulfill these needs that lure children into gangs? Parents can help their children . . .

Experience a sense of power by:
- Giving children an important role in the family. Younger children may simply take out the trash. Older children can take responsibility for the family pet, grocery shopping, tutoring a sibling, or other meaningful tasks. Chores and allowances are just as necessary today as they were in our grandparents' day. Earning money and having the power to decide how to spend it develops a child's decision making while giving them a sense of responsibility and power over their lives.
- Helping children set goals for themselves. The goals may be for school, for sports, or for anything the child considers important. Help the child see that effort is the key to achieving the goal. When a child realizes the power of effort, it is easier to set loftier goals--and more of them. Celebrate the accomplishment of all goals.
- Let children make some personal decisions. For example, give them the opportunity to decide how they study best. Some need a quiet room. Others like busy areas like the kitchen. Let the child decide where to study--as long as the results are positive!
- Avoid any behaviors or statements that make a child feel powerless or that his or her activities are unimportant.

Enhance their self-esteem by:
- Finding each child's strengths and interests and build upon them.
- Letting each child assume a leadership role each week.
- Recognizing or celebrate accomplishments, no matter how small.
- Encouraging each child to be the best he or she can be--verbally and nonverbally.
- Avoiding verbal statements or actions that might be perceived as putting a child down. Listen to the way you correct your child. Are your words telling the child something more than what you intend? ("Look at the way you're dressed today, Jason. You're never going to amount to anything." vs. "Look at your clothes, Jason. They're dirty and wrinkled. I know they have been in the floor in your room. Why don't you change into something clean? You want to look as handsome as you are!")

Develop feelings of connectedness and belonging by:
- Giving children a voice in family decisions that affect them.
- Holding family meetings to discuss important issues. On a rotating basis, let each child have a leadership role in the family meeting. Some families hold these meetings each week and ask one child to be responsible for selecting a fun activity or a topic for discussion.

Tool 2.3.10

- Involving children in planning family events.
- Finding at least one school activity that each child can participate in and make sure that the child participates on a regular basis. It isn't always the most talented children who succeed in sports, music, or clubs. It is often the ones who are always there that every one gets to know. The more the child participates, the more he or she will experience success, fun, and friendship.
- Taking advantage of after school programs, particularly in neighborhoods where there are no formal activities for children. Keep them involved with the school rather than allowing them to have idle time roaming the neighborhood.

Feel safe and protected by:
- Assuring that children's basic needs of nutrition, housing, sleep, and safety are met on a regular basis.
- Providing an emotional safe haven for children. Be sure they know they can share any problem, concern, or failure with you and that you will be there with unconditional support. This doesn't mean making excuses for children. It means supporting them when they make mistakes and guiding them as they correct them.
- Providing the same safe haven for the child's friends. Many children just need someone to talk to who will listen and help them sort out their problems.
- Be consistent. Make sure that your child knows what is expected of him or her. Praise the child for appropriate behavior and correct inappropriate behavior. Help the child realize that it was his or her choice to behave or not to behave and that, as parents, you will follow up when bad choices are made.
- Avoid making threats that you do not or cannot fulfill. "You're grounded for the next six months!" The child will ignore future threats or consider them merely hot air or tempers.
- Avoid overreacting to your child's behavior. Take a few minutes to think about what you want to say to a child before responding. This will help you think before you speak and say something you will later regret and the child will not forget.
- Make sure that adults in the home model the behavior they expect of their child. If we want to raise a child who is caring, polite, honest, and respectful, then we must behave that way also.
- Remember that punishment may only drive children away--into the arms of gang members. Focus on helping children achieve positive rewards. For example, goals, praise, allowances, privileges, and a sense of being an important part of the family and minimize the necessity of negative consequences.

Parents Can Give Their Children...

A Sense of Power

Let your child hold important roles in the family

Help your child set personal goals

Allow your child to make personal decisions

Avoid any behaviors or statements that
make a child feel powerless or unimportant

Enhanced self-esteem

Build on each child's strengths and interests

Let each child assume a leadership role each week

Recognize or celebrate accomplishments, no matter how small

Encourage each child to be the best he or she can be--
verbally and nonverbally

Avoid verbal statements or actions that might be perceived as
"putting the child down"

Use both positive rewards and punishment,
but focus on achieving the rewards

Parents Can Give Their Children...

**Feelings of Connectedness, Belonging, and Identity
"Part of the Family" and "Part of the School"**

Give children a voice in family decisions that affect them

Hold family meetings

Involve children in planning family events

Encourage and support participation in at least one school activity on a regular basis

Take advantage of after school programs

A Sense of Safety and Protection

Provide an emotional "safe haven" at home

Be consistent

Avoid making threats that you do not or cannot fulfill

Avoid overreacting to your child's behavior

Do not say something in anger that you will later regret . . . and the child will not forget

Model the behavior you expect of you child

Parents Can Give Their Children...

Feelings of Connectedness, Belonging, and Identity
"Part of the Family" and "Part of the School"

Give children a voice in family decisions that affect them

Hold family meetings

Involve children in planning family events

Encourage and support participation in at least one school activity on a regular basis

Take advantage of after school programs

A Sense of Safety and Protection

Provide an emotional "safe haven" at home

Be consistent

Avoid making threats that you do not or cannot fulfill

Avoid overreacting to your child's behavior

Do not say something in anger that you will later regret . . . and the child will not forget

Model the behavior you expect of you child

Violence Prevention: Questions for Self-Reflection

Tool 2.3.12

How successful are we at creating the type of school environment that discourages student conflicts and violence? By using the following scale to rate current effectiveness, we can begin to focus on improving future efforts. Have we created a school environment that...

Promotes the inclusion of all students.	1 2 3 4	Benefits most, but not all, students.
Promotes cooperation and sharing.	1 2 3 4	Promotes competition and winners.
Encourages students to work with and help others.	1 2 3 4	Focuses primarily on individual efforts and behaviors.
Formally and informally recognizes the accomplishments of students--large numbers, not just the top few.	1 2 3 4	Recognizes the accomplishments of top students in many areas. Honor rolls and awards assemblies are annual events.
Places a high priority on developing positive relationships among students and between students and faculty.	1 2 3 4	Does not take time away from academics to focus on social relationships among students.
Teaches students and parents strategies for conflict resolution and peer mediation.	1 2 3 4	Provides rules and expects students to follow them. Deals with conflicts as they arise.
Holds parenting workshops on preventing violence at home and in the community.	1 2 3 4	Shares information on violence with parents, but cannot get parents to come to school meetings.
Provides after-school activities to promote the active involvement of students in school programs.	1 2 3 4	Does not provide after-school programs other than athletics and clubs.
Provides students with strategies for problem solving and long term conflict resolution.	1 2 3 4	Teaches problem solving in some content areas. Some faculty members focus on conflict resolution.
Builds lasting partnerships with parents and community members.	1 2 3 4	Encourages parent and community participation in school events.
Follows state and school system policies for dealing with violence and teaches students with severe behavior problems how to handle anger and violent tendencies.	1 2 3 4	Follows state and school system policies for dealing with violence.

Tool 2.3.13

Faculty School Climate
Worksheet

▼ **What are we currently doing that is achieving our desired outcomes?**

▼ **What could we do to strenghten our current approaches?**

▼ **Is there anything we should stop doing after considering our individual reflections and research based ideas?**

Design 3

Communicating Effectively

Communication is....

- verbalized or written words and thoughts, nonverbal expressions, and unvocalized feelings (10% words, 30% sounds, and 60% nonverbal or body language).
- the way we connect with others by sharing thoughts and feelings.
- the basis for all human interactions, friendships, and relationships.
- one of the most important skills we can possess.
- a critical factor in parent and educator satisfaction with schools.

Effective communication positively affects the quality of our lives by fostering more supportive relationships. It promotes awareness of how others perceive us and helps us come to clearer self-understanding. It is through communication that we inform others about who we are and what we value. It enhances our ability to work together and to form productive partnerships. When we develop a climate that fosters open, honest, and direct interactions, people feel comfortable and accepted in their environment. They are more likely to be creative and take the risks necessary to accept new ideas and find different ways of doing things. And, perhaps most importantly, it is through effective communication that we enhance students' attitudes toward learning and the quality of our instructional interactions. Furthermore, it has also been confirmed that student achievement is enhanced when families are consistently informed about their children's progress (U.S. Department of Education, 1994).

Unfortunately, communication in schools is generally imperfect at best. Educators and parents agree that it is less than adequate and often a source of dissatisfaction. According to consultants who work with schools to improve the quality of school life, "In the majority of the schools with whom we work, communication is generally one of the most important factors; yet, it is one of the areas needing the most improvement." As educators and parents, we continually struggle with the more subtle and elusive aspects of communication in our efforts to have productive social and professional interactions. This Design provides opportunities to reflect on current communication practices as well as a variety of strategies to enhance the faculty's efforts to optimize communication within the school community.

What we hear from . . .

EDUCATORS

"Schools reflect their larger communities. It's sad that adults as well as children don't know how to listen and talk with one another without becoming tense or defensive."
(Elementary school principal)

"The media can make or break a school. Why do they seem to report stories about what is wrong with education rather than what is right? Why do any problems in education tend to appear as headlines or lead stories on the 6 o'clock news?" (Elementary teacher)

"I can't speak Spanish, so I'm not able to communicate well with some of my parents. And, to make matters worse, I really don't understand why they do some of the things they do -- like take vacations in the middle of the semester." (Seventh grade teacher)

"I do everything I can to keep my parents informed. When a problem arises, though, many of them act like they never heard of our policies." (Third grade teacher)

"Every time I tell Mrs. _____ something about her child, she seems to take it the wrong way. I'm almost afraid to say much more." (Elementary guidance counselor)

PARENTS

"I don't want to call the school and complain. They might take it out on my child."
(Parent of a third grade student)

"Every time I call they say the teacher is in class and that she'll call me back. We haven't connected yet - and it's been three days!" (Parent of a fifth grade student)

"This must be one of the worst schools in the area. I hear that there are so many fights and thefts that the principals can't ever get out of their offices." (Parent of a high school student)

"The report card just doesn't tell me enough. My daughter is a straight A student, but I know that she's just coasting. I worry that she's developing poor habits and not using her talents and creativity in the ways she could." (Parent of an eighth grade student)

STUDENTS

"We all like our teacher! She has a sense of humor and makes us laugh!" (Fourth grader)

"Our student teacher wants to show how smart she is and always uses words we don't understand." (Seventh grader)

"I always know that I can go to my science teacher and he will explain it to me over and over until I get it." (Eighth grader)

"I really liked being on the committee to develop our school's home page. I'm doing one on my computer at home and Mrs. _____ is still helping me!" (High school senior)

Shared Responsibilities

In effective partnerships, *both* educators and parents, families, guardians, or caregivers take responsibility for communicating effectively with one another. The following diagram illustrates the responsibilities that are unique to each group and those that both groups share.

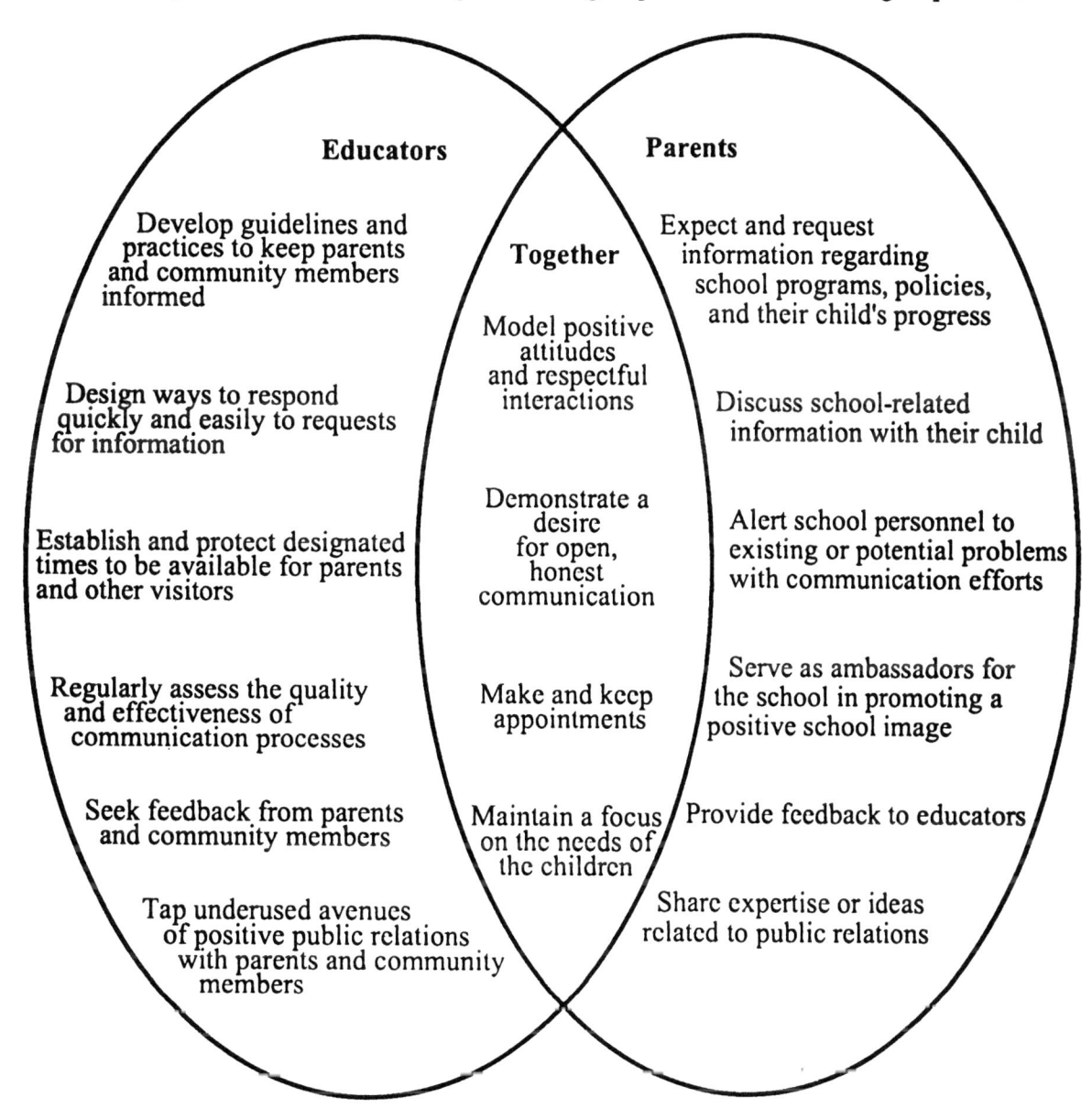

Educators
- Develop guidelines and practices to keep parents and community members informed
- Design ways to respond quickly and easily to requests for information
- Establish and protect designated times to be available for parents and other visitors
- Regularly assess the quality and effectiveness of communication processes
- Seek feedback from parents and community members
- Tap underused avenues of positive public relations with parents and community members

Together
- Model positive attitudes and respectful interactions
- Demonstrate a desire for open, honest communication
- Make and keep appointments
- Maintain a focus on the needs of the children

Parents
- Expect and request information regarding school programs, policies, and their child's progress
- Discuss school-related information with their child
- Alert school personnel to existing or potential problems with communication efforts
- Serve as ambassadors for the school in promoting a positive school image
- Provide feedback to educators
- Share expertise or ideas related to public relations

With all the time spent in communicating, it is critical that we do it well.

Steven Covey, 1990

Plans and Tools
for carrying out our responsibilities in designing effective communication

Plan 3.1. Overcoming Barriers to Effective Interpersonal Communication
Becoming aware of communication gaps, the impact of assumptions and inferences we make about others, and the ways information is misinterpreted will help educators and parents identify and understand communication problems that exist between the school and the home. Tools will help promote effective dialogue and communication skills to address existing problems and prevent others from happening.

Plan 3.2. Keeping Parents and Educators "In the Know"
This plan assists educators in designing guidelines for examining current communication practices and for improving processes that are not working as well as they should. Tools will help in designing handbooks, newsletters, calendars, electronic communications, and "forms" that facilitate home-school communication.

Plan 3.3. Making the Most of Parent-Teacher Conferences
This plan provides steps for assessing the effectiveness of current conferencing practices and ideas for enhancing them. It also includes sample communication forms for preparing for conferences, keeping track of information, reflecting upon the outcomes of conferences, and helping parents or guardians share what was discussed with their child.

Plan 3.4. Moving Beyond Report Cards in Communicating Student's Progress
This plan will help educators and parents rethink their assessment practices and move beyond typical report cards in describing student progress. Tools will provide guidelines for assessing the current system and identifying ways to make it more meaningful.

Plan 3.5. Promoting Positive Public Percpetions
This plan includes guidelines and strategies for enhancing communication throughout the school community and for "getting the word out" about school and student successes.

Three Key Indicators of Effective Two-way Communication

1. More families are involved.
2. Families are involved in a wider variety of ways over a significant period of time.
3. The involvement is experienced on both sides as constructive and purposeful.

Swap, 1993, p.62

Educator Reflection
Communication

How effective is communication at our school? What are we doing well? What could we be doing better? Take a few minutes to consider how frequently the following events or opportunities take place at your school. Put an "X" in the box that most closely reflects your perception.

	Often	Sometimes	Rarely
1. We attempt to understand parents' point of view and they do ours.			
2. All school personnel are available and willing to listen to parental concerns.			
3. All communications and interactions are characterized by mutual respect.			
4. Parents receive clear and timely information about school programs, rules, policies, and upcoming events.			
5. Most educators adequately communicate with parents through newsletters, notes, calls, recorded messages, etc.			
6. We make effective use of technology in communicating with parents and community members.			
7. Parents or guardians are contacted promptly about their child's problems and/or accomplishments.			
8. Parent-teacher conferences are productive for both educators and parents.			
9. Our parents receive adequate and meaningful information about their child's academic progress, social and personal development (accomplishments and difficulties).			
10. Our school's media image has a positive impact on it's reputation and public perception.			
11. We use the media to make the public aware of student and school successes.			

Plan 3.1
Understanding and Overcoming Barriers
To Effective Communication

One of the most frustrating situations for an educator or a parent is to try to discuss a problem, concern, or idea and to discover that what has been said has been misunderstood or misinterpreted by the listener. Sometimes, the misunderstanding escalates into an even greater problem than the one that was initially posed.

Why are effective interpersonal communications so challenging? There are several reasons. First, communicating involves many complicated processes--receiving, sending, interpreting, and inferring--all occurring simultaneously. While some people are more adept at these processes than others, most have difficulty with one or more of them from time to time. Second, each person brings his or her own unique perspectives to the conversation. In many of today's schools these individual perspectives represent a multitude of languages and cultures whose norms and subtleties are not known or understood by "outsiders." As a result, even the most well intentioned communications are often misunderstood. Third, communication is also highly situational. It occurs within specific contexts or situations that are highly changeable and dynamic. Words spoken effectively in one situation may be totally inappropriate in another. How words are phrased and who says them makes a difference in the quality of the interaction. Not only must communicators listen to what has been said, they must understand the varying interaction patterns and roles. When we realize all that is going on, it isn't surprising that communication is frequently less effective than it should be.

Peter Senge (1994), author of *The Fifth Discipline*, provides some insight into the difficulties with communication. He acknowledges the influence of our mental models on what we perceive. He describes mental models as "the images, assumptions, and stories which we carry in our minds of ourselves, other people, institutions, and every aspect of the world" (Senge, et. al., p. 235). These mental models function like a pane of bankers' glass with all of its bubbles and distortions. As we view the world through the distorted glass our mental models have created, we often see things quite differently from the way they really are or the way others see them. Furthermore, these mental models often contribute to our scaling the "Ladder of Inference" (Senge, 1994; Argyris, 1990). According to Chris Argyris, who is well known in the field of organizational dynamics and communication, this ladder image describes how individuals take in information, screen it through their mental models, and build responses that draw on their own prior beliefs or experiences with the information rather than what they have actually heard or observed. In short, as both parties engage in the process, they draw conclusions about each other based upon inferences that may be unfounded and untested. These inferences lead to words and actions that often escalate communication problems rather than resolve them.

In the *Fifth Discipline Fieldbook*, Senge (1994) also promotes the power of dialogue in enhancing communication. Dialogue is defined as "a sustained collective inquiry into everyday experience and what we take for granted" (p. 353). It is more than "active listening" that we all try to do in the course of a typical conversation. Dialogue requires both communicators to listen to the verbal and nonverbal messages sent by others while analyzing how they are responding to what has been heard. This involves understanding our own mental models and assessing their impact on what we hear as well as what we say. When educators focus on promoting dialogue, they create an environment that encourages learning from one another. At the same time, they promote individual and collective reflection and growth as well as open, honest, and trusting relationships. Dialogue takes time. It may require more conversations and more effort on the part of all participants. When used correctly, however, it has been found to be one of the most effective tools for overcoming barriers to effective communication.

How do we overcome these and other barriers to interpersonal communication? Basically it takes individuals who are willing to reflect, self-analyze, and commit to taking the steps necessary to develop communication patterns that will have a positive impact. At the same time, it takes an enhanced understanding of how to communicate effectively.

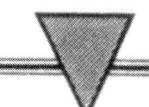

- Have someone on the faculty or an outside facilitator introduce the faculty to the concept of mental models. A brief explanation is provided in this plan and in Tool 3.1.1. more information is needed or desired, refer to *The Fifth Discipline Fieldbook* (Senge, et al., 1994) for a detailed explanation. The concept of mental models allows educators to become more aware of the way they view the world and to recognize the distortions in their windows of perception. According to the mental models analogy, the way individuals see themselves and others is determined to a great degree by perceptual filters used to interpret events and experiences. Tool 3.1.1 can be used to stimulate reflection and discussion regarding these filters and their impact. This discussion could be incorporated into a regular faculty meeting or an inservice session. Be sure to allow enough time for participants to think about the concepts, relate them to their own experiences, and share their thoughts with others.
  - Provide a brief explanation of mental models.
  - Allow a few minutes for each person to identify filters that have affected or shaped their mental models. Ask each person to write them down and share what they have written with others. Encourage them to consider the filters listed in Tool 3.1.1, but not to be limited by them. They may identify more than are listed in this tool.
  - Form triads and ask everyone to share their own personal mental models and filters. Pose the following questions for consideration: "How have your mental models been shaped?" "How have your mental models contributed to problems in communicating with others?" "Can you create new models?" (Answer: Of course!) Mental models can be changed just as we can develop new attitudes and perceptions. To do this we must confront our current ones before we can improve them. According to Senge, we can develop new mental models only when we are willing to link our imagination to action. For example, ask yourself, "How do my mental models influence my interpretation of our vision statement that 'all children can succeed?'" If I were able to remove the filters that screen out some children from my beliefs, how would I behave?

- Adapt the previous question to a specific concern at your school.
- Provide an opportunity to discuss the statement, "To understand the culture of a school or other organization, it is critical to understand the members' collective mental models" (Schein, 1993).

• Introduce the faculty to the "Ladder of Inference." Use Tool 3.1.2 as a visual explanation of the process. Sharing the information in creative ways (e.g., skits, posters, pictures) makes it more interesting and real life than just providing a written description. Tool 3.1.3 is a script of a skit that conveys a common teacher-parent scenario in which both parties scale the ladder. No matter how the information is shared, allow enough time to process the concepts and to link them to each individual's past and future actions.

• Provide an opportunity for faculty members to identify "real life" situations in which they climbed the "Ladder of Inference" when relating to a friend, colleague, or parent. Share these situations in small groups. Have each small group identify: (1) common situations that lend themselves to scaling the ladder, and (2) ways to avoid it in the future. Ask one person from each group to share the ideas generated with the total faculty. Look for common themes and write them down.

• Discuss ways to share the concepts of mental models, perceptual filters, and "Ladder of Inference" with parents. Identify appropriate groups of parents, times, etc. that would be conducive to sessions similar to what the faculty experienced. If this is not possible, discuss the possibility of other ways of sharing the information with parents such as through newsletters or one-on-one conferences.

• Refer to Tool 3.1.4 for information on promoting dialogue. The communication patterns and behaviors when individuals are engaged in true dialogue differ from those during other forms of interactions. When total faculties or smaller groups have learned about and practiced dialogue, their levels of understanding and trust have increased greatly.

• Each of us has developed particular ways of communicating with others. These ways become our routines which we perform almost automatically with very little effort. They are so common to us that they are almost invisible. Periodic reflection on our own interpersonal communication patterns help make them more visible to us. Use Tool 3.1.5 as a self-assessment of interpersonal patterns. By reflecting, we have become more conscious of our own interaction patterns. Awareness is the first step to enhancing our interactions with others.

• We live in a global society and increasingly more diverse communities. It is important that we as educators understand the cultural differences and develop an appreciation for the diversity. Educators and parents acknowledge that language and semantic differences can be barriers to effective communication. The difficulties need to be identified so that the ways around those difficulties can be discovered. See

Tool 3.1.6 for thoughts about challenges *and* opportunities of overcoming multicultural barriers to communication.

Other Possibilities ...

Recognizing Our Perceptual Filters

Tool 3.1.1

When looking through translucent glass, bankers' glass, or glass block, did you notice the lines and subtle distortions that makes this glass so beautiful? Did you realize that we see others and the world through our own mental window panes whose lines and distortions filter what we see? Senge's (1994) analogy tells us that if we are to improve our ability to communicate, we must become aware of our own mental models and learn to recognize the distortions in our own windows of perception. See if you recognize any of the following "filters" that affect how you view and respond to others.

Values and Beliefs Filters
What we value and what believe is right or wrong
affects our perceptions in all aspects of our lives.

Cultural Filters
What we have learned from our experiences and the way we have lived often
determines how we perceive and relate to other people, cultures, places, and experiences.

Family Filters
Family experiences often influence our perceptions. Positive experiences encourage a
positive outlook at life and opportunities. Negative experiences often pose limitations.

Religious Filters
Our religious beliefs and experiences guide the way we live our lives
and affect how we relate to others with differing religious perspectives.

Visual and Sound Filters
Often called "selective attention" and "overlooking details," this is when we
see and hear what we want to see and hear--whether it is sights, sounds, or words.

Memory Filters
Often called "selective memory," this is when we tend to screen out
what is too difficult or threatening to remember. Therefore, we often
remember the past and past events quite differently than they really were.

Appearance Filters
How we perceive people and places is often influenced by appearances
rather than what may be "below the surface." How many times are
people judged by their dress, their size, their occupations, or their homes?

Idealism Filters
We often see life in terms of how we think it *"ought to be."* These filters can cause
tremendous problems if we cannot separate *"what is"* from *"what ought to be."*

Tool 3.1.2

The Ladder of Inference

Communication is an overt act of connecting with other people. The ways we connect, communicate, and act are affected by our beliefs. What happens is that sometimes our actions are based on "misguided beliefs." These beliefs are based on conclusions drawn from what is observed and screened through personal filters and past experiences as opposed to those drawn from actual data. According to Chris Argyris (1990), individuals form these misguided beliefs by following a common mental pathway of increasing mental abstraction called the Ladder of Inference. Described in simple terms, individuals begin by observing data and then moving to other "rungs" of the ladder, not necessarily in a continuous path.

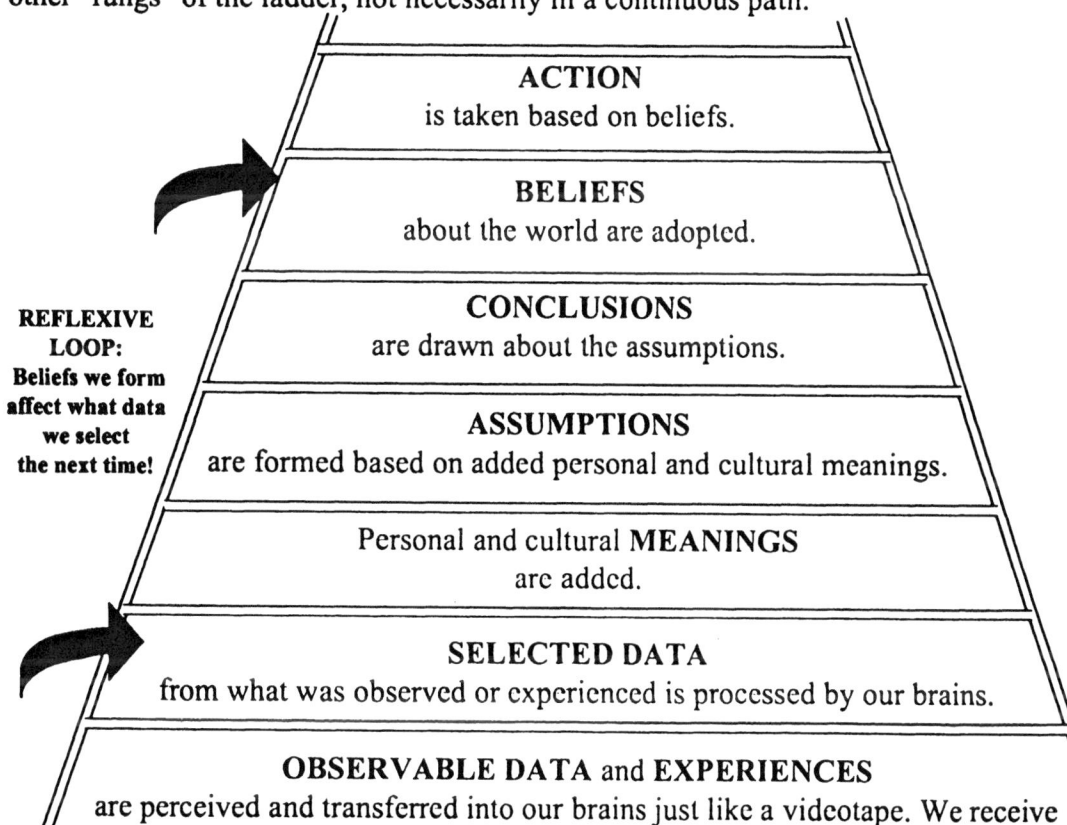

ACTION is taken based on beliefs.

BELIEFS about the world are adopted.

CONCLUSIONS are drawn about the assumptions.

ASSUMPTIONS are formed based on added personal and cultural meanings.

Personal and cultural **MEANINGS** are added.

SELECTED DATA from what was observed or experienced is processed by our brains.

OBSERVABLE DATA and EXPERIENCES are perceived and transferred into our brains just like a videotape. We receive facts, images, and information and screen them through our mental models. As a result, our perceptions are not always accurate. We may be taking in faulty data.

REFLEXIVE LOOP: Beliefs we form affect what data we select the next time!

How can understanding the "Ladder of Inference" improve communication? It helps us:
- understand how our mental models affect our responses to others.
- realize when we are basing our words or actions on inaccurate perceptions.
- make our thinking and reasoning more visible to others (becoming an advocate, taking a position and defending it, making it clear that we will not jump to conclusions).
- use inquiry to better understand the thinking and reasoning of others.
- recognize the dysfunctional ways individuals communicate in relationships, homes, and organizations.

Skit:
Climbing the Ladder of Inference

Tool 3.1.3

Introduction (Teacher)

I'm a teacher with very high expectations for my students. I communicate those expectations to both my students and my parents at the beginning of each year. I also model them for my students every day. I go out of my way -- and this takes nearly every evening and weekend-- to plan my lessons to ensure that my students are involved on a daily basis in challenging, hands on, enjoyable, and fun learning activities! Motivation is my bottom line!

I know my curriculum expectations, the abilities of my students, and ways to stimulate my students to want to learn--at least most of them. When I have a student who is not performing up to my expectations, I call the parents. Most are very concerned and willing to support my efforts to help their child.

Teacher: Then I called Mrs. _____ to tell her that I'm worried about Amy. I was surprised at her hesitancy to talk with me. I thought I had laid the foundation for this communication at the beginning of the year. She said she didn't have time to talk--and she knows how busy I am and that I wouldn't have called if it weren't very important! I guess her tennis schedule is a little too tight!

Parent: I hate that I couldn't talk with Amy's teacher today. My mother was on the other line telling me about yesterday's doctor's appointment and the latest problem that had shown up. I told Mrs. _____ that I would call her right back, but found that she was back in class. Each time I had a chance to call her, she wasn't available. The secretary is sounding a little more irritated every time I call. I know the call is about field trip money--I'll just send it in.

(Pause)

Parent: I've tried to call Mrs. _____ five times. This is really getting exasperating. What if this weren't about field trip money? I hate to keep bothering Mrs. _____, but maybe I should leave a message for her to call me back.

Teacher: After two days, I finally called Mrs. _____ again. By this point, I was really frustrated. Amy still hasn't turned in any assignments and is falling further behind each day. I can't believe her parents don't care enough to help. By the time I got her mother on the phone, I only had a couple of minutes before class to say what I needed to say. Needless to say, it wasn't one of my better parent communications!

Parent: I couldn't believe how brusque she was! And she's teaching my daughter? No wonder Amy is having a tough year. She puts you on the defensive right off the bat!

Tool 3.1.3

Teacher: I could tell that Mrs. _____ was totally disinterested in my concern about Amy. She acted like I have a problem! Since she's not willing to help me, I need to do something quickly--or Amy will fail this six weeks and be off to a terrible start for the year. I thought about it for an hour or so and called her back to tell her that I had scheduled a meeting for all of us in the principal's office. Someone needs to make her see how important it is to send Amy to school ready to learn.

Parent: What a phone call! A meeting in the principal's office over a few late assignments! Doesn't she realize that this is soccer season and these kids are playing or cheering at games every night? I guess she just picks on everybody--first Amy, now me. I wonder how many other parents she's infuriated? Maybe I should just call a few of my friends. . . .

Reflecting on the Skit

1. What rungs of the "Ladder of Inference" did the teacher and the parent climb? (See if you can explain their behaviors in terms of each rung.)

2. Thinking of the "reflexive loop," what might happen during the meeting in the principal's office?

3. How would this communication have been different if each party had been aware of the "Ladder of Inference" and modified their behavior accordingly?

4. Have similar situations occurred at our school? If so, describe one and explain what happened in terms of the "Ladder of Inference." What could be done in the future to avoid them?

Tool 3.1.4

Promoting Dialogue

> **Dialogue is ...**
> - collective inquiry and learning.
> - beyond conversation.
> - sustained interchanges leading to growth and change.
> - a means to help people talk together and learn from one another.

Dialogue requires ...

Individuals willing to be "equal participants" sharing their unique perspectives, knowledge, ideas, and resources (energy, patience, commitment).

Behaviors that promote dialogue ...
- posing essential questions that challenge thinking
- practicing "internal listening"
- identifying own perceptions (feelings, attitudes, assumptions) about what is being said
- listening to ourselves before listening to others
- questioning and confronting our own assumptions
- suspending judgment, restraining impulsivity, harnessing immediate reactions
- acknowledging defensiveness and probing for underlying reasons
- contributing relevant information, ideas, and experiences
- encouraging multiple perspectives and accepting differences of opinion
- being patient in coming to a clear, full understanding of what is being said
- paying attention to the words, but also the space between the words--pace, tone, timbre
- asking for clarification
- providing justification of one's position and requesting it of others
- enjoying the struggle by restraining the urge to reach consensus, decision, or closure
- reflecting on the dialogue process
- engage in a shared critique to improve the dialogue process

Dialogue occurs best when ...
- goals and guidelines are developed and communicated.
- essential questions are identified to focus the dialogue.
- dialogue is practiced. Identifying one or more process observers may be helpful.
- participants self-assess or debrief the dialogue process to improve future efforts.

Dialogue can lead to ...
- more productive collaboration, creative problem-solving, and coordinated action.
- higher levels of understanding and trust.
- increased interactive learning.
- enhanced growth for all participants.
- new and more effective ways of communicating with one another.

Improving Interpersonal Communication Skills

Tool 3.1.5

Take Time To Reflect
What behaviors do I exhibit when communicating with others?

- Am I judgmental in responding to others?
  OR
  Do I show acceptance by acknowledging what is said?

- Am I too aggressive in talking to others (saying "well, not really;" interrupting others; changing the subject abruptly)?
  OR
  Do I encourage and support what others are saying?

- Do I exhibit self-indulgence?
  OR
  Do I attempt to get beyond the limits of my own personal experiences?

- Do I block the opinions of others by pronouncing mine as the only "right" one?
  OR
  Do I take a more compromising position?

- Do I dominate the conversation and keep others from participating equally?
  OR
  Do I ask questions to elicit the contributions of others?

- Do I maintain eye contact and stay focused on the conversation?
  OR
  Do I become distracted and show a lack of interest in what is being said?

- Do I clarify and/or paraphrase in an attempt to fully understand what is being said?
  OR
  Do I contribute without fully comprehending?

Becoming aware of our behavior is the first step to changing!

Understanding Differences and Appreciating Diversity
Challenges *and* Opportunities of Multicultural Communication

For educators, parents, and students unfamiliar languages and cultural patterns can be viewed as significant communication challenges or as important learning opportunities. Educators are aware of the growing numbers of non-English speaking parents and community members, but they may not have developed their sensitivity to the unique cultural expectations of each language group. They may not know the most appropriate ways to communicate with those parents. In turn, these parents may be somewhat intimidated by an unfamiliar educational process and uncomfortable interacting with educators.

In addition to non-English speaking parents, educators may deal with a large number of adults who are otherwise not proficient with language. They may not have had the educational opportunities that allow them to competently and confidently communicate with educators. They have had limited experience in tactfully making their wishes known and in working collaboratively with others to bring about a constructive resolution to differences. Parents who have had less than positive school experiences themselves may be intimidated and somewhat threatened by formal communications from schools. Educators also need to interact with parents who are physically challenged or impaired. This requires that they develop communication modes or use technology that may be unfamiliar to them.

What happens when educators and families of various cultures try to communicate without understanding the differences that exist? They are more likely to misinterpret both verbal and written messages; make inaccurate or incomplete assessments of what has been communicated; or respond in ways that are interpreted by others as defensive, passive, or in other ways unsatisfactory. How can these pitfalls be avoided and mutual respect and understanding enhanced? Consider the following possibilities.

****

Identify knowledgeable people from each culture within the school system or community to consult with educators about communication patterns, both verbal and nonverbal. Their first hand knowledge and experience will enable educators to develop important guidelines (essential do's and don'ts) for communicating effectively. These "consultants" may be ESL teachers; translators; church sponsors; business persons or other community members; or area college or university professors, instructors, or graduate assistants.

****

Explore the interest of educators and community members in offering language classes. The classes would focus on conversational competence and cultural communication norms.

****

Tool 3.1.6

Promote school themes related to multiculturalism. Months or weeks could be dedicated to specific cultures represented by the school community. Students, parents, and community members could contribute to presentations, displays, ethnic food demonstrations, music, sports, celebrations, or other events that highlight various cultures. See Tool 2.2.3 for more detail on appreciating and celebrating diversity.

****

Engage students in research projects on different cultures. Their presentations and exhibits could be a catalyst for discussion and further investigations.

****

Listen to "the client's voice" (Rigsby, Reynolds, & Wang, 1995). Introduce faculty members and parents to the words and feelings of members of the school community who may come from backgrounds or cultures that differ from their own. Invite members of these cultures to share their feelings and perceptions through any means possible (interviews, tapes, videos, or face-to-face discussions, etc).

One school's experience...
A middle school principal in a rural southern town found a large "communications gap" between the teachers and the northern parents who had found employment in a large automobile assembly plant recently located in the town. Although many factors entered in, cultural differences appeared to have caused initial communications difficulties even between all English-speaking people.

Remember that there appears to be universal understanding of a need for an attitude of friendliness, acceptance, genuine interest and respect.
Attitude cuts across all cultures!

Plan 3.2
Keeping Parents and Faculty "In the Know"

How many times do parents tell us they "don't know what is going on in the school," "didn't realize that my child was responsible for...," or "don't know how to help?" As educators it is extremely frustrating when we spend so much time trying to keep them "in the know." At the same time, parents complain that they really do not know how to share their ideas or concerns with teachers and administrators. They are not always aware of the appropriate channels of communication and are, in many cases, intimidated about sharing their views. Schools that place effective communication as a top priority focus on improving dialogue and opening channels of communication between educators, parents, and community members.

Nearly every school uses newsletters, calendars, report cards, midterm reports, school handbooks, and hotlines--some more successfully than others. How can these and other avenues of communication be strengthened to maximize our efforts to keep all parents and the community informed? Working together to create a shared understanding of the purpose of communication and developing guidelines for communicating that everyone understands and follows are the keys to keeping everyone "in the know" and encouraging effective communication practices.

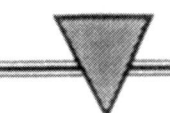

- As a total faculty (as one group or an appropriate number of small groups), engage in a discussion about communication. Specifically focus on:
  - Who are the important groups with whom the school should communicate?
  - What are the major reasons we feel we need to communicate with each group?
  - What are the main benefits of effective communication with them?
  - What problems generally arise when communication breaks down?
  - What are the best ways each group can communicate with educators?

- Continue the activity by identifying the ways communication is currently occurring with each of the identified groups. It may be helpful at this point to break into small groups if you haven't already done so. Each group could be assigned a specific population (teachers, parents, students, community members, politicians, etc.). Have them brainstorm:
  - The ways information is currently being shared (from educators and school personnel) with the group (newsletters, calendars, letters, homework hotline, telephone calls, notes to parents, etc.).
  - The ways information is currently being shared (from the group) to the educators or school personnel.

- Take each item identified on the "current" list and classify into two categories: "Working Well" and "Needs Improvement." From the "Needs Improvement" list, identify the specific problems. Also consider the "Working Well" methods. Some of them may need some adjustments to be even more effective. Also consider any situations that have been overlooked (such as the opportunities the groups have to communicate with the school).

- Now that current communication channels are known to all and some of the problems and gaps have been identified, the most appropriate way to proceed would be to preview the Tools provided in this plan. Tool 3.2.1 is a checklist for written communications. Tool 3.2.2 presents specifications for commonly used communication forms and formats. Both may be useful for teachers in assessing their own individual and grade level/departmental communications and in evaluating those sent on a schoolwide basis. Both Tools may provide suggestions for overcoming some of the problems in the current communication system. Review Tool 3.2.3 and Tool 3.2.4. Tool 3.2.3 provides a description of a Communication Web. This could also be called a telephone tree. If one is not functioning well in your school, reviewing this Tool may provide some good suggestions for making it work better. Tool 3.2.4 provides Parent and Student Communication Forms that may or may not be in existence in your school. Some schools have found it helpful to have a form available for parents or students when they are unhappy with some situation and want to lodge a formal complaint. The reason they are called Communications Forms is because parents and others may also want to commend someone's work or effort. It is a good idea to have a special place for such compliments. Tool 3.2.5 provides some additional Communication Extras that may extend the thinking about good communications.

- At some appropriate point in discussions about communication, specific guidelines should be developed to promote more effective practices. The following questions can guide the discussion to generate the guidelines:
  - Have all faculty members had input into developing the guidelines? This step is critical in developing a shared understanding and commitment to following them.
  - Have all faculty members had the opportunity to share their own ideas and practices? In every school, there are teachers who are using very effective techniques in communicating with parents, but many of their colleagues are unaware of their practices.
  - Do all faculty members understand the purpose for sharing information with various parent groups?
  - Are there differences at each grade level? Does everyone understand these differences and why they are appropriate?
  - Have parents been consulted in developing the guidelines and practices? (Using the *Building Community Parent Survey,* parent focus groups, or informal telephone polls can provide input that the faculty might have over looked without asking. Parents could also be included in the brainstorming.

- Have representative community members been able to share their ideas? It would be especially important to ask school partners or "adopters," local newspaper publishers, and business owners that are directly affected by the school. They could be included in the brainstorming sessions or their ideas could be gathered through the *Building Community Parent Survey* or telephone interviews.
- At appropriate grade levels, have students' opinions been considered?

• Before finalizing the guidelines and practices, be certain that they are realistic in relation to:
   - Time constraints
   - Costs
   - Availability of support from outside the faculty (e.g., parent volunteers, community members)

• Build in ways to assess the effectiveness of strategies to promote two-way communication. These strategies will enable the faculty to make minor revisions as they are implementing new approaches, rather than finding out "after the fact" that they were not as effective as they were designed to be.

Other Possibilities . . .

Checklist for Written Communications

Tool 3.2.1

(to be completed while designing and finalizing communications)

Have we . . .

_____ Developed a yearly schedule for major communications?
(This should be accomplished at the beginning of the year or prior to it.)

_____ Included the school name, logo, address, phone number/e-mail address, and appropriate individuals' names?

_____ Personalized the communications whenever possible?
(Never address any communications "To the parents of   Student's Name .")

_____ Translated the communications into languages spoken by our parents?
(Parent volunteers can be helpful!)

_____ Used an appealing layout?
(Consider font size; adequate spacing; highlighting with boxes, borders, and graphics.)

_____ Included "attention getting" devices?
(These include logos, mastheads, consistency or novelty in paper color and design.)

_____ Written in a clear, concise style? Avoided jargon, technical terms and acronyms?
(It is best to use simple sentences and easily understood wording.)

_____ Included all of the important information?
(All essential components of the particular type of communication should be included.)

_____ Checked for readability level?
(A 5th grade level is generally recommended.)

_____ Checked for accuracy of content?
(A knowledgeable person should review the information before it is distributed.)

_____ Spell-checked and carefully proofed?
(It is preferable to use an "objective" proofreader who was not involved in the writing phase.)

_____ Considered any interactive possibilities?
(Is there any response necessary from the reader? If a "tear off" form is used, be sure the essential information is duplicated so the receiver can retain a copy.)

Tool 3.2.1

_____ Involved students' work when appropriate?
(Students can serve as contributors for artwork, articles, layout or logo design, duplication, addressing, or other features. With appropriate curriculum integration, these could be excellent opportunities for authentic learning experiences.)

_____ Used high-quality reproduction techniques so the copy is clear and readable?

_____ Ensured distribution to the intended readers?
(U.S. mail, even with their glitches, is more reliable than student delivery systems.)

_____ Completed a spot check to monitor distribution and to ask for feedback?
(A few parents could be called at random to ask about the delivery and the quality of the communication.)

_____ Enlisted the assistance of parents, community members, or business representatives who may have the communications expertise to review communications and provide feedback for improvement?
(They may have ideas that we haven't considered.)

_____ Evaluated communications to ensure appropriateness in terms of tone, gender, assumptions (about marital status, resources of the parents), use of humor, etc.?

Communication Specs
(One-way and Two-way Types of Communication)

Tool 3.2.2

Parent Handbooks

Handbooks are a very important beginning of the year communication. For many parents, the handbook is often their "first impression" of the school. At a minimum, it conveys important content, but, more importantly, it presents an overall attitude about how the school views parents and treats their children. It contains a great deal of "need to know" information in addition to expectations and priorities. Pay careful attention to the content, the style and tone of the writing, and the attractiveness and appeal of the final product.

- Determine the appropriate content to be included.
    1. District information
    2. School philosophy, vision, mission
    3. Personnel and assignments
    4. Unique features, distinguishing qualities, recent distinctions and awards
    5. Governing structure, committees, and opportunities for parent involvement
    6. Programs (curricular, co-curricular, special) and services (food, transportation, clinic, counseling/advising, social services)
    7. Policies (attendance; tardy; early dismissal; emergencies; phone calls; home work; make-up work; dress code; fees; books and supplies; promotion/retention; security procedures--student ID, video scanners, metal detectors, searches; visitors; health-related procedures--immunizations, medication dispensing; student placement; transfer; and other policies that are important for students and parents to know)
    8. Grading system and reporting procedures
    9. Discipline guidelines or rules
    10. Celebrations, special and annual events
- Prepare a Table of Contents.
- Design a cover for final packaging. Students can be a terrific source for ideas.
- Decide on a procedure for distribution (person to person through parent helpers/room moms and dads, by child, sent through the mail). Ensure that each parent receives one. It may be helpful to have parents or guardians sign a statement that they have received the handbook.
- Provide opportunities for clarification. Encourage parents to ask questions.
- Review the handbook each year to ensure that the content is accurate. Depending on your distribution schedule, spring may be a good time so that revisions and printing can occur over the summer.

Tool 3.2.2

Informal Notes Home

The "surprise" message is often the one with the most meaning. Generally, these messages are positive and serve as "good news" about an accomplishment, recognition for a job well done, or just keeping in touch about a topic of mutual interest or concern. The messages are personal and spontaneous and can greatly increase feelings of trust and good will for all parties involved.

- Design a format that reflects your own style, is "age" appropriate for the students, is attractive, and communicates something about your classroom or the school (classroom theme, "nickname," etc.). Make an adequate number of copies to assure a ready supply.
- Design the forms with a dual purpose in mind. The notes could serve as a means to recognize accomplishments and contributions or could just communicate "good news" ("Happy grams," "Hats off" cards).
- Reproduce the note forms so that they are easily accessible for use. Use special paper that is reserved for your communications.
- Be sure to date each communication.
- It is an excellent idea to send an informal note home early in the year with some positive message. This helps set the expectation for productive communications. One variation is to address communications (or post cards) prior to the beginning of the year to distribute during the first 6-weeks of school. This is one way to keep track of who has received the communications and who hasn't!
- If the note requires a response from the parent, be sure to note a follow-up call if you have not heard within a given period of time. If the note does not require a parental response, be sure you don't close off the possibilities of continued communications (always extend the invitation, leave the door open).
- It may be helpful to designate intervals for sending notes home in your plan book.

Telephone Calls

Telephone calls can provide the two-way communication needed to initiate and sustain productive relationships. They can take many forms: an upbeat, "get acquainted" call; a progress check to see how plans are coming; an attempt to verify information or convey information about some school incident; or a more serious notification of a concern. While there are some difficulties with actually reaching some parents by phone, the benefits can be great. Telephone calls provide a timely exchange of ideas, information, and emotion and an opportunity to ensure understanding and respect. If a teacher perceives that there is a problem at school, the parent wants to know "before it is too late."

- Review the parent information sheet before calling the parent to determine if English is the spoken language. (See Tool 4.2.1)
- Rehearse the purposes of the call prior to making it. Is it to: share information? confirm information? request parental assistance? ask parents or guardians to engaged in shared problem solving? Make notes to keep the conversation on track.
- Identify yourself and confirm that you have reached the parent or guardian you want.
- Determine if "this is a good time to talk." Express that "I need just a few minutes of

Tool 3.2.2

Newsletters (and Newspapers)

Newsletters and newspapers are forms of ongoing communications that help parents and others feel "in the know." They are an excellent means for communicating announcements, requests, recognition, displays of student work, and in general, highlight the good work of schools and the excitement of learning.

- Determine the scope (schoolwide or for individual classrooms, grade levels, curriculum areas, and/or co-curricular areas).
- Decide on a format. Would it be beneficial to have regular columns or to change the format each time the newsletter is issued?
- Develop a distribution schedule (e.g., at a specific date each month, every two weeks).
- Include the date on the newsletter.
- Determine if seasonal, multicultural, or activity-oriented themes should be identified for each edition. If so, what should they be?
- Identify the timely and necessary information that should be included. Adequate notice of upcoming events is important.
- Identify additional highlights and topics that would be of interest to parents.
- Include recognition of special accomplishments.
- Request parental assistance in terms of needed materials, financial support, and/or preparation of the actual newsletter.
- Use a more conversational and spontaneous style of writing than is used in more formal written communications.
- Determine if a calendar should be included.

Calendars

Calendars are another form of ongoing communications that are intended to help maintain focus on day to day and important events at school. Often, calendars are included with the newsletters/papers, but they could be distributed separately before the beginning of each month. Identify the important information to be included, such as:

- Meals (for the month)
- Events
- Due dates
- Suggestions for parents about ways to reinforce school learning activities

One specific type of calendar is a Learning Calendar. These provide developmentally appropriate ideas for parent-child activities that can reinforce school learning. Highlights for the calendar could include: books to read together, videos to watch, local points of interest or special events, interactive opportunities, subject-related activities, study skills, and organizational skills. Additional suggestions for calendars are provided in *Design 7: Supporting Teaching and Learning Design*.

Tool 3.2.2

your time" and stick to it. An effective call can be pleasant, to the point, and also brief.
- Be sure that you probe for understanding and allow opportunities for questions and clarification. It is critical that the message is clearly understood by both parties. (This is tricky as probes are often perceived as "talking down." For example, the teacher might say, "It is very important to me that we fully understand each other. I'll review what we've said and I'll ask you to do the same. I'll review what my next steps are and . . .").
- End the conversation by sharing your appreciation ("I'm glad we had the opportunity to talk." or "Thank you for your time.") and leave an opening for continued interaction ("If you have any further thoughts or questions, please feel free to call me at ___.")
- Keep a separate notebook or listing of calls (in and out). Be sure to note date time, purpose of the call, what was resolved, and any needed follow-up. Be objective, try not to include your feelings or assumptions about the interaction.

Date/Time	Person Contacted	Purpose	Resolution	Follow-up

Suggestion Box

The physical presence of a suggestion box sends an important message that the school values the opinions and ideas of others and that there is a desire to do things in the best ways possible. When people see that their suggestions are acted upon, the communication process is enhanced.
- Create an attractive or unique "box"--one that will draw attention to it.
- Locate the suggestion box in a strategically appropriate place. For many reasons the office may be the best place, but just be sure that it is easy to reach and that paper and pen are available.
- Designate the appropriate person or persons to periodically review the suggestions.
- Develop a procedure that will encourage action on good ideas.
- Acknowledge suggestions that include an individual's name.

> YOUR SUGGESTIONS
> Help Us Grow!
>
> Please let us know if you have an idea
> that would help us improve what we are doing!

Outdoor Signs

Signs may only allow "short and sweet" messages, but they are a powerful way to keep parents and community members informed of upcoming events.
- Timeliness is the biggest concern. Post announcements well in advance of the event.
- Change the message fairly often and on a regular basis.
- Be certain every word is spelled correctly.

Tool 3.2.2

Videos

Videos could serve as a welcome to parents and new students or as an orientation to prospective teachers, interested community members, and business partners. While videos have many useful purposes, professional looking products require financial resources. Look for creative ways to defray the costs. Another idea is to have local high schools with technical capabilities produce videos as an authentic, "hands-on" learning experiences for the students.

- Get input from a wide variety of interested individuals (students, parents, community members, and business partners) about the contents of the video. The question they should address is: "What should we highlight to present 'who we are' as a school?
- The most appealing videos are those prepared by someone with technical and artistic expertise.

Parent Communications Form

Designating the form as a Parent Communications Form conveys the message that the report may be used for positive as well as negative information. When a parent comes in to commend a faculty or staff member for actions that are clearly "above and beyond," the form could be used to document the event. When a parent comes in expressing a "problem" with someone, the form could also be used when other avenues have been exhausted. A formal record should result from a parent complaint that cannot be resolved verbally to the satisfaction of both parties (or if school personnel determine it wise to have a record of the "alleged" incident). Often the parent will choose not to fill out the form, but, at least, the offer was made.

- See Tool 3.2.4 for a sample form.
- Decide upon procedures related to the use of the form.

E-mail

If you have the technical capability, e-mail may provide another avenue for parental communications. Some communities are incorporating e-mail into their regular communication practices--and are finding that more and more of their families with the financial means consider computers basic necessities for their children.

Home Pages

A school home page could be an important means of promoting the school. It can also encourage networking among professionals by connecting with other schools similar to yours.

- Students or former students (if elementary) are a great resource. The design could be a group or interdisciplinary project.
- Necessary information about personnel, programs, and services or highlights about special programs, grants, and activities could be easily accessed by interested parties. Key demographic features could also be of interest to others.

Tool 3.2.2

Automated Dialing Systems

Identify the features that would be the most helpful to accomplish intended purposes. Many schools use these systems to communicate specialized schoolwide, grade level, or class messages about a wide range of topcis: absences (student absences are listed and parents can call to confirm), when to return permission slips, report card distribution information, and important dates and times for open house, conference week, and other special events.

- Compose a message that conveys what parents need to know.
- Keep the message brief and to the point.
- Timeliness is an issue. Be sure to give parents ample notice.

Lesson Lines

Many schools provide telephone lines for the purpose of letting parents know what "today's homework" is and alerting them to upcoming projects, events, and parent involvement opportunities. Change the message on a regular basis. Nothing is more frustrating to a parent than calling the lesson line and hearing a message that is several weeks old.

Answering Devices

No parent should call the school and be unable to leave a message. If all personnel are occupied, it is critical to have a way for the parent, whose schedule may not allow another call, to communicate with the school. Answering machines may not be the best alternative, but they do allow parents' wishes to be heard.

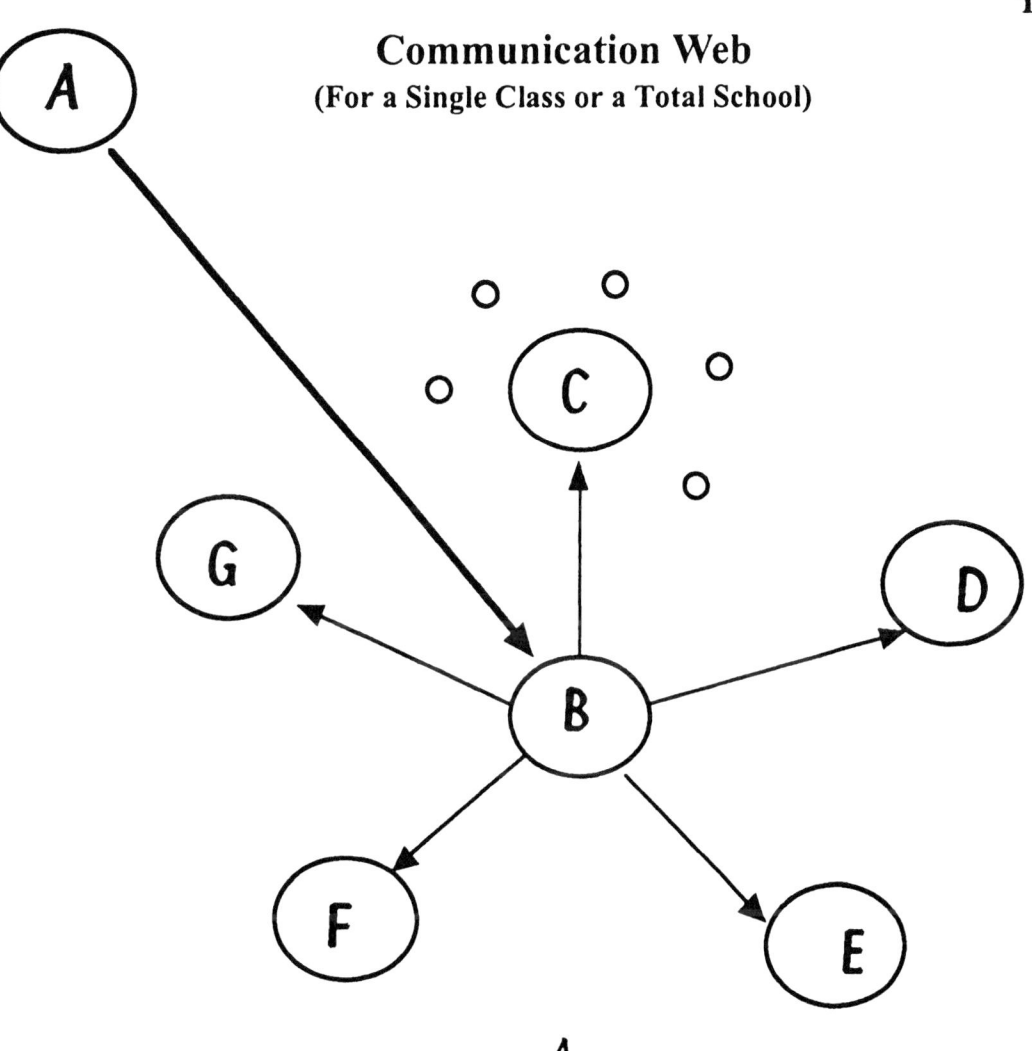

Communication Web
(For a Single Class or a Total School)

Tool 3.2.3

A
Initiator of the communication
Teacher, principal, parent, or anyone with authorized information to share

B
Facilitator for the communication web
Parent identifies "connectors" and begins the communication web

C - G
Critical "connectors" who make the web work.
Parent volunteers who are willing and able to make the connections when information is to be shared

---

Flow
A initiates message with B
B begins the web by calling C - G
C calls C1, C2, C3, C4, and C5
(**D** through **G** follows the same process)

Tool 3.2.3

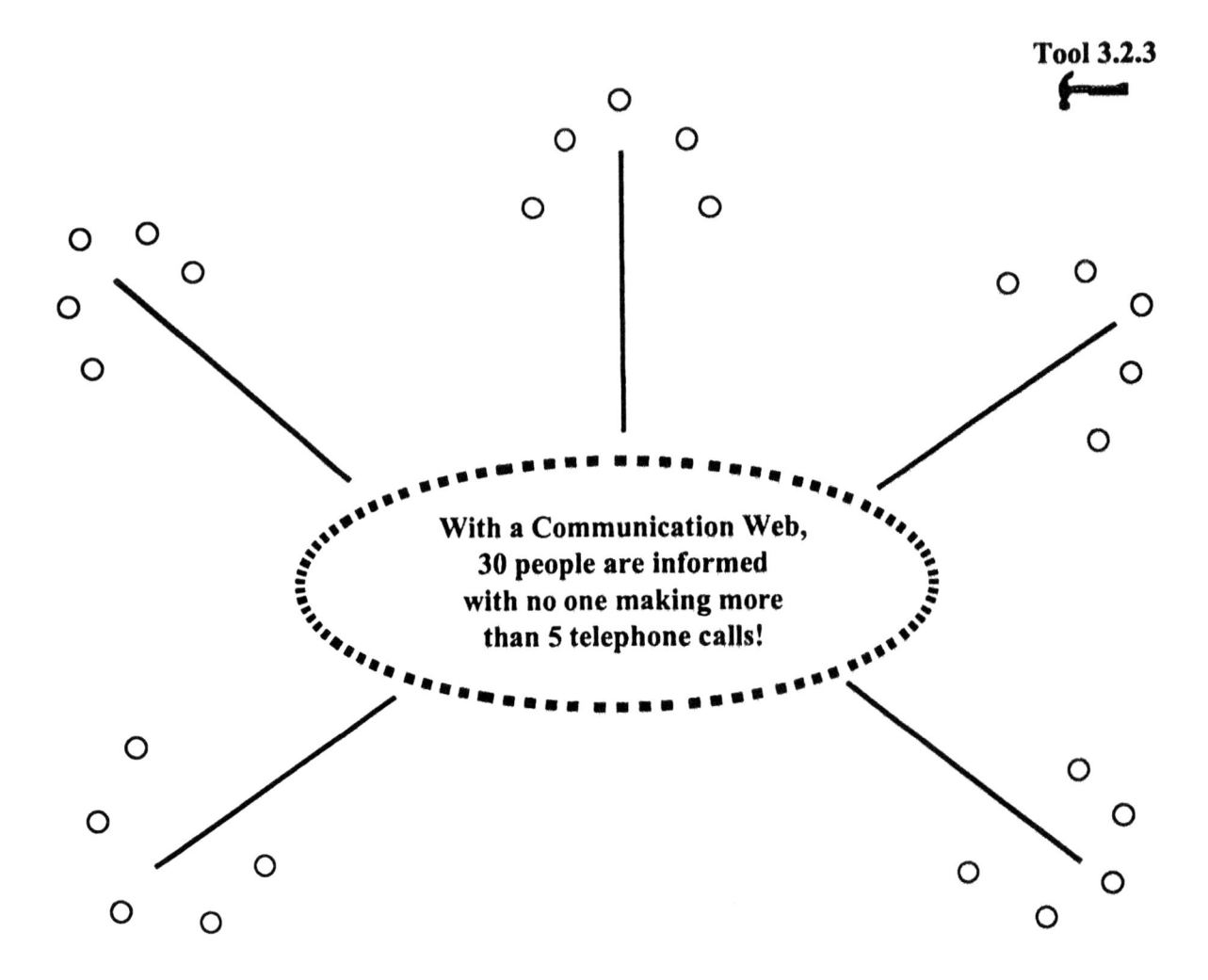

With a Communication Web, 30 people are informed with no one making more than 5 telephone calls!

Considerations:
- Whoever initiates the communication *must* be sure that the message has been authorized by a building administrator.
- Facilitators should select connectors who are dependable and who are willing to give the time to make the calls periodically throughout the semester or the year. This is often a good volunteer assignment for parents who work.
- If there are parents who are non-English speakers, be sure to select a "connector" who can convey messages in the native language.
- Add lines to the web so each position can be identified by name. The whole web can be reproduced for all involved.
- To reduce the number of calls each "connector" must make, increase the number of connectors.
- For a larger, schoolwide web, make each "connector" a "facilitator." Develop full webs for each of the connectors. It would be ideal to have at least one web per grade level depending upon the size of the school.
- Periodically the facilitator should do a random check to see how well the web is working.
- The accompanying worksheet may be helpful in making the web really work.

Communication WEB Worksheet

Tool 3.2.3

My position on the WEB is _____

I call--

Name	Home #	Work #	Child(ren)'s names
1.			
2.			
3.			
4.			
5.			

Participants' Promise

In my position as a "facilitator" or a "connector," I will . . .
- Complete my calls within 24 hours of receiving the message.
  (I understand that some emergency situations may arise and I will make every effort to make my calls as quickly as possible or enlist the help of someone else to do it if I am unable at that time.)
- Be brief and stay on topic.
  (I understand that everyone is busy and I will convey my message and not initiate chatting.)
- Be precise and accurate in conveying the authorized message.
- Ask if there are any questions or if there is a need for more information.

In my position as a receiver of the message, I will . . .
- Ask questions or request additional information if I need to.
- Not initiate any "off topic" discussions.

Parent Communication Form

Tool 3.2.4

We believe that parents deserve the opportunity to share successes or concerns. We truly appreciate your willingness to let us know what you are thinking.

Child's Name: _____

I would like to share the following: success story ____   concern ____   suggestion ____

_____
_____
_____
_____
_____
_____
_____
_____
_____
_____
_____
_____
_____
_____
_____
_____
_____
_____

_____   _____
Parent or Guardian Signature   Date

Note: This information will be shared with your child's teacher.

Communication Extras

Tool 3.2.5

Have You Thought About...

Teachers would be more successful in maintaining contact with their parents if they had adequate access to telephones. In most schools, teachers must share the few phones available making the access more difficult. In addition, the phones are usually not located in places that ensure privacy. The conversations between parent and teacher should be private, not public.

****

Should school to home communications be delivered by the children or sent directly to the home? Most school personnel feel that if the message is an essential one, the best route is the mail. It may be more costly, but the likelihood of the announcement "I left it . . ." is greatly decreased.

****

There are parents who may need more than encouragement to interact daily with their child about school events. Many teachers are especially creative in designing ways to promote that quality interaction. Some are using student agendas which alert parents to homework assignments as well as the child's activities for the day. One middle school teacher described her school's clever use of agendas. At this school, the agenda becomes a hall pass if students ask to go to their lockers or the restroom. However, the student must write down the destination and have the teacher initial it. It does not take long for teachers and parents to realize that a child is constantly asking to leave the classroom! Other teachers send notes home with questions posed for parents to ask their children. "Ask me about . . . " notes open the lines of communication about the school day and get better results than when parents ask their children, "What did you do today?"

****

Hold parent-teacher conferences at the closest fast food location. One elementary school enlisted the support of its local adopter, MacDonalds, to provide the site for the conferences. MacDonalds also offered a "free drink coupon" for each parent attending. The incentive of the free drink was appealing to the parents and MacDonalds gained community support as well as the additional money from food sold to the free drink recipients!

****

One teacher addresses a post card to each parent of her students prior to the beginning of the year. She sends them home throughout the first month of school. The communication is personalized by highlighting some specific positive contribution or characteristic of the child. This teacher has seen that this sets a positive tone for the whole year!

Plan 3.3
Making the Most of Parent-Teacher Conferences

Educators have an important responsibility in keeping families informed of their student's progress. Parents or guardians want and need information about their child's academic progress as well as information about social and personal development, accomplishments, and difficulties. When they send their children to school or to daycare, many of them feel the loss of the contact and minute to minute information about their children. For some this is traumatic, and for most, it is extremely uncomfortable. When they are with their children, they have immediate knowledge about how they are doing. When they "give up" their children to kindergarten teachers, they feel as if they are on the outside looking in. The problem increases as students enter the secondary levels. Families are even more reluctant to maintain the close contact with teachers that they had when their children were in elementary grades.

The challenge for school personnel is to capitalize on the needs and interests of families and channel them in ways that are helpful to children and to educators. If school personnel want to truly work in concert with families, they need to find ways to provide information that will productively engage them. It is also important to remember that when family members feel as if they are not getting the information they need or want, they may assume that school personnel do not care. That false assumption can become an extremely difficult obstacle to overcome.

According to many educators, parent-teacher conferences are extremely valuable opportunities for two-way communication with families. They are opportunities to share expectations, enhance mutual respect, and further understanding of one another and the child. It is a time when there is total focus on the child. Sharing information about the child's abilities and strengths, identifying concerns, and setting mutually desirable goals for the child, are productive ways to build collaborative relationships and two-way communication with families. Conferencing is also a positive way to reach parents--one at a time. Parents and teachers alike attest to the numerous benefits that can result from productive conferences. These positive outcomes would suggest that educators should be increasing the numbers of conferences they hold each year, but in reality many schools limit the number because of the time and effort they involve. While conferences are labor intensive, their impact on student achievement makes them a priority in many school systems.

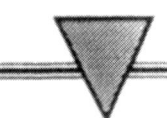

- Parent-teacher conferences are very visible activities. The way they are handled is a reflection on the whole school. Schools should provide opportunities for educator and parent feedback about the organization and effectiveness of the conferences. See Tools 3.3.1 and 3.3.2 for sample educator and parent assessments of current practices related to parent-teacher conferences. Information gathered by using these assessments (or adaptations) will provide insights that can provide direction for designing future conferences.

- For educators, conferencing is a true test of organizational skills as well as the ability to communicate effectively. Productive and positive parent-teacher conferences require attention to all stages of conferencing: planning, preparing, conducting, reflecting, and following up. Carefully review Tools 3.3.3 through 3.3.11. Regardless of whether you are novice or an experienced veteran, these Tools will provide useful suggestions for maximizing the quality and benefits of conferences. Some of the ideas can be incorporated on a schoolwide basis and others will be more applicable to individual teachers. It may also be helpful to review Tools 2.3.5 through 2.3.8 for additional guidelines to follow in managing and resolving conflicts in positive and productive ways.

- Some teachers are finding student led conferences with parents, caregivers, or significant adults in their lives to be a productive alternative to the traditional parent-teacher conference. In classrooms, more emphasis is being placed on portfolio development and goal setting. A natural extension is to guide students in structuring and preparing for their part in a parent-teacher-student conference. When students take an active role, more ownership and commitment for their own learning result. Tool 3.3.10 describes student-led conferences in more detail.

Other Possibilities . . .

Tool 3.3.1 (Option A)

Our School's Parent-Teacher Conferences: How Effective Are They?
(Educators' Reflection)

Which italicized statement most closely reflects your feelings about your experiences with parent-teacher conferences? Select one and complete the follow-up questions that apply.

_____ *The process we have seems to work well--leave it as it is.*
For me, the most positive aspects of the conferences are. . . . .

_____ *The process we have doesn't work as well as it should or could--it needs some minor adjustments.*
For me, the conferences are positive in many ways, but maybe we need to rethink . . .

_____ *The process we have does not work well--it needs a major overhaul.*
The main problem with the conferences is . . . .

I suggest that we . . . . .

_____ *The current process should be abandoned. We need to invent new ways to confer with our parents.*
A better way to confer with parents would be to . . . .

Tool 3.3.1 (Option B)

Our Parent-Teacher Conferences: How Effective Are They?
(Educators' Reflection)

My feelings about parent-teacher conferences are (check all that apply):

_____ We confer with most of our parents.

_____ We do not confer with many of our parents.

Over the last few years, it seems that the number of parents I see has
_____ increased.
_____ decreased.
_____ stayed about the same.

_____ The parents we do see are the ones with whom we already have a good relationship.

_____ Have more conferences.

_____ Have fewer conferences.

_____ Consider flexible or extended scheduling.

_____ Consider alternatives sites--neighborhood, home, parent employer.

_____ Offer more options in addition to face-to-face conferences such as telephone, computer, or small group sessions.

_____ Include the child in the conference.

_____ Provide more incentives to get the parents to attend.

_____ Provide teachers with more information about how to conduct positive conferences.

_____ Develop better ways to follow up on decisions or information shared during the conferences. (I don't feel that the conferences influence parents to act on what is discussed.)

I would also like to mention . . .

Tool 3.3.2

Our School's Parent-Teacher Conferences: How Effective Are They?

(Parents' Reflection for a Telephone Interview or a Questionnaire)

1. Did you receive adequate notice of your conference time? Did the teacher work with you to find a mutually agreeable time?

2. Were you able to attend the conference? Yes _____ No _____
   If not, would you mind telling me why not? Was it a school problem that prevented you from attending?

3. Were you made to feel comfortable and welcome at our school?

4. Did you receive information about your child that you wanted and needed?

5. Were you satisfied that there was enough time for both you and the teacher to share important information about your child? If not, did the teacher invite further discussion at another time?

6. Did you and the teacher develop a plan that will help your child's learning progress?

Tool 3.3.2

7. If you had any specific questions or concerns, were they answered?

8. Since your conference, how do you feel about the school's program and the educational goals (the teacher has) for your child?

9. Was the conference a positive experience for you?

10. Will you feel free to contact your child's teacher when you have questions or concerns?

11. Are there any other comments about the conference that you would like to make?

Instructions:

There are several productive ways to ask these questions. They could be used as a telephone interview or as a brief questionnaire. On a schoolwide basis, either approach could be used. The choice may revolve around how much time and energy could be devoted to it. Some schools enlist the assistance of parent volunteers if questions posed are not considered "sensitive." If they are, it is probably better to designate an educator to coordinate the effort. On a classroom basis, the teacher could have the option of either method and would be responsible for analyzing the responses he or she receives. Consider the following for either method:

Telephone Interviews: Identify who you are and verify that the person you are speaking with is the parent. State the purpose of the call: "I have several questions that will provide information about the parent-teacher conference held recently at the school. Your responses should only take a few minutes, but it is very important to have your input." Ask: "Is this a good time?" Be sure to say, "I will not ask you to identify your child's teacher nor will your name appear with your responses."

Questionnaires: Teachers could send the questionnaire to all parents in his/her classroom or a random sample of the parents (about 1/3rd of the total). If a sample is selected, be sure that it includes some parents who attend conferences and those who do not.

Tool 3.3.3

Initial Letter from Educator to Parent to Schedule a Parent-Teacher Conference
Sample

Date

Dear _____,
     (Parent's or Guardian's name)

Parent-teacher conferences at _____ School are scheduled for the weeks of _____. Our conference should take about **30 minutes**. Before we complete the schedule, we would appreciate some information from you.

- Your preferred day of the week:
  - ____ Monday
  - ____ Tuesday
  - ____ Wednesday
  - ____ Thursday
  - ____ Friday
  - ____ Saturday (morning only)

- Your preferred time of the day:
  - ____ Between 7 a.m. and 8 a.m. -- before school
  - ____ Between 8 a.m. and 12 (noon) -- mornings
  - ____ Between 12 (noon) and 3 p.m. -- afternoon
  - ____ Between 3 p.m. and 6 p.m. -- after school
  - ____ Between 6 p.m. and 8 p.m. -- early evening

- Who will be attending the conference?_____

- Will you need:
  - Child care?   Yes   No
  - Transportation?   Yes   No
  - A translator?   Yes   No   If yes, for which language?_____

Thank you for taking the time to fill this out. I will get back to you with a scheduled time and some questions to think about before the conference. I look forward to meeting with you.

Sincerely,

Teacher's Name

Follow-up Letter from Educator
Notifying Parent of Conference Time

Tool 3.3.4

Sample

Date

Dear _____,
(Parent's or Guardian's name)

Our conference has been scheduled for __(time)__ on __(date)__. We will be meeting in room__(place)__ for about 30 minutes. You may park in any space in the lot outside the front door of the school. If this time does not meet with your schedule, please let me know and I will reschedule the conference. The school phone number is _____. You may leave your message and I will get back to you as quickly as possible.

The main purposes for our conference are for us to get to know one another and to find the best ways we can work together for your child. In order for us to be as well prepared as possible, here are some questions you may want to think about before our conference. Feel free to discuss the questions with your child.

- Is your child having a good year in school?
- What has your child particularly liked about school so far?
- Is your child especially excited by or interested in anything happening at school?
- What has your child particularly disliked about school so far?
- Is your child especially frustrated by or anxious about anything that is happening at school?
- What talents or special abilities does your child have that I could reinforce at school?
- What are your child's special challenges or areas for growth that I could assist with here at school?
- Is there anything that I need to know about your child that will help make this year a successful one?
- Is there any specific way I could be of assistance to you?
- Are there any additional questions you would like to ask?

I'm looking forward to meeting with you.

Sincerely,

Teacher's Name

Details for Successful Parent-Teacher Conferences
(Reminders for Educators)

Tool 3.3.5

Schoolwide
- It may be helpful to send a brief note home or to make a quick reminder call the day before the conference (especially if it has been awhile since the conference was scheduled).
- Welcome signs
- Official greeters (older students or parent volunteers)
- Name tags
- Directions to rooms or volunteer to deliver parents to the room
- Room or area designated as hospitality room for before or after the conference
    - Coffee and drinks
    - Cookies
    - Student art work
    - Music
- Room designated as child care area
    - Qualified baby sitters
    - Toys for younger children to play with

Each Teacher
- Post the conference schedule on the door of the conference room.
- Post a welcome notice. (Example)
- Have students' materials ready for the conference.

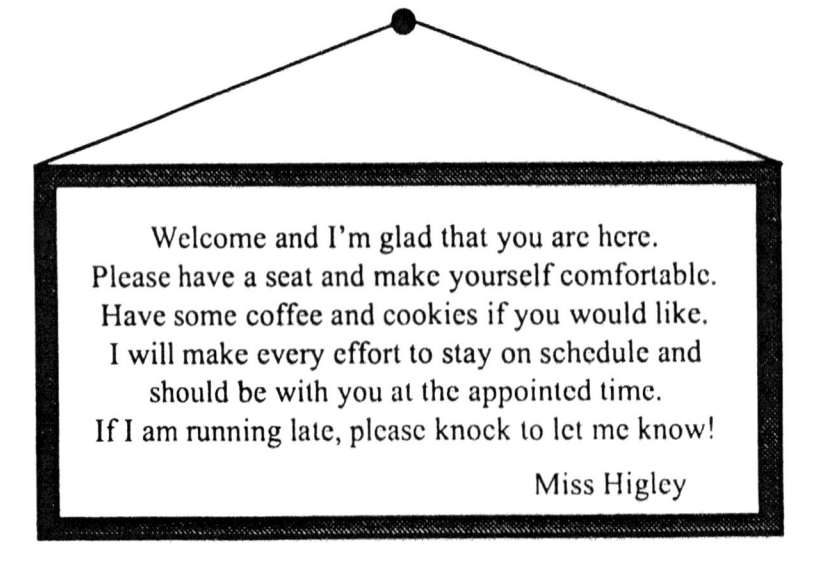

> Welcome and I'm glad that you are here.
> Please have a seat and make yourself comfortable.
> Have some coffee and cookies if you would like.
> I will make every effort to stay on schedule and should be with you at the appointed time.
> If I am running late, please knock to let me know!
>
> Miss Higley

Tool 3.3.6

Checklist for Verbal Communications
Especially for Parent-Teacher Conferences
(to be reviewed prior to conferences and after
interpersonal interactions for reflection)

Did I . . .

_____ Communicate the purpose of the conference?

_____ Provide a relaxed atmosphere and establish rapport early?

_____ Provide opportunities for parents to express their views, opinions, or questions?

_____ Maintain an appropriate percentage of "teacher talk" vs. "parent talk?"

_____ Begin by communicating something positive about the child?

_____ Share examples of the students' work?

_____ Listen intently and attend with energy?

_____ Maintain eye contact?

_____ Disregard any (minor) distractions?

_____ Accurately paraphrase and restate what others were saying?

_____ Ask for clarification and confirmation when necessary?

_____ Remain alert and respond appropriately to the feelings and emotions of others?

_____ Read both the verbal and nonverbal behavior accurately?

_____ Remain calm, if provoked? Avoid confrontation?

_____ Use nonjudgmental and supportive language?

_____ Use appropriate and easily understood language?

_____ Avoid jargon and technical terms?

Tool 3.3.6

_____ Model respect by using names, asking for opinions, acknowledging concerns, answering questions fully?

_____ Maintain focus on the main objectives/targets of the conference?

_____ Pace the conference appropriately?

_____ Use adequate "wait time" to encourage questions or responses?

_____ Emphasize areas of agreement?

_____ Emphasize cooperation, collaboration, and problem-solving? ("We're in this together and we can work this out!")

_____ Develop simple, reasonable, and focused plans for home reinforcement?

_____ Avoid offering advice before the parents had opportunities to share their opinions and suggestions?

_____ Note any needed followup or additional conferences? (Did I mark my calendar?)

_____ Summarize the main points as a closure to the conference?

_____ Express appreciation for the family's efforts?

_____ Gain insights about how to work better with the student and the parents?

_____ Feel well prepared and satisfied with the outcomes of the conference?

Personal Reflection
In the future, what is it about my verbal communication that I will . . .

Keep Doing?

Start Doing?

Stop Doing?

Tool 3.3.7

Preparing for the Conference:
Teacher Worksheet
(Complete before the conference)

Student's name:_____

Parent(s)' name(s):_____

Conference date, time, and place:_____

Purpose of the conference (general progress, specific purpose):_____
_____
_____

Goal for the conference: (To be a successful conference, what will be accomplished?)
_____
_____
_____

The child's strengths (in general or related to this issue):
_____
_____
_____

The child's challenges (in general or related to this issue):
_____
_____
_____

Examples of student work/portfolio needed:
_____
_____
_____

Additional documentation needed:
_____
_____

Tool 3.3.7

Questions I need to ask:
_____
_____
_____
_____
_____
_____
_____
_____

Materials to share:
_____
_____
_____

Other person(s) who should be present:
_____
_____

****
(Complete after the conference)

Parent or Guardian concerns or questions:
_____
_____
_____

Actions agreed upon?
_____
_____

Needed follow-up (mark your calendar now!)_____
_____

Next time I would_____
_____

Tool 3.3.8

Comments for Parents to Share with the Child After the Conference

(This could be filled out jointly by the teacher and parents as closure to the conference.)

Begin the discussion by letting the child know that you have discussed his or her status and that you are in agreement about what you are about to share. Initial comments could be:

"We are pleased that you are having a good year at school."

OR

"We are concerned that you are having a difficult year at school.
I/we will work with your teacher to help things go better."

Then let the child know the specifics of your discussion. The following are sentence stems that might be used to share both strengths and challenges in a positive manner:

"We talked about how good you are at . . .

"We said that together we would work on . . .

"Your teacher(s) said that he/she/they would . . .

"I said that I would . . .

"What can you do to make this year at school a good one for you?"

Tool 3.3.9

Follow-up Note or Phone Call to Parent(s)

For Parents or Guardians Who Attended the Conference

Date

Dear _____
(Parent's or Guardian's Name)

I was pleased that you were able to meet with me at our recent parent-teacher conference. It is always an important time when I have the opportunity to meet the parents of my students. I know that together we can make this year a good learning experience for your child. Please let me know if you would like to continue our discussion at another conference. I'll look forward to seeing you in the future or hearing from you anytime.

Sincerely,

Teacher's name

For Parents or Guardians Who Did Not Attend the Conference *

Date

Dear _____
(Parent's or Guardian's Name)

I'm sorry that you were unable to meet with me for our conference on _____ (date). I'll be calling soon to set up another appointment. It is very important that we work out a time that will be good for both of us to talk about your child's progress. I know that your child will have a better learning experience if we are able to work together. I look forward to meeting with you.

Sincerely,

Teacher's name

*Be sure to follow-up with a phone call to parents who did not attend the conference and did not respond to the second notice.

Student-led Conferences: A Positive Alternative

Some teachers are finding student-led conferences with parents or guardians to be a productive alternative to the traditional Parent-Teacher conference. In classrooms, more emphasis is being placed on helping students learn how to exercise choice, take responsibility for their own learning, and to set goals for improvement. A natural extension is to guide students in structuring, preparing, conducting, and evaluating Parent-Teacher-Student conferences. Middle school teachers who have tried it say that when students take a more active role in the assessment process, it generates more commitment and ownership. In addition, they found an unexpected bonus of the conferences to be the increased communication between students and parents. Parents and students also expressed benefits of the experience. Some parents felt that they were getting a more open and honest assessment of the performance of their child because "at times, what parents heard from their child was quite different from the picture the advisor painted" (p.65). Students enjoyed their more dominant role. One student said that "It was great to see the look on my parents' faces when they saw my good work."

A good source for additional information is an Educational Leadership article by L.L. Countryman and M. Schroeder, "When Students Lead Parent-Teacher Conferences," April 1996 issue.

Preparing for a "Challenging" Conference with Parent(s)

Tool 3.3.11

> "Difficult Situations" can be handled professionally and lead to a productive conclusion.

Suggestions for making the "challenging" conference go well . . .

▼ Sit side by side with the parent, not behind your desk. It is less intimidating and shows that you are willing to treat the parent as an equal in working together for the child's benefit.

▼ Communicate behavior descriptions. Give parents or guardians examples rather than opinions, feelings, or labels. The "evidence," such as samples of work, observations, grades, and anecdotal accounts, let them see for themselves how their child is behaving or progressing. They also allow parents to draw their own conclusions rather than listening to those provided by the teacher. Unless parents are particularly defensive or unaware, their conclusions will be very similar to those the teacher could have provided them. How much more powerful, though, when parents are given the opportunity to "see for themselves." For example, rather than labeling a student as "sloppy," show the parent samples of work that reflect sloppiness and ask them to compare what they see to what is expected of students their age. Rather than telling parents that their child is a "bully," show them discipline referrals or written documentation of the child's actions. The teacher is the professional who can then confirm or deny the parents' conclusions by offering additional information that would support a different perspective. This is not a guessing game and the teacher does want the parent to fully understand the situation, but work together to arrive at the understanding. This will take more time and effort, but it can be much more productive.

▼ If there are significant challenges and problems, don't minimize them. These issues are of immense importance to the parent--and to the teacher. Be tactful and truthful. Be certain that the parent has some reasonable and productive plans as to what to do. Be sure to not leave them with doubt about what the next steps should be. (Even if the plan is to "think about it and get back with one another next week or the next day.")

▼ Be sure to emphasize that the approach is "no blame" problem solving. Together "we will find ways to help." There is responsibility on all sides--teacher, parent, and child. Only make promises that can be kept.

Tool 3.3.11

▼ If the parent becomes defensive, try to find common ground that both teacher and parent can agree upon. One key phrase is: "We are both interested in doing what is best for your child." If the parent becomes hostile, bring the conference to a swift conclusion with statements such as one the following:

"It seems we have accomplished all we can for now. I'll call you next week."
"We can discuss this further at a later time if you would like."
"Let me think about this issue a little more and I'll get back to you."
"I'm sorry we cannot seem to reach agreement today. Let's both think a little more and we'll get together in a week or so."

The teacher may want to consider having another professional attend the next conference. Be sure to inform the parent before the conference.

▼ If the parent is questioning a teacher's action and the action is against school policy or not in the best interest of the child, it is best to admit the error and discuss what should have been done or what could be done to get beyond the immediate situation. The parent will see that the educator is also willing to accept responsibility for mistakes and to establish a plan for correcting the error.

If there are questions the teacher is unable to answer, it's okay to say that you do not know or are not sure, but that you will get back to them with the answer. Be sure to follow up!

▼ We all have "buttons" that usually produce negative reactions. It may be helpful to:

Avoid saying...	*Say instead...*
I really can't understand why you...	What was your thinking about...?
The way I did it with my children was...	Have you thought about...
You haven't had the experience or education I've had...	What I have learned from working children this age is that...
I hear from other parents that you...	How do you feel about...?
Does Demetrius act this way because he is--from a broken home, is the youngest in the family, is adopted?	Why do you suppose Demetrius acts this way? Is there something bothering him?
The problem with Sally is...	One challenge for Sally is...

▼ Be alert to parent questions that may not be on track and gently try to *educate* as you communicate.

"Why don't you just spank him when he disobeys? That's what we do."
"What is her IQ?"
"Why was he placed in --- this reading group, that track?"
"Is it okay to call you at home?"

Plan 3.4
Moving Beyond Report Cards
in Communicating Student Progress

> *"If you make the information clear and relevant, I'll feel more comfortable trying to help my child. I've looked at previous report cards and wondered—What does that tell me anyway?!"*   **Parent of a Sixth Grader**

Currently, in many school systems a students' yearly progress is reduced to a single letter grade assigned on a permanent record. Interim reports may provide more information, but are generally seen as less informative than desired. This situation is very frustrating for both educators and parents. For the next year's teacher, the letter grade tells very little about all that the child accomplished during the previous year. For parents who know that their child is a unique individual, the letter grade does nothing to inform them in meaningful ways. While both educators and parents agree about the need to develop better ways to report student progress, there is not much agreement about how to proceed to make it happen. Recently, there have been attempts by some schools and systems to move from the traditional approach to more sophisticated and detailed reports. One thing is clear: whatever the advocated format, designing it and selling it require a great deal of discussion and reflection by all parties involved.

Issues related to assessment of student progress are quite complex for both educators and parents. Educators are encouraged by researchers to promote more authentic learning and performance type assessments. These assessments often require new and different ways to evaluate student progress. As educators move in this direction, they find that the evaluative information generated by these assessments emphasizes the inadequacies of the current grading and reporting system. At the same time, computers and computer software are assisting in the task of assessment and can manage more data about student accomplishments than ever before. This poses a dilemma for many educators. There is more information available about student performance than ever before. How is this best communicated, given the structures that have been in place for decades? What additional training do teachers need to feel confident in assessing students and reporting their progress in these new ways? What are the most effective ways to reeducate parents and others about how student progress is assessed and reported?

For many parents, the area of grading and reporting student progress is often confusing and highly emotional. Parents have a great emotional investment in the judgments made about their child and are often unclear as to why the judgments have been made. The situation is worsened when they are confused by unfamiliar educational jargon used in the reports. It is equally upsetting when they do not know how to accurately interpret what is reported and do not feel that what is reported is what they want to know. Since many typical report cards reflect opinions (presented as grades) rather than actual evidence, parents may feel that they are not being given opportunities to know as much as they should about their student's progress, strengths, and challenges.

In reviewing the major purposes of grading and reporting, it becomes clear that the single letter grade approach is inadequate to achieve them. The purposes include: to communicate understandable and usable high-quality information to students, parents, educators, and others; to show current attainment of goals or current achievement status of students related in important educational goals; to provide information for students' self-evaluation; to identify students for particular educational programs; to provide incentives for learning; and to evaluate the effectiveness of the instructional program. As we know, the goals of schooling today are far more complex than they were in the past and the simplicity of the current system of grading is inadequate to provide the needed and desired information.

Whether the general perception about the reporting process is positive or negative, it is important that it be reviewed periodically by the appropriate interested parties. It should be noted that the scope of the review should take into account previous efforts and discussions. For this plan, the assumption is that the ways student progress is reported and communicated needs a major review. TheTools will assist educators in better understanding the current system, determining how well it meets the needs of all parties, and developing strategies to improve how student progress is reported to parents.

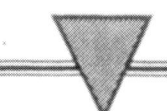

- Decide who should be included in the discussions. With such a complex and significant issue, it may be best to engage the total faculty. It would also be important to identify a representative group of parents to be included in the discussions. Some schools, particularly secondary and vocational schools, also include community representative and business representatives. These parents and/or community members could be included in faculty discussions or could participate in separate and fairly parallel discussions as focus groups. It would also be an option to have the faculty begin the review process and then include the parents and/or community representatives at a later time. Whatever approach is selected, it is critical to have parents and community members involved to some extent. See Tool 3.4.1 for a structure for using parent focus groups to improve reporting practices. Be sure to clarify the task for the group.

- For educator discussions, it is important to clearly set parameters. Are the discussions to enhance understanding or to make decisions? This topic can be an emotionally-laden one for many teachers because judgments involve a degree of subjectivity that is often difficult to defend. In addition, within most schools there is great diversity in the faculty's preferred approaches to grading, reporting, and communicating what students are learning. Many factors enter into their decisions. Likewise, parents have many definite ideas about the issue. Be aware that this can lead to discomfort for many participants. It may be important to provide reminders about expected behaviors during these discussions. Review the Rules We Live By before beginning (See Tool 1.2.5) Ask educators to fully describe the current process for grading and reporting. Use Tool 3.4.2 to guide the discussions. It addresses the major question: What is our current system? Following the discussion guide will lead to a full description.

- Now that the current grading and reporting system has been fully described, continue the educator discussions by addressing questions that are intended to gather perceptions about the adequacy of the current system and suggest possible areas of needed exploration. Use Tool 3.4.3 to guide this discussions. The questions in this Tool address the main issue: Does our grading and reporting system accurately and adequately reflect and clearly communicate student learning? The guide should lead to an assessment of the system.

- At this point in the discussions, it may be possible for the educators to reach some level of consensus about the adequacy of the current reporting system in meeting its intended purposes. Decide whether the group feels that they should keep as it is, make minor adjustments, make major revisions, or totally overhaul the process.

- If it is decided that the reporting system needs minor, major, or vast changes, develop a plan to make the revisions. Decide whether the total faculty or task forces should be involved. Could it be possible to break into subgroups to tackle specific tasks? Review what the research and professional literature suggests. Investigate what alternative forms other schools and school systems are using. Be sure to fully explore the potential of available computer technology to help manage the vast amounts of data that could be generated. Consult with a technology expert who has experience with the types of programs that could be used. Focus on answering the questions: What should be reported and how should it be reported? Tool 3.4.4 provides ideas for alternative reporting formats. Tool 3.4.5 describes a "Reverse" or "Interactive Report Card" which is an option that actively involves the parent in the assessment process. After exploring as many options as possible, summarize major ideas to share with others. Discuss, deliberate, and reflect.

- Design a first draft of a potential reporting system. Share the draft with others (teachers, parents, business leaders, community members, next school level representatives) and ask pointed questions to get their feedback. Make revisions. Pilot test, gain feedback, assess, and revise again.

- Provide high-quality training for the professional staff to help them develop a full understanding of the process; gain competence, confidence, and consistency; and to understand the implications of changing reporting systems. Remember that this will take some time--it will be a multi-year endeavor.

- Educate parents and community members. School personnel need to ensure full understanding and appropriate use of the information that is reported. Parents need to have accurate, adequate information and a clear understanding about what it means and what to do with it. Inadequate explanation and understanding can lead to misinterpretation and unsatisfactory or counterproductive follow through.

Other Possibilities...

Tool 3.4.1

Using Parent Focus Groups To Improve Reporting Practices
"What we want and need" vs. "What we currently get"

1. Organize a focus group of parents to gain parental insights about the current grading and reporting processes and related issues. Be sure that parents understand that their role is to provide information, not to make decisions. It would be best if at least one parent were from each homeroom. If the number of homerooms per grade is small, then 2 or 3 parents per grade would work well. Be sure that the group is heterogeneous and representative of all student groups at the school. If parents are unwilling or unable to attend meetings, similar information could be gathered through telephone interviews.

2. Communicate the task for the group: to help the faculty understand how well the current system of grading and reporting student progress meets their needs as "receivers" of the information? Then ask parents to identify the information they would like to receive from the school about their child's progress. Effective prompts might include:
    "I wish my child's teacher would tell me about . . ."
    "What I really want to know about my child is . . ."
Develop a collective listing of the group's suggestions. Categorize them by their main focus (e.g., academics, personal development, social adjustment, or "other).

3. Develop a parallel listing of the types of information and forms that are currently being given to parents. A simple discrepancy analysis could be done to determine the adequacy of what is currently provided and what they desire. The following questions could guide the discrepancy analysis:
    Which current practices "fit" with parents' wishes? Which do not?
    What areas are not being addressed by current practices?
    Is there consistency across and within grade levels? Where are the gaps?

4. Once the "ideal" information is identified, ask parents to make suggestions about frequency of reporting. Which information should be given on a regular basis? How often? What information should be given on a more immediate--need to know now--basis? How should that occur? It may be important to emphasize that when some potentially significant difficulty is noticed, it should be communicated to parents so that it can be addressed immediately. One consistent source of frustration for parents is not finding out about a problem in time to do something about it.

5. Ask parents if the language in the current progress reports is understandable to them. Educators tend to speak in a language of their own as do other professionals. The jargon is understandable to us, but may be confusing to parents. In addition, many academic and related issues are complex and require highly technical explanations. This may interfere with parents' comprehension.

Faculty Discussion Guide for Describing the Current Grading and Reporting System

Tool 3.4.2

Be sure to communicate the task and revise, omit, or add questions as needed. The responses should simply describe "what is." Avoid any judgments about the adequacy of the system at this time. Do not be surprised to find that responses vary by grade level and individual teacher.

What do we currently communicate?
Content knowledge? Life or workplace skills? Achievement? Progress? Effort? Standards? Student self-assessment? Student/teacher/parent goals? Others?

How is it communicated?
Letter grades? Numerical scores or percentages? Narratives? Checklists? Rating scales? Work samples or portfolios? Oral reports? Exhibitions? Student-led or teacher-led conferences? Record of project completion? Others? A combination of _____?

How often is student progress communicated?
Report cards? Interim reports? Daily or weekly reports? Daily or weekly agendas? Personal notes or telephone calls at designated times? Daily or weekly interactive communication charts? Daily or weekly e-mail notices? Others?

What data sources are used in determining the grades/information to be reported?
Test scores? Homework? Project grades? Portfolios? Team grades? Team and individual assessments of individual contributions? Observations? Others?

What do we see as the main purposes of our system of grading and reporting of student progress?
The responses to this question should identify everyone's assumptions about the reasons for the overall process. It may also point to the variations in beliefs about the rationale underlying the process.

For whom is the information intended?
Students? Parents? Teachers and administrators? Board of Education members? Policy makers? Post secondary institutions? Employers? The general public?

Does our system provide a longitudinal look at student progress or is it strictly a year-by-year report?
Is each child's progress from year to year shared with parents? Are there records that track the progress?

Is there anything else that should be included in this discussion?

Faculty Discussion Guide for
Assessing the Current Grading and Reporting System

Tool 3.4.3

Revise, omit, or add questions as desired. Judgments will be made at this step about the effectiveness and value of strategies currently in place.

1. Are all important aspects of student learning addressed in the report?

2. Are an adequate number of meaningful subcategories identified?

3. Are an adequate number of data sources used to provide information?

4. Are measures in place to ensure appropriate consistency in grading practices?

5. Do we engage in any grading and reporting practices that may have a negative effect on student learning and/or effective teaching (e.g., "grading on the curve" instead of against preset criteria, use of improvement grading)?

6. Do we engage in grading and reporting practices that have a positive impact on student learning (e.g., students learning from the assessment information; using test data to provide direction for teacher planning, student goal setting, or individual growth)?

7. Do we have adequate safeguards to reduce the influence of possible negative bias?

8. Does the system provide parents or guardians with the information they need and want to know? Is it presented in an understandable form? Is it comprehensive without being overwhelming? Is it perceived as personal and individualized? Is it "receiver friendly?"

9. Does it provide information about the adequacy of the progress achieved (i.e., status in regard to specific outcomes) and is that level of performance compared to expectations (i.e., below, at, or above expectations)? Does it address performance quality and work difficulty?

10. Does our system satisfactory fulfill its identified purposes?

11. Is our system consistent with our current curricular and instructional focus and our overall vision and mission?

12. Does our system appropriately reflect the recently developed national standards?

Designing Alternative Report Cards

Tool 3.4.4

Decisions need to be made regarding the specific components of the report. The following components should be considered in developing and designing alternative reporting formats.

Component 1: What are the major categories of information and/or behaviors that could and should be shared? This information will be apparent if Tool 3.4.1 has been used to determine what parents want and need to know. It will also build in the faculty's responses to Tool 3.4.2. (e.g., content knowledge, life or workplace skills, achievement, progress, effort, standards, student self-assessment, student/teacher/parent goals).

Component 2: What are the important subcategories that provide specific areas of focus? Begin to identify age-appropriate descriptors. Review by grade levels to determine if these categories and subcategories are currently being adequately and accurately assessed. If not, what changes should be made to improve them? Below are examples of categories and subcategories to initiate the discussion. Those schools that embrace *Dimensions of Learning* or multiple intelligences theory may want to incorporate specific attributes of those approaches.

Specific Content-related Skills and Knowledge
reading
mathematics
social studies, etc.

Interpersonal Skills
cooperates well with others
is sensitive to the needs and feelings of others
is friendly
relates well to other children and to adults

Intrapersonal Skills
is reflective
restrains impulsive behavior
acts in thoughtful ways
knows own strengths and needs
sets personal goals

Study Skills
management of time
management of materials
organizational ability

Learning and Motivational Behaviors
is attentive and eager
persists when faced with difficult tasks
takes risks
pushes the limits of ability
has a positive attitude toward learning
participates eagerly
works to completion
avoids frustration/anxiety

Readiness to Learn Behaviors
attends regularly
is on time
is self-disciplined
shows responsibility

Component 3: How should the level or quality of the performance in each of the categories and subcategories be expressed?
- Which of the following would be most appropriate for each subcategory: traditional letter grades, rating scales, numerical scores (what scale?), percentages, narratives, a combination (rating + comments or narrative), or descriptors?
- Decide what the grades reflect. Are they teacher judgments about current performance against expectations? Against past performance? Against peer performance (bell curve distribution)?
- Will some behaviors or accomplishments be weighted?
- Do we advocate improvement grading?
- Do we need to rate the quality of the performance and the difficulty of the task (like musical and some athletic competitions)?

Component 4: How will the level of performance be portrayed? The following are samples of descriptors used in a variety of school settings.

```
CO = consistently demonstrates behavior

DE = is developing this behavior as expected

DD = is experiencing difficulty developing this behavior

NC = is not currently developing this behavior
```

Tool 3.4.4

Degree of Performance Scales (2 Point)	
+ (does display/exhibit) Credit Satisfactory	− (does not display nor exhibit) No Credit Not Satisfactory

Degree of Performance Scales (3 Point)		
Basic	Proficient	Advanced
Needs Improvement	Satisfactory	Excellent
Not Seen Yet	Sometimes Seen	Often Seen
Novice	Proficient	Expert
In Progress	Competent	Exemplary
Quarter Moons	Half Moons	Full Moons
Not Yet Successful	Successful	Highly Successful

Degree of Performance Scales (4 Point)			
Unacceptable Unsatisfactory Amateur	Needs Work Limited Acceptable	Acceptable Proficient Admirable	Exemplary Distinguished Awesome

Degree of Performance Scales (5 Point)				
Exploration Emergent	Emergent Beginning	Beginning Developing	Developing Experienced	Capable Exceptional

Use these ideas to guide your thinking, but be sure not to overlook others that might be especially important in your setting.

Tool 3.4.5

Reverse/Interactive Report Card

On an interactive report card there are questions that require parental responses. Instead of evaluative information only going one way--from the school to the home, this provides opportunities for the communication to become two-way. This component could be an added dimension to the typical ways schools report student progress. Reverse/interactive report cards provide parents with opportunities to more actively participate in their child's educational process. They are also a way to convey the expectation that parents will be partners in the evaluation process.

Here are some ideas to consider if you plan to incorporate this component into your grading and reporting plan:

- ▼ Supply space for Parent Comments (seen now on many report cards). Also supply space for Student Comments (not currently seen on many report cards). This would provide the opportunity for students to contribute to the process.

- ▼ Ask the parent(s) and student to identify any particular strengths (i.e., abilities, talents) and challenges (i.e., needs, areas for growth) that may have contributed to the progress or problems during the grading period.

- ▼ Use the reverse/interactive report card to establish one or two high priority goals for the next grading period. (See Plan 5.4. for ideas about goal setting.)

- ▼ Ask parent(s) to evaluate how well their child applies what is learned in school to home, work, or social situations. This might relate to interpersonal skills, problem solving, decision making, communication, and work related behaviors. It might also be that the student is making use of concepts learned in the various content areas.

Plan 3.5
Promoting Positive Public Perceptions

While the public's perception of schools appears to be on the rise, school personnel have long felt (and endured) the less than desired levels of public confidence in the educational process. And with the discussions about school choice and vouchers, they have had to shift from the passive approach ("If we are really good, everyone will know it") to a more aggressive one. They have begun to realize that positive perceptions by the public cannot be left to chance. The subtleties of schooling may or may not be perceived in a favorable light by their public.

Perhaps the most important action school personnel can take to promote a positive perception is to build their reputation from "within." There are many resources to draw upon, but one significant one is the students. According to Joyce Epstein (1995), "Students are a critical key to establishing effective school, family, and community partnerships." Over the course of their school careers, students spend over 15,000 hours in schools and classrooms. They have ample opportunity to observe "what is going on." As we know, they also add their own interpretation to it and share their perceptions with others on a regular basis. Teachers and other school personnel are an equally important resource. They are entwined in the community in many other roles. They can be our own "best friends" by publicly conveying the positive aspects of our schools and privately working to make the school even more responsive to the needs of its stakeholders. They, in addition to the students, can contribute significantly to the public's image of our schools. Additional resources are the many volunteers and visitors to our schools. When they are treated well and have positive experiences at the school, it can strengthen their support and encourage their good words in the community.

Once the "inside" connections are strong, the connections to the outside can be significantly enhanced. It is critical that school personnel maintain their existing positive relationships and develop new connections to bring more interested and eager individuals into the school community. They must develop proactive measures to establish a firm base of public support, but they must also design reactive approaches to minimize the effects of potentially negative events.

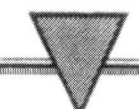

- School personnel should communicate (clearly and often) their belief in community ownership of the schools. The line of reasoning is obvious. If the school is a reflection of the community, then each member of the community has a responsibility to promote the most positive reflection as possible. If there is a problem, it is "our" problem and "we" need to deal with it. The understood obligation is to go directly to school personnel and work collaboratively to a constructive resolution of the problem. Having a suggestion or comment box in several visible locations is one way to facilitate this ownership and ongoing participation. (See Tool 3.2.2 for more information.)

- The appearance of the school facility and its surroundings can send the message that all within the school take pride in how it looks. Visible signs (e.g., beautification projects) and public displays (e.g., "permanent" gifts contributed by individuals or classes) are perhaps small, but important indicators of the sense of pride the members of the school community have in their school. Individuals from each group within the school community (students, educators, parents) will have ideas to share. See Tool 3.5.1 for a strategy to use in working with any or all of these groups in promoting school pride. Also refer to Tools in *School Environment* for additional suggestions.

- Identify a specific individual or individuals within the school and/or school system who will accept responsibility for communicating with the larger community. An appropriate individual is one who has expertise in the area of communication and one who would be a good spokesperson and represent the school or school system well. This individual is the one responsible for getting the positive words out; notifying the newspaper(s) and radio/television station(s) of upcoming cultural, athletic, or academic events of interest; and responding to the press in times that are not so pleasant. When incidents or accidents occur at school, the public needs access to information. It is better that they have first-hand knowledge, the facts, rather than hear-say or rumor which is open to many interpretations. Some school systems hire consultants with communications and PR expertise.

- Explore all potential avenues for increasing the public's awareness of the many activities, successes, and innovations going on in the school. See Tool 3.5.2 for ideas about some possibilities for getting the word out.

- An Ambassador program is described in Tool 3.5.3. Ambassadors could be secondary students (or adult volunteers) who are knowledgeable about the school and its programs and activities or who have talents and expertise to share. They can serve as spokespersons to interested groups such as civic or school groups. For students, it is an opportunity to serve as a shining example of young people who are willing and able to contribute talents and energy to the community.

- Nurture all existing connections to the larger community and forge new ones. If the current relationship between the school and the press is not a positive one, work in as many ways as possible to establish one. Identify additional supporters (individuals and/or groups) and solicit assistance from each of them. The initial requests could be as simple as asking for permission to post notices and announcements or volunteering to give a presentation about the school or particular school activities or programs. These beginning alliances have the potential for developing into more substantive and lasting partnerships.

- Tool 3.5.4 provides a description of one successful media campaign. One local television station showed its commitment to the community and to education by becoming the driving force and co-sponsor with other local businesses of an extensive pro-education media campaign, *Ten for the Future.* Working in collaboration with local educators and interested others they have brought public awareness to significant topics of interest and increased public knowledge of educational programs.

Other Possibilities . . .

Communicating School Pride

Tool 3.5.1

Engage interested groups in a creative brainstorming activity. IWWMW, a creative problem solving strategy used by Richard Villa, means In What Ways Might We . . . . In this case, the task becomes "IWWMW . . .Communicate Pride In Our School." See tool 1.2.17 for a description of the IWWMW process. It is a technique to help capitalize on the positives within a situation and to identify additional ways to enhance it.

- Focus on identifying as many ideas as possible with no time spent in evaluating each suggestion.
- Encourage everyone to participate since the purpose is to build on the ideas of others. No idea is considered too silly or outrageous at this point in the process. Groups enjoy the opportunities to exercise their creativity, especially when it is for an important purpose and there is a commitment to following though on their suggestions.
- After numerous possibilities have been identified, they should be screened against criteria to determine their worth. One is feasibility. Are there resources (expertise, time, energy, and money) available? Another is the anticipated positive impact. Will it make a difference to enough people to be worth the effort? An additional important criterion could be the potential the proposed project has for an authentic learning experience for students.
- After a discussion of the worth, feasibility, and impact of the proposed projects, a ranking process could be used to allow each individual to have their say in the final selection(s).
- Once the priorities are determined, the responsibility for planning should be delegated to a team of willing volunteers who have an interest in the project. The team could make decisions about the extent to which students, parents, and community members could be involved and take responsibility for seeing the project through to completion.
- To the extent they are able, it would be highly desirable to have students design, plan, research, and implement the project. When a project is relevant for students, it has a higher potential for meaningful learning and long-term effect. The project could be a vehicle for integrating content-area learning and for promoting lifelong learning skills as well. The project could also be a way to generate community participation in supporting learning experiences for students.

**At an elementary school in Dallas, Texas,
a circular bench surrounds a large shade tree near the playground.
A small sign presents the dedication:**

> To Mrs. _____.
> You will always have a place to sit at
> _____ Elementary School.

To visitors to the area, this was a very inviting scene.
But even more, it said so much about those who live here.

Getting the Word Out
So--What's So Great About This School?

Tool 3.5.2

Have you thought about...

Videos. Professional quality videos could be produced to portray the school in its most positive light. Many school systems have the technical expertise and equipment to create an exciting and engaging video. Students could be enlisted to plan, shoot, edit, and complete the final product. Elementary schools could look to some of their former students at the high school level who might be eager to become involved as a community service project.

Home Page on the Web. Special programs and academic or extracurricular highlights could be presented in ways that would reflect positively on the school. Again, students can be very creative and technically proficient in helping in the production.

Inviting media to film, photograph, or report special school events. Don't let a "photo op" pass without contacting local television, radio, and newspaper representatives. Educators and students alike seem to appreciate the extra recognition that comes with the spotlight.

Submitting student work to local media. Whether it is a poem, piece of art, or dramatic scene, if it is high-quality, let others know about it. Lobby for their support, rather than waiting for them to ask.

Brochures. An appealing way to introduce your school and/or grade level or department to others is to develop a professional looking brochure. With a quick glance, the special qualities could be communicated. The brochure could be included with materials sent home at the beginning of the year or displayed in the office for visitors or newcomers to pick up as they enter the office.

> **Getting it done...**
> Thinking of good communication avenues is one thing, getting them done is another! School personnel may have thought about these possibilities, but opportunities are often lost because no one was specifically identified to the assume responsibility for them. Remember to involve students to the greatest extent possible as many of these projects provide authentic learning opportunities that can promote genuine motivation and pride. While some of these projects are fairly involved, they will not be as complicated or time consuming once initial contacts have been established and plans have been developed and implemented. After the initial development work, it will only require "fine tuning" for future years to continue to build pride and ownership throughout the school community.

Tool 3.5.3

Students as Ambassadors to the Community

> *Capitalize on the potential within—the students.*

Who are ambassadors?

Qualified student leaders at the middle school and high school levels who would be positive representatives of the school in the community could be appropriate ambassadors. In elementary schools, parents and retired teachers or administrators might be a source for ambassadors at that level.

What are their responsibilities?

Ambassadors would need to be knowledgeable about the school and school activities. They could serve as spokespersons to interested groups (e.g., civic organizations, retirement homes, elementary or middle school groups). The ambassadors could also coordinate invitations to other students (members of drama club, chorus, band, foreign language clubs, etc.) to share their talents and expertise with community groups.

How to begin an ambassadors program?

Decisions need to be made about who should be an ambassador. Input from faculty members and parents should help determine the selection criteria for students applying to be ambassadors. Decide on the appropriate number of ambassadors. Consider having students work in teams or pairs that cross all grade levels. This structure would provide mentoring and learning opportunities for the younger students which would help with their readiness and ability to serve as ambassadors as they advance. It would be necessary to identify a faculty member and parent sponsor for the group. Once the ambassadors have been selected, their role and responsibilities should be clearly communicated and discussed. They need to have a full understanding of what it means to represent the school well. Initial decisions about potential audiences and topics appropriate for ambassador presentations could be discussed. The students will have ideas, but it might be helpful to ask representatives of the targeted audiences for their suggestions. As the students prepare and practice their presentations, be sure to enlist the help of individuals who have the expertise (e.g., drama/speech; technology) to help shape the presentations to a high level of quality. Decide about how best to publicize the availability of the ambassadors.

What are the potential benefits of an ambassadors program?

Benefits are to all involved. The school enhances its status within the community and support for its programs. This increases the possibilities for new relationships with community members and groups. The students involved gain confidence and competence in their interpersonal and communication skills. These experiences in the community are excellent leadership development opportunities for them. The community members benefit in terms of increased awareness and understanding of the future leaders of their community. The potential for intergenerational connections also can be an added dimension within any community.

Media Support For Education
Ten for the Future: A Model

Tool 3.5.4

Knoxville is the third largest metropolitan area in Tennessee, a state that historically has not given strong financial support to education. Knoxville is also the home of the state's largest university and with that connection come many cultural and academic opportunities not available throughout the state. The city and its surrounding area are an interesting mix of individuals who are highly educated and pro-education with those who are of a more rural orientation with traditionally less emphasis on formal education.

Knoxville is also fortunate to have a television station committed to its community and to education. For the past five years, WBIR (Channel 10) has been the driving force and co-sponsor with other local businesses of a pro-education media campaign, *Ten for the Future*. The station personnel have contributed their considerable talent and expertise to producing "Town Meetings" which are public forums to discuss important educational issues. The station personnel have worked in collaboration with local educators and interested others on their advisory board to bring public awareness to significant topics of interest and to increase public knowledge of educational programs. "Town Meetings" are held on a regular basis about five times a year and address such topics as "Financing a College Education," "Parent Involvement in Education," "Innovative Curriculum and Instructional Programs," and "Vocational Education." Local schools host the show from their facilities. This and special media spots provide opportunities to invite the public into different schools for a first hand look at what's going on.

In addition to the "Town Meetings," WBIR and the other co-sponsors also coordinate an "Our School Needs Campaign," "Teacher Grants," and "Student Scholarships." Through "Our Schools Needs," schools are able to request needed equipment and supplies not accommodated for in local budgets. The record of requests and contributions is a very impressive one. "Teacher Grants" are awarded to teachers who submit a proposal for important professional development activities that contribute to the educator's renewal and to their students' academic growth. "Student Scholarships" are awarded each year to outstanding area students. The scholarships are based on the student's financial need, academic record and potential, leadership and honors, and community service. Five of the six scholarships are awarded to college-bound students with one going to a deserving vocational student. The emphasis is on excellence and service regardless of the academic program. The scholarship program has provided opportunities for students who may not have been otherwise able to pursue an advanced degree.

Ten for the Future has been a most productive collaboration between the media and education. The benefits have been to all individuals involved as well as to the public at large.

Design 4
Promoting Supportive Relationships

Supportive Relationships...

- contribute significantly to an individual's quality of life and a student's success in school.
- help us connect with others in ways that are mutually beneficial.
- allow educators and parents to work as a team in helping each child reach his or her potential.
- enhance the efforts of schools, community service agencies, and individuals in providing services and assistance for children, parents, and their schools.

The quality of relationships is a dominant concern in America's schools. Interpersonal problems among students are escalating. Tensions between students and educators are more prevalent than ever before. To make matters worse, the gulf between educators and parents has also grown wider. In too many cases, parents and educators do not view each other as allies in helping children cope with the tremendous pressures of growing up, learning, and becoming the best they can be.

According to *Voices from the Inside: A Report on Schooling from Inside the Classroom* (1993), the poor quality of relationships is one of the most serious problems in schooling in the U.S. The researchers concluded from their extensive study of the perceptions of students, educators, parents, and support personnel that "no group inside the schools felt adequately respected, connected, or affirmed" (p.19). For students, teachers who care about them as individuals and take the time to establish personal relationships are a key to positive feelings about school. However, too many students do not experience this type of relationship. While educators perceive themselves as caring individuals who entered the profession to make a difference in the lives of children, many feel that others do not care about them or the important role they play. According to this study, "most teachers also feel isolated and unappreciated inside schools by students, administrators, and parents, as well as inside the larger society" (p.21). At the same time, most parents want a positive school experience for their children and are willing to do whatever they can to help their child succeed, even if it means more effort on their part. However, *Voices from the Inside* also found that parents often "feel isolated and not respected by participants inside school communities" (p.24). The result: well meaning and caring adults working toward the same or similar goals, but sometimes not in the most supportive ways. Building supportive and lasting relationships is the key to achieving these goals.

What we hear from ...

EDUCATORS

"We try to present an open, accepting climate to our community. Everyone tries to make parents and community members feel welcome." (Fourth grade teacher)

"We make every effort to help parents with the problems they are facing with their children. What we do goes way beyond our roles as educators." (High school guidance counselor)

"I don't care how hard I try to work with some parents, they just ignore me. I know they don't realize how much I care about their child and their family." (First year teacher)

PARENTS

"I used to share my real concerns with my daughter's teachers. Then I realized that an assistant principal used the information against her. Now I'm afraid to tell them anything." (Parent of a high school student)

"You can tell how friendly the school is when you walk in the front door. You're greeted like a friend and treated as if you're a special person in the school." (Parent of a middle school student)

"No one seems to care about my child and the problems she has to deal with. Just whether she is in school every day and has her homework. That's all." (Parent of a fifth grader)

STUDENTS

"My favorite teacher is Mrs. _____. She helps me with everything. Not just schoolwork, but also the problems I have with my friends." (High school junior)

"This place hurts my spirit."
    (Voices from the Inside: A Report on Schooling from Inside the Classroom, 1993)

"I don't like the way some students think about me." (Sixth grade student)

"Some of the kids are real nice and some of the teachers are, but I would like to change it. I want to have a safe school where you don't get pushed around, but where everybody is nice as they can be." (Seventh grade student)

"You can come to school and not be harassed, bothered, called names, and, I hate to say it, but beaten. Because some kids have those types of parents that beat their children and some of them can come to school and feel happy for eight or so hours a day." (Eighth grade student)

Shared Responsibilities

Although educators must take the lead in developing productive, supportive relationships, both educators and parents have an important role in establishing and maintaining them. The following diagram illustrates the responsibilities that are unique to each group and those that both groups share.

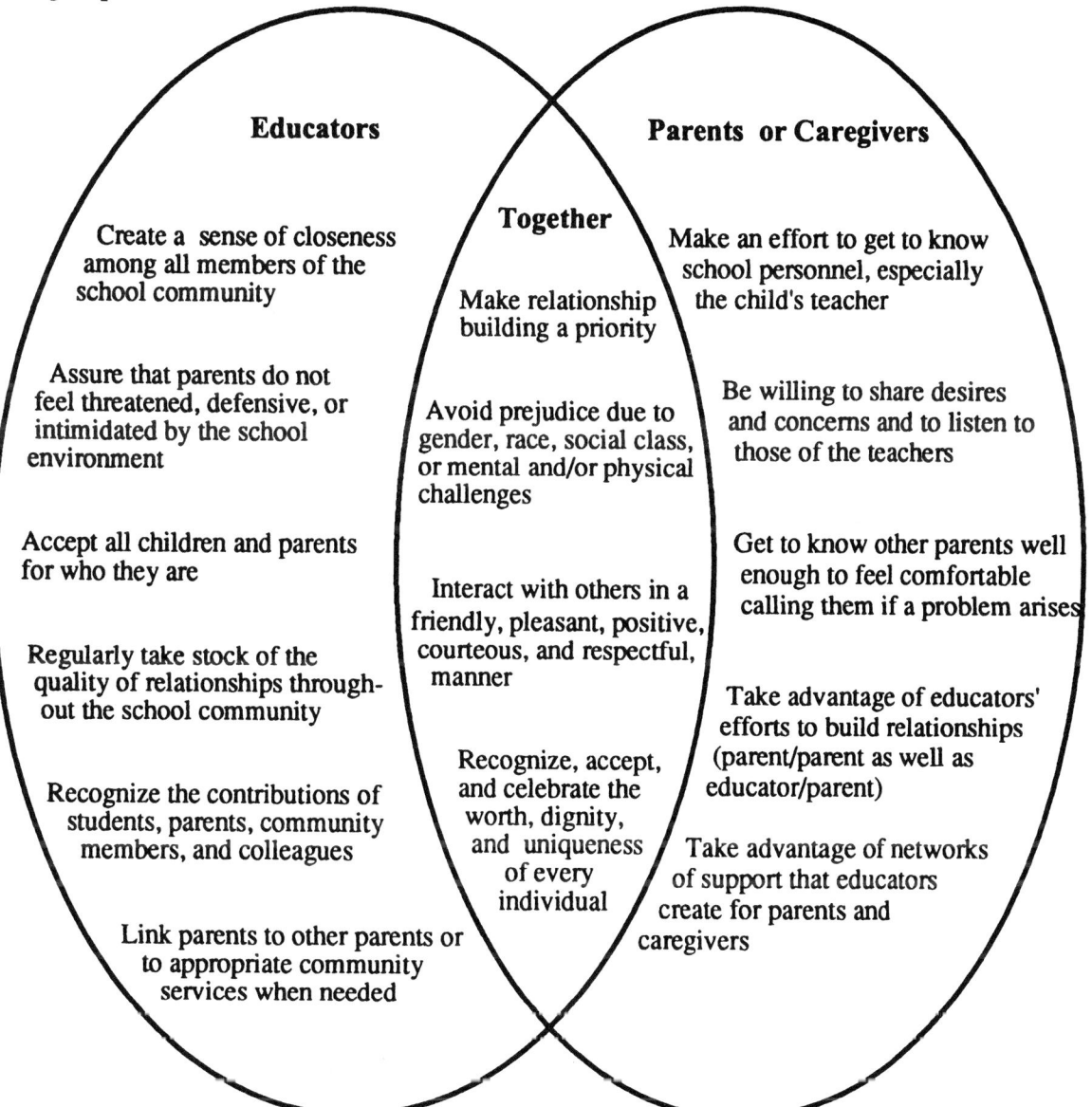

Educators
- Create a sense of closeness among all members of the school community
- Assure that parents do not feel threatened, defensive, or intimidated by the school environment
- Accept all children and parents for who they are
- Regularly take stock of the quality of relationships throughout the school community
- Recognize the contributions of students, parents, community members, and colleagues
- Link parents to other parents or to appropriate community services when needed

Together
- Make relationship building a priority
- Avoid prejudice due to gender, race, social class, or mental and/or physical challenges
- Interact with others in a friendly, pleasant, positive, courteous, and respectful, manner
- Recognize, accept, and celebrate the worth, dignity, and uniqueness of every individual

Parents or Caregivers
- Make an effort to get to know school personnel, especially the child's teacher
- Be willing to share desires and concerns and to listen to those of the teachers
- Get to know other parents well enough to feel comfortable calling them if a problem arises
- Take advantage of educators' efforts to build relationships (parent/parent as well as educator/parent)
- Take advantage of networks of support that educators create for parents and caregivers

The crisis inside schools is directly linked to human relationships.

Voices from the Inside, 1993, p.12

Educator Reflection
Promoting Supportive Relationships

How supportive are relationships among faculty members, students, parents, and community members at our school? What are we doing well to establish and maintain positive relationships? What areas should we be addressing that are currently being overlooked? Take a few minutes to reflect on the following statements. Put an "X" in the box that most closely reflects your perception of the relationships within our school.

	Often	Sometimes	Rarely
1. Educators make an effort to get to know parents and to work with them throughout the school year.			
2. School personnel help parents feel welcome and ensure that parents do not feel threatened, defensive, or intimidated when they come to school.			
3. There is a "we" feeling in our school community. Educators, students, and parents feel a sense of closeness, acceptance, and support.			
4. As an educator, I am generally satisfied with the relationships I have with most parents.			
5. Educators help parents get to know other parents.			
6. Educators, students, parents, and community members treat each other with kindness and respect.			
7. Students, parents, and community members are treated fairly by school personnel.			
8. Our school has a positive peer culture. Students are pleasant, positive, courteous, and friendly toward each other.			
9. Educators make an effort to help students develop social skills and supportive relationships with their peers.			
10. The diversity within the community and the uniqueness of each individual is recognized, accepted, and celebrated.			
11. Relationships with community businesses and social service agencies have been established and allow educators to link families with needed support.			
12. School personnel recognize the contributions and achievements of students, parents, community members, and community businesses and social service agencies.			

Plans and Tools
for carrying out our responsibilities in promoting supportive relationships

Plan 4.1. Reaching Out
Establishing positive relationships with new or uninvolved parents and community members often requires educators to seek innovative ways to reach them. This plan includes ideas for overcoming barriers to positive school, home, and community relationships; for making the most of regularly scheduled school events; and for capitalizing on the diversity within the community.

Plan 4.2. Making Connections
Making connections assists educators in helping parents connect with the school. It suggests ways for educators, parents, and community members get to know one another on a personal basis, identify and capitalize on individual talents and strengths, and make relationship building a priority.

Plan 4.3. Developing and Maintaining Relationships
This plan provides strategies for enhancing established relationships, creating a school environment in which new relationships can flourish, building a network of supportive relationships throughout the school community, and making the school the hub of the community.

Plan 4.1
Reaching Out

Before we can get parents actively engaged in school activities or their child's education, we have to entice them into the school. Some parents are excited about the opportunity to visit the school and learn about their child's new world. Others are so consumed with their own careers and interests--or with survival issues--that they rarely have the time or make the effort to attend school events. A larger percentage than we would like to acknowledge remember school as a source of frustration, alienation, and failure. These parents will tell you that although they do not want their cycle of failure repeated for their children, they are afraid to reenter an environment that still conjures up unpleasant memories. The result? Those parents who enjoyed school during their youth and who help their children experience the same success are at school almost as often as they are invited. Unfortunately, the parents who would gain the most from working as a team with their child's teacher do not or cannot take advantage of available opportunities. A parent once said, "I was a mess when I was in school and I'm more of a mess now. I just don't want my child's friends to see me look stupid at school." A colleague, well known in her community as an outstanding teacher, also told us that she was afraid to go to school meetings for fear of intimidating her child's teacher. What do these individuals at opposite ends of the spectrum have in common? They are both reluctant to take the first step in developing relationships that can make a tremendous difference in student success.

Our challenge is to find traditional and nontraditional ways to reach out to parents in ways that will entice them to take the first step toward parent involvement--entering the front door of the school. This may only require minor adjustments such as reinstituting, refining, or expanding strategies that have been successful in the past. On the other hand, it may call for a more comprehensive approach that involves rethinking all parent activities directed toward attracting all parents, even the reluctant ones, to the school.

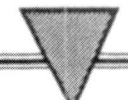

- Involve parents in the process of identifying and assessing current practices. They are able to provide perspectives that might not be apparent to faculty members working alone. Include parents who are currently actively involved as well as others who are not regular participants. It is also important to seek parents who represent the various socio-economic levels and cultures represented by the student population. The varied perspectives of these different groups are essential to understanding why some of their peers are not responding to current efforts to attract them.

- Identify current strategies for reaching out to families who are not participating at desired levels. What are individual teachers doing to encourage uninvolved parents to participate more in their child's education and school activities? What schoolwide efforts are being implemented? What is the parent-teacher association doing? Tool 4.1.1 provides a structure for identifying the current practices.

- Gain an indepth understanding of the reasons for the success of strategies identified as "best practices." Are there some beginning of the school year or special activities that the school community looks forward to each year? Determine why people have such strong feelings about them. Which activities seem to draw the most parents? Determine why parents respond to them. Ask enough questions to determine if it is the activity or the way parents are invited to attend that makes the difference. Are there any that attract parents who are not typically involved? Find out why. Are there activities that were successful in the past, but have had lower than desirable attendance rates recently? Determine what has caused the change. Are there some that were successful, but were discontinued for some reason? Tool 4.1.2 suggests a format for assessing the effectiveness of current and past practices.

- Consider how to enhance or refine the best practices to reach as many parents as possible. In planning any activity, focus on how to help parents get acquainted with school personnel and each other. Once they meet educators and other parents, they usually feel more comfortable initiating communication or attending other events. Tool 4.1.3 provides numerous strategies for making acquaintances and creating networks throughout the school community.

- Sometimes it is the informal interaction between parents and school personnel that makes parents feel the most comfortable. Capitalizing on planned or unplanned visits to school or encouraging parents to schedule visits lets them know that their presence is valued. Tools 4.1.4, 4.1.5, 4.1.6, and 4.1.7 include strategies many schools use to reach out to parents through informal events, Open House, performances, and holiday celebrations.

- Determine which activities have the potential to become traditions or rituals. These are the activities that parents look forward to and plan their schedules around. When a large percentage of the school community knows that the Fall Festival is a time for parents to have fun while assuming leadership roles for special events, many look forward to participating and encourage others to join them. Tool 4.1.8 illustrates a variety of approaches that schools have taken to develop traditions and customs that encourage parents to reach out to other parents.

- Brainstorm strategies to reach out to reluctant parents that go above and beyond what is implemented for the majority of parents. Tool 4.1.9 highlights a number of innovative strategies that have been used by schools to reach parents who cannot be attracted by more traditional means.

- Periodically assess how parents view efforts to reach out for their participation. Tool 4.1.10 is a sample Open House evaluation that could be applied to any event.

Other Possibilities ...

Current Practices to Reach Out To Families

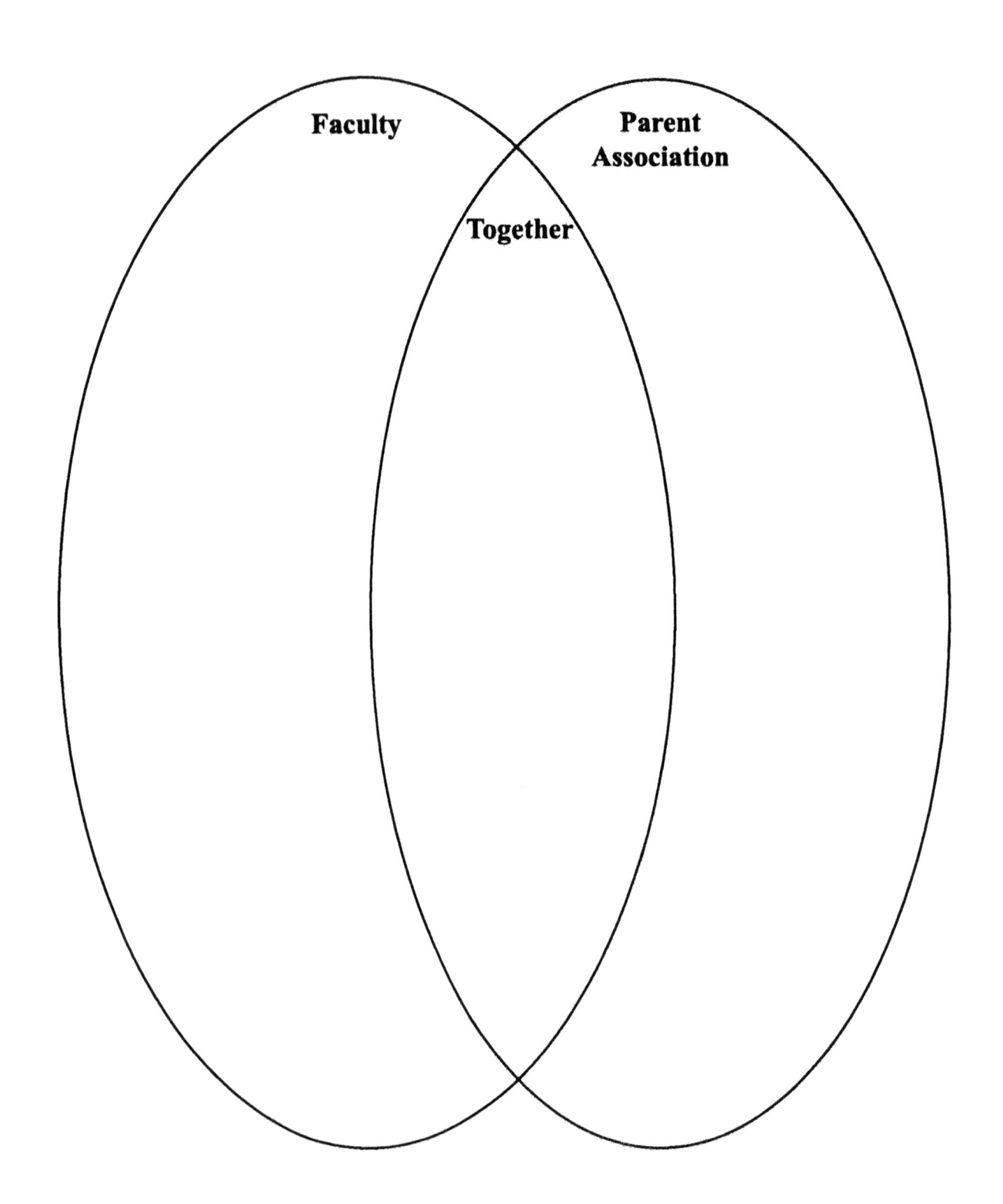

Tool 4.1.1

Faculty

Parent Association

Together

How Effective Are Our Practices to Reach Out to Families?

Tool 4.1.2

Which current practices . . .

Do parents look forward to each year?

Draw the most parents and families?

Attract parents who are not typically involved?

Were successful in the past, but are no longer attracting as many parents?

Previously worked well, but are not currently being used?

Getting Acquainted

Tool 4.1.3

There are three key ingredients in the formula for encouraging family members get to know one another and the faculty.

Communication + *FOOD* + *Networking*

Communication opens the door and generates interest...

Personal Telephone Calls
A three minute telephone call sends a message that family members are important enough for someone to take the time to talk to them. Even telephone messages left on recorders are impressive. The call can be made by the teacher or a parent volunteer, but the personal touch is the key.

"Hello, I'm Your Child's Teacher" Calls
If home visits are not a possibility for you, schedule a time for an informal conversation with every parent. Tell parents about yourself, your classroom, and your goals for the class and their child. Ask them to share their goals for their child. Use this call as an opportunity to encourage the parent to work with you to see that the child is as successful as possible in reaching your agreed upon goals. Also invite parents to come to Open House, to attend parent activities, and to visit the classroom whenever they can. Some schools send a note home prior to calling to be sure that parents are prepared for them and available to talk.

Success Calls
A brief telephone call to share a child's achievement or an incident in which the child used exceptional judgment will reinforce the child's efforts as well as the parent's commitment to supporting and working with the teacher.

"Here's an Upcoming Event You Won't Want to Miss" Calls
Once you have made initial contacts and talked with the parent at least once, you are ready to focus calls on specific purposes. Educators spend a tremendous amount of time planning parent involvement events to find that only the "few same parents" are likely to attend. Sometimes other parents are not even aware that the activities are taking place. For them, a quick call to alert them or remind them might make the difference in attending or not attending. While you have them on the telephone, you can also ask if they have any questions or concerns about their child at this point in the year.

Tool 4.1.3

Notes from Teachers

Taking the time to write a personal note to a nonparticipating parent may prove to be time well spent. Sometimes parents feel that they are really not that important to their child's educational experience. A personal note makes the point that they are valued and that their participation really is important.

Getting to Know You Letters

Some educators send letters to parents at the beginning of the year to let them know about their goals and plans for the year. These letters, especially those sent before the mountains of paperwork that accompany the opening of school, let parents know that the teacher is willing to make an effort to communicate. This should encourage the parent to contact the teacher at any time--especially before a little problem becomes a big one.

Post Cards

Some teachers address post cards to parents or caregivers as soon as they receive their class rosters (usually during the summer when they have more free time). Then they are able to send personalized notes to parents with little difficulty during the first weeks of school. Some teachers address multiple post cards for each family and continue the practice throughout the school year.

FOOD is Always an Incentive for Participation...

Getting Acquainted Breakfasts

Why not ask moms, dads, or other parenting adults to come by the school on the way to work and find out a little about their child's school? It's a good time to meet the principal on an informal basis -- and any teachers who are free at the time. One school set up different days for moms and dad and called them: "Donuts for Dads and Grandads" and "Muffins for Moms and Grandmoms." Another school decided to invite all parents for "Donuts at Dawn" from 7:30 a.m.until 8:15 a.m. over a consecutive three day period. Parents could attend together or separately to have coffee and a donut with their child before school. Special materials to highlight upcoming school and parent projects were displayed around the cafeteria and baskets of donuts were on each table to avoid any potential waiting in line. The attendance was so satisfying that the parent committee decided to have several "Donuts at Dawn" sessions throughout the year.

Tool 4.1.3

Getting Acquainted Lunches

Some elementary and middle schools invite "new" parents to have lunch with their children in order to help their children make friends. At the same time, the parents are able to meet the principal and the child's teachers. In other schools, principals have invited "new" and "nonparticipating" parents to lunch to talk about specific issues. Some even send special invitations to encourage participation.

Getting Acquainted Meetings

At an elementary school, teachers at each grade level met with parents as a team. As a panel presentation, they introduced themselves, told about their own families and children, and talked about their goals for the year. At the same time, they explained rules and policies and asked for parent questions or concerns. Parents left the meeting feeling that they knew their child's teacher--and others as well. Of course, tasty refreshments were served during the meeting. Why not try this at the secondary level? It could be clustered by team or by subject area.

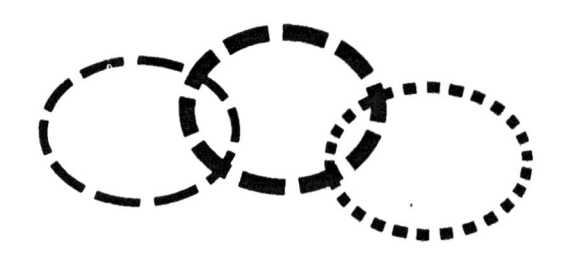

Informal Networking Broadens Contacts...

Newcomers Coffee

Newcomers are invited to meet other parents who are new to the community at regularly scheduled monthly coffees. Some schools hold the coffees on a monthly basis and others on an alternating monthly basis. Some hold them in homes and others meet at restaurants or local fast food stores. At the coffees they share information about the community as well as the school. Once new families are familiar with the community, they can take the lead in welcoming other newcomers. Many schools with large ethnic populations select leaders from the various cultures to welcome new residents. The dates for the coffees are included in the school's monthly calendar included in the school newsletters. As new students check in at the school office, the secretary is sure that each new parent is aware of the date and location of the next meeting.

Welcome Wagon

Many schools use a Welcome Wagon to introduce the school to community newcomers. School personnel and parents on the Welcome Wagon committee design information packets to share with parents new to the school and community. When a new family registers at the school, the school secretary alerts a parent representative from the parent-teacher organization or the Parent Welcome Wagon committee. A parent representative from the Welcome Wagon committee contacts the new family and sets up a meeting -- or coffee or lunch. At the meeting, the Welcome Wagon representative shares information about the school, how parents are encouraged to be involved, and the parent-teacher organization's plans for the year. The Welcome Wagon representative also identifies information about the parent that might be helpful to faculty members or the parent-teacher organization (e.g., talents, interests, and expertise the parent might be willing to share), whether the parent has been active in previous school settings; and any particular needs the family has in adjusting to the new school.

Parent to Parent

Some parents, whose schedules do not allow them to be part of the formal parent organization, are more than willing to welcome new parents to the school community. Ask parents with similar backgrounds to talk to the newcomer and share upcoming events. All it takes is providing the parent volunteers with information and allowing them to operate on their own schedule.

Communication Web

See Tool 3.2.3 for a process for involving parents in sharing information with other parents. The communication web is a simple method for linking parents into an information sharing network.

Students Recruiting Parents

In some schools, students are urged to recruit the parents of their friends to major school events. These students convey invitations to parents who are less likely to participate than their own parents. They are a great vehicle for sharing both information and excitement about school events.

Making the Most of Informal Events

Tool 4.1.4

Unplanned Visits to School

Every school and classroom has parents who drop by when a child is tardy or when they need to bring lunch money or supplies. Why not capitalize on their presence in the building? As they check in, they could be encouraged to see displays in the library or other areas of the school, bulletin board announcements of upcoming events, and children's work that is displayed in the hallways.

Send an Open Invitation to Visit

In the beginning of the year correspondence that is sent to parents, include a note to encourage parents to "drop by" at any time to observe their child or the class. Let them know that you welcome them at any time! Tell them not to worry about interrupting the class. You will continue to teach and they can observe or participate. It might be good to include a "How to Observe Guide" similar to the following one to prepare them for the visit.

How to Observe Guide

We're glad you're here to visit our class.
We want you to see as much as possible, so feel free to:
- speak briefly with your child
- walk to the centers to watch children working
- ask children questions about what they are learning
- look at all of the children's work hanging on the classroom walls

In order not to interfere with the children's learning, please do not:
- ask me questions that take my attention away from the children
- help the children do their assigned work
- distract your child fom learning

Enjoy your visit. I know your child loves having you here.

Send a Special Invitation to Visit

Sometimes it would be valuable to have parents in the classroom as extra pairs of eyes and hands! Other times it would be helpful for parents if they could see how their child interacts with others or functions in a particular learning situation. If there is a good "match" between an upcoming activity and what a parent could provide or benefit from, send an informal invitation to the parent -- or call to see if the parent could be available. It is often the simple personalized invitation that makes the difference! See Tool 7.1.1 for a sample invitation.

Tool 4.1.4

Use Parent Bulletin Boards to Spark Interest

Put a parent bulletin board outside the classroom door or in the hallway outside the school office to let parents know that they are important partners in their child's education. Include anything on the bulletin board that might encourage a parent who just "drops by" to consider becoming more actively involved. Pictures of parents helping children in the classroom or on schoolwide projects, plans for upcoming parties or events, a "Wish List" of everyday items needed for a project, and suggestions on how parents can work with their child at home are only a few of the items that could be included.

Coat, Toy, Book and Software Swaps

Schedule times every two to three months for parents to meet at school to exchange children's coats, toys, books or computer software. This will provide an opportunity for parents to clean out their closets while saving money on needed items. More importantly, it will help them get to know other parents and to realize that others are just as interested as they are in saving a little money on children's clothing and educational materials. Put announcements for the swaps on calendars that are distributed with or included in school newsletters. It is also a good idea to send notes or to use the communication tree as a reminder several days before the swap.

After School Hours Visits

Seize the moment while parents are sitting in the car waiting to pick up their child--or ask a volunteer to ride the bus routes to say hello to parents who are waiting for their children. A warm hello and short conversation with the principal or a parent volunteer is not what every parent has experienced in the long traffic lines. The parent who is greeted pleasantly one day may become an active supporter the next.

Share Flyers About Opportunities for Parents

Any time a notice about events or activities that involve parents is sent home to parents, make a few extra copies to share with the parents as they drop their children at the school door or wait for them in the afternoon. It's just one additional way to be sure the flyers get into parents' hands--at least a few! They might also spark a question or comment that would open informal lines of communication.

Ask Parents to Help Recruit Less Involved Parents

The fact that parents are at the school or bus stop to pick up their children reflects their desire to be involved in their child's education. They may have some good ideas for encouraging others--that they might not be available to share in more formal meetings. Would they like to come to school even earlier and help out? If they are not available or willing, maybe they could suggest another parent who is. If there is enough time, they could be encouraged to fill out volunteer forms or a talent book entry. See Tools 6.2.4 and 6.2.6b for sample talent book and volunteer forms.

Tool 4.1.5

Making the Most of Formal Events: Open House
Make it special!

Make Arrangements to Accommodate All Parents
It is important to schedule meetings so that parents from more than one class have enough time and space to visit. Do specified time slots guarantee each parent or care giver ample time with the teacher? Should Open House be extended over several days?

Send Written Invitations
Clever, creative invitations can make parents feel that this Open House will be one that should not be missed. School houses, apples, and creative designs are better than sophisticated invitations. Use your or your students' creativity, but include the necessary basics on this more formal design. With computer imaging capabilities, what about a computer generated invitation with a picture of the child?

YOU
are the most important reason for our
OPEN HOUSE

(Date and Time)

You will be able to:
Meet your child's teacher.
Meet the parents of your child's classmates.
Learn about the teacher's plans for the school year.
Find out how to help your child.
Ask any questions you have about the school or classroom.

Help Parents Get to Know Other Parents
With Ice Breaker Activities

People Search
Greet parents as they enter the room and give them a list of "generic items" such as "Admits to watching 'I Loved Lucy' reruns," "Watches Star Trek more than 5 times a year," "Reads romance novels," "Works at a restaurant," "Loves to shop," "Loves to work puzzles," "Is a jigsaw puzzle genius," "Was born in ____," etc. Let parents find others who fit their categories as they mingle before the meeting.

Tool 4.1.5

Two Truths and a Lie

Put parents into groups of three or four. Ask each individual to identify two truths and one lie that they are willing to share with others. Encourage teachers to define the lie as a "slight misrepresentation" since honesty is valued at school. Remind parents that this is just for fun. Allow time for the groups to share and see if others can guess which are true and which are fabrications. Ask each group to share their most outrageous or funniest lie.

"Who is the Parent?" Game

Give each parent a slip of paper with a question such as the following. As they are waiting for the more formal part of the meeting to begin, ask them to find the answer to their question by talking with other parents.

> "Who has the most unusual pet?"
> "Who has the most children in our school?"
> "Who surfs the Internet the most?"
> "Who drives the farthest to get to school?"
> "Who is involved in the craziest sport?"

Include Food

Was it our mother or grandmother who always said, "Food warms the heart?" This age old belief is still at the heart of any gathering. Why not involve parents in helping with this important part of Open House? Parents are wonderful about bringing homemade cookies and cakes--and even ethnic foods. Open House is a marvelous time to share our cultures through our foods.

Give Parents Something to Take Home

Schedules, classroom goals, discipline plans, student work or folders, guidelines for parents visiting classrooms, pamphlets, flyers, or anything that will help the parent understand the "inner workings" of the classroom are helpful to the parent in digesting all that is taken in during Open House. This is especially helpful if the parent has more than one child in the school--or in several schools! Prepare something tangible such as the first or next edition of the class newsletter. Refer to Tool 3.2.1 for guidelines to follow in sending communications to the home.

Involve Parents in Evaluating the Event

This is a terrific opportunity to find out why the parent came to the Open House, what they liked best, what was least beneficial, and what they think is necessary to improve future Open Houses. See Tool 4.1.7 for a sample evaluation form.

Contact Parents Who Did Not Attend

Make a special effort to let parents know that they were missed at Open House. View their absence as an opportunity to connect with them through a personalized note. Include information that was provided at Open House and ask what school personnel could have done that would have made it easier for them to have attended.

Making the Most of Formal Events: Performances

Use these events to attract parents other than those of students who are performing.

Send Invitations

The parents of the performing students know about the performance and will most likely be on the front rows. Take this opportunity to reach out to other parents and community members. Encourage them to take advantage of the interesting events happening in the school. Be sure to let them know that they can enjoy and learn about music, dance, art, or other programs from the performances, even if their child is not performing. Encourage them to bring their child along to see what other students are doing.

> Please join us
> for the performance
> of the
> Middle School Orchestra and Chorus
>
> Wednesday, December 4th
> 6:30 p.m. - 7:30 p.m.
> Jefferson Middle School Auditorium
>
> We especially encourage parents whose children are not involved in the orchestra to join us and to learn about the wonderful opportunities available to your children through our music program. The performance is also an opportunity for parents to see how our music students are progressing throughout their middle school years. Bring your child and enjoy an hour of music and refreshments in the cafeteria following the performance.

Ask Parents to Invite Two Other Parents to Attend

The parents of performing students will generally be thrilled to ask others to watch their child exhibit his or her talent. By asking these parents to help "reach out" to other parents who are less involved, the parents feel that they are helping the school while they are celebrating their child's accomplishments!

Include a Social Time After the Performance

Refreshments in the school cafeteria following a performance provide a casual setting for parents get to know one another. This does not have to be a major expense or a tremendous amount of work for anyone. It is the opportunity to chat after the performance that is enticing!

Ask a Group of Parents to Share Their Impressions

A few days after the performance, ask a small group of parents to provide feedback about the evening. Avoid critiquing the performance. Focus on the steps taken to "reach out" to parents and to make the event one that would encourage further participation.

Tool 4.1.7

Making the Most of Formal Events: Holiday Celebrations

Make them a time to reach out to parents from different cultures and religions--and a learning experience for all.

Guidelines

Identify the various cultures and religions represented by the student population. If the school population does not include a major religion and culture, try to find someone in the school community who might be willing to share with the students, parents, and faculty.

Ask a few parents from each of the selected cultures and religions to meet with a committee of educators to decide how "educate" others about their heritage.

In meetings and in sharing sessions with students and parents, maintain the focus on including everyone. Avoid making any student or family feel different, excluded, or inferior--at all costs!

Use creative means to teach others about each culture or religion. These might include:
- Demonstrating ceremonies
- Displaying clothing or artifacts
- Sharing special foods, music, and dance
- Involving students and parents in "hands on" activities
- Poster sessions where students and parents rotate from group to group to learn about different cultures and religions.

Decide on a means for informing parents about the cultural awareness activities. Use this as a means to "reach out" to parents who might have been afraid to become involved because they are different than the majority of families.

Make the meetings fun, as well as educational. Remember, these important occasions may be one of the best vehicles for reaching out to parents and community members.

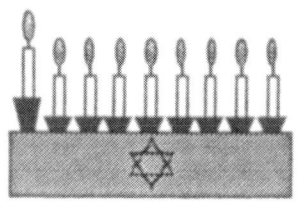

Traditions That Encourage Parent Participation
Only a few of many traditions . . .

Annual Christmas Shopping Spree for Primary Students
Parents of one school's Academic Booster Club hold an annual sale of small items for primary students to purchase for their parents. The parents have had such a tremendous time planning and running the sale for the past few years that their club's membership roster has grown steadily. They are also proud that their profits sponsor major academic activities.

Welcoming Party for Kindergarten Parents
Each year at one elementary school, the parents of fifth grade students give a welcoming party to parents of kindergarten students. They share important information about the school as well as their perspective after five years of participating in school activities. Each year the parents work to make this a special introduction for the new parents--and talk about how to prepare their own children for their next transition.

Fall Festival or Homecoming
Every school has some type of festival at some point during the year. In some schools, however, these events are special times for parents. One school turns the entire event over to a parent committee that plans the evening, asks the faculty for input on an ongoing basis, and implements the plans without teachers having to do any of the work. Teachers are appreciative of their efforts and get to know the parents as they engage in the ongoing planning sessions.

Graduation Night Party
High school parents who work together to plan and implement the "all night" graduation parties often learn a valuable lesson too late for their own benefit. The process of working together on such a critical event opens lines of communication among families, encourages new relationships and friendships, and helps parents deal consistently with serious problems facing their adolescents (e.g., drugs, drinking, and driving). Many wonder why they didn't start working together on similar events as their children entered high school.

State History Day
In one rural community, state history day is an opportunity for everyone in the community to share something about the town's history, music, traditions, and culture. Parents and faculty members initially reached out to local community members in asking for help with what would become an annual event. After five years, this traditional event involves every classroom highlighting a special aspect of the culture from bread making to quilting to sheep sheering. Family members spend many afternoons displaying materials to be used for the event. Musical groups, some comprised of great grandparents of students, play at various locations. As the principal said, "This is the one day of the year that we are truly a school community."

Tool 4.1.8

Annual Hamburger Cookout

One elementary school invites parents to help organize and enjoy a fall cookout. Local businesses and community members donate supplies, parents help with the set up and clean up, and the principal cooks. At another middle school, a similar event is held in the spring on the day that annuals are presented to students. While parents talk to each other and to teachers, students are engaged in signing annuals.

Dedicating a Special Place in the School to Honor Students' Accomplishments

One high school has an entire room dedicated to athletes who have graduated and have been outstanding during their college or professional careers. At this school the room is named for one nationally recognized athlete. Other schools have "halls of fame" or similar places where pictures of current students or graduates are displayed along with their achievements. Parents are invited to ceremonies when pictures are added to the walls.

Going "Above and Beyond" Tactics
Sometimes traditional means just aren't enough.

Neighborhood Coffee Hours
With the help of involved parents, informal coffee hours can be held in homes within the community to allow parents to get to know teachers or school representatives on an informal basis. In this relaxed atmosphere educators can share information, discuss ideas, or answer parent questions. More importantly, parents have the opportunity to see educators as just another person who enjoys coffee and conversation.

Workplace Visits
School personnel and parent volunteers schedule visits to workplaces and factories where large numbers of parents work to meet with parents informally on their breaks. They use the short periods of time just to get to know the parents at first and to share what is happening at school. Once the parents feel more comfortable, the visits can be used to encourage other means of involvement.

Community-Centered Visits
Rather than asking parents to enter the school building, some schools take Open House and Parent Meeting nights to the community--to community centers, housing developments, churches, and local restaurants. Using a setting that is familiar to parents reduces their anxiety and enhances attendance.

Community Center Homework Help Sessions
Along with educators or parent volunteers who are available to help with homework, someone who can interact well with members of the community goes along to chat with parents who may bring their children to the session. Knowing that this person will be there on a regular basis provides an opportunity for parents to open up to someone linked to the school and to their community.

Visits to Community Churches
Although some parents are afraid to walk through school doors, they may be actively involved in their churches. Why not ask the minister to help parents become more involved in their child's education? Perhaps the minister would allow meetings to take place at the church or would distribute information that might encourage involvement or attendance at another site.

One-on-one Visits at a Safe Spot
Sometimes parents have issues that are concerning them that they are afraid to share in a setting where others might see them. Sometimes their concern or fear is related to their child, the child's peers, or family members. Other times it might be personal, but the parent does not want to be seen at the school. Find a place like a fast food restaurant, a library, or another neutral setting to meet. By helping the parent resolve the concern, you may be laying a foundation for a true partnership.

Tool 4.1.10

Evaluating Formal Events
Adapt this Open House evaluation to any other event.

Dear Parent,

Thank you for attending our Open House. In order for us to continue to make this a special evening for parents and teachers, please take a few minutes to help us by answering the following questions. Please feel free to add any notes to explain your responses. When you complete this evaluation form, leave it in the box by the front door of the school. Thank you for coming and for sharing your feelings about our Open House.

How did you feel about . . .

- Communication about the Open House?
    _____ very helpful   _____ adequate   _____ more information needed

- The time, date, and length of sessions?
    _____ excellent   _____ adequate   _____ needs improvement

- The usefulness of the information you were given?
    _____ very helpful   _____ adequate   _____ more information needed

- The amount of time you had to visit with your child's teacher?
    _____ what was needed   _____ adequate   _____ more time needed

- Refreshments?
    _____ excellent   _____ adequate   _____ needs improvement

- Child care (if provided)?
    _____ excellent   _____ adequate   _____ needs improvement

What did you find most helpful?

What would you suggest to make future Open Houses even more effective?

Plan 4.2
Making Connections:
Really Getting to Know One Another

Reaching out to parents might get them through the school doors for an initial visit, but what must educators do to convince them to keep coming back? How do we build on initial interest and curiosity to develop the types of relationships that will enhance student learning and success? How do we help parents feel connected to the school and their child's education? These are serious questions that most educators are asking. Some have found solutions by placing a high priority on positive interpersonal relationships and feelings of connectedness throughout the school community.

Making connections focuses on learning more about each other. In order to develop relationships built on understanding and trust, we must begin by getting to know one another on a personal level. Parents are introduced to teachers and other parents at the school's Open House, performances, and meetings. On these occasions, teachers meet so many parents that they cannot be expected to do much more than put a face with a name by the end of the evening. Do educators or parents really *know* anything about each other at this point? Of course not. It takes continued opportunities to meet, work side by side, and communicate in nonthreatening environments before individuals know more about each other beyond superficial information. Without making these "real" connections, parents do not feel that they are a part of the educational process and often perceive school personnel as merely "going through the paces" of asking for their support and involvement.

- Gain as indepth an understanding of the parent population as possible. It is critical to know if children live with two parents, one parent, grandparents, or guardians and how to reach them. All schools have forms to record this information. It is also helpful to know the socio-economic level of the family and its unique needs. If the family is receiving special services, educators who are aware of them can work with service providers to help the family. If the family needs services or assistance that they are not currently receiving, educators should be able to link them to the appropriate providers. At the same time, educators who find out what types of interactions would be most interesting and accessible to parents (e.g., one-on-one meetings, conferences when the need arises, informal small or large group meetings, formal parent-teacher organizational meetings, coffees, e-mail connections, regular notes to and from home, home visits, retreats) are better able to plan for them. Knowing what time of day they prefer also helps with scheduling meetings, conferences, or telephone calls. See Tool 4.2.1 for a parent information and interest inventory to use in gathering information that is not readily accessible in school records and Tool 4.2.2 for a chart to organize the information. It may also be worthwhile to find out what talents, interests, or cultural information they would be willing to share. See Tool 6.2.4 for a model of a parent talent book to gather this information.

- Maintain a focus on creating an environment where parents feel that they are a valuable part of the school. Work on breaking down barriers that make school intimidating for parents. The initial goal is to help parents feel emotionally safe and secure in trying to establish relationships. The long range goal is to promote feelings of inclusion and belonging that encourage parents to view themselves as partners in their child's education. How can educators promote such an environment? They can avoid using educational jargon and nonverbal actions that may be perceived as power plays. They can create opportunities for parents to get to know them as *real people* with the same desires for their students that parents hold for their child. They should clear about parents' opportunities for involvement at school so that they know when it is appropriate to visit the school and when it is not. Teachers and administrators should find out how parents would be most comfortable interacting with them. Are they intimidated by formal meetings of any kind? Would they prefer to drop by and get to know educators on an informal basis? Set special times aside for these visits? Tool 4.2.3 provides a form for administrators to use in reserving time slots for informal meetings with parents. Could teachers set aside informal meeting times after school hours?

- Determine the best possible structures for getting to know parents. The information that has been gathered should provide direction for selecting the most appropriate methods for making connections. Consider the following in making decisions about the most appropriate structures. How many of the parents are willing to attend meetings or take part in activities at school? If most indicate that they would be comfortable at school, take advantage of their willingness. Meeting in the school allows educators to share school and student materials as well as information about the facility that cannot be shared as easily in other settings. If it appears that some parents are less willing to attend functions at school, could an additional meeting be held in another setting? Would faculty members be willing to meet in the community center or at a church or at a local fast food restaurant? Are home visits a possibility? Research has shown that home visits are an excellent means for establishing relationships with families, especially those with special needs or anxieties about attending school functions. For guidelines for home visits, see Tool 4.2.4. Would a retreat be a possibility? Retreats, because of space and cost limitations, generally involve representatives of various parent populations, rather than *all* parents. Might the representative parents involved in the retreat be able to recruit others to future meetings at the school? Tool 4.2.5 provides guidelines for hosting a successful retreat. Are there ways to build upon parents' interests and concerns regarding their child's transition to new grade or school levels? Tool 4.2.6 suggests ways to assure smooth transitions.

- Develop strategies for helping parents to get to know each other. In some schools, a space is set aside for parents to meet and talk. Tool 4.2.7 describes how to develop a parent center that could become more than a meeting room. In some schools, parent centers have become the impetus for more focused activities for parents such as literacy training and parenting skills.

Other Possibilities . . .

Parent Information and Interest Inventory

Tool 4.2.1

In planning for this school year, it is very important to be sure that what I am considering is the most appropriate for all of my students. As a result, I would like to learn about your child from his/her most important teacher: *you*.

Would you please take a few minutes to answer the following questions? Some relate to your child and others to you and your family. A few also ask how you can or will be involved in our classroom this year. Please feel free to rewrite these questions, add comments, or make any suggestions that might make this the best possible year for your child. I hope this is just the first of many opportunities for us to work together this year.

About your child . . .

1. How does your child learn best? (Check all that apply.)
   _____ By following an example
   _____ By experimenting on his or her own
   _____ By reading
   _____ By listening to instructions
   _____ Other (Please describe.)

2. What does your child like the best or seem to do most easily?
   _____ Use words (understanding meanings, explaining, remembering information)
   _____ Use numbers and identify patterns and relationships
   _____ Body movement activities
   _____ Draw, form images, copy pictures, use an active imagination
   _____ Musical activities, creating rhythm or melodies
   _____ Relate and work well with others
   _____ Think about a topic or concentrate on an activity for a long period of time
   _____ Other (Please describe.)

3. Does your child have any special talents or areas of interest that I could use to encourage future learning?

4. Does your child have any special needs or problems that I should know about?

Tool 4.2.1

5. What experiences would you like for your child to have at school? (If you could have one thing happen to your child at school this year, what would it be?)

6. What would you like your child to be able to do by the end of the year?

About you and your family . . .

1. Do you have any special interests or talents that you would be willing to share? (Art, music, sports, writing, computers, religion, culture, gardening, etc.)

2. Do you have any special needs or concerns that I should be aware of?

3. Is there anything that you would like me to know that I did not ask?

4. Do you have any questions about our classroom or our school that I can answer before we have an opportunity to meet?

Thank you for taking the time to complete this *very important* information sheet. I look forward to teaching your child and to meeting you as soon as possible. Do not hesitate to call me if I can be of help to you.

Parent Information Chart

Tool 4.2.2

Student	Parent or Guardian	Home or Work Phone	Family Needs or Services	Desired Interaction (Phone, conferences, groups, E-mail, Home Visits, Notes)	Best Times	Notes (Previous experiences, talents, skills culture to share)

Parent Visits with the Principal

Tool 4.2.3

The following times are reserved for parents to schedule a visit with the principal. Please stop by to share your ideas, ask questions about the school, or make suggestions. We truly want you to help us educate your children.

Tuesday _____

Time	Parent/Guardian
9:30 a.m. - 9:45 a.m.	_____
9:45 a.m. - 10:00 a.m.	_____
10:00 a.m. - 10:15 a.m.	_____
10:15 a.m. - 10:30 a.m.	_____

Thursday _____

Time	Parent/Guardian
9:30 a.m. - 9:45 a.m.	_____
9:45 a.m. - 10:00 a.m.	_____
10:00 a.m. - 10:15 a.m.	_____
10:15 a.m. - 10:30 a.m.	_____

Important

If more time is needed, block out two time slots.

If these times are not convenient for you, please schedule an appointment.

If you have question related to your child's classroom,
you will need to schedule an appointment at a time when the teacher can be involved.

Home Visits

Tool 4.2.4

Why are home visits important?
Home visits allow teachers to learn from the families of their students. They may be the *only* way for teachers to understand the ethnically or racially diverse family's experiences, customs, values, and expectations for their child. They also provide an opportunity for parents to get to know educators on their own turf rather than in the intimidating educational setting. Many educators have said that home visits are critical to establishing partnerships with parents. When parents realize that teachers or school representatives are willing to go beyond what is expected to come into their homes to listen to them and to learn about their child, it inspires confidence and a commitment to working together in the best interests of the child.

Home visits can provide . . .

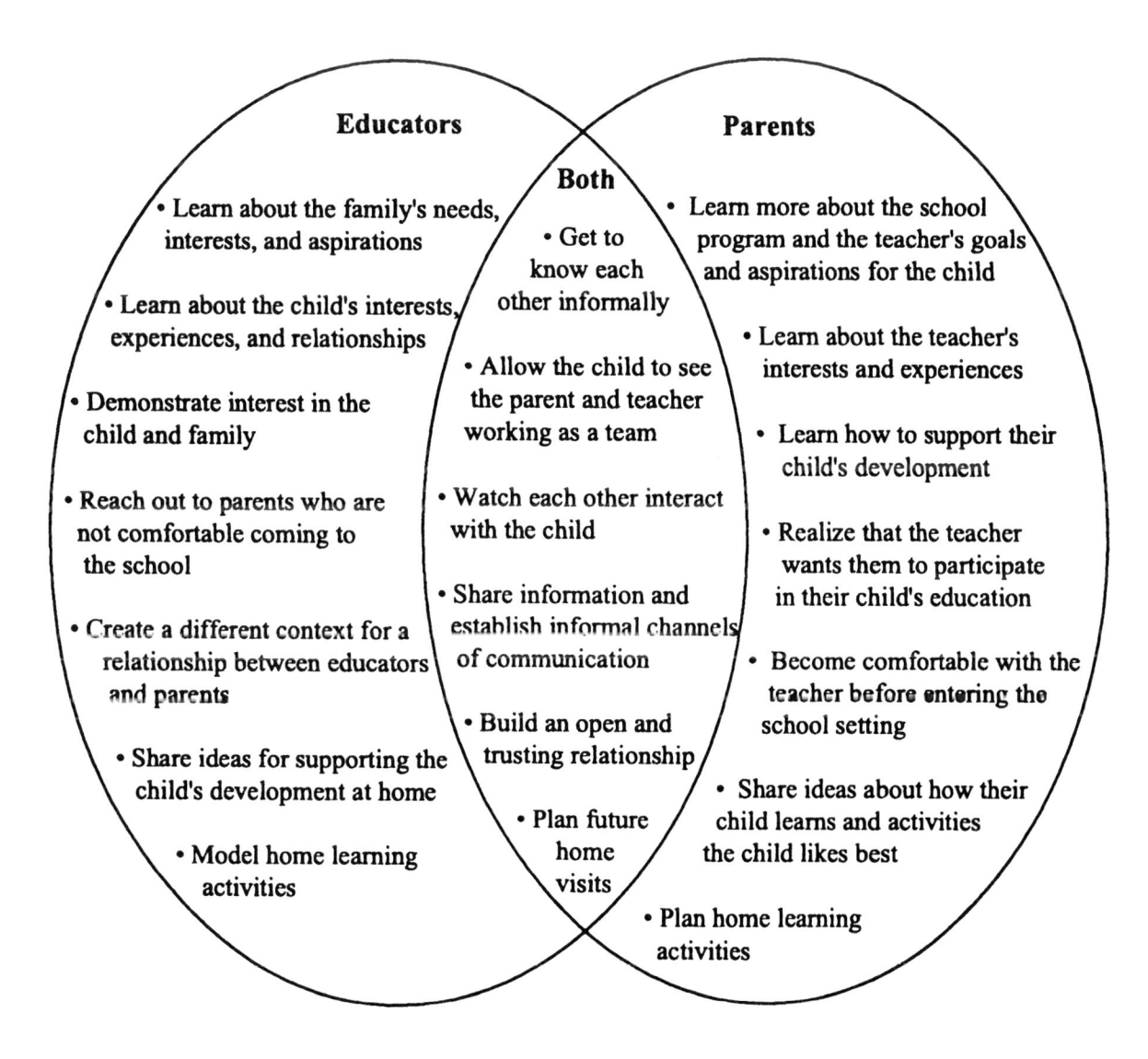

Educators
- Learn about the family's needs, interests, and aspirations
- Learn about the child's interests, experiences, and relationships
- Demonstrate interest in the child and family
- Reach out to parents who are not comfortable coming to the school
- Create a different context for a relationship between educators and parents
- Share ideas for supporting the child's development at home
- Model home learning activities

Both
- Get to know each other informally
- Allow the child to see the parent and teacher working as a team
- Watch each other interact with the child
- Share information and establish informal channels of communication
- Build an open and trusting relationship
- Plan future home visits

Parents
- Learn more about the school program and the teacher's goals and aspirations for the child
- Learn about the teacher's interests and experiences
- Learn how to support their child's development
- Realize that the teacher wants them to participate in their child's education
- Become comfortable with the teacher before entering the school setting
- Share ideas about how their child learns and activities the child likes best
- Plan home learning activities

Tool 4.2.4

Types of Home Visits . . .

Teacher "Before School Begins" Visits

Establish a relationship with the family during the time when children and their parents are most excited about the upcoming school year--and are not as harried as they will be once school begins! Take a picture of the child for the "Welcome Back to School" bulletin board! Learn about the child's home, siblings, interests, and hopes. Teachers find that this is a terrific time to answer the family's questions about what to expect for the year.

Teacher "During the School Year" Visits

Decide how many visits you plan for the year. Some schools or teachers feel that one visit is critical to establish a relationship with the family. Others plan two or three to continue building the relationship and to incorporate some one-on-one parent training and modeling. Once plans are developed, contact families to let them know why you want to visit in their home, what you will do during the visit, and what you think it will provide for their child. If parents are totally opposed to your visit, suggest a meeting at school.

Home Visit Schedule				
Family	Telephone	Visit Date	Reminder	Follow Up

Visits by a Team of Educators

Sometimes it is helpful for parents to meet several members of the child's educational team, especially when the child and the family have special needs. This visit might include a combination of the teacher (or teachers) and a counselor, specialist, or administrator. Visiting in the home helps the team members work together more effectively to address the needs of the child, but also allows parents to get to know the various team members in ways that would be impossible in formal meetings at the school.

Visits by Parent Supporters

Visits by volunteer supporters or paid parent coordinators may not be as effective as those made by the child's teacher or a team of educators, but they are still quite a valuable tool. Parents who are informed, genuinely interested in building a positive relationship between parents and the school, and able to communicate effectively can serve as effective liaisons to other parents. These parent supporters can communicate the school's expectations, provide information about curriculum and academic requirements, and share ways that parents can help their child succeed. They can also listen to family members' concerns and needs and communicate these to the educators. Parent visitors are often able to reach peers who are intimidated by educators or the parent elite as many parent/teacher organization leaders are perceived. They can also play a persuasive role in encouraging reluctant parents to become more involved in the school and in their child's education.

Guidelines for Home Visits

Tool 4.2.4

- Set a goal for visiting every family at least once a year. Tentatively schedule days available on the calendar.

- Keep the focus of home visits on developing open and trusting relationships, increasing communication, and helping parents become more confident, competent, and independent in helping their children.

- Determine the specific purpose for each home visit--and communicate it. Remember that home visits are not a time to focus on problems at school. Instead, they are opportunities to establish a partnership--that may be critical in handling problems at another time.

- Contact families concerning the visits through letters, telephone calls or notices well in advance of the visits. Remember, they have busy schedules, too. Do not bring other visitors unless you have the parent's permission.

- Offer to include other members of the family in the visit.

- Dress comfortably and casually. Stepping out of professional attire helps create a less intimidating environment.

- Be prompt, confident, and yourself! Let parents get to know you as a person who is also a teacher.

- Be observant, but remember that the parent is also observing you.

- Be respectful of cultural and ethnic values--and do not impose your own.

- Build on the parents' goals and agenda for the visit. Be flexible enough to let them share what is most important about their child.

- Be a good listener and communicator. Avoid any verbal or nonverbal messages that might make parents feel that their home or hospitality are being judged. Build on parents' ideas, concerns, or suggestions.

- Accept the family's hospitality. If you are offered something to eat or drink, enjoy it.

- If your home visit plan involves helping parents learn how to work with their child, begin working on a specific activity during the first home visit. Help parents learn why the activity is important and how to develop and lead it. This will help them realize that they can and do teach their children. Activities that revolve around daily routines are easiest for parents to do on their own.

Tool 4.2.4

▼ Do not ask parents to do something you would not do.

▼ Expect progress, not perfection. Remember that progress is a series of small steps that lead to big improvements.

▼ Ask the parent to help you assess the effectiveness of the home visit and plan for future visits.

▼ Do not share anything you learn about the family in public. Respect the parent's willingness to confide in you.

▼ As you leave, invite the parent to visit the school. If there are school or classroom events planned within the next month, encourage the parent to participate.

▼ Call the parents or send a thank you note to let them know how much you enjoyed the visit. The special extra touch will be greatly appreciated.

Hosting a Retreat

Tool 4.2.5

A retreat provides a relaxed, comfortable atmosphere for developing relationships. In an environment away from titles, roles, and responsibilities, educators and parents can get to know one another as individuals who share a common interest and concern for the well being of the children. Retreats can be as simple as an evening or Saturday morning at the school or a local meeting room or as grandiose as a weekend at a resort. Whatever the setting, there are a few simple guidelines that should be followed to assure that any type of retreat accomplishes its intended purposes.

> **Create a "We" feeling.**
>
> **Accentuate the positive.**
>
> **Look to the possibilities.**
>
> **Seize the opportunities.**
>
> **Plan! Plan! Plan!**

▼ **Determine the desired outcomes of the retreat. Building relationships is generally one desired outcome. What are others?**

One school advisory board expressed concerns over high school students' escalating use of drugs and alcohol. They felt that if parents could get to know one another in an informal setting, they might be more willing to contact each other when their children planned to party or spend the night together and might, as a result, have a positive impact on the escalating problem. Their specific purposes were to: 1) bring as many parents of students at a specific grade level together as they could; 2) let the parents get to know each other informally; 3) share statistics on students' self-reports on a national drug and alcohol survey; and 4) encourage parents to contact each other when they had any concerns about their child's out of school plans. They arranged a Thursday Night Retreat for each grade level at the school with a special dinner and a speaker to explain the drug and alcohol survey results. Parents paid a minimal fee for a ticket to the dinner (which was augmented with school funds so that it was a good value). Parents who could not afford to attend were provided with a complimentary ticket. One interesting note to this school's planning: students tried to divide and conquer by convincing their parents that they would be the only ones attending. School personnel mailed reminders to the parents which included the large numbers of parents who had made reservations. The result? Over three-fourths of the parents attended what became the first of a series of parent meetings for the school.

245

Tool 4.2.5

▼ **Determine the structure of the retreat.**
How will the intended outcomes be accomplished? How will the participants interact? At one elementary school, the faculty and the parent teacher organization spent one year focusing on long range planning. While both groups proceeded along the same paths of identifying strengths and challenges throughout the first semester of the school year, neither group had shared what was being developed with the other. The principal decided that a Saturday morning retreat in the spring might be the best means for bringing the two groups together. The retreat was structured around four areas: 1) processes and procedures that assured that neither group would feel intimidated or put down by the other; 2) a focus on common themes from the combined plans; 3) time devoted to celebrating successes; and 4) group assignments that required educators and parents to work together to find solutions to common concerns.

▼ **Select the retreat participants.**
All faculty members and support staff who have a professional interest in the goal of the retreat or topics to be addressed should be encouraged to attend. While it is not economically or physically possible to involve all parents, those who are selected should represent a wide range of student interests, abilities, and levels of school success. A retreat is an ideal time to help parents overcome their own limitations in dealing with others from different religious, ethnic, or racial backgrounds. It is also an opportunity to help parents realize the common concerns of parents of children with disabilities.

▼ **Decide how the retreat will be funded. Are grant funds available? Will school adopters provide support?**
One school simply asked their Central Office for funds for a minimally expensive retreat. With clearly delineated goals, objectives, and task structures, their proposal was deemed too valuable not to finance. Another school secured a small grant from a local funding agency. Others have asked for assistance from community agencies or adopters. It is important to secure the funding before proceeding with the planning!

▼ **Delineate roles and responsibilities and determine whether outside facilitators or consultants are needed.**
One high school school used outside consultants as retreat leaders to conduct and coordinate the various sessions and to coordinate follow-up activities. The principal and teacher leaders attended to all details and focused primarily on building inclusion among the participants. Several teachers were asked to assume leadership roles by serving as facilitators. In a series of pre-retreat meetings, the consultants, principal, teacher leaders, and facilitators worked to set the stage for a successful retreat. They shared information about the context of the school and discussed possible strategies before agreeing upon the final plans.

Tool 4.2.5

▼ **Select the most appropriate retreat activities.**
Most initial retreats focus on some type of team building activity which allows participants to get to know one another in a task-oriented, nonthreatening situation. Work groups of about six to eight members including representatives from all groups are ideal. Brainstorming activities allow all participants to share their ideas or perceptions without fear of repercussions. Reflective activities encourage groups to sort through the various ideas identified to select those that have the greatest potential worth, feasiblilty, and impact. Refer to Tool 1.2.5 for rules to guide the interaction and to other appropriate Tools in *Design 1* for enhancing collaboration and long range planning.

▼ **Decide upon appropriate post-retreat activities.**
The desired result of any retreat is a future course of action. Questions such as the following should be answered either during or shortly after the retreat:
- What will be needed to carry out the plans made during the retreat?
- How will school personnel and parents continue to build upon the relationships that were formed during the retreat?
- Should target dates be selected to continue the dialogue begun during the retreat?
- Should "Thank You" notes be sent to retreat participants or others?
- Are there any specific participant's requests that must be acted upon?

Guidelines for Creating a Parent Center

Tool 4.2.6

> *"The first time I came, I was terrified. Now I feel that I have friends at the school--other parents and some teachers!"*
> Parent of an elementary student

Several schools have developed Parent Centers to address the need for greater parent involvement in school activities and in the education of their children. The following guidelines assure that planning a Parent Center addresses critical issues of importance to educators and parents.

▼ *Develop goals.* Begin by articulating what faculty members and parents want the Parent Center to achieve. Goals will provide direction for those involved in planning how to implement Parent Center activities. The following are one center's goals.

Parent Center Goals

To make the school the "hub of the community"

To enhance family involvement in the education of their children

To promote the competence and confidence of family and community members in helping children develop their talents and abilities

To strengthen linkages among adult care givers throughout the community

---

▼ *Transform a room at the school into the Parent Center.* Ask teachers, parents, businesses, and community members to donate comfortable furniture (couches and a table and chairs) to help create an informal and welcoming atmosphere. While soliciting donations, ask for children's books, toys (for younger children), educational materials, or cash contributions to defray the costs of establishing the center. Treat their contributions as a donation to charity and provide them with a receipt for the value of their contribution. Make the most of the contributions by painting or decorating the room to make it as welcoming and comfortable as possible.

▼ *Develop a code of conduct.* It is important that parents realize that they will rarely know all of the details about events that happen at school. Since they may witness students' misbehavior or conflicts, they must agree not to discuss what happens at school with others. Parents who have a tendency to gossip or spread rumors are not good candidates for involvement in a Parent Center. They may carelessly cause more harm by sharing information about events or actions they do not fully understand.

Tool 4.2.6

▼ *Invite parents and community members to volunteer to staff the Parent Center.* Schools that have been successful have placed a high priority on recruiting the most positive, influential, and hardworking volunteers available. These are the people who make visiting parents feel welcome and comfortable. In some cases, the Parent Center is staffed by a combination of paid staff members and unpaid volunteers. The staff members are paid on a part-time hourly basis to coordinate the volunteers and to take responsibility for the schedule, activities, and staffing of the center. Most schools feel that paid staff members are more consistent in their attendance and have a greater stake in assuring that the center is working well. See Tool 6.2.3 for information about parent involvement coordinators.

▼ *Decide what parents will experience when they visit the Parent Center.* A goal of most centers is to provide parents with a place in the community where they experience a sense of belonging and support from other parents and from educators. Many of the centers began by offering parents a place to have a cup of coffee while talking with other parents about what their children were experiencing at school. Eventually they expanded into welcoming and nonthreatening places where parents could get information about health and/or social services, ESL or GED classes; assistance with transportation to classes or agencies; ESL, GED, parenting classes, or computer classes; parenting materials; and clothing, books, and toys through periodic "swaps." Nearly all help parents develop relationships with other parents and teachers, often sponsoring informal get togethers. While each center offers different activities, all focus on the goal of making the center and the school accessible to *all* parents.

▼ *Market the Center.* In most cases, parents who visit the Parent Center one time will return. The critical step is in getting parents to make the first visit. Flyers, announcements at parent-teacher organization meetings, telephone calls, and parent-to-parent or home visits are all strategies that have been used to establish a Parent Center. Post upcoming activities on the wall in the center and in other places in the school building so that parents who do visit can see what is planned or is currently happening. Generally word of mouth advertising builds participation after parents begin using the center. At first, however, this is an area where parent volunteers will spend a great deal of time.

▼ *Involve community members in the Parent Center.* Many businesses will make a commitment to adult literacy and to enhancing parenting skills. In many school districts they provide contributions that range from financial donations for materials and supplies to releasing employees to serve as one-on-one tutors. By involving community members, the Parent Center contributes significantly to the school being perceived as the "hub" of the community.

▼ *Make the Parent Center accessible to other parent groups.* If parent groups (band, music, athletics) need a place to meet, suggest that they use the Parent Center when it is not being used for other activities. This will help to develop a sense of ownership among all parents and may encourage these parents to participate in other activities sponsored by the center.

Assuring "Smooth Transitions" to New Schools or School Levels

Tool 4.2.7a

Educators spend a tremendous amount of time preparing students for new experiences. They assess their readiness and make plans to capitalize on their current knowledge, skills, and attitudes. They also work diligently to prevent problems from arising that could have been anticipated and avoided. Think of all the work involved in introducing new kindergarten students to school and how diligently fifth and eighth grade teachers work to prepare their students for their middle and high school years. In some schools, elaborate plans are also in place for introducing new students to the school. Wouldn't it be even more beneficial if these efforts were augmented by a plan to help parents assist their children with these same transitions? The following process enables educators to identify and implement strategies designed specifically to help parents assure that their child's transition is a smooth and positive one.

Reflect

In grade level groups, brainstorm what is currently being done to prepare the following groups of parents for new experiences and to assist them in helping their child make the necessary adjustments.

- Parents new to the school or community
- Parents whose children are entering a new grade level at the same school
- Parents whose children will be leaving the current school to enter another school level (intermediate school, middle school, junior high, or high school)

Tools 4.2.8b is a form that can be used to list ideas generated. Share the grade level group ideas with the total faculty. Are there other schoolwide efforts that have not been included? If so, add them to the list. Review the lists generated during the brainstorming session. Assess the effectiveness of the current strategies by considering the following:

- Who is currently responsible for helping "new" parents? Is it a few faculty members or everyone? Who should be involved?
- Are efforts consistent throughout the school? Should they be? Should some be consistent and others differ according to the grade level of the child?
- Do all faculty members and office personnel know the processes and procedures that are currently in place? Do they assure that current practices are implemented as planned?
- Are all affected parents aware of the processes and procedures that are in place?
- Are parents currently involved in helping other parents make transitions?

Project

What is needed to make the transitions smoother for each of these groups? As part of the brainstorming process, consider the same critical components that guide planning for students: *readiness, knowledge, skills, and attitudes.* Remember to build upon the strengths of processes and procedures already in place. Brainstorm with grade level groups of faculty members and list ideas on the form provided by Tool 4.2.8c. Grade levels are important at this point since parents at each grade level may have different needs.

Tool 4.2.7a

Connect
Talk with educators at other affected grades or school levels. Gather information about what is expected of students and parents. Ask school personnel to identify parents who would be willing to meet to discuss issues they faced as their children made the transitions between elementary and middle or middle and high school levels.

Prioritize
Determine what is needed most: 1) at each grade level, 2) at important transition years, and 3) for the total school. Once priorities have been established, decide if it would be helpful to ask parents to provide some input or to help in planning the most appropriate strategies to address the priorities. Identify any other resources that may be needed.

Develop a Plan
Brainstorm grade level and schoolwide strategies for each priority and determine which offer the greatest potential benefits. Select one or two to implement *this year* at each grade level. As a total faculty, select one or two that could be accomplished on a schoolwide basis. Establish a timeline and assign responsibilities. Each faculty member should contribute so that this plan does not become "more work" for an individual or a committee. This tool is, after all, designed to help the faculty as well as the parents.

Implement the Plan
Secure resources, develop the necessary materials (letters, forms, certificates), hold meetings with parents (if they are included in the plan), and put the plan into action. Then watch the effort that is being spent pay dividends.

Evaluate and Revise
Collect information that will help determine which strategies are working best and which need to be revised in the future. There are a variety of ways to collect this information:
- Keep a file for notes or comments from parents. Include notes of any successes or problems encountered in implementing the plan.
- Develop a short survey or conduct telephone interviews with a sampling of parents to get their feedback. Parent volunteers can actually make the calls.
- Ask a group of parents who are new to the school or grade level to meet with you to discuss their experiences and to help plan future efforts.

After the first year, meet as a grade level to share the data that has been collected. Celebrate successes and rethink any strategies that could be improved.

Transitions
Helping Parents Help Their Child

Tool 4.2.7b

Current Practices for Parents Who are...

Entering a new grade level	New to the school and/or the community	Preparing for a new school level

Transitions
Helping Parents Help Their Child

Tool 4.2.7c

New Practices to Strengthen Parent *Readiness, Knowledge, Skills,* and *Attitudes* . . .

Entering a new grade level	New to the school and/or the community	Preparing for a new school level

Ideas for Helping Parents and Students Make Smooth Transitions

In every school there are formal and informal strategies for making new students and their families feel welcome. The following ideas have been shared by schools that have made this an important priority.

Graduating Parents' Night
"Preparing Your Eighth Grader for High School"

Before the end of the eighth grade school year, the combined faculties at one middle school and one high school invite parents to a meeting at the familiar middle school. During this meeting, they share information about differences in expectations for middle school and high school students, how middle school teachers have worked with their children to prepare them for the transition, and what they could do during the summer to continue the preparation. Information is also provided about grading policies, attendance policies; the importance of involvement in extra-curricular activities at the high school level; the types of sports, clubs, and academic activities available to students; and the role of guidance counselors and deans. At this meeting, parents are invited to a New Parents' Night at the beginning of the school year to become more comfortable with the school and to get to know other parents.

New Parents' Night

At one high school, parents of incoming ninth graders are invited to attend an evening filled with information and fun. Invitations are mailed to parents that include the traditional time, place, and purpose as well as cleverly described hints about what they can learn that will help them "stay two steps ahead" of their incoming freshmen. Food and drawings for dinners at local restaurants are also built in as enticements to get parents in the door.

Welcoming Lunch with the Principal

Once a month, the principal at one middle school invites parents new to the school for lunch. Parents sign up for the luncheon as they enroll their child in the school. Invitations are sent out a week before the luncheon to serve as a reminder and to provide the time and location of the luncheon. A table is set in the school cafeteria with a "Parent Luncheon" sign in clear view. Teachers of the parents' students are asked to join the luncheon or to stop by and say hello. According to this principal, "Parents need to see how we operate, how students dress and interact with each other, and how we monitor behavior. Where else can you see all of that but in the cafeteria!" The principal's other goals for the luncheon are to answer parents' questions about the school, communicate expectations, and open the door to future communication.

Ice Cream Social

An elementary school invites parents and students who are "new" to the school to an ice cream social that is held on a monthly basis. Teachers who have new students in their classrooms are also invited to attend. As part of this "informal" meeting, parents are given special information sheets and are encouraged to sign up for classroom and schoolwide activities. Some are even asked to help with future "Ice Cream Socials" as a way to meet others new to the community.

Tool 4.2.7d

Parent to Parent Preschool Networking

Parents zoned for one school in Charlotte-Mecklenberg, North Carolina, have realized the importance of sending their children to school ready to handle the academic and social challenges of kindergarten.* Parent leaders in the community work with school administrators to identify families in the school zone who have preschool aged children. The parents then contact these families to invite them to participate in a *Preschool Play Group*. As parents and children participate in the playgroup, they get to know each other, have opportunities to learn about the school, and overcome fears about the transition from home to school. As the *Play Group* parents share leadership roles in planning their children's activities, they are also networking and preparing to assume similar roles at the elementary school. According to a parent who has been instrumental in developing this program, involvement has grown significantly over the last several years and some parents who thought they wanted their children to attend private schools have reconsidered that choice as a result of their involvement in the playgroup.

*Thank you to Allison Warren, a parent volunteer at
Selwyn Elementary School, Charlotte-Mecklenburg, South Carolina

Plan 4.3
Developing and Maintaining Relationships

Establishing relationships with parents and community members that will withstand the test of time and inevitable conflicts requires more than making acquaintances. The key to long term supportive relationships is nurturing, one family at a time. This nurturing can take many shapes. At the simplest level, educators nurture relationships with parents each time they open doors for visitors. Parents or caregivers who visit the school or volunteer on a regular basis develop a greater understanding and appreciation of what is taking place at school. When they know educators on a personal level, they are more likely to initiate dialogue, seek help when problems arise, or offer their talents or services.

Many parents, however, are fearful of the school environment and typically do little more than is required of them. For these parents, many of whom are struggling with survival issues, nurturing relationships is more complicated. It may involve providing food and transportation or establishing contacts with social service agencies. When their basic needs are met, these families are better able to recognize educators' willingness to help them with the problems they are facing. In reflecting upon a one year grant funded literacy program for homeless families, McGee (1996) concluded that "our most important discovery was that human relationships must precede academic pursuits. Only if our parents trust and believe in us do we stand a chance of teaching them anything. To earn their trust, we had to accept them for who they were" (p. 32). Acceptance took many forms: providing food when it was apparent that nutrition was a critical issue for these parents and their children, assuring predictability in their unpredictable world, making opportunities to interact with educators fun and nonthreatening, and overlooking behaviors that did not align with educators' expectations.

Nurturing also means meeting the needs of families who are not at a survival level, but who may not be actively involved in the school. For these parents, it may require providing educational or dialogue sessions for those who are trying to cope with their child's academic, social, or behavioral problems. In most cases, it revolves around establishing networks among parents to allow those who have established positive and productive relationships to help their peers who do not feel the same sense of belonging at school.

This plan proposes that educators develop strategies for creating collaborative relationships in an atmosphere that is positive, open, and guided by principles that all understand. At the same time, it also focuses on making the school the "hub" of the community by expanding relationships, building a network of parent support for the school and for each other, and serving as a linkage with community services when the need arises.

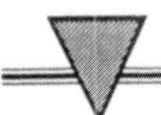

- Lay the foundation for a collaborative relationship. Foundations for relationships, like those for stable buildings, must be strong enough to withstand the obstacles that will inevitably arise. What many schools have found is that clear expectations for how all interpersonal encounters will be experienced; a common purpose; open, honest dialogue; and trust are basic elements in developing this foundation. Without any one of these, the likelihood of maintaining mutually supportive relationships is greatly diminished. The *Rules We Live By* (Tool 1.2.5a) will be useful in articulating desired expectations. Plan 3.1 may also be helpful for promoting dialogue.

- Develop strategies to form networks of support for students, parents, and educators. According to Winter (1994) parents in today's society cannot successfully raise their children in isolation. They never have. Parents have always talked to each other, shared concerns, and developed "united fronts" in dealing with their children's desires and behaviors. However, in our busy, transient, and media-controlled world, this has become more difficult for families to do on their own. Many parents, especially in low income areas, move frequently and are not able to establish the types of relationships that allow this sharing. Even the most stable families find their children, particularly once they have reached adolescence, traveling in circles they know nothing about. They simply cannot know the parents of all their child's friends. This is why some schools and communities have created parent networks. They are a way to overcome the "disconnectedness" many parents feel in dealing with their children. At the same time, they are a means for parents to help each other and themselves enhance their parenting skills and their relationships with their children. Parent networks range from telephone trees (Tool 3.2.3) to formalized programs. There are as many types of networks as there are needs to be met through encouraging parents to get to know one another and to work together for a common purpose. See Tool 4.3.1 for ideas to promote parent networking.

- Broaden the focus of networking to include social service agencies within the community. Researchers have shown that schools, families, and communities are far more effective when working together than when operating in isolation. Who is in a better position to link children and their families with the services they need? A major premise of this book is that families should be directly involved in the education of their children. When circumstances get in the way of parents being able to work with their children, school personnel may be their only resource. Why not involve the parent-teacher organization or interested community members in serving as a liaison between the school and local social service or support agencies? Tool 4.3.2 provides guidelines for assuring success in connecting parents and families with community agencies and services.

- Include local businesses in the network. According to Richard Riley, U. S. Secretary of Education, "The support of business is crucial to improving education in America. When businesses get involved, schools get better and our nation's prosperity is insured." When educators and business representatives work side by side to improve opportunities for children, everyone benefits. Educational experiences and opportunities for students are the primary benefit. At the same time, school-business partnerships provide the business sector with meaningful opportunities to share their talents and resources. As they work together, educators and business representatives generally develop relationships that extend far beyond their roles in the partnership. When they combine their talents and energy, school-business partners often develop programs and activities that are uniquely suited for the local community and are more exciting and motivating than either could have provided on their own. Take advantage of the opportunity and look beyond typical volunteering in working with businesses. Tools 4.3.3a and 4.3.3b provide suggestions for structuring school-business partnerships. Tool 4.3.4 includes a variety of activities that have resulted from school-business partnerships.

- Why not make the school the hub of every community? Family oriented events can help even the most reluctant parents view the school as a nonthreatening and enjoyable place. Schools that provide families with needed assistance, from counseling to recreation, often find that they can break down barriers and stimulate participation among the most resistant families. Many educators are surprised to find how willing parents are to help their children once they overcome their fear of entering an educational environment. Tool 4.3.5 includes several ideas that schools have used to create the feeling that the school is an integral part of the community.

- While we do not like to dwell on "what ifs" in education, we do need to be prepared when tragic circumstances occur. Building relationships means that school personnel must be there for students, parents, and community members in their time of need. Are there any plans in place to help a student whose parent has died? To help a frightened or grieving parent whose child has been hurt or killed in an accident? To help the entire student body cope with the suicide or death of a peer? Tool 4.3.6 provides guidelines to consider in developing a crisis intervention plan.

- Celebrate accomplishments. Make the recognition of students, parents, community members, and business representatives a high priority. Educators know how important it is to acknowledge and recognize their students' achievements and contributions. They are also acutely aware of focusing on character, citizenship, cooperation, and doing one's best as well as accomplishments and winning. In most schools, they are making a concerted effort to expand schoolwide and classroom recognition beyond the twenty to thirty percent of the student population who are academically, athletically, musically, or artistically talented and traditionally receive all of the honors. Recognizing and celebrating the accomplishments, contributions, and efforts of parents, community members, and business partners is equally important. It lets the givers know that their contributions are truly appreciated. See Tool 4.3.7 for a variety of recognition strategies for each of these groups that have been used successfully by schools across the country. See Tool 6.2.11 for recognition strategies for school volunteers.

Other Possibilities . . .

Parent Networking Strategies

Tool 4.3.1

The Community Lifelines Project
Frank Barry, director of Community Lifelines, one of nine demonstration projects funded by the National Center on Child Abuse and Neglect, describes several parent networks that have been established through Community Lifelines. In one project, part-time parent volunteers in three schools invited parents into the schools each afternoon for coffee and for the opportunity to get to know one another. Slowly but surely, the parent partners encouraged reluctant parents to attend and began to see results far beyond what they had initially intended. Parents at one school became upset by how their children interacted on the playground and developed strategies for working with the teachers to change the children's behavior. At another school, parents have helped each other with their own literacy and parenting needs. Another parent group organized after school activities for children who were unsupervised after school. Yet another group of families have been working together on the issue of adolescent drug abuse. As the director of the project pointed out, "it can be very painful to share worries about your children in a small town where everybody knows everybody else. But that's exactly what they're doing. This group is meeting a real need" (Winter, 1994, p. 13).

Community Lifelines Radio Spots
Community Lifelines uses public service announcements to develop networks for families. "We Can Help!" is the title of one series that provides parents with suggestions for coping with the difficulties of parenting and helping them with their parenting skills. A one minute message closing with "Smart people, successful parents - get help when they need it" provides a variety of parenting tips. Some of the tips help parents handle frustration in critical moments, such as asking a neighbor to watch a child for a half hour to allow the parent to cool off. Others simply encourage effective parenting, such as "hug your children to let them know you think they're special and you love them absolutely." Another spot, called "We're Part of the Solution" asks business people, older members of the community, and families without children to take small actions to help others with their parenting. Providing books, crayons, or games in offices; taking a child for a walk, calling a parent to acknowledge something a child has done well are some of the tips this spot suggests (Winter, 1994, pp. 12-13).

Grade Level Parent Dinners
In one school district a dinner was held for parents of middle and high school students by grade level. The purpose was not to share any school information. It was simply to provide a way for parents to get to know each other well enough in an informal setting that they might be willing to call each other if their children wanted to go somewhere together or spend the night at each other's homes. This plan was devised to help parents maintain more control of their teenagers--as was instituted at the request of a parent committee.

Tool 4.3.1

Parent to Parent Informal Networking

Some parents do not want to be a part of a formal committee or group. They are willing, however, to work with another parent on a one-on-one basis. Once schools identify these parents who are willing to network on an as needed basis, all that is needed is someone to coordinate their activities. This could be a Spanish speaking parent who would be willing to help another parent overcome a language barrier. It could be another who knows social service agencies and could help direct a parent who is too intimidated to talk to school personnel. Parents who have lived through and overcome problems with adolescents are often willing to help others who are in the midst of behavior, drug, alcohol, or pregnancy crises.

Father-son Breakfasts and Man-to-Man Workshops

These are two of many approaches to networking supported by The National Network of Partnership-2000 Schools at Johns Hopkins University. In several Baltimore, Maryland, schools grandfathers, fathers, uncles are invited to attend sessions that include guest speakers and home-cooked food. The purpose is to encourage fathers to become more involved at the school and in their child's education and community life (Sanders, 1996).

Pops on Patrol

Another strategy of the Baltimore Schools is a program at one elementary school where the action team started a volunteer program for grandparents to help in achieving the school's goal of becoming more pleasant, productive, and school. Six grandfathers and grandmothers donned hats and vests and patrolled the school each morning and afternoon. They greeted students, encouraged their attendance and punctuality, and provided a sense of security as students walked to school. School personnel also felt that the grandparents provided excellent role models for some of their younger parents (Sanders, 1996).

Computer Networking

In this day of computer networking, some schools are establishing links between classrooms and parents, community members, businesses, and university programs. At one university, students in an undergraduate class are paired with students in an elementary classroom as writing mentors. The elementary students send their articles or stories to the university students who, in turn, provide feedback and ideas. At other schools, parents serve as mentors for individual students or as resources for classes on special topics. This helps parents and community members get to know students while never having to leave their offices or interrupt their busy schedules. The ideal has been realized in one new residential community in North Carolina in which every new home is built with a computer already connected to the school! The system is in place for each family to network with the school and each other.

Guidelines for Connecting Parents and Families with Agencies and Services

Tool 4.3.2

▼ Appoint or hire a parent or community member to take responsibility for making the appropriate connections. This person could work with the school social worker or nurse on small problems. If there are a large number of families with these types of needs, a committee could be used to carry out some of the duties. It would be critical, however, for one person to assure that contacts have been made and that positive relationships are being established.

▼ Establish a working relationship with key social service agencies. Once the parent volunteer has made the initial connection, invite them to the school. Share the unique socioeconomic conditions of the school population as well as past problems that might have been handled more productively if the school and the agency had been able to work as a team with the student, the parent, or the family. At the same time, find out how the school can enhance the work of the agency. Could referral procedures be improved? Could the parent-teacher organization be of assistance, particularly with services provided to the school community?

▼ Consider designating an office to the parent volunteer. A desk and a telephone would be essential. Having a place to keep records, to make the telephone calls necessary to establish relationships, and to create needed materials is a necessary expense.

▼ Develop a system for monitoring school-social service agency teamwork. Keeping records of what has been accomplished as the school and the social service agencies work together is imperative. As new parent volunteers assume leadership roles, they can replicate or build upon what has taken place as they work with new families. They can also develop strategies for overcoming obstacles.

▼ Celebrate accomplishments. At the end of each school year, make an effort to recognize the contributions of the social service agencies and the parent volunteers. They are the backbone of this endeavor that enhances both students and the school. A breakfast, luncheon, or ceremony are well worth all the hours these individuals have contributed to the well-being of students and their families.

What Educators and Business Leaders Can Do to Promote Effective Partnerships

Tool 4.3.3a

Educators	Both	Business Leaders
• Secure commitment of the faculty and staff to participate in the partnership. • Clearly articulate school-wide needs. • Develop strategies for working effectively with business partners--and for making them feel welcome and comfortable at the school. • Plan ways to link business employees to students or student activities as early as possible. • Develop meaningful ways for employees to participate in school activities. • Identify a variety of ways to recognize the contributions of the business employees.	• Identify a coordinator at each site who has the responsibility for overseeing the partnership and assuring that it is achieving its goals. • Communicate regularly. • Share needs (school) and available resources (business). • Assess options and decide upon those that are mutually beneficial. • Develop plans with goals, objectives, activities, and timelines. • Specify dates for major activities. • Develop a contract that specifies what each partners will accomplish. Post at each site. • Translate the commitment to action--begin activities as early as possible and maintain momentum. • Celebrate the partnership.	• Secure commitment of employees to participate in the partnership. • Determine what type and amount of resources (personnel, time, money, or matierials) can be donated to the partnership. • Allow employees to volunteer at the school during work hours. • Develop schedules to accommodate employee and student needs.

Be aware of possible problem areas:
  1) inadequate planning (haphazard efforts that leave both parties unclear about activities, roles, and responsibilities or that result in too many volunteers at one time)
  2) overzealous planning--trying more than can be accomplished successfully
  3) lack of buy in and real commitment from educators or employers
  4) allowing a slump or low period to squelch enthusiasm

Criteria for Successful School and Business Partnerships

Tool 4.3.3b

- *Concern for public relations*

- *Desire to build lasting relationships throughout the community*

- *Awareness of the expectations of the partnership*

- *Careful consideration of potential benefits and sacrifices*

- *Awareness of what the partnership has to offer both parties--and students*

- *Commitment to fulfilling responsibilities of the partnership*

- *Willingness to make the coordination of partnership activities a formal work responsibility, not an after hours "add on"*

- *Enthusiasm*

- *A sense of humor*

- *Energy to maintain momentum or persevere if the partnership hits a slump*

- *Sprit of adventure and involvement*

- *Sense of responsibility*

School and Business Partnerships
One School System's Ideas for What Each Can Provide

Tool 4.3.4

Educators	Business Partners
• Use of the school facility for partner functions • Artwork displays • Performances • Treats for their partners • Cards to partners or specific employees on special occasions • School banners	• Job shadowing • Mentoring • Field trips • Classroom visits • Computer equipment • Student incentives • Student awards • Classroom and office supplies • Personnel to assist at school events • Landscaping • Teacher appreciation awards • Recycling projects • In-service programs • Judges for student contests • Bus transportation to special events • Purchase of playground equipment • Publishing of student handbooks, annuals, or other publications • Medical screening (e.g., cholesterol) • Stress management workshop for faculty members • Free videos for classroom use • Speakers' bureau • Trips • Technical support

Thank you to Scott Bacon, Knox County Schools, Knoxville, Tennessee

Strategies for Making the School The Hub of the Community

Tool 4.3.5

School-Based Family Counseling

Many families, particularly those with adolescent children, would seek the advice of counselors, but cannot afford the luxury. Some schools have asked guidance counselors or counselors within the community to hold sessions throughout the year on topics such as parenting skills, parent-child relationships, dealing with adolescence, recognizing warning signs of drug or alcohol abuse or gang membership, dealing with stress, time management, and other issues facing today's families.

Parent Help Sessions

Some schools are surveying parents to find out what topics they would seek help with if given the opportunity. Then they are holding sessions on the topics of greatest interest. As a result of a survey, teachers at one school are taking one evening during each grading period (rotating among teachers at each grade level) to teach parents the skills they need to help their children with upcoming assignments.

World of Work Courses

Many parents are seeking advancement in their own workplaces which often requires additional training after work hours. At the same time, previous generational welfare families are now seeking preparation for entry into the work force. Why not use the school to offer some of these training sessions? They could be university or technical school courses or more informal sessions on topics such as "Preparing for Interviews" or "Work Habits of Successful Employees." While the college level courses may be costly, others may be able to be provided by community members who want to help the unemployed or underemployed improve their work lives. Members of civic organizations are often willing to lead sessions such as these.

Family-Oriented Events

Picnics, bazaars, Fun Fairs, bingo, parent-child athletic events, and family night dinners (at a minimal cost) are a few ideas schools have used to encourage parents and their children to spend time together. They also have an opportunity to get to know educators on an informal basis as they participate in something for their family.

Family Night Dances

Why not use the schools as a vehicle for educators and parents to have some fun? Learning unfamiliar dances puts educators and parents on an equal footing in an atmosphere that is uplifting and enjoyable. Learning traditional ballroom dances, line dances, or country and western steps might even be fun for their children! Evenings where parents and children have a place to enjoy themselves at no cost (or very little cost, if necessary) are enticing to most families.

Tool 4.3.5

Parent Library
In some schools, the library sets aside a special section for parents or care givers. Parents are encouraged to drop by and check out books on parenting just as they would at the public library. At one school, the librarian also posts lists of books that are particularly interesting and appropriate for each grade level and encourages parents to read them to their children.

Parent Resource Center
Several schools have developed parent resource centers that house information about community agencies, social services, health services, and employment services. Some also have this information on computer disks so that parents can check out a disk and take it home to study. School personnel who have made an effort to identify appropriate resources for their school community and to establish working relationships with the providers can give families valuable support in seeking the resources they need.

Recreation Activities
Schools and churches are realizing the need within their communities to use their recreational facilities for adult physical fitness and recreation when they are not being used for their main purposes. When the gym is not in use, why not allow parents to have basketball leagues, workout sessions, or an indoor track? Outdoor facilities could also be used.

Computer Linkages
Is it possible to provide linkages to homes that have computer e-mail and internet capacity? Why not involve technologically talented parents and community members is looking into creative ways to link the school community?

Craft Activities or "Make and Take" Classes
Helping families create crafts or games to use for decoration or for playing with their child provides a number of benefits for parents as well as educators. First, it gives parents an opportunity to make something rather than having to purchase it, which saves money and time and builds confidence in one's creative abilities. Second, it provides a reason for parents to get together, which helps them get to know one another on an informal basis. Third, it allows parents to get to know teachers in a fun, nonacademic setting. When teachers and parents are learning or doing something together, it creates a sense of being in the same boat which can be carried into classroom interactions.

Partnerships for Students Activities
In one school system, a "Partnerships for Students Week" is held each year to encourage parents and community members to visit the school or to participate in school activities. Activities include receptions for representatives from local businesses, inviting community members and business leaders in the community to have lunch with teachers and students, having students write thank you notes to area businesses and community members that have supported the school during the school year.

Tool 4.3.6

Guidelines for Supporting Members of
The School Community During a Crisis

▼ Designate a faculty member who will have the responsibility for initiating crisis intervention activities. This could be one individual or a committee or team, but one person should be in charge. It is to this person all information about a crisis should be directed. If a committee or team has been set up to handle the crisis, the designee would call the committee members to initiate the process. In many schools, the principal is the official designee who works with a Crisis Intervention Team, which can include parent volunteers.

▼ Determine what assistance is to be provided. While this will differ with each situation, the Crisis Intervention Team will determine what the needs are and how they are to be handled. The following are a list of services that might be helpful:
- Notify friends, relatives, or other families in the school community
- Deal with the press
- Arrange for or provide: transportation, food, babysitting, shopping, etc.
- Contact agencies for additional support
- Visit the hospital
- Help with arrangements if there are no family members to assist
- Talk or be available to talk

▼ Determine what follow-up is needed. Crisis intervention is not a one time process. Develop procedures that identify how the committee or team will assure that the family's needs are met after the initial crisis is over.

One Family's Story

This is a story that could be told in every community in our country. The characters might be different, but the situation is all too familiar. Two days before Thanksgiving, a young father died unexpectedly. His wife and two sons, seven and ten years old, were in shock as any family would have been. While family and friends were focused on helping them through their loss, it was the ten year old who thought to notify the schools. Once they were alerted to the tragedy, teachers at each of the boys' schools called daily to talk to the children, the faculties sent home made food, and the guidance counselors scheduled meetings with the children to help them cope with their loss. The counselor also talked with the mother about how important it was for her and her sons to go through the steps of the grieving process. The teachers and counselors assured the family that they would be there for them in the months to follow--and they were. All of the family members were amazed at how caring the faculties at these two schools were. While we are always concerned about situations such as this one, do we always act upon our concern as these educators did? As the old adage goes, "Actions speak louder than words." This school's efforts were noticed and appreciated by more than the family they were trying to help.

Tool 4.3.7

Recognizing and Celebrating Accomplishments

Recognizing the accomplishments of "more than the few top students"...

A Central Bulletin Board or wall space used to highlight students' accomplishments related to character development, citizenship, or contributions to the school
When parents enter the school, the display should grab the parents' attention.

A school-wide effort to highlight a student each day who did something kind or special
Use parent, community member, or business volunteers to write a note to alert parents of their child's recognition.

Special rewards or events for students when they have worked to achieve a challenging goal
(One school provided a special dance for high achievement on the state achievement test. Smaller groups are often rewarded with certificates, rewards, lunches, or parties.)
Involve parents in the celebration and include the success in the parent newsletter.

"Be Prepared" awards for students who attend class fully prepared to learn each day of the month. Each student who wins a monthly award is eligible for a drawing for 20 students to receive awards donated by community organizations and businesses.
As part of beginning of the year activities, such as Open House or Parent Night, be sure to alert parents to the effort being made to encourage students to do their homework and to come to class prepared to learn. Let them know some of the exciting rewards that will be given during the year.

Recognizing team efforts
Invite all the parents of the team members to enjoy the celebration. This may be the first time they have met each other and may be a good way to develop parent to parent relationships.

"Most improved student or the month" and/or "Citizen of the month" for each class, grade level, or school
Invite parents to the school when students are recognized either individually or in small groups.

Tool 4.3.7

Appropriate awards for student improvement rather than for As and Bs
(One school recognized those students who have improved by
40 percent, 30 percent, 20 percent, and so on.)
*Notes to parents or invitations to celebrations make these events even more
special to the students and the families.*

Awards for dress and courtesy standards
Be sure that parents realize that their efforts in these areas are noticed!

Student birthday club
*This may be the only recognition some children receive. Be sure their parents realize
the school is doing something to recognize each child each year!*

Display of student work in the main office
*The display should be in an area visible to parents and community members.
It is an opportunity to share outcomes of the school's various programs.*

Display of student work (drawings, paintings, photographs, writing, projects) on
storefronts, in parks, and on community education bulletin boards
*This is another opportunity to share outcomes of the school's various programs --
and to spark community interest in what students are achieving.*

Varying ways to celebrate students' successes . . .

Academic letters, like athletic letters, for consistent honor roll achievements
*Banquets, receptions, or special meetings make parents as much a part of students'
receiving academic letters as they are when their students earn athletic letters.*

A "Hall of Fame" complete with photographs of meritorious students.
Let students decide on the categories. Academic, citizenship, willingness to help others,
improvement, conservation, fundraising, safety, health, and recycling achievements are
just a few examples. Have students write a one page paper to nominate their peers.
*Make a ceremony out of adding students' pictures to the wall,
inviting parents, community leaders, and business representatives.*

Tool 4.3.7

Inclusion of students' honors in the monthly newsletter to parents
*A "Did You Know..." column allows space for highlighting a variety
of student achievements in addition to those generally announced.*

Banquets to recognize school "pacesetters," with transportation
provided to the front door of the school in a limousine
Parents love to be a part of a surprise!

Copies of yearbooks, school newspapers, and literary magazines offered to
doctors and dentists for display in their waiting rooms to alert
community members to students' accomplishments
Parents also love to see their children's accomplishments "in print."

Initiating recognition programs as incentives for students who are not currently being recognized...

Goal Achievement Awards Program involves all students in setting personal goals
and writing a contract with specified outcomes, standards, and timelines. Personal goals
should be challenging and important to each student--
which also places them on an even playing field. Celebrate the
achievement of the goals as well as steps toward achieving them!
Involve parents in the goal setting process and in helping their child achieve the goals.

An academic incentive program, awarding students color-coded identification cards
based on grades during the preceding quarter, for which they receive corresponding
privileges (free admission to all school activities, reserved parking, a full day of
independent study, a free coke) encourages involvement as well as academic success
*When parents understand incentive programs, they can encourage and reinforce
students' efforts to achieve their goals.*

A student incentive program in which fifteen students per grading period
can win $10.00 each for excellent citizenship, honor roll status, and no
discipline referrals, with students having perfect attendance and no tardies
receiving free certificates from local restaurants or stores
These are incentives most parents will help their children achieve.

Tool 4.3.7

A pizza and soft drink lunch or an ice cream sundae with the principal
program for students who are nominated by their teachers for:
- good behavior and academic performance
- making significant academic improvement
- exhibiting good citizenship
- doing something special for someone else

(Large schools often hold a lottery to select
a given number of students each month.)
*Parents should be alerted to the child's selection
so they can talk about the special lunch that evening.*

A student of the month program with students chosen by teachers getting a special T-shirt
and certificate and having their pictures taken for the display case
*Students will tell their parents about the pictures in the display case. Why not
let them know before the students are told so they can be part of the celebration?*

Poster Contests, Bulletin Board Contests, and Honor Roll Contests
Involve parents in judging and displaying student work or honors.

Recognizing parent, community member, and business contributions . . .

Personal notes from the teacher of principal
Model good etiquette.

Articles in the school or parent newsletter
*Most parent groups will make this a special project.
All the school personnel must do is provide the information for the article.*

Bulletin Boards
*When children see their parents recognized for their efforts and contributions,
it helps them see the importance of doing their best and doing for others
-- not to mention making them proud.*

Special rewards or events
*Receptions, banquets, and recognition at meetings are just as
meaningful for adults as they are for children.*

Tool 4.3.7

Lunch with the principal
Invite parents each six weeks who have done something special for the school.

Principal for a Day
At one school, active parents and community members are invited to shadow the principal for a day. They attend early morning staff meetings and accompany the principal in working with faculty and students. The day selected is generally one which involves recognizing students for their accomplishments. The Principal for a Day has the honor of participating in the recognition process.

Other . . .

Design 5

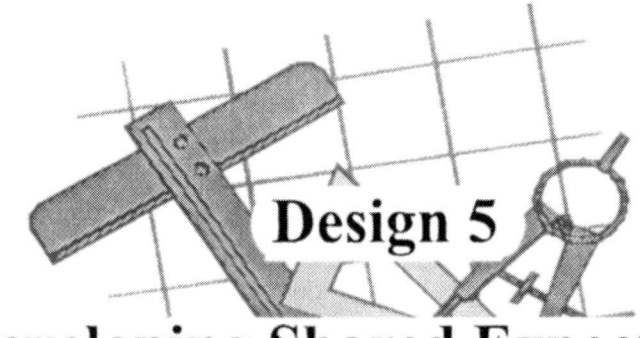

Developing Shared Expectations

> **Expectations...**
> - are visions, aspirations, and hopes--dreams for the future.
> - reflect the goals we hold for ourselves and those others hold for us.
> - guide our everyday thoughts and actions, consciously and unconsciously.
> - become a catalyst for action and basis for long range planning.
> - are critical determinants of a child's success in life.

Expectations are the force that energizes individuals and organizations to higher levels of commitment and performance. When the desires and hopes of all members of the school community are identified and articulated, they become the basis for a vision for the school's future and for long range plans to achieve the vision. Schools that work collaboratively toward a vision will undoubtedly be more successful than others working without clear direction and focus. They will be more purposeful in their day to day actions. They will reach for greater heights, individually and collectively. They will also be more likely to perceive obstacles as opportunities and "problems as our friends" (Fullan, 1993, p. 21).

Shared expectations and visions also have a direct impact on student success. The research clearly indicates that teachers' beliefs about students and their expectations for their performance affect the way they structure learning experiences and respond to students. There is also evidence to support a tendency for parents to respond in similar ways with their children. When teachers and parents hold high expectations for students, they challenge them and provide the support and encouragement needed to succeed. Without the high expectations from teachers or parents, the impetus for students to work hard is reduced. It is critical, however, that educators or parents avoid expecting more than is mentally or physically possible. A child who is struggling and unable to attain the expectation is likely to develop feelings of inadequacy and failure. When there is an awareness of holding high, but attainable expectations, extraordinarily positive results can occur. Children are stimulated to assume responsibilities and undertake challenges they might not have thought they could handle successfully. They rise to the occasion, work hard, and succeed at whatever they do--partly do to their own efforts and partly because of the support system encouraging their success.

As overlapping spheres of influence in a child's life, educators and parents who work together to communicate high expectations can also have a significant impact on children's overall growth and development (Epstein (1995). When children consistently hear the same messages and see similar behaviors being modeled by teachers, parents, and others, they are more likely to develop in ways that are consistent with those behaviors. How can they make this happen? They can collaborate to determine shared expectations and can communicate and model them. They can give their time, talents, and energy to bringing them about. In these significant ways, members of the school community can bring about a positive future for themselves and their children. In a very real sense, "It takes the whole village to raise the child."

What we hear from ...

EDUCATORS

"Look around at our fine athletic facilities--ball fields, stadium. You know what we value here. That's where the money goes." (High school teacher)

"Everything is a priority around here. We try to do it all. Any new program that comes along--we'll be on board." (Elementary school teacher)

"Most of our students really don't have any ideas about their future. No wonder they don't see the need for an education. They don't have any goals." (High school principal)

"All this planning is really exciting. Now I hope we follow through." (Middle school teacher)

PARENTS

"We need to think about what the future holds for these children. We have to prepare them for jobs that don't even exist today." (Middle school parent)

"I don't know why we need all those computers and fancy stuff. Back in my day, we didn't have all that and I learned just fine." (School Board member)

"Going through the process of creating a vision with the teachers has helped me see that we really want the same things for our students." (High school parent)

STUDENTS

"I think our school is one big 'thon.' There's a walk-a-thon, read-a-thon, and now a jump-a-thon! Sometimes I think that we're relying too much on students to raise money." (High school senior)

"Now--finally--I know I can do this! I never really thought I could." (College student)

"If I don't get a scholarship, I can't go to college. I know what courses I have to take and the grades I need to make." (10th grade student)

"I'm going to be an engineer for architectural purposes. I learned that at career day." (Second grade student)

Shared Responsibilities

In effective partnerships, *both* educators and parents, families, guardians, or caregivers take responsibility for establishing expectations and for developing strategies to achieve them. The following diagram illustrates the responsibilities that are unique to each group and those that both groups share.

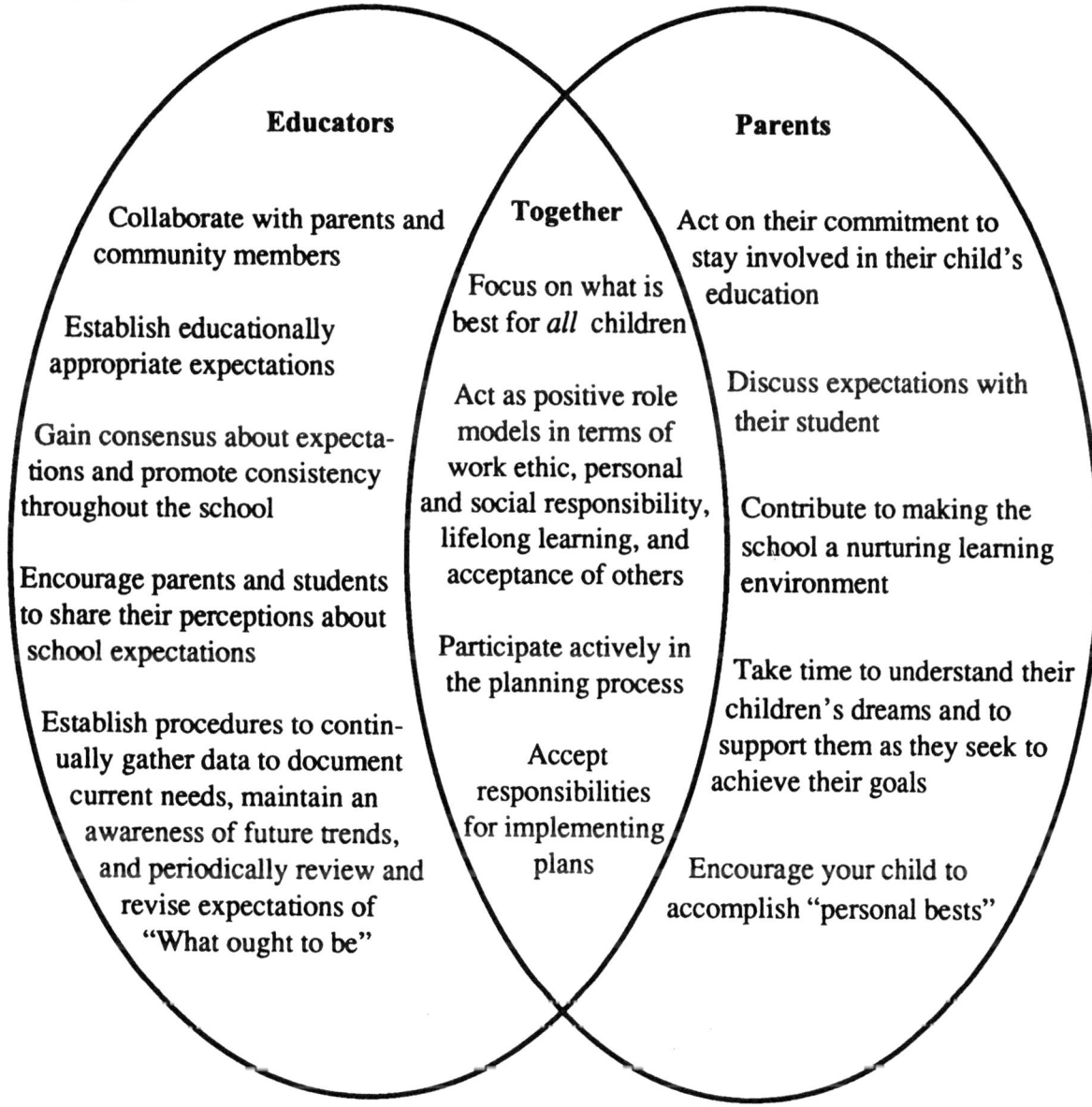

Educators

- Collaborate with parents and community members
- Establish educationally appropriate expectations
- Gain consensus about expectations and promote consistency throughout the school
- Encourage parents and students to share their perceptions about school expectations
- Establish procedures to continually gather data to document current needs, maintain an awareness of future trends, and periodically review and revise expectations of "What ought to be"

Together

- Focus on what is best for *all* children
- Act as positive role models in terms of work ethic, personal and social responsibility, lifelong learning, and acceptance of others
- Participate actively in the planning process
- Accept responsibilities for implementing plans

Parents

- Act on their commitment to stay involved in their child's education
- Discuss expectations with their student
- Contribute to making the school a nurturing learning environment
- Take time to understand their children's dreams and to support them as they seek to achieve their goals
- Encourage your child to accomplish "personal bests"

In our rapidly changing environment, it is critical to have some control over the future direction of our schools. While it is not possible to control the future, it is possible to know how the changes in our environment will impact our schools.

Bellon et al., 1993

Plans and Tools
for carrying out our responsibilities in establishing expectations and developing plans and strategies to achieve them

Plan 5.1. Understanding Current Needs: Collect, Portray, and Analyze Data

Understanding current student needs is an important first step in developing shared expectations. This plan provides guidelines for a needs assessment process that includes data collection, portrayal, and analysis. The end result of these activities will be a format and a system that will ensure easier assessments in future years.

Plan 5.2. Establish a Vision for the Future

The essence of shared expectations for the future is developing a vision for the school. This plan describes a process for establishing a vision with strategies for accomplishing the process in the most beneficial ways. Tools also address strategies for communicating the vision and accepting responsibility for achieving it.

Plan 5.3. Moving the Vision to Action Through Collaborative Long Range Planning

This plan presents a long range planning process that is collaborative and moves the vision to action. The Tools detail the important steps and provide formats and processes to build further commitment and ownership in achieving results.

Plan 5.4. Reinforcing Learning Expectations

This plan focuses on ways parents and educators can reinforce learning expectations at school and at home. Tools provide strategies for monitoring the level of optimism and expectancy for success, setting goals for student growth, and being positive role models for students.

Educator Reflection
Developing Shared Expectations

How effective are we as a faculty in collaborating with parents and community members to establish expectations for students and the school? Are we developing strategies to achieve the expectations? Are we involving parents and community members in the process? Take a few minutes to consider how frequently the following events or opportunities take place at your school. Put an "X" in the box that most closely reflects your perception.

		Often	Sometimes	Rarely
1.	Our school has a vision and/or mission that communicates current and appropriate expectations of "what ought to be."			
2.	Our school's vision and/or mission were developed with the involvement of educators, parents, community members, and students.			
3.	We collaborated on developing long range plans that will move our vision to action.			
4.	Our long range plans accommodate current and anticipated future needs.			
5.	As an educator, I am given adequate opportunities to share my opinions and provide input on school issues that are important to me.			
6.	In this school, students and parents are given ample opportunities to express their opinions about important school issues.			
7.	As educators, our day to day behaviors, actions, and decisions are consistent with our vision and mission.			
8.	School and classroom rules and policies are aligned with our vision and are monitored for positive results.			
9.	In general, everyone in the school expects success and exhibits a "can do" attitude.			
10.	Expectations for student learning and behavior are attainable, yet challenging and clearly understood by all.			
11.	Every student is encouraged and provided with needed support to work to his or her ability.			
12.	All educators and school personnel are positive role models for students.			

Plan 5.1
Understanding Current Needs:
Collect, portray, and analyze data

The goal of any effective school, home, and community partnership is to work together to make a difference in the lives of students. The first step in making this happen is to develop a clear understanding of students' needs as well as those of parents and community members. By developing a database of relevant information, partners are better able to make informed decisions about appropriate expectations for students. Shared expectations, then, are built upon a clear understanding of the current needs of the school community.

Part of determining the needs of students is understanding the numerous societal influences that place many children at a survival level. High levels of poverty, unemployment, homelessness, emotional dysfunction, tension and violence permeate many homes within our communities. In addition, a child's sense of belonging and attempts at socialization can be threatened by the high rate of mobility, diversity of cultures, isolation within neighborhoods, and contemporary family structures. As educators are aware, children must feel safe, secure, and able to think about their futures. When they are consumed with anxiety over their basic survival needs, they do not have the mental or physical energy to think beyond the present. They cannot focus on becoming self-actualized or the best that they can be--when they are unsure what tomorrow will bring. As Maslow (1943) reminds us, only healthy individuals whose basic survival and belonging needs have been met can capitalize on the present while designing their futures. It is imperative, therefore, that educators and their parent and community member partners make a conscientious effort to identify and understand the context in which students are functioning. Only then can appropriate expectations be established.

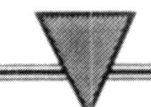

- Convene a representative group of educators and parents, if desired. Inform them about the process of data collection, portrayal, and analysis and the reasons for doing it. (See Tools 5.11 and 5.12 for visuals to use in explaining the process and the rationale for it.) This is a multi-step process requiring time and effort. It will take several sessions to complete all the tasks. The important point to convey to the participants is that once baseline information is generated, the process of updating is a much less time consuming and complex. Continue to review and update the data base on a regular basis--every three to five years.

- The first task is to identify the types of information or data that would be helpful in gaining a clear understanding of the needs of the school community. Information could relate specifically to the students and their levels of performance, but could also relate to the community in general. See Tool 5.1.3 for examples of potential data sources that are generally available to school personnel at the building and/or district level and a grid that can be used to identify the most important sources.

- Engage in fast-paced brainstorming to identify any and all possible types of relevant data. (See Tool 1.2.6 for a sample brainstorming process.) As a result of this process, develop a list of data sources that the group feels will be helpful.

- Review and assess the list. Screen the list against the following questions and follow through where appropriate.
    - Is there redundancy in the types of data identified? (Consolidate.)
    - Are some not really relevant? (Delete.) Remember to only gather information that is relevant and significant or informative to the task.
    - Is the information readily accessible? (Go for it--gather it.)
    - Are there "gaps" in the information? (Identify a way to collect it.)
    - Is there a feasible way to generate the information (through survey, focus groups, interviews)? (Do it, referring to the Plans in *Design 1--Gathering Perceptions and Collaborating on Results.*)

- Once the list of data sources is finalized, designate responsibility for physically acquiring the data. Keep in mind that some will be relatively simple (one person now has the information) and some will be more difficult to acquire (not currently collected or in the possession of more than one person). Current participants may accept responsibility for completing data collection or may prefer to enlist the help of others in gathering it. Agree upon a timeframe for completing the data collection.

- Identify ways the data should be portrayed. Charts, table, graphs are options. These visual presentations, such as the example provided by Tool 5.1.4, may be more readily understood. In developing a format such as the one illustrated in Tool 5.1.4, it is important to identify the significant groups within the student population (e.g., gender, ethnicity, grade level) and disaggregate or present the data for each group. Portraying the data for each group provides a more indepth analysis of the data, rather than one that is generalized across all groups. It is also important to set up databases in such a way that it will be easy to update with new figures each year to portray multiple years of data. The resulting longitudinal database will be extremely helpful in identifying patterns or trends that may not otherwise be apparent.

- Analyze data to determine significant findings. What is most important in the data? What do the figures or patterns indicate about each of the significant groups? About the total population? Are there specific areas that are as important as the patterns that emerge from the data? See Tool 5.1.5 for an examples of findings that have been drawn from a data base.

- Future trends are important influences on expectations and on planning efforts. School personnel need to remain in touch with the trends and needs of the larger community--locally, nationally, and globally. Tool 5.1.6 highlights trends identified by futurists as having an immediate and long range impact on students and their schools.

- Identify needs by conducting a discrepancy analysis. A discrepancy analysis is a systematic way to determine the gap between actual student performance ("what is") and the desired future state ("what ought to be"). See Tool 1.2.7 in *Design 1* for a detailed description of this process. A discrepancy analysis (comparing the current state with the desired future state) will identify specific "gaps" in student performance which indicate needs.

Other Possibilities . . .

Tool 5.1.1

Data Collection, Portrayal, and Analysis Results in . . .

a database of relevant, objective information

and

specific data that provides an accurate picture

of the needs of the school community.

Data Collection, Portrayal, and Analysis can . . .

- help us understand the numerous factors that affect our students' attitudes toward learning and their academic performance.

- lead to the identification of the "real" needs within our school community—based on facts and figures rather than intuition and subjective information.

- provide baseline data for evaluating the impact of future school improvement efforts.

- encourage collaboration and cooperation by actively engaging important school community stakeholders.

- promote a higher level of commitment to meeting the needs.

Steps in Developing A Database
(Data Collection, Portrayal, & Analysis Process)

Tool 5.1.2

Identify the types of information or data.
- Brainstorm information needed
- Objective and subjective data

Review & assess data sources.
Redundancy, Relevancy, Accessibility, Completeness, and Feasibility

Acquire the data *or* generate it.
- Persons responsible for each source
- Timeframe for data collection

Portray the data in charts, table, and/or graphs.
- Identify significant groups to disaggregate the data
  (e.g., gender, ethnicity, grade level)
- Construct longitudinal databases

Analyze data & identify significant findings.
- Patterns in the data
- Significant occurrences that may not be patterns, but are important

Identify important local, national, and global future trends.
- Community demographic changes
- Family structures
- Futurists' predictions

Conduct a discrepancy analysis to identify needs.
"What is" vs. "What ought to be"

Goals are what fill the gaps.

Potential Data Sources

Tool 5.1.3

Student data could include:
Enrollment figures
Profiles of at-risk students
Numbers of students living in homes where English is the second language
Numbers on free and reduced lunch
Numbers who are gifted and talented
Numbers who have had successful prekindergarten experiences
Numbers living in homeless situations or group homes
Attendance rates
Graduation rate
Grades
Discipline referrals
Test scores
Post secondary success
QSL (Quality of School Life) or other School Satisfaction Studies

System data could include:
Per pupil expenditures
State Department of Education "Report Cards"
Alcohol and Drug Surveys
Pregnancy rates

Community information could include:
Designbook parent and community member survey information
Percentage of unemployment in the local area or families in various SES categories
Local employment opportunities
Real estate projections
Mobility rate
Recent surveys or questionnaires from community agencies which provide information about opinions and are considered expressed needs.

Potential Sources of Data Grid					
Data Source	Objective	Subjective	Readily accessible	Requires effort, but would be helpful

The ultimate questions to evaluate the quality of the data sources identified:

- After we collect and portray all this information, will we have a full understanding of the influences that affect our students and their prospects for success in school?

- Do we have information about current as well as future needs?

Data Portrayal:
Longitudinal and Disaggregated

Tool 5.1.4

Data become more informative when tracked for several years. The long-term portrayal becomes very significant in helping identify trends and new influences. The following example illustrates a longitudinal portrayal.

ELEMENTARY
Grade 3 Statewide Testing Results

		Norm Referenced						Criterion Referenced		
Stanine	Year	Vocab	Comp.	L Mech	L Exp.	WAnaly	Spell	Domains	Non Mastery	Partial Mastery	Mastery
								Mechanics			
1	95	11%	9%	15%	4%	13%	13%	95	26%	34%	40%
	96	7%	7%	9%	7%	12%	12%	96	16%	42%	42%
	97	12%	7%	12%	12%	14%	10%	97	12%	19%	69%
	98							98			
2	95	7%	2%	7%	13%	13%	13%	Lang Use			
	96	7%	2%	2%	5%	2%	7%	95	25%	40%	35%
	97	7%	7%	2%	5%	10%	10%	96	14%	33%	52%
	98							97	17%	17%	67%
								98			
3	95	17%	13%	33%	19%	22%	22%				
	96	12%	2%	26%	16%	7%	19%	Sentence			
	97	5%	10%	10%	17%	7%	14%	Paragraph			
	98							95	29%	35%	35%
								96	19%	29%	52%
4	95	20%	17%	24%	26%	13%	13%	97	17%	31%	52%
	96	9%	19%	26%	16%	14%	14%	98			
	97	21%	14%	21%	7%	17%	19%				
	98							Spell			
								Word Id			
5	95	15%	28%	4%	15%	11%	15%	95	13%	32%	55%
	96	26%	19%	14%	21%	23%	12%	96	12%	9%	79%
	97	17%	12%	29%	21%	24%	12%	97	10%	24%	67%
	98							98			
6	95	17%	15%	13%	15%	15%	13%	Comp			
	96	16%	19%	16%	14%	21%	21%	95	24%	26%	50%
	97	14%	29%	10%	21%	10%	24%	96	21%	14%	64%
	98							97	19%	21%	60%
								98			
7	95	13%	11%	4%	4%	7%	7%				
	96	19%	14%	2%	9%	7%	12%	Ref			
	97	21%	12%	12%	10%	2%	7%	Study			
	98							95	13%	20%	67%
								96	10%	14%	76%
8	95	0%	4%	0%	4%	4%	2%	97	5%	19%	76%
	96	2%	7%	5%	5%	7%	5%	98			
	97	2%	2%	5%	7%	7%	2%				
	98										

Data are also more descriptive when disaggregated by significant groups within the school community. The chart above is an example of disaggregated data analysis. It looks at third grade students' scores rather than the total school population. This analysis may be even more meaningful if it were disaggregated by gender, ethnicity, or other significant subcategories.

Identifying Significant Findings from the Data

Tool 5.1.5

Here are a few examples ...

Findings related to academic performance:
1. Failure rates are highest for ninth grade students.
2. Ninety percent of the students who failed English and mathematics courses performed in the below average range on standardized achievement tests.
3. Students who participate in extra curricular activities tended to have average or above average grades.
4. Fewer ninth grade students were involved in extra curricular activities than any other grade level.

Findings related to standardized achievement test scores:
1. As of 1996-97 the percentage of students in the lowest stanine group (1-3) has decreased in social studies, science, and study skills and has increased slightly in spelling (.4). At the same time, the percentage within the median percentiles (4-6) has increased in all areas and has shown a sizeable increase in social studies and study skills.
2. For 1996-97, the percentages of students in the top stanine groups remained the same or fell slightly below the 1995-96 levels in all subtest categories.

Findings related to attendance:
1. Absenteeism varies by grade level.
2. High school students who have been retained one or more times have higher absenteeism rates than their peers.

Findings related to student behavior and discipline:
1. Factors thought by guidance counselors, principals, teachers, dropouts, and parents to be contributing to student discipline problems or poor academic performance included lack of student preparation and attention to school work, lack of parental support, conflicts between teachers and students, assignments perceived as too difficult or irrelevant to student lives, student interpersonal relationships, and excessive demands on students.
2. The majority of office referrals were for fighting, inappropriate language, and failure to follow the teacher's directives.
3. Office referrals and suspension rates (in-school) have decreased significantly in the past two years. The decline coincides with the faculty's emphasis on developing appropriate social skills.

Findings are facts or patterns that can be identified from the data— not opinions about what the facts and figures imply.

Future Trends That Will Shape Our Lives and Our Schools

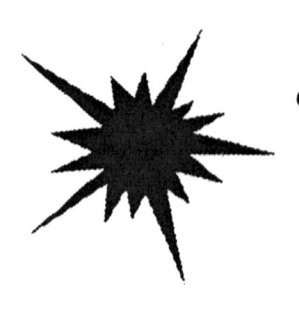

changing demographics

changing family structures

information explosion

technology explosion

age of convenience

age of globalization

rising numbers of at-risk students

growing need for "knowledge workers"

citizens with more than academic skills

fewer jobs requiring college degrees

changes in the structure of schooling

changes in the way learning occurs

Questions to Consider:

What local, national, and global future trends seem to be the most significant for our students?

What must we be aware of as we attempt to reach our goals?

Plan 5.2
Establish a Vision for the Future

The school's vision and/or mission communicates the collective expectation of "what ought to be." A vision, according to Bennis (1985), is a waking dream that provides a bridge from the past to the future. Garfield (1989) describes a vision as "seeing something that you want so passionately that it calls forth your whole hearted commitment"(p.83). While a vision describes the desired future state, a mission identifies the ways in which we intend to achieve the vision. Visions and misions should be developed in ways that motivate people to make a commitment to developing long range solutions to important problems (Bellon & Bellon, 1993, p.2). They should communicate deeply held beliefs and values and provide focus, priorities, and a sense of purpose.

When developed in a truly collaborative way with widespread involvement and input of educators, parents, students, and community members, a vision or mission can achieve numerous results. Appropriately done, the process helps people see themselves and their organizations in different ways. It can also promote cooperative and meaningful relationships which may significantly alter the culture within the school community. It can invigorate people with renewed energy and optimism in bringing about their shared vision for the future. Participants see themselves as significant contributors to the important work of the school and realize that their efforts can produce a more effective and satisfying organization. Most importantly, a vision calls for the commitment of all stakeholders to act in ways that will make it happen.

It may be helpful to think of the vision setting process as both top-down and bottom-up. An individual school may be in a school system that has established a vision. That vision may influence the thinking at the individual school site, thus resulting in a top-down process. It is also important for the vision to be developed from the bottom up incorporating the hopes and dreams of those at the school. Integrating both is what will make the vision unique and inspiring.

- Assemble a group of individuals with a strong interest in the future of the school. Make decisions about the appropriate size of the group. Develop ways to ensure appropriate representation from each of the significant groups within the community (parents, educators, School Board members, community members, business persons, and older students). Sending a letter to potential participants with a brief description of the process and the time it will require may be helpful.

- Prepare the group for the task of establishing a vision. For groups that have not engaged in such a process, start by defining a vision and how it differs from a mission statement. Tool 5.2.1 is a visual that could be used to clarify these terms. Tool 5.2.2 for an example of one school's vision and missions that could be used as an example.

- Establishing a vision is neither an easy nor quick task. It requires time to allow for reflection about what really matters in schools. In most cases, it is important to engage in pre-vision activities that focus on what is important and what is valued. Once this important information is articulated, developing a vision is much easier. Tool 5.2.3 describes a pre-vision activity that focuses on the underlying values that become the basis for the vision. Tool 5.2.4 is a scenario of how one school fashioned their vision activities incorporating some creative features reflecting the personalities of the facilitators and planners of the session.

- Ask the participants to take a few minutes to reflect over the most significant educational experiences they can remember--the high points.
  - The experiences do not have to be linked to any particular school.
  - Encourage participants to think back as far as possible. The experiences could be as a student, parent, or as an educator.
  - Write a brief statement or description of the experiences.
  - Tell the participants that they will not have to share these high points with others. They do not need to worry about how odd or insignificant they may seem.

- Give the participants approximately ten minutes to think and write. To debrief, ask questions such as:
  - How far back did you remember? How many years ago did the memories occur?
  - Did you think at that time that the experiences you remembered would be significant events?

  Allow any volunteers to share.

- Now, ask the participants to take several minutes to project into the future. What are some high points or peak experiences they would like to see in the future as an educator, member of the school community, parent, student, etc.? Encourage them to think beyond the next year or even two or three years. Think more in terms of five to ten years.
  - Ask each participant to write three, four, or five peak experiences or high points they envision--for education in general or related to the school.
  - Encourage them to take advantage of the opportunity to think beyond the current situation, the status quo, and all constraints.
  - Provide advance warning to the participants that they will be sharing their ideas with others.

  Provide at least ten minutes--maybe more--to think and to write.

- Cluster participants into triads or groups of four to share what they have written. Once they have had time to share and elaborate, ask:
  - Are you able to identify any common themes?
  - Could these individual vision statements be combined into one?

- If time permits, cluster a second time. Increase the size of the groups by moving two together. This time have them write a vision that is inclusive of the various visions the group members hold. This could be written on butcher paper or on a blank transparency to share with the total group.

- Ask each group to share the "rough drafts" of their visions with the total group. There will be many common themes across the groups, just as there were within their individual groups. At the same time, some groups may suggest some unique ideas or perspectives. A vision for the school could be fashioned by combining the key points of each small groups' efforts.

- To develop the "final" draft, the individual vision statements can be consolidated by a team of volunteers who represent each group involved. After the "final" draft is ready to be shared with the original group, reconvene them with the task of further refining the vision and deciding the next important steps to bringing it about. Some schools have found it desirable to develop the "final" draft and let it sit for awhile to allow everyone to think about it. The time allowed for reflection may produce a more meaningful vision. A time could be designated to revisit the vision and finalize it later in the year. In finalizing the vision, it is important to have criteria to use as a guide. Tool 5.2.5 is a reflection and assessment guide that can be used by all or a representative sample of participants to evaluate the quality of the vision as well as the vision setting process.

- Once a vision is established, it should be shared with any and all interested members of the school community. See Tool 5.2.6 for ideas about how to make the vision public.

- Establishing a vision is one thing. Accepting responsibility for achieving it is another. Every individual within the school community should feel some responsibility for bringing about the desired future state. See Tool 5.2.7 for an example of how one school promoted that sense of responsibility. It emphasizes the importance of periodically reviewing the responsibilities to see how well everyone is doing in acting on their obligations to achieve the school's vision.

- Another positive impact of a vision is that it can be used as the major criterion when educators and/or parents are involved in making school related decisions. Tool 5.2.8 focuses on ways to ensure that actions and decisions align with the school's vision of "what ought to be."

- It is advised that the vision should be periodically (every 3-4 years) reviewed and revised, if necessary. This will help keep the vision alive and will serve as a reminder of its importance. Remember that situations and major participants change and those new influences and perspectives need to be incorporated in the vision.

A special thank you to Jerry J. Bellon and Elner C. Bellon
Shared Leadership Projects
Tennessee and Illinois

Other Possibilities:

How do a Vision and Mission Contribute to a School?

Tool 5.2.1

A vision . . .

describes a desired future state.

is the collective expectation of "what ought to be."

is a bridge from the past to the future.
(Bennis, 1985)

is "seeing something that you want so passionately that
it calls forth your whole hearted commitment."
(Garfield, 1989, p. 83)

A mission . . .

identifies the ways in which we intend to achieve the vision.

Visions and missions can . . .

motivate people to make a commitment to develop
long range solutions to important problems.
(Bellon & Bellon, 1993, p.2)

provide focus, priorities, and a sense of purpose.

help people see themselves and their organizations in different ways.

promote cooperative and meaningful relationships and
significantly alter the culture within the school community.

invigorate people with renewed energy and optimism in
bringing about their shared vision of the future.

One School's Vision and Missions

Tool 5.2.2

Vision

"Every child will become more than he or she ever hoped to be."

Mission

To maintain a focus on learning as our main priority

Mission

To provide a positive climate for learning

Mission

To foster positive and nurturing relationships throughout the school community

Mission

To model a commitment to excellence and to promote positive attitudes toward renewal

PreVision Activities to Identify Important Beliefs and Values

Tool 5.2.3

Building a "Strong Foundation" for Establishing a Vision

Developing a vision is like building a house. Regardless of the design of the house, it is critical that it be built on a strong foundation. As "builders" of a vision, participants need to identify those essential "building blocks" that will become the foundation. The building blocks are the beliefs and values that will support the load of all that goes on top of them. Take time to engage in a discussion of the essential "building blocks." What values are essential to our structure? What values must be in our foundation so that the building will remain secure for years to come?

1. List beliefs and values individually.

2. Share individual lists with one other person.

3. Share those that both individuals agree upon with a small group.

4. Share group lists with the total group. Make a list of the beliefs and values that were mentioned by several groups. Add others that may have been mentioned by only one group, but were readily accepted by the total group.

> This is not yet a vision, but the values that are essential to a vision will be known and incorporated into the vision.

Core Ethical Values

caring, honesty, fairness, responsibility
and respect for self and others

The Character Education Partnership

Big Rocks and Little Rocks

If we were to build our vision upon specific beliefs and values, which would be the most important ones? They would be our big rocks. Others that are also extremely important, but not as important as big rocks become little rocks. We all know that both are needed for any enduring building project. This same analogy works well with big bricks and little bricks.

Setting the Stage for Establishing a Vision
(Sequoyah Elementary School, Knoxville, TN)

Tool 5.2.4

An elementary school faculty decided that they wanted to establish a vision for their school. Their feeling was that it would provide the direction they felt was lacking. This school enjoys a strong reputation within the community and high and energetic levels of parent involvement and community support. They want to keep it that way. They are a good example of a really good school that is working to become even better! The faculty felt that it was time to start a new learning curve rather than remain the same and possibly stagnate. They felt that it would be important for them to go through a process that might reunify and possibly refocus their efforts. Rather than yielding to the urge to "get it done and get it on paper," they chose a more leisurely--and enjoyable route. Here's what the school's leadership team decided to do.

▼ Invitations were distributed to all faculty members for "Lunch with Miss Daisy." A fresh daisy was taped to the colorful, computer generated invitation. The luncheon was to take place on an early dismissal day provided by the school system for professional development.

▼ The library was transformed into an inviting gathering place. The decorating theme was daisies--daisy paper plates and napkins, fresh daisy flowers in apple "vases" at every table, and a daisy bouquet as a center piece on the serving table. Classical music played softly in the background as the faculty entered created a relaxing and comforting atmosphere.

▼ After enjoying a delicious lunch and having time to socialize, participants were invited to relax and listen to a tape of a storyteller's reminiscence of an extraordinary fourth grade school year. With an engaging "southern" voice, delightful sense of humor, and captivating style, the storyteller shared his most memorable events of that year in Miss Daisy's classroom. The memories he shared were those one would hope every student would have the opportunity to experience. The listening activity successfully engaged the teachers. Laughter as well as tears occurred at numerous points in the story. Without giving it away, one favorite saying of Miss Daisy's was that "on the wings of butterflies--you can go anywhere you want to go."

▼ After the tape, the teachers were asked to reflect on their own schooling experiences--as students or as educators--and to remember and jot down those memorable events or times. Several volunteered to share their memories. They were then asked to write down their "dreams" for the future of this school. What did they hope would be memorable and positive experiences for their own students? They were encouraged to extend their thinking five to ten years into the future. They were then asked to share their individual visions with the colleagues seated at their tables.

Tool 5.2.4

▼ After each individual had time to share, the groups were asked to look for common themes and to write the ones the group identified as most appropriate and appealing on colorful butterfly cutouts provided at each table.

▼ A spokesperson for each group shared the group's butterflies with the total group. As they were shared, the butterflies were posted on the blue "sky" creating a colorful mural of the goals this faculty has for their school.

▼ The butterflies were posted on a bulletin board in the main hallway where they remained for several months. The butterfly theme will continue as the faculty reflects and works together throughout the year. Other butterflies may be added as the year progresses.

> *Please join us*
> *for lunch*
> *with*
> *Miss Daisy*
>
> *September 30th*
> *In the Library*
> *12:00*

Information about the audio tape:
Title: Miss Daisy
Storyteller: Donald Davis
Producer: August House Publisher
1-800-284-8784
201 E. Markham
Little Rock, AK 72201

Criteria for a Good Vision and Vision Setting Process

Tool 5.2.5

Our Vision _____
_____

	Yes	No
Is our vision . . .		
Future-oriented?	___	___
More than a slogan?	___	___
Stated positively?	___	___
Does our vision . . .		
Have meaning and relevance to each participant? (Can each person repeat it from memory?)	___	___
Communicate well to others?	___	___
Incorporate and communicate our deeply held values and beliefs?	___	___
Reflect the uniques perspectives of the school?	___	___
Generate commitment and enthusiasm?	___	___
Link to the vision of the school district?	___	___
Did our vision setting process . . .		
Include input from representatives from all groups within the school community (parents, educators, School Board members, community members, business persons, and older students)?	___	___
Encourage participants to be thoughtful and reflective?	___	___
Promote discussion, dialogue, and sharing of perspectives?	___	___
Help develop positive relationships among the participants?	___	___

Sharing the Vision

Tool 5.2.6

Who Should be Aware of Our Vision?

Identify the individuals and groups you would want to be aware of your vision.

How Should We Communicate Our Vision?

Any number of ways! You're only limited by your own creativity.

By day to day actions and decisions

By making it an integral part of educator's daily conversation

Predominantly displayed on walls

As part of the letterhead on school stationery

Magnets for refrigerators

On individual's business cards

Shared at any public event or community gathering

Reported in the community newspaper--as a media release

Shared with focus groups as a "set" to their collaborative activities

Reported as updates linking school activities with the vision

Stated as a pledge

Included on contracts with parents

Remember . . .
Behavior speaks louder than words.

Our Vision is Our Shared Responsibility
at _____

Tool 5.2.7

As School Board Members, we will...
exercise wise judgment in hiring expertise and in providing
resources and policies to support learning.

As Central Office Personnel, we will...
provide leadership in carrying out policies to benefit all our students.

As the Principal, I will...
maintain a safe, supportive, and enriching learning environment.

As Teachers, we will...
provide high quality instruction to stimulate and challenge students
to productive levels of thought and action.

As Support Staff, we will...
contribute in all ways possible to meet the needs of all students.

As Students, we will...
dream the impossible and prepare for it.

As Parents and Guardians, we will...
stay involved in the education of our children
and model the importance or learning.

As Community Members, we will...
support education and promote the growth
and development of each individual student.

This is one school's articulation of individual responsibilities in working toward reaching their collaboratively developed vision. At this school, everyone was asked to become committed to the vision and to acting in ways that would support translating the vision to action. These important statements were prominently posted in the school and have been used in many ways to communicate their vision.

Aligning Actions and Decisions with Vision

Tool 5.2.8

The vision and mission of the school come alive when behaviors are modeled, decisions are made, and rules are developed and implemented. If the vision is consistent with the faculty's and community's collective beliefs and is internalized, it should be reflected in everyday behaviors, interactions, and decisions.

For Example...

Behaviors Modeled

If the vision is "to graduate life-long learners who are fully capable of functioning as responsible citizens, productive workers, and caring members of the community"...

Then all individuals within the community, both children and adults, should exhibit those characteristics and act in ways consistent with the vision. For example, they could be observed:

- expressing curiosity about new ideas and positions different from their own
- engaging in unfamiliar pursuits and developing new talents, skills, and interests giving words of encouragement to learn
- recognizing improvements and accomplishments
- promoting a love of learning and beliefs that *all* students are capable of learning
- incorporating self-regulation in curriculum, instruction, and assessment practices
- providing service learning opportunities for students
- engaging students in "problem-based" learning (encouraging students to identify and attempt to solve "real world" community problems
- including students in developing school and classroom rules for behavior and cooperation
- training students in conflict resolution and peer mediation to enable them to monitor the enforcement of rules
- allowing students significant input into decisions affecting them
- permitting students freedom to exercise some degree of personal choice

Decision Making

The vision also becomes the screen for all decisions. Decision making can become less arduous or ambiguous when the major criterion for a good decision is "How will this help us achieve our vision?" In schools, there are numerous requests for educators' time, attention, and energy. These are valued resources in schools. It is sometimes very difficult to deny those requests that may be somewhat worthwhile, but are not directly in line with identified priorities. However, if the time and attention spent on these activities will not result in helping achieve the vision, then the decision as to whether or not to engage in theses activities would have to be "No."

Decision Process: Tool 5.2.8

Decision Question: Should we _____?

If we were to take this action ...

Then, how would it help us accomplish our vision?
- **No:** Discard the idea or revise it and try again
- **Yes:** Proceed by screening the decision question against additional criteria that would make for a "good" decision (state each criterion as a question).

Then, what are the specific benefits for all our students? for a particular group of students?
- **No:** If very few or no worthwhile benefits that support the vision can be identified. Stop here.
- **Yes:** Because the benefits are consistent with our vision.

Then, is this the only way students might gain these benefits?
- **No:** If there are other sufficient opportunities for students to receive the benefits and/or they are not worth the time and effort (cost vs. benefit).
- **Yes:** This is the only or best way for the students to gain these benefits.

Then, will only positive effects for all students result?
- **No:** Discard due to the possible negative consequences of the action.
- **Yes:** Because all possible negative effects have been fully considered.

Then, will the benefits be equal to or greater than doing something else?
- **No:** Don't do it.
- **Yes:** The benefits will be equal to or greater than doing other alternatives

Then, is it feasible?
- **No:** Discard because we do not have the necessary resources to be successful.
- **Yes:** It is within our capability to accomplish.

Plan 5.3
Moving the Vision to Action Through Collaborative Long Range Planning

> **Vision and Change**
> Vision without action >>> Dream
> Action without vision >>> Just Passing Time
> Vision with action   >>> Successful Change
>   (unknown)

Shared expectations become the collective vision for a better future. It is through collaborative long range planning that the vision is translated to action. Planning is a natural extension of the vision process. Whether the process is called strategic planning or multi-year planning, the goal is to define the desired future state and to develop strategies and activities necessary to reach it. Two considerations should precede the actual development of plans. First, it is critical to scan the environment both within and outside the school. Internal and external scans identify the current state of the organization and target the strengths and areas for improvement. This process highlights challenges and opportunities that should be addressed in the plan. Second, maintain a focus on any future trends and external threats or constraints that may positively or negatively impact the organization. Strategies to avoid negative impacts and to capitalize on the positive ones should be incorporated into the plans.

While long range planning can be a rigorous and fairly tedious process, it can result in a clear direction and assurance that resources will be available to meet high priority needs. Increased accountability, efficiency, and confidence are inherent parts of the process. Once a systematic planning process is in place, updating will be considerably easier. It is important to remember that any planning process is a cyclical one. Data are gathered and analyzed, findings are used to develop plans, plans are implemented, plans are evaluated, evaluation data are gathered and analyzed, plans are revised, and the process continues.... Planning is the key to growth and must be viewed as an integral and ongoing part of a school's work.

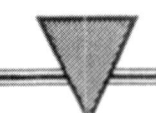

- Once a representative planning team is assembled, the planning process may begin. (Review Involvement Tool 6.3.1 for considerations about team membership.) If the steps in Plan 5.1 were followed, the databases and significant findings will be the starting point for the planning process. It will be helpful to review the vision with the planning participants to set the stage for planning activities. The wording of the vision may be inspirational, but they soon become hollow if not translated to actions.

- Then proceed with the steps. Tool 5.3.1 can be used as a handout for planning participants. It outlines the main steps in the planning process. Note to facilitators: accomplishing this plan requires the use of several important collaborative strategies presented in other Plans. The Tools will be noted so they may be reviewed, if needed.

- "Taking Stock" implies taking time for self-assessment. Taking Stock is the process of identifying strengths and successes and then identifying continuing challenges or unfinished business. This is an appropriate time to recognize progress and to celebrate successes. It is important that the focus remain on the positives. It is not that the school is in great need of a major overhaul, but that any excellent school will not stay that way unless it continually strives to get better. Maintaining the status quo is not a realistic approach in ever changing world. Review the databases developed in Plan 5.1 and the survey results generated from Gathering Perceptions Surveys using Tools 1.1.1 and 1.1.2. The actual identification of strengths and challenges can be accomplished through brainstorming. See Tool 1.2.6. for a brainstorming strategy.

- Clarify continuing challenges. The challenges identified are potential targets for improvement efforts. Tool 1.2.7. provides a variety of approaches to understanding challenges. Before jumping to solutions or talking in circles, take the time to be sure that all involved understand the challenges as thoroughly as possible. An effective way to develop this understanding is to discuss each challenge area in terms of "what is" vs. "what ought to be." First, list what is currently working well in this area. Then identify what is not working as well as it could be. If only a few people within a school have access to needed information on the issue, ask them to participate as resources to the group. Once everyone has an understanding of the current state, identify the "ideal state." What desired outcomes do we want? It is helpful to remind the group not to let any constraints limit their thinking about the ideal state. As we all know, many constraints are imagined rather than real. Even real constraints can be addressed later in the planning process. At this point, encourage participants to visualize the best that can be imagined. The discussion of each challenge should also include determining the benefits of pursuing the challenge. This is the time to rethink it's connection to the vision. If we pursue this challenge, would it help us achieve our vision? -Is this challenge worthwhile in terms of effort and resources? If we were successful in overcoming this challenge, could it have a positive impact?

- At this point in the discussion, it would be helpful to examine each challenge by looking at the factors within and outside the school that may facilitate or impede planning efforts. This discussion could give a more realistic appraisal of the feasibility of the challenge. First, identify the obstacles or barriers that may negatively impact the improvement efforts and then, be creative in thinking about the possible strategies that will help overcome them. See Tool 5.3.2 for a strategy for capitalizing on strengths and finding ways around obstacles.

- Identify priority target areas for improvement. Review Tool 1.2.7 for prioritizing strategies. While all challenges are important, some are perceived by the majority of the participants as most in need of attention or most likely to make a significant difference if attended to successfully. The discussion about "what is" and "what ought to be" should have prepared the group for determining priorities. What we know from the military is that too many battle fronts lessen the likelihood of winning a war. In schools as well in other organizations, it is necessary to identify the challenges that are priorities so that limited resources can be committed to winning the war--and making a difference. Therefore, decide on a limited number of target areas as a total school community. Making significant progress in a few priority areas is seen as more desirable than minimal progress on several. It may also help gain the needed consensus and support.

- Develop Action Plans. Identify goals and objectives for each of the priorities. See Tool 5.3.3 for a visual depiction of areas one school translated into goals to achieve their vision and mission. Before identifying specific activities, it would be helpful to engage in a process for exploration. Others beyond the planning team could be involved at this point. One structure is to establish idea, study, and scout groups. The idea groups can be responsible for brainstorming the currently known possibilities; the study groups can explore research and professional literature to identify additional "proven" options; and scout groups can visit any sites that are known to have exemplary programs. See Tool 5.3.4 for more explanation.

- Specific activities can now be identified on the Action Plan. After the idea, study, and scout groups have completed their tasks and shared their finding, an expanded planning team can engage in further creative problem solving. Tool 1.2.17 illustrates the IWWMW process ("In what ways might we") that could be used to encourage creative thinking. This process, building on effective practices and incorporating fresh, creative ideas and futuristic possibilities, can only enhance the quality of the resulting plan.

- Develop evaluation criteria or indicators of success to be used for formative and summative evaluation activities. Look back to the identified objectives to guide the thinking. Evaluation criteria should align with objectives which are stated as measurable outcomes. Identify dates as check point opportunities prior to implementing the plan.

- Put the plans on paper. See Tool 5.3.5 for Planning Guides which provide the structure necessary to translate ideas to action. In addition to the above information, the plans will specify the anticipated timeframes (beginning and end dates), resources needed (money, information, people, etc.), and responsibility (who will be responsible for coordinating the activities and tasks).

- Distribute the proposed plans to others for input and suggestion. Once they have been refined to everyone's satisfaction, ask permission of the total planning group or other important groups such as the total faculty. Consent should be gained from the necessary stakeholders before moving ahead. In addition, it is desirable to have everyone's best ideas about how to proceed.

At this point, the plans are ready to implement. Evaluation activities should also be initiated at the same time.

- Publish and distribute the plan. The detailed plans should be shared with all important stakeholder groups. Besides showing commitment to the proposed actions, sharing the written document can help others see ways they can become involved. Support from the total school community is important in bringing the vision to reality.

- Capitalize on the feedback loop. Formative evaluation information from the check point opportunities will provide guidance in adjusting the activities--as they are being implemented rather than when it is too late.

- It is also important to use the summative evaluation information to "take stock" at the end of the year and each year after that. Take the time to reflect about what has taken place in terms of successes and continuing challenges. Be sure to incorporate what has been learned to guide future action. Tool 5.3.6 is provided to guide the reflection on the planning process.

- Remember to celebrate successes. All too often we forget to focus on those accomplishments, both large and small, that are sources of pride. Celebrating success can be very motivating and encourages us to capitalize on the things we are doing well. Successful planning should result in knowing where we are going, what got us there, and specifically how we are going to achieve our future vision.

Other Possibilities . . .

The "product" will be the PLAN, but the more important "by products" are the stakeholders' increased understanding and perspective taking ability, commitment and support for proposed actions, and creative problem solving abilities. It's the planning PROCESS that can create the enthusiasm and energy to get it all done!

Tool 5.3.1

Moving the Vision to Action Through Collaborative Long Range Planning

Vision and Change
Vision without action   >>>   Dream
Action without vision   >>>   Just Passing Time
Vision with action   >>>   Successful Change (unknown)

Steps:

1. "Take stock."
Identify strengths and successes
Identify continuing challenges or unfinished business
Recognize progress and to celebrate successes

2. Clarify continuing challenges.
"What is" vs. "What ought to be"
Determine the benefits of pursuing the challenge
Clarify the connection to the vision
Understand obstacles and develop ways around the obstacles

3. Identify priority targets for improvement.
Select a limited number of target areas as a total school community

4. Develop action plans.
Identify goals and objectives
Establish a process for exploration
  - idea groups - brainstorming possibilities
  - study groups - research and literature
  - scout groups - visit exemplary sites
Engage in further creative problem solving (IWWMW - "In what ways might we")
Develop evaluation criteria or indicators of success
Distribute the proposed plans to others for input and suggestion
Implement and evaluate the plans

5. Publish and distribute the plan.
Share the detailed plans with all important stakeholder groups

6. Capitalize on the Feedback Loop
Use evaluation information to "take stock" each year
Reflect about what has taken place (successes and continuing challenges)
Use what has been learned to guide future action

Capitalizing on Strengths and Finding Ways Around Obstacles

Tool 5.3.2

What are the STRENGTHS, opportunities, or assets within our school community that will facilitate us in achieving our vision?	What are the OBSTACLES, the real and perceived barriers, within our school community that might hinder us in achieving our vision?

How can we CAPITALIZE on our STRENGTHS
in OVERCOMING potential OBSTACLES?
(For each of the obstacles, identify one or more of the strengths
or assets that may help in finding ways around the barriers.)

Think in the longer term—progress and change takes time, patience, and a positive attitude.

Tool 5.3.3

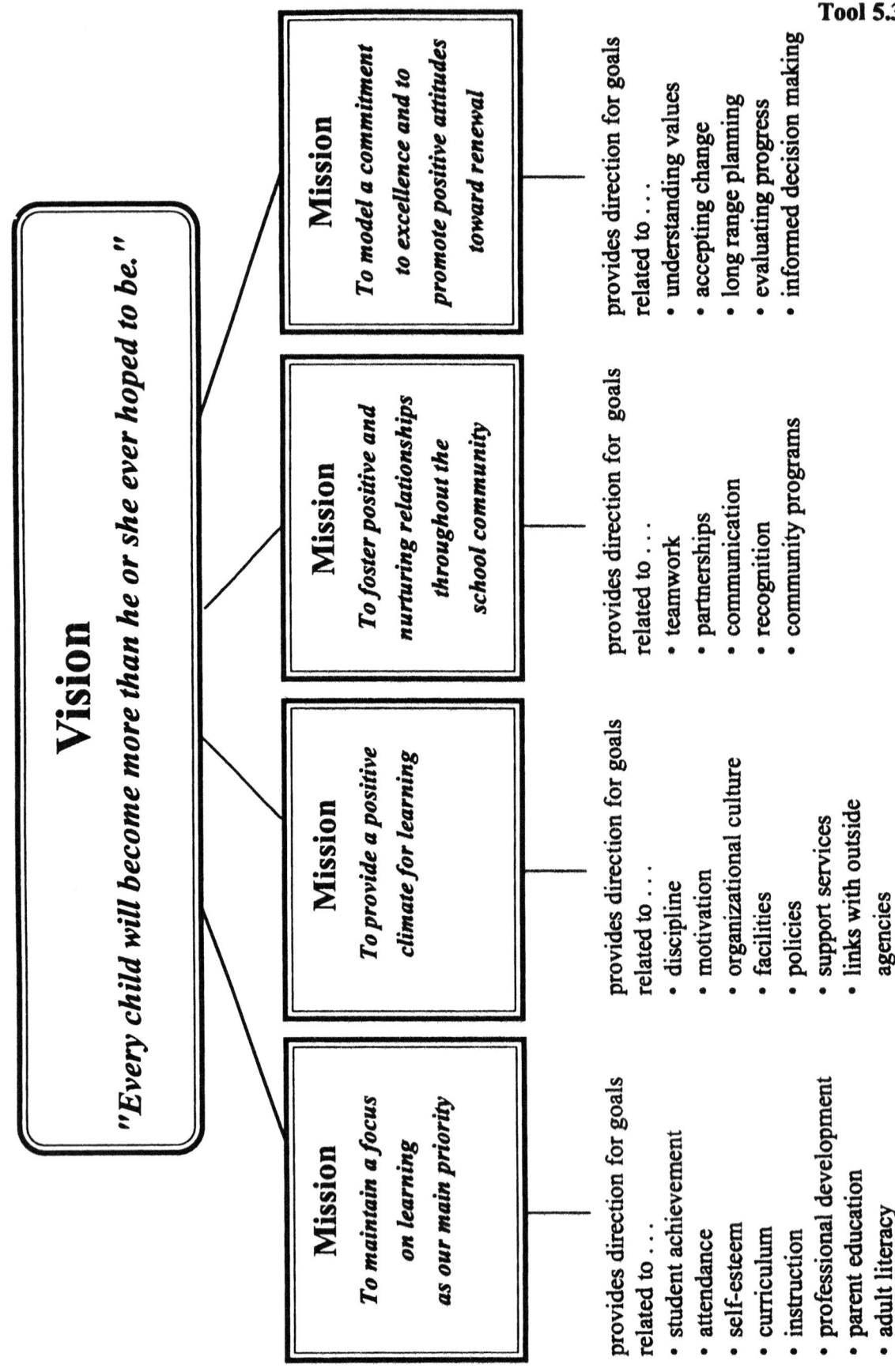

Vision
"Every child will become more than he or she ever hoped to be."

Mission
To maintain a focus on learning as our main priority

provides direction for goals related to . . .
- student achievement
- attendance
- self-esteem
- curriculum
- instruction
- professional development
- parent education
- adult literacy
- community programs

Mission
To provide a positive climate for learning

provides direction for goals related to . . .
- discipline
- motivation
- organizational culture
- facilities
- policies
- support services
- links with outside agencies

Mission
To foster positive and nurturing relationships throughout the school community

provides direction for goals related to . . .
- teamwork
- partnerships
- communication
- recognition
- community programs

Mission
To model a commitment to excellence and to promote positive attitudes toward renewal

provides direction for goals related to . . .
- understanding values
- accepting change
- long range planning
- evaluating progress
- informed decision making

Finding New Alternatives

Tool 5.3.4

Identifying some innovative strategies with a good track record may be one of the most exciting aspects of collaborative planning. There is a desire to move ahead, but also a caution to move ahead in thoughtful, purposeful ways. All three types of groups can be very productive in identifying new approaches and strategies. The structures allow participants to capitalize on existing exemplary programs that may just be a key to school improvement and renewal.

Participants can form groups based on their individual interests, skills, and available time. The number of group members may vary. Be sure that each group is clear about the focus of their work. It is helpful to identify ways to share the results of their efforts with the total planning team, the total faculty, or other interested groups.

Idea Groups

Their task is to identify currently strategies, activities, or approaches through brainstorming. If the group membership is diverse, the collective list will reflect some current and productive strategies; some current strategies that need some modifications; some previously, but not currently used strategies; some approaches members have experienced in other settings; and some activities that they have heard about that are being used in other settings.

Study Groups

Their task is to identify proven research-based strategies from the professional literature. Some individual schools may have limited professional libraries. Perhaps the school district or another school has a greater selection of professional journals. Educators who are members of professional organizations also have access to some relevant and current information. In some districts, an individual is responsible for completing database searches on specific topics. The Internet can be a very helpful tool in finding some interesting possibilities.

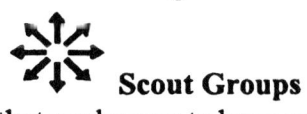

Scout Groups

Their task is to visit any sites that are known to have exemplary programs in place. Of course, resources limit the range and extent of the visits, but on even a limited basis, they can be extremely helpful. It is advisable to visit a school of similar grade levels and size, if possible. Sometimes when the school characteristics are very dissimilar, it is more difficult to see how what is being observed can be applicable in one's own setting. It is also extremely helpful for the group, with the input of others, to develop a "Visit Guide" prior to the site visit. This will help the visitors be more consistent in what they attempt to observe at each site.

Tool 5.3.5

Planning Guide

Goal: _____

Objective(s): _____

Major Activities	Beginning Date	Ending Date	Persons Involved * Responsible	Resources Needed	Indicators of Success

Reflection on the Planning Process

Tool 5.3.6

The "product" is the PLAN, but the more important by products are the stakeholders' increased understanding, commitment and support for proposed actions, and creative problem solving abilities. It's the planning *process* that can create the enthusiasm and energy to move the school to new heights.

The Product—the Plan
Will our plan help us achieve our vision?

	Strongly Agree				Stongly Disagree
Overall, the plan . . .					
1. is of high quality.	O	O	O	O	O
2. is worthwhile (worth our time, energy, and resources).	O	O	O	O	O
3. should have the desired impact on all students.	O	O	O	O	O
4. is feasible and "doable" in terms of available resources. (Some of the proposed activities may require funds for professional development, materials, technology, etc.)	O	O	O	O	O
5. capitalizes on our strengths.	O	O	O	O	O
6. maintains currently strong programs and uses available potential to the fullest.	O	O	O	O	O
7. was developed from a comprehensive needs assessment. The data base adequately and accurately reflects the "current state."	O	O	O	O	O
8. provides clear direction to overcome our most significant challenges.	O	O	O	O	O
9. is focused on a limited number of priorities.	O	O	O	O	O
10. is future-oriented.	O	O	O	O	O
11. incorporates current "best practices" as well as valid innovative approaches.	O	O	O	O	O
12. identifies adequate evaluation procedures that provide needed information about effectiveness of the activities.	O	O	O	O	O

Tool 5.3.6

The Process
Was our planning process productive?

Overall, our planning process . . .	Strongly Agree				Strongly Disagree
1. improved understanding and relationships.	O	O	O	O	O
2. had the support, commitment, and active involvement of the school leader(s).	O	O	O	O	O
3. was initiated with up front commitment to follow through-- before planning began.	O	O	O	O	O
4. involved the "right" people (adequate representation from all groups within the school and those with the necessary skills).	O	O	O	O	O
5. incorporated creative problem solving and a persistence to discover the best ways around obstacles.	O	O	O	O	O
6. promoted a "we can" attitude.	O	O	O	O	O
7. accomplished objectives and tasks efficiently and in a timely manner.	O	O	O	O	O
8. provides a tool for future planning. Now that the process is in place (format, database), it will encourage effective planning in the future.	O	O	O	O	O
9. involved others at key times. For example, the "draft" was shared with the faculty and parent leaders to gain their input. Their suggestions were incorporated into the final form which was distributed to all interested stakeholders.	O	O	O	O	O
10. resulted in monitoring procedures that will ensure progress on the proposed activities.	O	O	O	O	O

Suggestions to make our future planning more effective . . .

Plan 5.4
Reinforcing Learning Expectations

The vision is the collective view of a desired future and a powerful motivator for both educators and parents. If the vision is to become reality, it must be translated to challenging expectations for all members of the school community. Expectations, both conscientiously and unconscientiously, become a driving force for educators, parents, and community members.

When the school and home environments are both focused on achieving the expectations, children perceive the consistency. When adults in both environments continually communicate their importance, model appropriate behaviors, and celebrate achievements, children realize their value. When children from these homes come to school understanding why it is important to study and to do their best, they are more likely to be successful than their peers who come from homes that do not hold similar expectations. They understand the reasons behind the expectations held for their educational success and are supported and rewarded for achieving them.

Parents are equally influenced by the expectations they hold for their children. Expectations can be seen in their interactions. When talking with their child about immediate or long range plans, parents subtly guide the child's decisions in ways that are consistent with the expectations they hold. As they help their child set goals or their own expectations, they are using one of the most powerful tools for motivating their child (Youngs, 1989). How different these parents are from those we have all heard saying something similar to, "Look at you. You'll never amount to anything." Many of these parents would never again utter these words if they knew the power of positive expectations.

- Access relevant information about developmentally appropriate expectations. Guidance counselors, school psychologists, and others are knowledgeable about appropriate expectations for students at specific grade levels and can make this helpful information available to everyone. Recent work in establishing national standards and benchmarks also provides important information for consideration. Hold discussions with parents, community members and educators about ways the school's vision could be translated into shared expectations that would be consistent with the age and/or maturity level of the children. See Tool 5.4.1 for an expectation discussion guide.

- Reflect on the emphasis given within the school community to developing a "Can Do" attitude. Use Tools 5.4.2 and 5.4.3 as a beginning point for assessing the level of expectations and optimism. The concept of "high expectations" is an appealing one for teachers, parents, and other adults. The challenge of high expectations comes in aligning our everyday behavior with our expectations. Use the Tools to identify behaviors that are consistent and those that are not. Discuss the changes that need to occur to align expectations with actions.

- Increase the use of goal setting for students and for adults within the school community. Motivational literature supports the positive impact of goal setting. Garfield (1986) says it best when he encourages everyone to be a peak performer. He describes peak performers as individuals whose theme is "I have done well, and I am capable of achieving much more. I am not finished yet. There is much more to me than this" (p.20). Tools 5.4.4, 5.4.5, 5.4.6, and 5.4.7 will be helpful guides in working with students in setting goals. Tool 5.4.4 outlines a collaborative goal setting process. Tool 5.4.5 is a worksheet to use with students as they identify goals and work through the complete process. Tool 5.4.6 provides sentence stems that could be used as journal entries requiring written student responses. They could also be used as interview questions. Tool 5.4.7 is a form to guide parents or care givers in observing their child's behavior. What they observe about their children provides an important perspective for the goal setting process. Taken together or in part, these tools can guide students to be the best that they can be.

- Tool 5.4.8 is a report card for parents.* It has been used as a way for adults to reflect on the expectations they hold for their child and the actions they take to ensure the child achieves them. When teachers have asked for their return, they have been surprised at how honest the parents are.

- Adults who take responsibility for achieving expectations serve as positive models for students. Modeling is more powerful when a strong partnership exists between home and school. Teachers are encouraged to establish the most appropriate and challenging education for students because they know that parents will do their part. Parents reinforce expectations by linking what is expected and learned in school to everyday family living. While a great deal of effort is required in being consistently appropriate role models, the payoff in terms of motivation and achievement is reaped by all. Tool 5.4.9 allows educators and parents to reflect upon how students exhibit expectations they hold for themselves. Tool 5.4.10 encourages them to reflect upon their own effectiveness as role models.

*Thank you to Barbara Clark, principal of New Hopewell Elementary School, Knoxville, Tennessee

Other Possibilities . . .

Expectation Discussion Guide

Tool 5.4.1

Our Vision is _____

To bring the vision to life, translate articulated expectations into realistic, yet challenging goals.

1. Desired Behavior

(specifically stated--appropriate for all children/students)
Students will develop pro social interpersonal skills

2. **Optimistic Expectation**
   (ideal state)
   All students will consistently exhibit courtesy to peers and adults

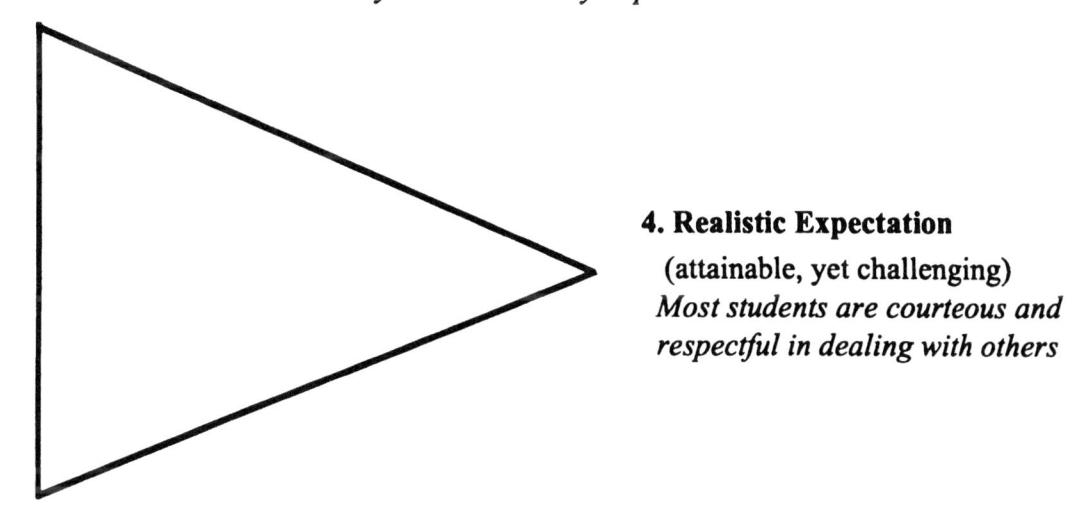

4. **Realistic Expectation**
   (attainable, yet challenging)
   Most students are courteous and respectful in dealing with others

3. **Pessimistic Expectation**
   (unacceptable)
   Students will always show disrespect for peers and adults

5. *How* the desired behavior will be *communicated* and *modeled*

6. *How* the desired behavior will be *monitored*

7. *How* the desired behavior will be *reinforced* and *celebrated*

Developing a "Can Do" Attitude

Tool 5.4.2

Successful schools are characterized by a "can do" attitude. Adults and children within the school expect success and work to achieve it. For all of us, expectations for success are powerful motivators. When individuals are working toward a goal they value and believe that they will be capable of achieving with reasonable effort, their feelings of efficacy and control are greatly increased. This sense of efficacy, of feeling able and capable, can lead to ever increasing motivated and optimistic behaviors (Bandura, 1977).

The schooling experience for all children should result in increased confidence and excitement about learning. Stipek (1986) reported a study that illustrates the extreme confidence and optimism of kindergarten students as opposed to students further along in their school careers. When asked to identify the smartest child in the class, nearly every kindergarten student readily identified himself or herself as the smartest student. When this question was posed to third graders, the response had changed significantly. These students identified others as the smartest students. This study verifies the trend seen by other educators that the positive attitudes of students entering school generally give way to more negative feelings of inadequacy and withdrawal. Many studies have shown that perceptions about self-worth and self-esteem greatly impact the learning process. It is clear that individuals who expect to succeed make different choices and act in different ways from those who expect to fail.

Epstein (1995) supports the contention that expectations for success reside within each individual. She says, "The inarguable fact is that students are the main actors in their education, development, and success in school" (p. 702). While certain aspects of motivation must be dealt with on an individual basis, schools can also make sure that the most positive schoolwide and classroom conditions are in place to energize and encourage students to their own successes. Educators and parents can work together to ensure that all children become "more than they ever dreamed they would be."

Overall, the school should be what Glasser (1986) describes as "a place where almost all students believe that if they do some work, they will be able to satisfy their needs enough so that it makes sense to keep working" (p.15).

Checklist: Are We A "Can Do" School?

Tool 5.4.3

Rate each of the following items. After compiling individual ratings, look for areas of common agreement. Applaud those that are nearly always in place. Look for ways to improve those that are rarely or never exhibited.

	Always	Sometimes	Rarely	Never
1. The peer culture promotes motivation to do one's best. All students may not attain perfection, but they are all striving for excellence. They are proud of personal bests. Students feel that it is okay to do well, acceptable to be smart and to provide encouragement to one another.	O	O	O	O
2. Risk taking is valued and errors are seen as signs of learning rather than sources of embarrassment. Each individual is regarded as "a work in progress."	O	O	O	O
3. Team efforts are recognized and celebrated. Working together to accomplish important tasks is valued. Opportunities for competition are reduced and those for cooperation are increased.	O	O	O	O
4. Confidence is communicated to students by saying, "You can do it!" Student success is then ensured by appropriate modifications and accommodations to tasks (allowing more time, taking smaller steps). Success is always within reach.	O	O	O	O
5. Teachers, parents, and other adults model statements of attribution and help students attribute their own success to effort (e.g., attending to the task, listening to directions, persisting when the task is difficult). As students move through the elementary years, they are helped to understand the relationship between effort and success.	O	O	O	O
6. Students persist when faced with difficult tasks. They seem convinced that they can succeed if they try.	O	O	O	O
7. Unique attributes and talents of individuals are highly prized. It is not just okay, but desirable to be different.	O	O	O	O
8. Students are aware of their unlimited potential. They exhibit a sense of challenge and energy to "push the limits" rather than becoming stagnant or complacent.	O	O	O	O
9. Students are helped to realize that personal competencies and positive results are brought about by effort, not luck or coincidence.	O	O	O	O

Tool 5.4.3

	Always	Sometimes	Rarely	Never
10. The faculty focuses on helping students develop feelings of competence—of being able and capable of achieving expectations.	O	O	O	O
11. Although students continually encounter seemingly unsurmountable obstacles, for the most part they remain resilient, hopeful, and optimistic.	O	O	O	O
12. Students are not aware of their status (high or low) within the classroom. Individual student success is not in comparison to others.	O	O	O	O
13. Adults directly attempt to develop the self-efficacy of students. They focus on helping students acquire skills and knowledge rather than emphasizing "hollow" self-esteem campaigns that may make the students feel good about themselves, but do little to contribute to the student's core capabilities.	O	O	O	O
14. Appropriate praise is given to individuals and groups to reinforce, encourage effort, and provide needed corrective feedback.	O	O	O	O
15. Criticism is never used to demean or humiliate, but is only given with the understood intent of helping the child improve and is interpreted by the child as supportive.	O	O	O	O
16. Student grades reveal a low failure rate with most students succeeding academically.	O	O	O	O

Collaborative Goal Setting for Student Growth

Tool 5.4.4

GOAL SETTING is . . .
- translating expectations into action.
- a way to help students become the best they can be.
- a means to tap students' previously ignored and unlimited potential.
- self-regulating one's behavior to work at the edge (rather than at the center) of one's competence.

GOAL SETTING can:
- result in a sense of pride in accomplishments.
- increase responsibility for actions.
- foster greater commitment and ownership.

GOAL SETTING requires:
- introspection and reflection about "who I am" and "who I want to become."
- visualization beyond the present to some desired future state.
- identification of goals the student cares about achieving; goals that will energize to action, truly excite, and sustain their attention and effort.
- commitment to achieving the goals.
- formulation of a plan of action.
- assessments about progress and replanning.
- self-reinforcement and support from others for the progress made.

① REFLECTING
② DREAMING
③ COMMITTING
④ PLANNING
⑤ PROGRESSING
⑥ CELEBRATING

GOAL SETTING

317

Tool 5.4.4

REFLECTING: Through formal and informal self-assessments, the student develops an understanding of "who I am" (the person I am now) and "who I want to become" (the person I will be in the future). Sources for reflecting include the student, parents, previous teachers, siblings or anyone who knows the student well. The following tools will be helpful with this step:
- Student Worksheet (Tool 5.4.4)
- Informal interviews/sentence stems/journal prompts for students (Tool 5.4.5)
- Informal interviews/discussions with parents
- Parent "Kid Watching" Observation Form (Tool 5.4.6)
- Formal or informal interest inventories
- Informal observations that reveal interests--teachable moments
- Student-produced Booklet--All About Me
- Multiple Intelligence assessments
- Learning style assessments
- Academic records, progress reports, readiness assessments
- Career and aptitude inventories

DREAMING: The student must dream beyond the present. Help the student visualize himself or herself as an inventor, talented musician, pro football player, renowned lawyer, the physician who discovered the cure for _____, author of a best selling book, etc. Guide the student to think in terms of a well-rounded person who has talents in many areas. Consider the following categories as areas of development: social or interpersonal; mental or cognitive; emotional, affective, or altruistic; physical, kinesthetic; and artistic, musical, or aesthetic.

COMMITTING: Assist the student in choosing one or two challenging goals that he/she is excited about and willing to commit to achieving. Choice helps with ownership.
- Think about starting with short term and very specific goals that describe particular behaviors and actions.
- Help frame the goals so that they are challenging and "push the limits" of the student's abilities, but within reason.
- Assist the student in understanding the personal benefits of achieving the goal.

PLANNING: The student's plan of action should provide the structure needed to achieve the goal. It should include the smaller, perhaps more doable steps required in accomplishing the goal and the target dates for reaching the steps. It should also note the resources and support that may be needed.
- Assist the student in identifying the specific and possibly unfamiliar behaviors that will need to be developed, a realistic estimate of the amount of practice required to reach the goal, and the possible reminders or incentives that may help keep progress on track.

Tool 5.4.4

- Help the student identify the resources (things, time, money) and the assistance or support (people, structure) that may be needed in order to accomplish the goal.
- It may be helpful at this point to talk with the student about any obstacles that may get in the way of achieving the goal. Obstacles may be personal (a tendency to procrastinate) or contextual (constraints within the student's world). Also focus the discussion on the strengths or opportunities the student may use in achieving the goal.

PROGRESSING: Plan with the student to incorporate periodic check points for assessing progress.
- Students can develop skills to self-assess and reinforce their own progress. Adults can model the process by giving constructive feedback and asking "guiding" questions about progress.
- It is important for the student to recognize the small steps forward. Some goals may be long term and require multiple steps to achieving it.
- If some problems have been encountered, encourage the student to be flexible, identify some creative ways (possible assistance and/or resources) around the obstacles, and adjust the plan. Gaining commitment is important, but maintaining a positive, optimistic attitude is the real key.
- Encourage the student to believe in himself or herself. Anyone can succeed if they want to badly enough. The key is really wanting to succeed, which may involve reassessing personal goals.

CELEBRATING: Open to endless possibilities--based on individual preferences.

REFLECTING: The cycle starts over--hopefully with increased motivation and confidence to achieve!

Student Goal Setting Worksheet

Tool 5.4.5

Reflecting

What area do I want to work on?
- ____ personal
- ____ social
- ____ academic
- ____ caring for others
- ____ physical
- ____ artistic
- ____ other (describe)

Dreaming

What are two or three possible goals you would like to achieve?

1. _____

2. _____

3. _____

Picture yourself achieving your goal. What will success look like?

Committing

	Yes	No
Evaluate each of the potential goals.		
Is this goal a priority for me? _____	____	____
Is the goal doable and realistic? _____	____	____
Would it be a challenge for me? _____	____	____
Do I really care about achieving the goal? _____	____	____
Is achieving the goal going to be helpful to me? _____	____	____

My goal is . . .

_____

_____

Tool 5.4.5

Planning

Decide how long it will take to achieve the goal. Will it take a week, a month, several months, a grading period, a semester, a year, several years?

The target date for achieving the goal is _____.

Develop a plan with specific activities and steps--small steps.

#1 _____

#2 _____

#3 _____

#4 _____

Think about: Now that I am committed to my goal,
- what will I do differently tomorrow and every day after that?
- how much practice is required for me to accomplish my goal?
- what do I need as a reminder (e.g., "To Do" list)?

What resources (things, time, money) do I need to accomplish my goal?

What help and support from people do I need to accomplish my goal?

What obstacles do I need to overcome to achieve my goal (in myself, in my world)?

What strengths or opportunities do I have to build on in achieving my goal?

Go For It! You Can Do It!!

Reflecting about Possible Goals
(for students)

Sentence stems
- People comment about my (or how good I am at) . . .
- I have received many compliments about my . . .
- I know I am good at . . .
- I wish I could . . .
- I've been told that I'm a great_____ . I guess that's because I . . .
- I'm okay at ----, but I want to get better (or know more) . . .
- My teacher says that I should (or I need to) . . .
- My parent tells me that I need to . . .
- I am embarrassed that I can't _____ very well . . .
- I dream that one day I will be . . .
- I dream that one day I will . . .
- One of my proudest moments (or thing that happened to me) was when . . .
- I feel best when I . . . or I feel satisfied when . . .
- In my leisure time, I like to_____ because . . .
- For recreation, I like to_____ because . . .
- My favorite extracurricular activity is _____ because . . .
- The five words that describe me best are . . . (Why?)
- The job I one day will have will be . . .
- In 10 (or 20) years I see myself as . . .

Open-ended questions

My most outstanding physical characteristic is my . . .
(strength, appearance, fitness)

My most outstanding social characteristic is my . . .
(ability to make and keep friends, ability to influence others, to get along with others)

My most outstanding personal characteristic is my . . .
(responsibility, care and concern for others, sense of humor, initiative, positive attitude, persistence)

My most outstanding talent is my . . .
(academic ability, technical ability and computer skills; ability to work with my hands, to put things together; artistic or dramatic ability; athletic ability; fluency with words; ability to work with others and/or work independently)

Parent Observation Form
"Kid Watching"

Tool 5.4.7

My child . . .	Most of the time	Sometimes	Rarely	Never
seems to like going to school	___	___	___	___
likes to be read to/read	___	___	___	___
has many interests and hobbies	___	___	___	___
watches too much TV	___	___	___	___
makes friends easily	___	___	___	___
keeps friends	___	___	___	___
is outgoing	___	___	___	___
is shy	___	___	___	___
is alert and aware of surroundings	___	___	___	___
is the first one to join in	___	___	___	___
is reluctant to join in activities with other children	___	___	___	___
is creative	___	___	___	___
needs constant reinforcement	___	___	___	___
is cooperative and gets along well	___	___	___	___
is respectful and considerate of others	___	___	___	___
maintains attention	___	___	___	___
gives up easily when tasks are difficult	___	___	___	___
is very bright, but acts unsure or lacks confidence	___	___	___	___
is content to work or play alone most of the time	___	___	___	___
is happy most of the time	___	___	___	___
becomes angry quickly/looses temper easily	___	___	___	___
follows parents' requests	___	___	___	___
talks back	___	___	___	___
enjoys physical activities	___	___	___	___
enjoys playing games	___	___	___	___
is good with numbers	___	___	___	___
enjoys music	___	___	___	___
enjoys art activities	___	___	___	___
is very concerned about what others think	___	___	___	___
is physically about the same as peers	___	___	___	___
is less mature than children the same age	___	___	___	___
cries easily/becomes upset easily	___	___	___	___

One thing I've noticed about my child is . . .

One thing I'd like to talk with you about is . . .

Tool 5.4.8

Parent Report Card

Rate yourself A B C D F (Needs Improvement) on the following items:

As a parent, I always . . .	A	B	C	D	F
• Express optimistic expectations for my child.	O	O	O	O	O
• Model courteous, respectful behavior.	O	O	O	O	O
• Give encouragement and support to my child.	O	O	O	O	O
• Express the importance of going to school and being a good student.	O	O	O	O	O
• Monitor my child's attendance and punctuality.	O	O	O	O	O
• Model conscientiousness and persistence in attending to my own responsibilities.	O	O	O	O	O
• Work cooperatively with others.	O	O	O	O	O
• Resolve conflicts in constructive ways.	O	O	O	O	O
• Set goals for my own growth and actively strive to achieve them.	O	O	O	O	O
• Try to learn new things, take risks, and learn from my mistakes.	O	O	O	O	O
• Set aside time each day to talk with my child about school and activities.	O	O	O	O	O
• Spend some of my time with my child reading aloud or silently.	O	O	O	O	O
• Provide time, appropriate place, and needed assistance and/or support with my child's homework.	O	O	O	O	O
• Help my child make decisions about which television shows or movies to watch.	O	O	O	O	O
• Discuss television shows and movies with my child.	O	O	O	O	O

Reflecting on Expectations
Our Children Hold for Themselves

Tool 5.4.9

How often do we see our children exhibit the following behaviors? If the answer is *always* for every question, the child will undoubtedly be successful in school and in life. If the responses are not what you would want them to be, consider focusing on expectations as a way to build the child's self-esteem and motivation to be the best he or she can be.

	Always	Sometimes	Rarely	Never
• Do our children hold high expectations for themselves?	O	O	O	O
• Do they have a strong identity and clear sense of who they are?	O	O	O	O
• Do they exhibit confidence in their abilities and talents?	O	O	O	O
• Do they appear to be well adjusted, interested, and active?	O	O	O	O
• Do they exhibit high self-esteem and positive self-regard?	O	O	O	O
• Do they strive to achieve at their highest levels or do they just do enough to "get by"?	O	O	O	O
• Are they active, resourceful learners acting in ways that will bring about successful outcomes?	O	O	O	O
• Are they resilient having the skills to cope and work their way through obstacles?(actively seek new and different strategies)	O	O	O	O
• Do they learn from their mistakes and look forward to challenging situations?	O	O	O	O
• Do they readily accept responsibility for their actions?	O	O	O	O

Being Positive Role Models for Children

Tool 5.4.10

Do we as adults (educators, parents, and community members) hold high expectations for ourselves and for our children? Use the following checklist to reflect upon our effectiveness as role models for children.

	Always	Sometimes	Rarely	Never
• Do we express optimistic expectations for the children of our community?	O	O	O	O
• Do we help all children feel accepted, respected, and loved for who they are?	O	O	O	O
• Do we expect the best from children and act in positive and supportive ways towards them?	O	O	O	O
• Are we a positive influence on our children by expressing the value of education and learning?	O	O	O	O
• Do we encourage attendance, punctuality, and courteous, respectful behavior?	O	O	O	O
• Do we model conscientiousness and persistence in attending to our own responsibilities?	O	O	O	O
• Do we exhibit a sense of efficacy believing that they are able and capable of making competent decisions and taking charge of their own destiny?	O	O	O	O
• Are we able to solve problems and work cooperatively with others on tasks of mutual interest?	O	O	O	O
• Do we provide our children with opportunities to share their talents and caring with others? (providing them with a sense of self-worth, accomplishment, and belonging)	O	O	O	O
• Do we strive to be peak performers who exhibit a strong commitment to lifelong learning?	O	O	O	O
• Do we set goals for our own growth and actively strive to achieve them?	O	O	O	O
• Do we try to learn new things, take risks, and learn from our mistakes?	O	O	O	O

Design 6

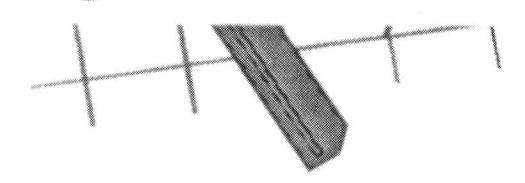

Involving Others Productively

> **Involving Others Productively...**
>
> - provides meaningful and rewarding opportunities for parent, community member, and student participation in school activities.
> - uses the best skills and talents of volunteers to maximize their contributions.
> - involves developing strategies that allow and encourage parenting adults to take a more active role in supporting their children's education.
> - requires structures that encourage parents, community members, students and educators to work collaboratively as highly effective teams.
> - involves providing adequate and diverse opportunities for student participation in school sponsored activities.

Providing meaningful and rewarding ways for parenting adults to be involved in their children's education benefits the child and the school. When volunteer work is well organized, it can generate feelings of efficacy and strengthened commitment for everyone involved. When volunteers feel that the work they are asked to do is important and they see that what they do makes a difference, they gain a sense of satisfaction, accomplishment, and ownership. Successful parent involvement programs provide a range of ways for parenting adults, community members, and students to be involved. They provide for working and non working adults by including formal and informal opportunities and tasks that require varying levels of commitment and time. At the same time, they continually explore ways to allow students to contribute productively to their school community. These schools have realized the benefits of using the school's most underutilized resource well.

    Many educators have found that productive involvement can help them achieve their goals for their students while reducing their tremendous work load. However, most continue to struggle with finding more efficient ways to accomplish their tasks. Working productively with others on teams helps all participants work smarter, not harder. We know that most educators cannot put in more hours or work any harder than they currently do. If volunteers are carefully placed and are prepared to carry out their assigned roles, they can free educators to use their expertise instructing students rather than doing noninstructional tasks. If meetings are conducted in an expedient and efficient manner and paperwork is reduced to a minimum, educators can devote more time to productive partnership activities. When educators and parents learn to work together efficiently as team members, their collaboration brings about more positive results for students and all of the adults involved.

What we hear from...

EDUCATORS

"As a new teacher, I'm learning the value of parent involvement. In my co-teacher's class parents help with activities, bring in toys, food, and other fun things for the kids. I only have one parent who is willing--and one can't do it all. I feel that my class gets left out."
(First year preschool teacher)

"I have spent a tremendous amount of time setting up a learning center for my volunteers to help with. The kids love it, but are also very disappointed when the volunteer doesn't show up. It's not an activity they can do on their own without guidance." (Second grade teacher)

"It seems that no matter what we do, we cannot get the parents (we want) to become involved with us in educating their children. It's the same parents who attend everything-and it's their children you see on every honor roll." (Elementary school principal)

PARENTS

"I can't believe how the PTA dies when the students get to the middle school level. I know I'm an officer and that means I want to be actively involved, but why don't others at least attend our meetings?" (Parent and PTA officer)

"As a retiree and a Rotary Club member, I volunteer my time in local elementary schools tutoring students. One school is especially well organized and prepared to use our services, while the others appear to not be interested in the extra help." (Community volunteer)

"Our parent-teacher organization decided to give our students immediate access to the Internet. We used our parent talent book to identify parents with computer and technology skills who organized the installation of the wiring. Others raised money from local businesses. We set up a Saturday in the fall, had everything ready (including donated food and drinks), and had every classroom operating in less than 10 hours. Just shows what parents, and organizations can do when we work together!" (Parent of a middle school student)

STUDENTS

"It's neat when my Dad comes to school to help us on computers. We get to do some really cool things when he's here!" (Elementary school student)

"Channel 10's weatherman came to school today. We got with Mrs. Stafford's class to listen to him tell us about the remote weather station they are setting up at our school. Every night on the 6 o'clock news, they're going to report the weather conditions from our school!" (8th grade student)

"Julia's mom is here all the time. I wish my mom would do that." (Elementary school student)

Shared Responsibilities

Although educators must take the lead in involving parents and community members in productive ways, parents also have important roles to play. The following diagram illustrates the responsibilities that are unique to each group and those that both groups share.

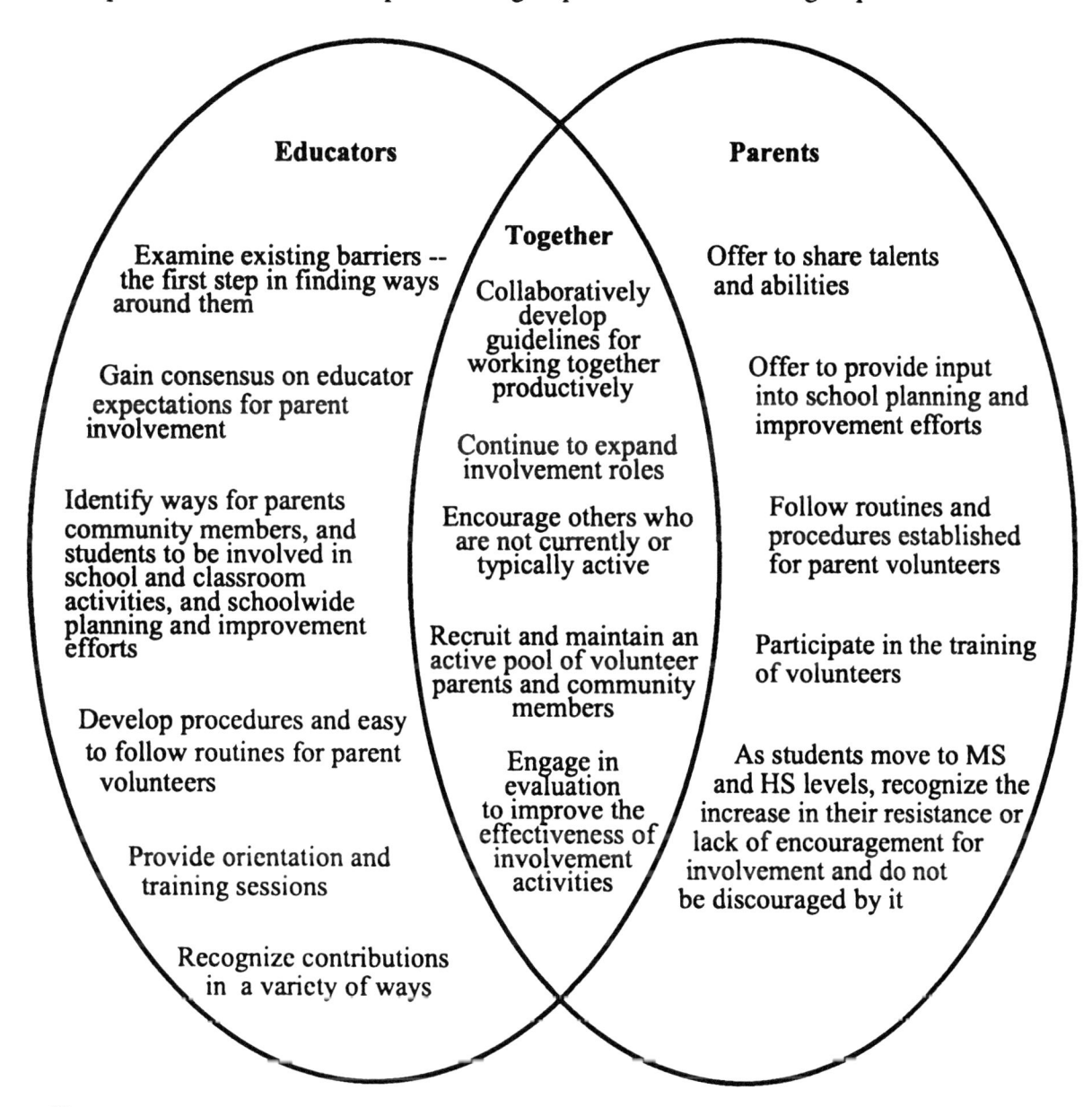

Educators

- Examine existing barriers -- the first step in finding ways around them
- Gain consensus on educator expectations for parent involvement
- Identify ways for parents community members, and students to be involved in school and classroom activities, and schoolwide planning and improvement efforts
- Develop procedures and easy to follow routines for parent volunteers
- Provide orientation and training sessions
- Recognize contributions in a variety of ways

Together

- Collaboratively develop guidelines for working together productively
- Continue to expand involvement roles
- Encourage others who are not currently or typically active
- Recruit and maintain an active pool of volunteer parents and community members
- Engage in evaluation to improve the effectiveness of involvement activities

Parents

- Offer to share talents and abilities
- Offer to provide input into school planning and improvement efforts
- Follow routines and procedures established for parent volunteers
- Participate in the training of volunteers
- As students move to MS and HS levels, recognize the increase in their resistance or lack of encouragement for involvement and do not be discouraged by it

Schools with successful parent involvement programs have reengineered their approach to include traditional and nontraditional means for productive participation.

Blank and Kershaw, 1997

Plans and Tools
for carrying out our responsibilities for involving others in productive ways.

Plan 6.1. Increasing Opportunities for Parent and Community Involvement

This plan presents some possibilities for increasing opportunities for parent and community member involvement. Tools provide guidance in rethinking involvement. They will assist in examining the effectiveness of current roles and levels of involvement and in expanding opportunities to reach others who traditionally have not been involved to any great extent.

Plan 6.2. Maximize the Potential of Volunteers

The plan provides a recommended structure and many basic requirements for making a volunteer program successful. Strategies are proposed to maximize the potential of volunteers. Many of them have proven to be effective ways to overcome the typical obstacles many parent volunteer programs experience.

Plan 6.3. Working as a Team

Effective teamwork is the focus of this plan. It provides guidelines for selecting team members and defining roles and responsibilities. To help teams function at an optimal level, this plan includes reinforcement strategies and ways to assess team functioning to identify goals for improvement.

Educator Reflection
Productive Involvement

Educators should periodically assess the opportunities they provide for parent, community member, and student involvement. In some large schools, teachers in the same building often do not know what many of their colleagues are doing to involve others productively. Furthermore, as conditions within the school community change, efforts at involvement need to change in order to remain beneficial to all. Take a few minutes to reflect on the following statements. Put an "X" in the box that most closely reflects your perception.

	Often	Sometimes	Rarely
1. In general, school personnel provide adequate opportunities and encouragement for others (parents and community members) to become involved in school activities.	☐	☐	☐
2. As a classroom teacher, I have adequate and appropriate involvement from parents and community members.	☐	☐	☐
3. As a classroom teacher, I have had adequate training (and/or experience) in using volunteers well.	☐	☐	☐
4. In general, most of our parents are actively and appropriately involved in school activities.	☐	☐	☐
5. In general, our parents are actively and appropriately involved in their child's education.	☐	☐	☐
6. School personnel ask for and encourage suggestions and input from parents on important school issues.	☐	☐	☐
7. Most opportunities for parent involvement are well organized and worth the parents' time.	☐	☐	☐
8. Parents are provided with guidelines for their involvement and adequate orientation and training to participate effectively.	☐	☐	☐
9. As a school, we have developed and enforce appropriate policies and guidelines for parent involvement.	☐	☐	☐
10. Schoolwide, we provide adequate recognition and appreciation for the contributions of parents and community members.	☐	☐	☐
11. Schoolwide, we provide adequate and interesting opportunities for students to become involved in activities.	☐	☐	☐

Plan 6.1
Increasing Opportunities for
Parent and Community Involvement

Parent and community members come in all shapes and sizes--some with confidence and competencies to contribute and others with insecurities and limited skills; some with all the right intentions and some with their own (and possibly competing) agendas and needs; some who will serve as true advocates for the school and others who may be only detractors; some who are the over-participators (those who do or want to do everything) and those who are silent or physically and emotionally detached from the school communities. The point is--regardless of their particular personal characteristics, schools need to find productive ways to use their talents and energy.

There is no better time than now to rethink involvement. By looking at this important topic in some different, and hopefully, more creative ways, the traditional views of parent involvement may be greatly expanded. By approaching involvement more systematically and attentively, educators will be in a better position to align the talents of the individuals with the tasks the school needs to accomplish. Through partnership activities, it is possible to reengineer parent and community member opportunities for more productive involvement.

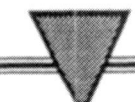

- Meet as a faculty to discuss the topic of parent and community involvement. Review the research in the introductory chapter related to involvement and select information that would be appropriate for initiating faculty discussion. As an ice breaker, see Tool 6.1.1 for a "Here they Come--Ready or Not! Just for Fun" list of volunteer types to add to the research.

- Assemble a group of interested participants who are willing to tackle the challenge of increasing opportunities in our school for greater parent and community member involvement. For this topic, it would be helpful to have representatives from each of the stakeholder groups. While this would naturally involve educators, parents, and community members, be sure these individuals also represent various cultures, grade levels, or other population characteristics. Also consider retired members of the community, perhaps retired teachers. Depending on the number of participants, it may be appropriate to stay as a total group or break into smaller groups. If the small group option is selected, see Tool 1.2.3.

- Review Tool 6.1.2 which presents possible categories of involvement opportunities and types of tasks or jobs that are representative of each category. This may be a helpful starting point for discussions. Given the realities of today's world, schools need to provide options for involvement that can accommodate varied schedules, needs, desires, capabilities, and other demands. Working from the categories and jobs identified in the Tool, develop a list of roles that reflects the specific needs and opportunities of your school. This list will need to be updated periodically. Tool 6.1.3 provides a grid to illustrate the need for volunteers in all areas and at all levels of time commitment. Contemplating the grid may spark some creative thinking about additional possibilities.

- Of the roles and jobs identified, which ones have been used in the past or are currently used? Which ones have been the most productive? Which ones have been problematic? Why?

- Since involvement opportunities require time and resources, make decisions about how to support them. Tool 6.1.4 provides guidelines for making it happen--monetary commitment, parental involvement policy, and formal contracts among the parent(s), the educators, and the student.

- Consider ways students could be involved beyond their regular classes. Many schools are developing community service expectations and opportunities for them. Others are adapting the concept of community service to their own school. Discuss these possibilities as a faculty and identify ways that they could be used to enhance student learning and personal development. Tool 6.1.5 includes questions to guide a discussion on community service opportunities for students.

Other Possibilities . . .

Tool 6.1.1

Here They Come--Ready or Not!
Just for Fun

It is possible for educators to identify individuals within the community who are: 1) The Highly Desirables; 2)The Coachables; and 3) The "Tries Everyone's Patience!" types. Where do the following volunteer types fit on this scale? Which can we recall from past experiences? Which do we want for future experiences?

Self-starters
want to be involved in absolutely everything.

Non-initiators
are willing do whatever is asked of them, but must be asked. They are the "troopers."

Whiners and complainers
will not be satisfied--no matter what.

Gossips or self-appointed "conduits" to the community
delight in spreading stories or rumors to anyone who will listen.

Overprotectors
want everything for their own child,
*but have difficulty focusing on the best for **all** students.*

Bosses
use their favorite words very often: "You ought to ..." or "What you should do is ..."

Power seekers
seem to acquire a great deal of authority from holding certain positions.

Yea-buts
respond negatively to most suggestions and seem to have a reason why they will not work.

Know it alls
seem to have all the answers and usually begin their statements with
"The way we did it at _____ School was . . . ."

Unpredictables
are very difficult to read and are volatile or inconsistent in their reactions.

Procrastinators
initially supportive and have good intentions, but rarely follow through satisfactorily.

Collaborators
are willing to look at the possibilities and see the perspectives of others.

Partners
want to work collaboratively with school personnel to make the
educational experience for children the very best it can be.

Worksheet for Identifying Possible Roles

Tool 6.1.2

Identify a range of options for parental and community member involvement. The following are a list of possible roles and the many specific jobs they could include.

GOVERNANCE
- ____ member of school leadership team
- ____ member of planning team
- ____ parent organization leader
- ____ provider of input on surveys/interviews
- ____ participant in focus groups

INSTRUCTIONAL SUPPORT
- ____ tutor
- ____ mentor
- ____ reading in class
- ____ listening to students read
- ____ instructor of adults
- ____ library assistant
- ____ computer assistant
- ____ coverage instructor (e.g., music, art)
- ____ laboratory assistant
- ____ paper grader
- ____ instructional materials preparer
- ____ monitor of learning at home

TECHNICAL SUPPORT
- ____ clerical help
- ____ typing, copying
- ____ receptionist
- ____ telephone answerer
- ____ translator
- ____ financial advisor
- ____ "nurse" in health clinic
- ____ contributor to grant writing activities

ORGANIZATIONAL SUPPORT
- ____ coordinator of volunteers
- ____ class parent
- ____ organizer of awards and recognition
- ____ contributor/committee member
- ____ chaperone
- ____ advocate (formal and informal)
- ____ spokesperson
- ____ parent organization member

ENVIRONMENTAL AND RESOURCE SUPPORT
- ____ grounds and display beautification coordinator
- ____ grounds and display beautification helper
- ____ coordinator of commemoratives
- ____ host/hostess
- ____ greeter
- ____ information person
- ____ provider of food
- ____ guest for lunch or breakfast
- ____ resource contributor

OTHER
- _____
- _____
- _____
- _____
- _____

Range of Involvement Roles

Tool 6.1.3

Does the school offer opportunities for involvement that fit with individuals' levels of time, energy, skill, and mobility? Examine the range of volunteer roles in terms of commitment of time and energy, level of skill required, and the amount of time required at the school site.

Range of Involvement Grid

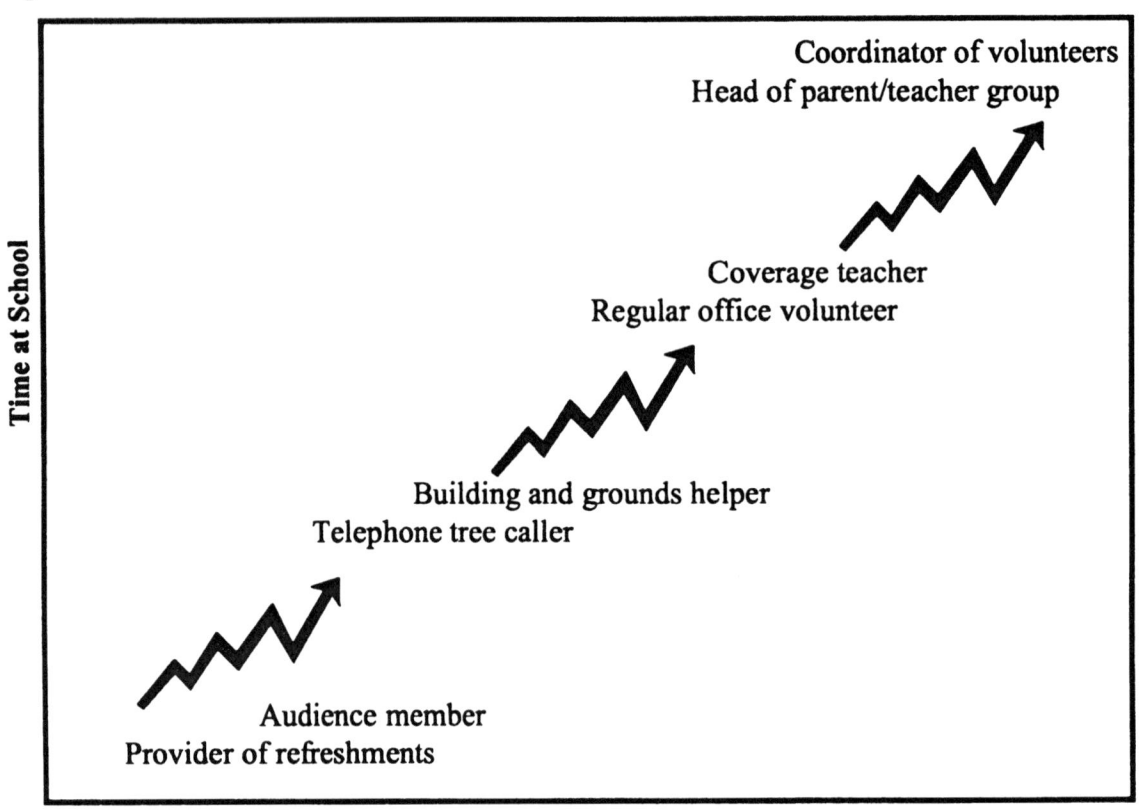

Y-axis: Time at School (Low to High)
X-axis: Level of Expertise (Low to High)

- Low expertise / Low time: Audience member; Provider of refreshments
- Mid expertise / Mid time: Building and grounds helper; Telephone tree caller
- Higher expertise / Higher time: Coverage teacher; Regular office volunteer
- High expertise / High time: Coordinator of volunteers; Head of parent/teacher group

Supporting Parent and Community

> What is most important is providing parents and community volunteers with opportunities that match with their abilities, interests, and schedules.
> Are we asking too much of our volunteers?
> Are we recognizing and utilizing their expertise and time as effectively as possible?

Involvement Opportunities

Tool 6.1.4

If involving parents and community members is a priority for your school, then ...

Money: Helps Make It Happen
A specified amount of money should be dedicated to parent involvement projects and activities. Joyce Epstein (1991) recommends that $25 per student be designated annually for such activities. However, any amount of money committed to this purpose is better than none.

Policy: Makes the Commitment More Visible
A fully described and collaboratively developed policy supporting parent and community involvement should be presented in writing. The policy should be well aligned with the school's vision and provide definite guidance to the involvement program.

Contracts: Secure Commitment
A number of schools require parent(s) to formally commit a designated amount of their time (one hour/week) to school involvement activities. At the same time that parents register their child in school, they sign a three-way contract specifying their commitment to be involved with their child's learning at home and with school-related activities during the day. While it may be difficult to get away from work to come to school, many parents are finding that it is definitely worth the effort. The students take a great deal of pleasure in not letting their parent forget their agreement. Managers in the work force are also seeing the benefits in terms of satisfied and fulfilled workers. They are increasingly more willing to flex and make accommodations for workers requiring lunch time away from the site, late arrivals, or early departures. One school reduced the key points of the contract and made a magnet for each parent to put on the refrigerator door as a daily reminder.

Sample contract

As a parent of _____, I promise to:
- send my child to school ready to learn (rested, healthy, with a good attitude and materials),
- check teachers' weekly communication sheets to monitor my child's progress,
- be sure that time and space are provided for my child to study at home,
- attend parent conferences,
- communicate with teachers if my child or I have a problem or concern,
- participate in at least one volunteer activity each grading period, and
- have lunch with my child or visit in classes at least once a month.

Signed: _____   _____   _____
             Student   Parent   Principal

Commendations: Acknowledge All Contributions
Let volunteers know that their efforts are recognized, appreciated, and valued. A simple "thank you" means a lot! See Tools 4.3.6 and 6.2.11 for additional recognition strategies.

Opportunities for Student Involvement

Tool 6.1.5

Use the following worksheet to guide the discussion on the benefits of student involvement and how to incorporate it most effectively into the current program.

1. **Brainstorm: What types of student involvement activities would enhance their academic, social, or behavioral growth? Then, compile a list for each category.**

    Academic:

    Social:

    Behavioral:

2. **Looking over the list of potential activities, decide which could be carried out at school and which should be conducted within the community.**

    School:

    Community:

3. **How could these activities be incorporated into the regular instructional program?**

4. **What do we think their impact will be on:**

    The student involved:

    The total student body:

    The school:

5. **What guidelines should be developed to monitor students' progress?**

Plan 6.2
Maximizing the Potential of Volunteers

The more adult help in the school, the better--if educators and volunteers can find ways to work effectively, efficiently, and cooperatively with one another. There are many obvious benefits to students and educators, but there are also numerous benefits to those who volunteer as well. Many school are finding that parents, community members, and educators willingly support the use of volunteers when it is a well planned and effectively run endeavor. An increasing number of local, state, and federal mandates require schools to involve parents and community members as volunteers. It is to everyone's advantage to develop truly collaborative relationships and partnerships that are productive.

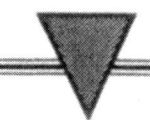

- Secure administrative commitment to a volunteer program. Having overt and continued support from building-level leadership is critical to making the volunteer program a success. The specific leader may not matter greatly--whether it is the principal, assistant principal, department chair, or lead teacher. What seems to make the difference is when someone with schoolwide responsibility has commitment to the program and will ensure effective operation.

- Generate educator, parent, and community member support for the volunteer program. One productive way to do that is to engage educators and volunteers in safely sharing their existing attitudes about involvement. By making their attitudes known, it will then be possible to work together to establish conditions that will ensure maximum potential for the program. Productive collaboration to find opportunities and ways around the barriers to involvement will lead to a more successful program and satisfaction for all involved. Two Tools will be helpful. See Tool 6.2.1 to elicit teachers' and volunteers' opinions about volunteering. It includes sample questionnaires and steps to follow in analyzing the perceptions. Tool 6.2.2 provides a model to follow in identifying strategies to overcome identified barriers to successful volunteer programs.

- Identify a capable individual to coordinate volunteers. Depending on the situation, one individual could be selected as coordinator for the entire school or several people could be chosen to serve as coordinators for one or several grade levels. It is important to determine the specific responsibilities for the coordinator role. Tool 6.2.3 provides a brief description of the volunteer coordinator's job with a listing of major duties. Review and revise the duties to ensure that the essential ones are designated including those that are most appropriate for your school. Then decide how best to fulfill those responsibilities.

- Recruit appropriate candidates to be volunteers. Effective volunteers are those who are dependable, conscientious, caring, respectful of teachers' and students' rights, ethical, congenial, cooperative, and supportive. Capitalize on their interests and talents. Tool 6.2.4 can be used to identify the "talent pool" in the community. They are in our communities and are often more than willing to work with schools when they are asked. See Tool 6.2.5 for a sample recruiting poster. Once they are inside our doors, we need to ensure that they are using their best talents to help us accomplish significant tasks. Tools 6.2.6a and 6.2.6b are forms that can be used to identify parents, community member, and educator interests and needs.

- Orient volunteers to their roles and responsibilities. See Tool 6.2.7 for a suggested Orientation and Training Agenda. It is advisable to schedule several of these sessions per year not just at the beginning of the school year. Holding sessions during the fall, winter, and spring may better meet the needs. Volunteers want and need direction, but caution is advised in thinking about the extent of the training. Studies have found that a little is better than a lot. Too much may be perceived as overtaxing or overwhelming.

- Enter into a contract with any volunteers in the building. The contract serves to emphasize the important expectations on both sides. Difficulties arise when there are no clear "do's" and "don'ts" or when there are unspoken rules rather than well communicated expectations for involvement. One expectation would be that when volunteers have questions or concerns about anything seen or heard, they should know to talk with the administrator (or volunteer coordinator) first. The opportunity to share perceptions would help ensure that accurate data were gathered. This could lead to a clearer understanding of what was observed. Volunteers are in situations that allow them to become aware of privileged information and it is critical that teachers' and students' rights be respected. Volunteers also need to understand how important it is that anything that may be possibly perceived as negative should not be shared throughout the community. The obligation on both sides is to work together to make the school as responsive to the needs of the students and its clients as possible. Tool 6.2.8 provides a sample contract that clearly specifies the expectations of volunteers.

- Establish quality control measures for the volunteer program. As stated earlier, extensive planning and preparation can prevent many potential problems, but if difficulties arise, some effective form of quality control can help work through even the toughest challenges. Tool 6.2.9 describes a quality control can be helpful to the volunteer program.

- Periodically conduct evaluations of the volunteer program. Conduct both formative evaluations during the year to fine tune it and summative evaluations at the end of the year to determine its overall effectiveness. It would be ideal to have the formative evaluations occur through brief face-to-face interviews (coordinator and teacher and coordinator and volunteer) near the end of every grading period. Summative evaluation could also be conducted as a brief interview or in a short written form. If individualized contact is not an option, forms could be distributed to everyone involved at designated points throughout the year. See Tools 6.2.10a, 6.2.10b, 6.2.10c, and 6.2.10d for sample formative and summative evaluations for educators and volunteers. Decisions about adjustments or changes could then be made after the responses (written or oral) are analyzed. As with all evaluations, the information collected must be kept in strictest confidence and reported anonymously--without identifying any individuals.

- Privately and publicly recognize and show appreciation for volunteers. There are many appropriate ways to show that they are valued. The important point is to do it--in many formal and informal ways on a regular basis. Don't wait until the end of the year. Tool 6.2.11 provides suggestions for recognizing volunteers and showing appreciation.

Other Possibilities . . .

Discovering Barriers to Involvement

Tool 6.2.1

The most appropriate time to examine opinions and beliefs about any volunteer program is in its beginning stages. Since most schools have had or currently have experiences with some type of volunteer program, most faculty members have some firmly-held and widely-mixed opinions about the use of volunteers. Some teachers openly welcome the extra help, know what to do with the helpers, and function very smoothly with other adults in the classroom. In some schools, it is not uncommon to see as many as four adults in most classrooms on a regular basis. Other teachers find it very difficult to manage classroom conditions satisfactorily to accommodate other individuals; no matter how capable and well intentioned they are. Spend some time reflecting on educator and volunteer attitudes. By making the attitudes known, it will then be possible to work together to establish conditions that will address existing concerns and ensure maximum potential for the program. Productive collaboration to find opportunities and ways around the barriers to involvement will lead to a more successful program and satisfaction for all involved.

▼ Ask educators and volunteers to anonymously share their feelings about volunteers in the classroom. Brief questionnaires (like the ones that follows) could be developed to gather their opinions.

Educator Questionnaire
(Sample Questions)

The reasons I like having volunteer help are . . .

The reasons I do not like (or am not comfortable about) having volunteer help are . . .

Having volunteers seems to work the best when . . .

Having volunteers does not work well when . . .

My suggestions for making our volunteer program as successful as it could be are . . .

Volunteer Questionnaire
(Sample Questions)

The reasons I like being a volunteer are . . .

The reasons I do not like (or am not comfortable about) being a volunteer are . . .

Being a volunteer seems to work the best when . . .

Being a volunteer does not work well when . . .

My suggestions for making our volunteer program as successful as it could be are . . .

Tool 6.2.1

▼ Analyze educators' opinions. Identify the major patterns in the responses and summarize to share with others. The goal is to learn about the conditions for successful volunteer programs and to capitalize on the opportunities that exist within the situation--and even expand them.

▼ Analyze the opinions about why volunteers do not work out well. Identify the major patterns in the responses and summarize to share with others. The goal is to learn about the major obstacles to successful volunteer programs and to find creative ways to work around them so that they will be minimized or eliminated altogether.

Barriers To Successful Volunteer Programs
and
Strategies to Overcome the Barriers

Tool 6.2.2

Teacher Barrier—"I'm too anxious with another adult in the classroom. I feel like my every word is being judged."

Way Around--Request that volunteers make instructional materials, listen to students read, handle some clerical tasks--anything that would contribute, but that would not require the adult to be in the room. The best strategy is probably a gradual process with the parent first assigned to outside the classroom activities to spending some time in the classroom. The contract between parents and the school will also convey a "we" approach rather than a judgmental relationship.

Parent Barrier—"I don't feel that what I do for my daughter's teacher is very important."

Way Around--Give the parent a grade level or school wide assignment. When it is an individual teacher's responsibility to identify tasks, it can be too demanding. When there is a coordinator for the school, grade level, or both, the assignments can be more diverse, interesting, but also meaningful.

Teacher Barrier—"Some parents are not conscientious and have left me in a real crunch. They are just too unreliable."

Way Around--Working through the coordinator, a second volunteer could be identified for those critical activities. Then if the first volunteer does not fulfill the obligation, there is one prepared to step in. A contingency plan should be developed so that the activity could work if both or one of the volunteers showed.

Parent Barrier—"I show up and it doesn't seem that I'm expected, much less welcomed."

Way Around--Having an official greeter for parent volunteers, a parent room to go to, a coordinator to make arrangements, and an overall attitude that is very supportive of visitors and volunteers should help the volunteers see that they are more than welcomed, but also a valued member of the school community.

Tool 6.2.2

Teacher Barrier—"It takes so much time getting volunteers broken in so they know the routines and how they can be helpful."

Way Around--The coordinator can provide some initial training and orientation so individual teachers do not have to. The coordinator needs to communicate with the teachers about the training agenda (even develop it collaboratively with the teachers). Teacher volunteers could provide some more specific instructional techniques to the volunteers. Perhaps model volunteers could serve as mentors for the novice volunteers giving them their best advice and tricks of the trade.

Parent Barrier—"I don't have a high school diploma. I don't know how I can be of help at my child's school."

Way Around--Attend school with your child. Some schools offer programs that provide general education diploma (GED) assistance as well as baby sitting or child care instruction (parent-child interaction time). A person with limited educational experience could also help by preparing instructional materials such as cut outs or manipulatives. Teachers could prepare intact kits or full instructions that could be ready for any volunteer to do.

Parent Barrier—"I'm worn out from work and the things I have to do around the house. I don't have the time or the energy to volunteer."

Way Around--Help the parent understand that spending quality time with the child is of utmost importance. One way these parents can volunteer their time to help with their child's learning. Formalize their involvement commitment by agreeing to listen to the child read, model own enjoyment of reading, check on homework completion, and monitor television watching.

Volunteer Coordinator's Responsibilities

Tool 6.2.3

The Volunteer Coordinator should . . .

- Determine educator needs (by conducting surveys, questionnaires, discussion, or interviews)

- Organize recruitment efforts

- Interview volunteers to determine areas of expertise, interest, availability, schedule, etc.

- Maintain records of volunteers (names, phone numbers, areas of expertise and interests, availability, and hours worked)

- Provide or oversee appropriate orientation and training for volunteers

- Finalize and monitor the signed contract between the volunteer and the school

- Establish oversight procedures to deal with unsatisfactory situations or placements

- Organize and coordinate formative and summative evaluations of placements and overall effectiveness of the program

- Maintain regular contact and open communication with administrator, teachers, and volunteers

- Confer with the administration regarding decisions related to volunteers and/or the program

- Make necessary adjustments and needed changes in volunteer placements, work assignments, or procedures for the program

- Provide private appreciation and public recognition for the volunteers

Note: If there is more than one coordinator, decisions will need to be made about how to most efficiently and satisfactorily fulfill the responsibilities.

Tool 6.2.4

Parent Talent Book

Name	Talent/Topic You Are Willing To Share	Are you willing to work with Classroom? School? Either?	When You Are Available?	Resources Needed?

Tool 6.2.5

We need you

at our school!

Educator Need Form

Tool 6.2.6a

School Year: _____

Name: _____

Please indicate the ways volunteers could be of the most help to you:

Preferred times to have volunteer help:

   Day(s):

   Times:

Are there other ways that volunteers could help with grade level activities that would be beneficial?

Are there other ways that volunteers could help with schoolwide activities that would be beneficial?

Be sure to ask teachers, administrators, and support personnel.

Parent/Community Member Volunteer Form
School Year: _____

Tool 6.2.6b

Name: _____

Child's Teacher(s): _____

Please indicate your preferences for volunteer activities

_____ **At-home activities**

What types of activities would you prefer?

_____ **At-school activities**

What types of activities would you prefer?
_____ Schoolwide activities
_____ Grade level
_____ Child's classroom
_____ Other (Please describe)

If you are interested in at-school volunteer activities, please indicate the days and times that you would be available.

Days:
- _____ Monday   _____ Thursday
- _____ Tuesday   _____ Friday
- _____ Wednesday

Times: _____ Morning   _____ Afternoon   _____ Full days

Orientation and Training Agenda

Tool 6.2.7

1. **Welcome and introductions**

2. **Orientation to the volunteer program**
   Purposes
   Characteristics of effective volunteer programs (from the information in the plan)

3. **Characteristics of effective volunteers**
   Expectations for Volunteers
   Expectations for School Personnel

4. **Explanation of possible roles**

5. **Additional training opportunities (or information) available**
   List the type of training available such as . . .
      How to listen to children read
      How to read to children
      How to tutor
      How to mentor
      How to work together as effective teams
      How to do office procedures
      How to be a greeter

6. **Fill in volunteer information form**

7. **What to do when things are not going well**
   Oversight procedures
   Evaluation activities

8. **Sign contract/agreement**

Volunteer Contract

Tool 6.2.8

Our Agreement

I,_____(Name of Volunteer),

as a volunteer in _____(Name of School) agree to:

- work cooperatively with school personnel,

- fulfill my volunteer assignments and responsibilities conscientiously and to the best of my ability,

- ensure that information about students is kept confidential,

- serve as a positive role model for the students,

- contribute to improving the educational process, and

- act in ways that will promote parent and community pride in our school.

I understand that working as a volunteer with school personnel will help achieve our goal of providing the best possible learning conditions for our children. Together we can make a difference.

_____   _____
Signature of Volunteer   Date

_____   _____
Signature of Administrator/Parent Coordinator   Date

Quality Control Measures for the Volunteer Program

Tool 6.2.9

Why is Quality Control Needed?

Dissatisfaction with the volunteer program can occur on either side--the volunteer or the educator. It is important to have an identified course of action and someone or some group designated to serve in a quality control or oversight capacity for the volunteer program. The coordinator(s) or administrator(s) are the logical choices, but it might be helpful to also have other educators or volunteer representatives involved. Although a great deal of planning and effort goes into making the program a success, there are always some unpredictable problems that occur which have the potential to undermine its effectiveness. While issues of incompatibility or minor irritation can be dealt with satisfactorily by the coordinator or administrator, more complicated ones may require additional advice and counsel.

What Purposes Would Quality Control Serve?

It would be the responsibility of the quality control group or individual to intervene when a problem is identified that . . .
- cannot be solved satisfactorily by the designated coordinator or administrator,
- is too sensitive to be handled through the normal channels,
- may involve dissatisfaction with the coordinator or other volunteer, and/or
- involves a breach of the contract between the volunteer and the educators.

In general, any situation that may cause hurt feelings or negative consequences to the program should be dealt with immediately by the individual(s) serving in this position.

What Are the Benefits of Quality Control?

The major goal is to deal with the situation with the utmost confidentiality and tact and always with the vision of the school in mind. The coordinator's actions must be aligned with what is best for all students and members of the school community. Therefore, keeping the volunteer program on track and functioning well can provide many benefits to the school and the individuals involved.

Tool 6.2.10a

Educator
Formative Evaluation
of the Volunteer Program

Date: _____

Name: _____

What assignments have the volunteers had?

The volunteers are working out . . .

_____ very well

_____ just fine

_____ not too well

_____ very badly

If it is going well, why?

If it is not going well, what is/are the causes of the problem(s)?

What suggestions do you have to remedy the situation? (What changes do you feel need to be made?)

Would you like to discuss this more?

Tool 6.2.10b

Volunteer
Formative Evaluation of the
Volunteer Program

Date: _____

Name: _____

My main jobs as a volunteer have been . . .

My volunteer assignment is working out . . .

_____ very well

_____ just fine

_____ not too well

_____ very badly

If it is going well, why?

If it is not going well, what is/are the causes of the problem(s)?

What suggestions do you have to remedy the situation? What changes do you feel need to be made?

Would you like to discuss this more?

Tool 6.2.10c

Educator
Summative Evaluation of the Volunteer Program

Please rate each component using the following scale:

1 = strongly agree   2 = agree   3 = disagree   4 = strongly disagree

The assistance provided by the volunteers was of benefit to me and my students.	1	2	3	4
I felt comfortable working with volunteers.	1	2	3	4
The relationship I had with the volunteers was positive.	1	2	3	4
The volunteers understood the goals of the program.	1	2	3	4
The volunteers understood their roles and responsibilities.	1	2	3	4
Volunteers lived up to the terms of their contract.	1	2	3	4
Volunteers had the skills and personality to be effective.	1	2	3	4
I clearly understood my role and responsibilities.	1	2	3	4
The program was well organized and ran smoothly.	1	2	3	4

What did you like best about having a volunteer?

Did you experience any problems associated with your volunteer(s) or the volunteer program in general?

What suggestions do you have for making the volunteer program better?

Will you request a volunteer next year? If not, why?

How do you think we could go about interesting other parents and community members in being volunteers?

How do you think we could go about interesting other educators in having volunteers?

Volunteer
Summative Evaluation of the Volunteer Program

Tool 6.2.10d

Please rate each component using the following scale:

1 = strongly agree   2 = agree   3 = disagree   4 = strongly disagree

As a volunteer, I felt ...

The work I did was meaningful (not busy work).	1	2	3	4
The work I did was helpful to the students and the teacher.	1	2	3	4
The work I did was comfortable for me to do.	1	2	3	4
The work I did required about the right amount of time.	1	2	3	4
The relationship I had with the educator was positive.	1	2	3	4

Orientation and training

The orientation to program was helpful and informative.	1	2	3	4
The training we received helped me be a better volunteer.	1	2	3	4

Roles and responsibilities

I clearly understood my role and responsibilities.	1	2	3	4

Appreciation

My efforts were appreciated.	1	2	3	4
I made a contribution to the school.	1	2	3	4
I felt welcomed in the school.	1	2	3	4

Coordination and organization

The program was well organized and ran smoothly.	1	2	3	4

What did you like best about being a volunteer?

What suggestions do you have for making the volunteer program better?

Will you volunteer next year? If not, why?

How do you think we could go about interesting other parents and community members in being volunteers?

Ways to Recognize Volunteers
and
Show Appreciation

Tool 6.2.11

- ▼ Acknowledge efforts face-to-face. Take the time to find them and tell them how much their assistance has made a difference to you, your class, or the school.

- ▼ Write personalized thank you messages. These could be from the teacher or from students.

- ▼ Create a Wall of Appreciation to display pictures, articles, notes or anything else that would recognize volunteers' efforts and contributions. Display individual portrait type or action shots and change them periodically. In one school, pictures are mounted on butcher paper with room left for educators to write thank you notes. Other schools designate bulletin boards in the office or lobby for this purpose.

- ▼ Include notes or articles in classroom and school newsletters. Highlight specific volunteer activities or individuals who have gone beyond the call of duty. Include action shots with the articles if possible.

- ▼ Have a thank you Food Day. Provide snacks throughout the day or a special breakfast, brunch, lunch, or after school reception.

- ▼ Give volunteers small mementos (with school logo, vision, personalized) to recognize their efforts.

- ▼ Establish a parent workroom so parents can have a place to be and a place to leave some necessary items, materials or supplies.

- ▼ Offer reduced priced lunches while volunteers are working at school.

- ▼ Provide special name tags (that could change seasonally) or more permanent badges.

- ▼ Participate in the Recognition Assembly or program that typically occurs at the end of the year.

- ▼ Offer the chance to win door prizes. Some kind of equalized opportunity system could be designed so everyone would have a chance to win. Choose one week a month and enter everyone's name who has provided some type of volunteer services during the week. Another option might be to hold the drawing once a month and put volunteers' names in the pot one time if they worked during the month--not once for every time they worked.

Plan 6.3
Working as a Team

The business world believes in the power of teamwork. Business leaders are seeing greater pride in quality products, more creativity and innovation, and increased accountability and sense of responsibility. They have seen that the adage, the sum of the whole can be more than the potential of the individual parts is true. Since effective teamwork is so critical to positive outcomes, employees who cannot get along with others or function as team players are seen as negative influences. CEOs of major companies are saying that a main reason for an employee's dismissal from a job is not the inability to do (or to learn how to do) the job, but the inability to get along with others. Educators are responding to their call for team players. They understand that their students need preparation for this aspect of the world of work and are providing more opportunities for students to work as teams and to cooperate to accomplish important goals. By using cooperative learning strategies, they are seeing impressive cognitive gains as well as affective benefits they did not see when students only worked on their own.

Educators are also focusing more on effective teamwork for the adults who are attempting to accomplish the important work of schools. Parents and educators are coming together as leadership or advisory teams to cooperate and collaborate on significant challenges. Whether their participation is voluntary or assigned, the challenge is to shape that collection of individuals into fully functioning teams that are able to and experience all the benefits of productive teamwork. We can learn from successful athletic coaches who have long capitalized on the force of teamwork and have not left its development to chance. They know that their emphasis on team building will create a strong sense of belonging, intense pride, and energizing spirit. By using strategies similar to those employed in coaching and cooperative learning approaches, productive adult teams can be developed that energize their members and generate commitment to accomplishing important long term outcomes even when the work may be unfamiliar and difficult.

In order to ensure the most positive outcomes of teamwork--sense of belonging, efficiency, accomplishment of goals, and pride in the team's functioning and outcomes, certain guidelines need to be addressed. It is important to use these guidelines proactively to prevent problems and negative influences from impacting the performance of the team. They will be helpful in the development of the team, but also in helping the team reflect upon their progress after they have been functioning for a period of time. Even though the team has ideal membership and initial commitment has been given, teams often function at less than desired levels. Taking the time to formally evaluate their collaborative efforts is not generally a high priority when the team appears to be working well. It is only when things are not going well or when the team is "stuck" that the need to assess its functioning becomes apparent. However, if the ultimate goal of a team is to work smarter, not harder, reflecting on how the team is performing can help even the best of teams improve their efficiency and performance.

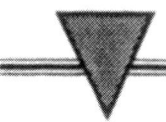

- Establish the need for the team and clarify its purpose. There should be a clear and compelling reason for the team to exist with tasks to be accomplished that are of significant challenge. A committee or task force could accomplish tasks that are of lesser impact and of shorter duration, a task that requires a team effort will probably require longer term commitment.

- Determine the appropriate representation and the skills needed by team members. The exact number of team members can be determined after those questions are answered. By first determining which groups (and subgroups) should be represented, the desired number of team members will become more evident. From 2 to 20 members is acceptable, but 6 to 8 may be more workable and still provide the diversity of perspectives and expertise needed. See Tool 6.3.1 for considerations in determining team membership. A grid strategy is also provided that may guide in selecting team members.

- Discuss the important goals for the team and the way the team should function to fulfill its purpose. Tool 6.3.2 is a worksheet to facilitate the group's discussion. At the same time, involve team members in developing their own rules to live by or code of conduct that will help them accomplish their goals. Tool 1.2.5 in *Design 1: Gathering Perceptions and Collaborating on Results* can be used as a guide.

- After members have been selected and they have accepted their positions, a first level of commitment can be gained by discussing several important issues. Is each member clear about the team's purpose? Does everyone understand the expectations for their involvement? Should the length of team membership be determined? Are the limits of decision making responsibility clear? Is each member willing to make a commitment to the success of the team and to be held mutually accountable for outcomes?

- Team members should spend some time discussing what an effective, efficient team would look like. This could be accomplished through a brainstorm activity. Many educators are familiar with cooperative learning teams and what effective teamwork looks like in those classrooms. Include their experiences in the discussion. Tool 6.3.3 can be used as summary to the brainstorming session to see how closely the team members' thinking aligns with that of researchers in the field.

- At this point the team should determine the roles necessary to accomplish their tasks, to maintain necessary records of events, and communication with others. Some teams or projects are better served by appointing members to the roles for the duration while others rotate them on a periodic basis. See Tool 6.3.4 for a listing of typical team roles and responsibilities.

- Develop strategies for making team meetings most effective. When should they be held? Where? How long should they last? How can they be conducted in the most efficient manner? Tool 6.3.5 provides guidelines for productive meetings that may assist in making these decisions.

- After the team has been working together for a period of time, time should be taken to assess the ways team members have contributed to the progress of the team and the ways the team has worked together. The intent is to promote reflection to determine the behaviors and conditions that are helping members work together well and those that are hindering their progress. See Tool 6.3.6 for a description of developmental stages and growth challenges of teams (Dornseif, 1996). Tool 6.3.7 provides several important team building strategies that can help teams function more effectively. These activities can be targeted to teams functioning at particular stages of development. Tools 6.3.8a and 6.3.8b provide sample self-assessments that can be used with individual team members or the group as a whole. Tool 6.3.9 is an interaction chart that can be used as an observation instrument by an outside facilitator or by one team member serving in that role.

Other Possibilities . . .

Tool 6.3.1

Determining Team Membership

Develop criteria for team membership (if members are to be selected). Some of the most frequently identified desirable traits of team members include optimistic attitude, the ability to see problems and obstacles as opportunities, sense of humor, communication skills, flexibility, credibility, and ability to cooperate and be supportive of team decisions. Consideration should then be given to the specific skills or qualities that would be necessary for the team to function efficiently to accomplish the identified tasks. In addition to appropriate representation (e.g., important groups, grade levels, departments that should have a voice), consider areas of expertise, access to information, previous experience, available time to fulfill the commitment, etc. The following strategy using a grid can help guide team member selection. First, identify the major criteria for team membership. The criteria could become evident by answering the question: What skills and characteristics are needed by members in order for the team to function effectively and accomplish its goals? Second, identify potential team members by name. Finally, complete the grid by checking off the traits and skills exhibited by the proposed individuals. When there are some skills and traits not represented by the proposed individuals, it may be that additional members should be suggested or that different individuals should replace some who are being considered.

Name	Stakeholders				Knowledge	Writing Skills	Credibility	Dependability	Available Time	Link to Agencies	Experience
	Educators	Parents	Supp. Pers.	Comm. Member							

Special thanks to Jerry J. Bellon, USDA Curriculum Workshops (1994) for team building suggestions.

Team Worksheet

Tool 6.3.2

Purpose/Mission
What are the major responsibilities or tasks of our team?

Code of Conduct
If we are to work together cooperatively and collaboratively as a team, what rules can we agree upon as those we will live by? (See Tool 1.2.5 for an example.)

Roles
If we are to fulfill our purposes, what roles should team members play?

Roles	Responsibility
_____	_____
_____	_____
_____	_____
_____	_____
_____	_____

How often should the role assignments change?

Self-evaluation
How and at what points should we assess the effectiveness of our team and set improvement goals?

Productive Team Behaviors

Tool 6.3.3

Researchers suggest that members of high performing teams . . .

Seek Information
Ask questions
Ask for help
Ask for clarification, facts, and opinions

Give Information and Opinions
Contribute ideas, expertise, materials
Elaborate by giving examples and personal experiences
Offer differing perspectives

Coordinate/Make Sense
Suggest or show relationships
Pull ideas together

Summarize
Listen actively, reflect on what others are saying
Paraphrase, restate positions, comments

Encourage
Express feelings
Express warmth and empathy toward group members
Acknowledge contributions of others
Reinforce others' ideas
Express support and acceptance
Ensure everyone's participation--not forcing contributions but allowing them

Mediate
Reconcile differences, seek common ground
Suggest options
Offer compromises
Test to see if nearing consensus
Suggest criteria

Relieve Tension
Use humor to enhance group cohesiveness
Exhibit self-control
Disagree without criticizing
Work to resolve conflicts productively

Stay on task
Continue to engage in activity
Keep each other focused on the issue

Potential Roles for Team Members

Tool 6.3.4

Leader
Develops the Agenda
Sets the Task
Begins the Discussion
Defines and Redefines the Problem
Formulates the Decision Questions

Runner
Acquires Necessary Materials and Equipment
Arranges the Room

Facilitator
Serves as Timekeeper
Checks on and Encourages Participation
Promotes Attending to Task

Reporter
Communicates to Others
Responds to Inquiries
Sends Necessary Correspondence

Recorder
Develops Written Records of Meetings
Denotes Action(s) Taken
Identifies Next Steps

Observer
(At Designated Intervals)
Records Interaction
Diagnoses Difficulties
Analyzes Obstacles
Holds Members to Standards of Performance
Provides Constructive Feedback

****

Roles should be appropriate for the particular task. Select all or some of the roles to achieve the group's purposes or define others that may be more useful. Roles could be permanent (for a designated period) or could rotate at appropriate times.

Guidelines for Productive Meetings
Working Smarter, Not Harder

Tool 6.3.5

▼ Begin and end at agreed upon times. Set an approximate time limit for the meeting and attempt to stick to it. Begin promptly and adjourn at the designated time or reach agreement about extending the time.

▼ Provide introductions, if necessary, or acknowledge the presence of each participant.

▼ Clearly communicate the purpose of the meeting as soon as it is appropriate. If there is a preset agenda, be sure to provide the opportunity for participants' input into revisions or additions. Another good option is to create the agenda together--a shared agenda. This communicates that everyone's input is needed. It is helpful to post the agenda so all can see what is being suggested (e.g., butcher paper, on a transparency, on a chalkboard).

Agenda

Date: _____

Items

1.

2.

3.

4.

5.

Unfinished business or Items for next meeting:

1.

2.

▼ Before proceeding with the agenda, begin with something positive. This could be an accomplishment, progress, special effort, support or comments received, etc. An appropriate cartoon or quote may also be helpful.

Tool 6.3.5

▼ Identify someone to develop a brief written summary of the meeting, if a member has not been designated as the recorder. This person may volunteer at the meeting or could have been volunteered prior to the meeting. The role of recorder may rotate.

▼ When there are multiple teams operating within the school, it is helpful if every team uses an agreed upon format for written summaries of meetings and activities. After each meeting or event, the form should be completed by the designated individual. The sheet is then placed in a notebook established for that purpose. Maintain the notebook in an accessible place for all interested people to see.

Team
_____

Date:

In attendance:

Major points of discussion:

Decisions made:

Further follow-up action required:

Items for next meeting agenda:

Succeeding at TEAMWORK

Tool 6.3.6

Is our school leadership, grade level, or departmental team a high performing one? In what developmental stage is our team? What do we need to do to develop into a fully functioning team?

*A team in the **FORMING** stage is one whose members are just beginning to work together. This could be a newly formed team whose members are all new--or one that has had some recent major changes in membership.*

We are FORMING if we are . . .
- Acting politely to one another
- Looking to the principal for leadership
- Operating at a high energy level
- Doing what we are told to do
- Expressing negative feelings privately and politely
- Beginning to see cliques and hidden agendas
- Obeying the rules
- Accomplishing some real work

What we need to do at this stage of development . . .
- Develop a code of conduct
- Engage in team building activities to develop trust
- Learn and practice effective communication skills

*A team in the **STORMING** stage can be productive and function adequately, but their actions may not be the best. In addition, relationships and team spirit may suffer.*

We are STORMING if we are . . .
- Freely expressing our ideas, opinions, and positions
- Exhibiting hostility or passive aggressive behavior
- Some members are striving for power and influence
- Resolving conflicts through ineffective and destructive means
- Doing what is required, but not approaching tasks with enthusiasm or creativity

What we need to do at this stage of development . . .
- Promote a win-win philosophy
- Monitor adherence to a code of conduct
- Develop constructive conflict resolution strategies
- Periodically review and revise the purposes and functions of the team
- Decide on appropriate roles for each member to ensure that everyone has productive ways to contribute
- Designate someone, possibly an outsider, to serve as facilitator if the team is stuck

Tool 6.3.6

A NORMING team has developed some maturity having survived the trials of the first stages. There is a sense of accomplishment, trust, excitement, and readiness for more substantive challenges.

We are NORMING if we are . . .
- Actively listening to one another
- Beginning to develop a trusting relationship
- Valuing creativity and diverse opinions
- Tackling difficult issues with enthusiasm
- Changing preconceived opinions when credible information or data challenge them
- Using effective processes for decision making and conflict resolution
- Making progress toward goals
- Building team spirit
- Developing shared leadership

What we need to do at this stage of development . . .
- Periodically assess the performance by all members
- Involve groups members in self-assessment
- Provide opportunities for reflection and action to improve team functioning

Teams that are PERFORMING are aware of their abilities and are competent in handling even the toughest tasks with ease and confidence. They are living up to the vision they established for themselves.

We are PERFORMING if we are . . .
- Efficiently and effectively identifying problems and potential solutions
- Progressing smoothly on action plans
- Willingly holding ourselves accountable
- Identifying evaluation criteria to measure our progress
- Accepting leadership and responsibility
- Developing the highest levels of trust and camaraderie exhibiting relaxed interactions and positive humor

What we need to do at this stage of development . . .
- Welcome, orient, and mentor new members to expectations and procedures
- Periodically reassess strengths and contributions of individual members
- Regularly assessing teams' functioning and identifying challenges for action

Summarized from Dornseif, Allan. (1996). *A Pocket Guide to School-Based Management. Number 7: Succeeding at Teamwork.* Alexandria, VA: Association for Supervision and Curriculum Development. Included in that document is a brief questionnaire that helps teams identify their current stage of development.

Team Building Strategies: Developmental Activities for Teams

Tool 6.3.7

▼ Engage in trust building activities. Many teams have found ropes courses or trust walks to be helpful activities. In general, trust among team members develops gradually as they work together on meaningful tasks and succeed at significant challenges. Trust evolves from knowing the individual strengths of members and being able to rely on them, gradually developing a shared sense of purpose and belonging, and feeling a growing commitment from all members to the success of the team.

▼ Plan informal socialization opportunities. Having refreshments available before the meetings begin and at breaks is always welcome. Collegiality is enhanced when members get to know each other on a personal level.

▼ Identify and share the strengths and perspectives of individual team members. A Multiple Intelligence Inventory will identify each person's areas of natural intelligence and will illustrate the collective sources of intelligence within the team. The Myers-Briggs personality assessment or a Learning Styles assessment will indicate members' interests and work preferences. Any of these options could serve as a springboard for promoting awareness of team members' strengths and their potential for contributing to the team.

▼ Become more knowledgeable about effective communications. Engage in exercises on various types of communication. There are a wealth of resources available. One of the best is *Reaching Out: Interpersonal Effectiveness and Self-Actualization* by David W. Johnson.

▼ Develop constructive conflict resolution strategies. In developing teams, minor to major conflicts are nearly inevitable. Mediation strategies can be very helpful in finding common areas of agreement and ways to move beyond the dispute. If a particular member is continually exhibiting negative group behaviors (e.g., being aggressive, blocking or interfering with the progress, being disruptive through excessive joking or clowning, or withdrawing from the activities), those behaviors need to be controlled for the good of the team. When the overall team spirit is healthy, it is a matter of confronting the negative behavior. If confrontation is necessary, it is important to focus on the behavior (not the person) by giving behavior descriptions and by emphasizing the effects of the actions. Providing the member with alternative ways to act that are more productive frequently eliminates the negative behavior. (See Tool 2.3.7.)

▼ Use specific problem solving and decision making processes. The ways problems are solved and decisions are made can promote a win-win philosophy or can lead to win-lose confrontations. (See Tools 1.2.9 through 1.2.15 for descriptions of the processes.)

Tool 6.3.7

▼ Decide on appropriate roles for each member to ensure that everyone has productive ways to contribute. (See Tool 6.3.4.)

▼ There are times when teams appear to be stuck. That is, the team is not functioning smoothly, is unable to overcome an obstacle, or is ineffective in moving ahead. It may be necessary to identify an individual who can serve as facilitator to get things back on track.

▼ Designate times to monitor how well the team is functioning. Several important questions should be answered: Are we living up to our code of conduct? Are we still clear on the purposes and functions or our team? Are all members performing to expectations? (See Tool 6.3.6 for criteria that could be used to monitor the team's progress.) If the team is not achieving at its desired level, it would be a productive time to develop mutual goals for growth.

▼ Mentor new team members to help them learn the teams' expectations and procedures. If members rotate off and on the team, be sure that the new members join at staggered points to maintain continuity.

▼ Celebrate successes. Periodically take time to reflect on the team accomplishments and progress. Mark tentative dates to celebrate on the calendar at the beginning of the year.

▼ Convene team meetings with something positive--acknowledgments, special efforts by individuals and groups, a humorous event, or meaningful quote.

▼ Develop a log of accomplishments--dedicate a spiral notebook, stack of index cards, or a word processing document to jotting down the group's feelings, insights, descriptions of team high points, and successes.

Teamwork Assessment
Team Member Reflection

Tool 6.3.8a

As a team member, to what extent do I . . .	I Could Do Better	I'm Okay	I'm Doing Very Well
Support team members	O	O	O
Listen attentively	O	O	O
Communicate openly and honestly	O	O	O
Commit to group decisions (and actions)	O	O	O
Encourage participation and contributions of others	O	O	O
Remain open to new possibilities	O	O	O
Accept others' ideas	O	O	O
Fulfill roles and responsibilities	O	O	O
Arrive on time and remain focused	O	O	O
Help resolve conflicts	O	O	O
Defuse potentially negative situations	O	O	O

At this point, I feel my major contributions to the team are . . .

In the future, to be a better team member, I will . . .

Teamwork Assessment
Team Reflection

Tool 6.3.8b

As a team, to what extent do we...	We Could Do Better	We're Okay	We're Doing Very Well
Set realistic goals and follow through on expectations	O	O	O
Meet deadlines	O	O	O
Exhibit appropriate team behaviors	O	O	O
Capitalize on the talents and diversity of the members	O	O	O
Maintain a future orientation	O	O	O
Stay open to innovative ideas	O	O	O
Approach tasks creatively	O	O	O
Hold efficient meetings	O	O	O
Maintain necessary records and communications	O	O	O
Celebrate successes	O	O	O
Recognize and reward contributions of team members	O	O	O
Exhibit interdependence of team members	O	O	O
Show care and concern for one another	O	O	O

At this point, our best qualities as a team are...

In the future, to be a better team, we will...

Interaction Chart

Tool 6.3.9

An interaction chart is an observational tool that can be used by a team member or outsider serving as a process observer. It can be an objective record of participation during a team meeting or activity providing important information about how well the team functions. To create the chart, draw the physical arrangements--table, seating positions identifying individuals, any equipment, etc. As the meeting progresses, log the interaction that takes place. At the simplest level, each comment by any participant can be numbered (1-2-3-4-5 . . .). It could be noted if the comment was brief (BC) or if it were an extended comment (ExC). This will give some indications of the dynamics of the interaction. A more complex possibility is to label the contributions made by each member (or develop a verbal log). It is possible to note each time a member asks a question (?), provides encouragement to others (E), interjects humor (H), comments off topic (OC), etc. If abbreviations are used, be sure to note them on the form so they will not be forgotten when the team looks at the chart.

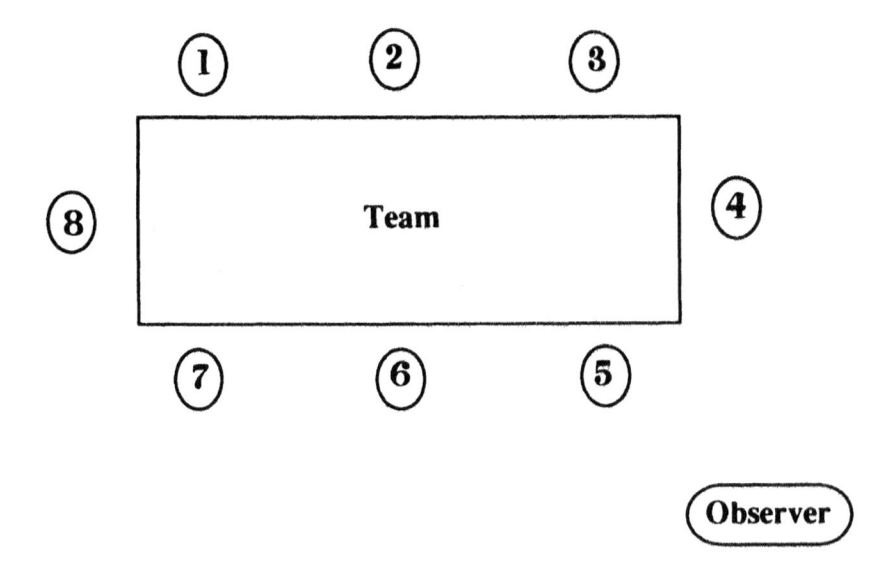

```
        ①      ②      ③
      ┌─────────────────┐
   ⑧  │      Team       │  ④
      └─────────────────┘
        ⑦      ⑥      ⑤

                         (Observer)
```

Design 7

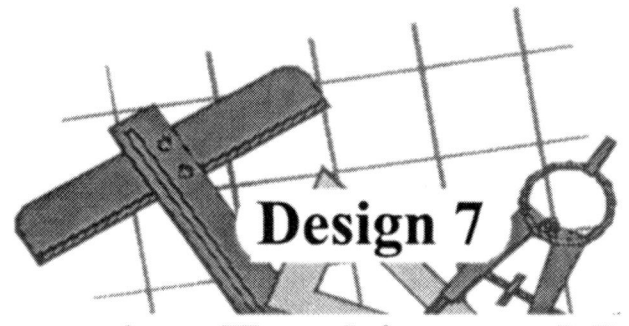

Supporting Teaching and Learning

> **Supporting Teaching and Learning is ...**
> - translating high expectations into clear goals and positive action.
> - helping each child become the best he or she can be.
> - striving for high quality, interactive instruction; providing challenging, coherent curriculum; and expanding co-curricular activities that enhance learning and expand academic experiences.
> - ensured by the active support and productive involvement of parents and community members.
> - providing appropriate home supports for homework, behavioral expectations, and social skills.
> - assisting adults within the community in their lifelong learning pursuits.

Teaching and learning is the heart of the matter in our schools. Students spend about 15,000 hours attending school throughout their K-12 years and it is critical that those hours be spent in learning experiences that challenge, intrigue, and stimulate. Educators realize the importance of making every minute count and are continually expanding their repertoire of research based strategies to enhance student learning. They concur with parents in the belief that every student has the right to expect high-quality learning opportunities. As a society, all races, socioeconomic levels and cultures also have a right to expect that *alll* students are allowed and encouraged to function at their highest levels of capability.

Partnerships focus on generating strong support for teaching and learning to achieve these desired results. Successful teachers know that their students' academic, personal, social, and civic growth is far greater when what they are learning at school is supported and extended at home. The research clearly shows that student learning can be greatly enhanced if parenting adults reinforce and promote positive academic attitudes and provide adequate conditions for students to attend to school requirements. Collaboration between parents and educators is the key to developing consistency in home and school approaches to learning. Working together in partnerships, parents and educators can mutually enhance and reinforce efforts at "good parenting." Partnerships allow educators the opportunity to help parents see and believe that they *do* make a significant difference in their child's learning.

Another benefit of the partnership's direct focus on teaching and learning is the potential for emphasizing and extending learning beyond the school walls. Many educators are establishing relationships within the public and private sectors which result in meaningful, "real life" learning experiences for students. The schools that are becoming true "laboratories for learning" are also producing growth and renewal opportunities for the adult learners in the communities as well.

What we hear from ...

EDUCATORS

"Our mentoring program has been extremely successful. The students gain first hand experience about career possibilities and what is required to be successful. This brings a whole new meaning to the student's school work." (Secondary supervisor)

"Homework can be a source of frustration for everyone. The students hit a roadblock--they don't come to get the help they need--they fail--their parents get mad. It seems to start a very negative scenario. I think it's time to rethink our whole approach." (High school math teacher)

"One of my most satisfying roles this year has been as a facilitator for our parenting classes. It has been rewarding to work with such dedicated and interested parents. The only negative factor is that we haven't been able to involve as many of the parents as we had wanted." (Elementary teacher)

PARENTS

"It bothers me that I don't know how to help my child learn." (High school parent)

"I've gone to many of the Parent Academy sessions. I've learned a lot and enjoyed talking with other parents who have similar interests and concerns. I hope the school continues them." (Elementary parent)

"At my grandson's school, teachers have 'make and take' workshops in the spring before school is out. We get so many ideas and materials to use with our children during the summer. It really helps make the summer less boring for the kids--and for me!" (Grandparent of a third grader)

STUDENTS

"I used to have a hard time understanding, but now that I'm in this team--it just goes a lot easier. And it is a lot more fun!" (7th grader)

"My mom works all the time. Even when she's home, she doesn't have time to help me with my homework." (5th grader)

"I learned that two of my stronger intelligences are musical and interpersonal. This helps me understand why I enjoy being the chorus so much!" (10th grader)

Shared Responsibilities

In effective partnerships, *both* educators and parents, families, guardians, or caregivers take responsibility for supporting teaching and learning. The following diagram illustrates the responsibilities that are unique to each group and those that both groups share.

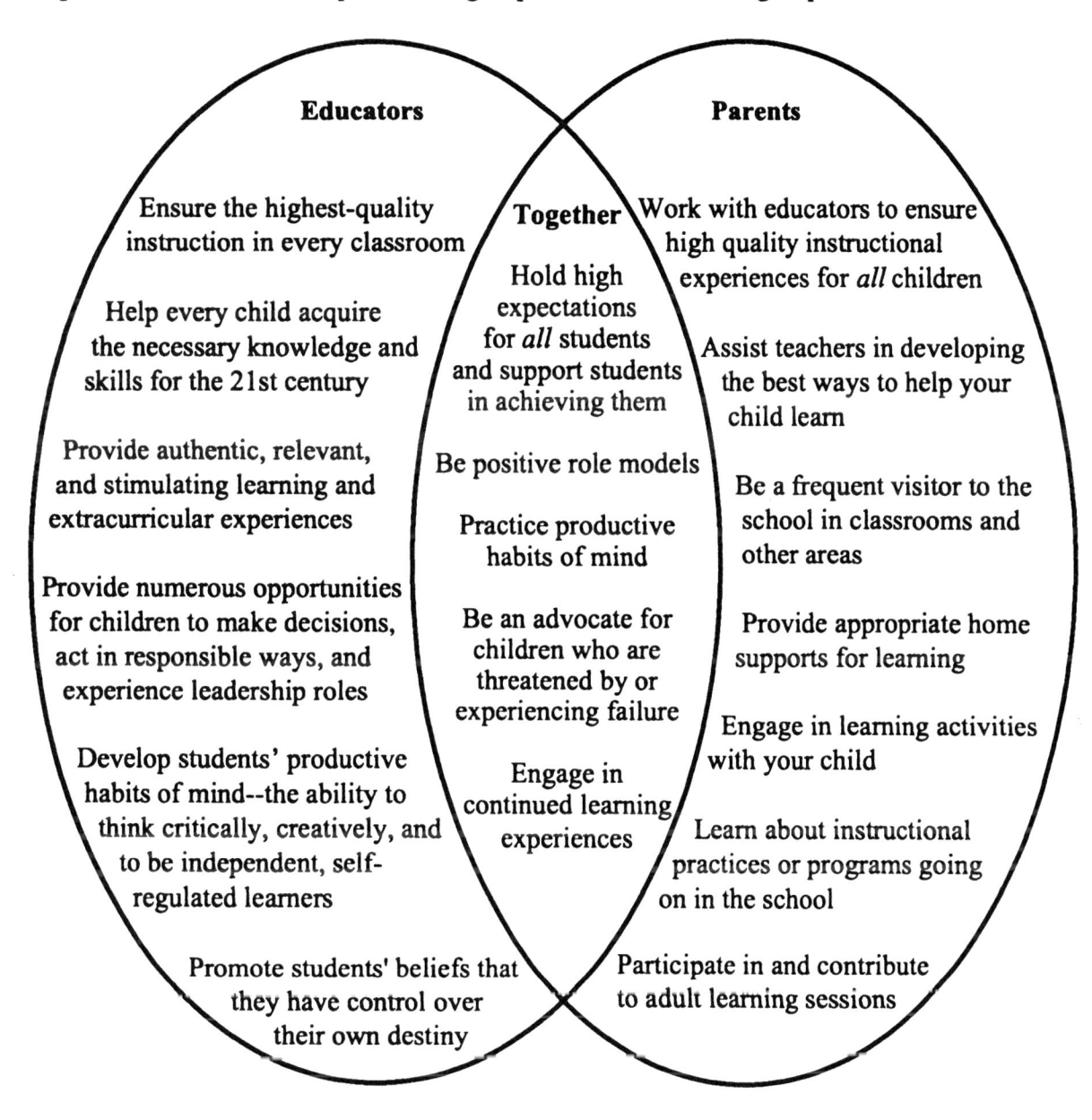

Educators

- Ensure the highest-quality instruction in every classroom
- Help every child acquire the necessary knowledge and skills for the 21st century
- Provide authentic, relevant, and stimulating learning and extracurricular experiences
- Provide numerous opportunities for children to make decisions, act in responsible ways, and experience leadership roles
- Develop students' productive habits of mind--the ability to think critically, creatively, and to be independent, self-regulated learners
- Promote students' beliefs that they have control over their own destiny

Together

- Hold high expectations for *all* students and support students in achieving them
- Be positive role models
- Practice productive habits of mind
- Be an advocate for children who are threatened by or experiencing failure
- Engage in continued learning experiences

Parents

- Work with educators to ensure high quality instructional experiences for *all* children
- Assist teachers in developing the best ways to help your child learn
- Be a frequent visitor to the school in classrooms and other areas
- Provide appropriate home supports for learning
- Engage in learning activities with your child
- Learn about instructional practices or programs going on in the school
- Participate in and contribute to adult learning sessions

It may seem surprising, but surveys show that most parents, regardless of their background, want guidance from the schools on ways to help their children learn better.

Oliver C. Moles, 1996, p. 1

Plans and Tools
for carrying out our responsibilities in supporting teaching and learning

Plan 7.1. Engaging Parental and Community Support for Learning
This plan addresses the need to engage parent and community member support for learning. Tools include promising strategies for helping parents and others understand and support classroom instructional practices. They also highlight ways that educators, parents, community members, and businesses can collaborate to broaden the learning experiences for students.

Plan 7.2. Supporting Learning at Home
This plan focuses on promoting positive home supports for learning. Tools include strategies for helping children with homework, study skills, and life skills. They also suggest ways to develop productive habits of mind and lifelong learners. Potentially effective parent-child projects are suggested as ways to involve parents in homework in ways that will extend the learning and enjoyment for the child--as well as the parent.

Plan 7.3. Promoting Lifelong Learning
The theme of this plan is "You're never too old to learn." Considerations are provided for making adult learning opportunities as productive as possible. Educators' attempts to help parents deal with areas of mutual interest can be highly effective when important guidelines are followed. The Tools provide strategies to facilitate "lifelong" learning in the most appropriate ways for adult learners.

Educator Reflection
Supporting Teaching and Learning

In order to engage parents and community most effectively in supporting what educators are trying to accomplish in their schools and classrooms, it is important to begin by reflecting on current practices. Consider each of the following items that relate to various aspects of the instructional program. Put an "X" in the box that most closely reflects your perception.

In general . . .   Often   Sometimes   Rarely

1. teachers hold adequate expectations for student academic growth and behavior.

2. educators in this school make every effort to address the needs of *all* students.

3. educators generally go out of their way to help students who need extra help with assignments or problems.

4. the grades and recognition children receive generally reflect their effort.

Classwork and homework . . .

5. adequately cover required academic content.

6. are interesting and useful to students.

7. appropriately emphasize personal, social, and civic learning.

8. incorporate innovative strategies (e.g., cooperative learning, technology).

School personnel make an effort to help students . . .

9. become more organized, responsible, and self-disciplined.

10. develop their talents and interests.

11. develop their leadership abilities.

12. develop skills required for success in life (e.g., problem-solving, decision making, conflict resolution, and communication).

	Often	Sometimes	Rarely

Educators are provided with adequate or appropriate . . .

13. opportunities for professional development.

14. time to prepare for lessons and classroom responsibilities.

15. class sizes to allow enough time for individual student needs.

16. recognition and support for quality instruction (e.g., from administrators, parents, students, others).

In terms of parents and community members, . . .

17. adequate home support for learning is provided by most of our parents (e.g., appropriate conditions-time and place, expectations).

18. most parents take advantage of opportunities to become more informed about parenting skills or topics of interest.

19. school personnel provide adequate and appropriate learning opportunities and programs of interests for parents and community members.

20. this school has a strong reputation within the community.

Plan 7.1
Engaging Parental and Community Support for Learning

In today's world, educators are finding it necessary to take a proactive position in "instructing" others about what should be going on in schools. There are several reasons why this is necessary. First, as educators continue to enhance their knowledge of effective practices and quality programs, they realize the need to inform their public about changes in school and classroom practices. This reduces the likelihood that they will be confronted by negative perceptions about their efforts or objections to particular innovative practices. Why should this be a concern? Schools are the only professional setting where everyone over the age of five years has had first hand experience. As a result, many parents and community members feel that this experience makes them qualified to judge any aspect of schooling. Schools that are most successful in introducing new practices have found that keeping parents and community members informed and enlisting their support thwarts potential confrontations.

Second, the increasing complexities of schooling and raising children have brought about new challenges and demands. Society holds schools responsible for far more than academics. The business community and general population want schools to produce knowledgeable students with good character, social skills, and a commitment to civic responsibility and lifelong learning. These challenges make it even more important today that educators and families work as partners to support the academic and personal growth of their children.

Third, to the casual visitor and interested parent, the changes taking place in our schools and classrooms may appear a bit confusing and overwhelming. In some cases, they may oppose the changes, primarily from lack of knowledge. However, when educators take the time and effort to help them understand the program or instructional strategy and how it can improve their child's learning, they are more likely to be supportive of the teachers at school, at home, and in the community.

This plan will highlight strategies that many successful schools have used to "instruct" their parents and community members about their overall school program or specific innovative components. It is not a comprehensive approach to all current innovations, but rather a guide to assist educators in gaining the support of their constituents on any aspect of the school program.

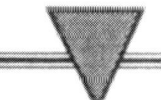

- Send invitations to parents and community members to visit the school and individual classrooms. It would also be a good idea to include invitations to school board members, politicians, and others who are in decision making roles. Tool 7.1.1 is a sample invitation for a classroom visit. The purpose is not to "put on a show," but to allow others to see the extraordinary things that go on every single day.

- Decide on the best ways to educate parents, community members, and others about what effective schooling involves. Provide easy to read information to parents about effective practices used by classroom teachers and the high-quality programs going on in the school. Tool 7.1.2 is a sample communication to parents that illustrates what a visitor would observe in any of the learner-centered school's classrooms. A written document similar to this could be shared as new parents enroll their children in the school, at open house, at conferences, or any other appropriate time. An enticing description of what is taking place inside classrooms is an important first step in engaging parents' long term support. As it opens the door for meaningful discussion, questions, or clarification, it may also encourage more active participation in volunteer activities that support what has been described.

- Use these written materials to help parents and community members understand specific instructional strategies that might appear confusing or counterproductive at first glance. Cooperative learning is a popular and productive instructional practice, but not one that many parents experienced as students. As a result, many view it as a new term for group work. The term group work conjures their own images of some students doing all the work while others sat back doing little or nothing and everyone sharing the same reward or grade. They fear that their child will be harmed by such experiences, either by not being made to work or doing all the work while others receive credit and grades they do not deserve. While cooperative learning strategies have been thoroughly researched and their benefits have been well documented, educators realize that they must help parents see how it will benefit their child as well as or better than other instructional practices. Tool 7.1.2 is a model for sharing the facts about cooperative learning. Other important instructional topics could be summarized and provided as a written communication or as a topic of a focus session. Whatever means is selected, educators are finding it helpful to share the reasons for using the approaches and their benefits in encouraging more efficient learning and more positive attitudes towards learning.

- Many individuals, groups, and businesses within the private sector have tremendous talents, knowledge and experiences to share with students. Those who have become involved in partnerships with schools are finding that they reap significant benefits in return. The quality of the potential work force is improved, the current work force is more satisfied (not feeling divided between obligations of work and those of parenthood), and employees are experiencing positive rewards from giving to others and making a positive difference in the lives of children. At the same time, establishing partnerships with community members who do not have school-aged children also increases their understanding of the challenges and opportunities educators are facing. The more aware they are, the more likely they will be to support the financial needs of schools--individually and as citizens voting for adequate financial funding. When schools are open to the community as true laboratories for learning that encourage student and adult learning in a variety of contexts, community members and business leaders can see for themselves that their tax dollars are well spent. Tool 7.1.4 provides some suggested strategies for involving community members in the public and privates sectors in the educational process. This Tool highlights several of the many significant and meaningful ways they can contribute.

Invitation to a Classroom Visit

Tool 7.1.1

Date:

Dear _____,

We invite you to come to our classroom to see for yourself what a busy place it is! The month of November would be a good time for us. Our instructional program involves the students in a variety of ways. You will see them participating in "hands-on" experiences, interesting research investigations, technology-based learning, and cooperative learning. We would enjoy your being with us to see it all first hand. Unfortunately, I will only be able to talk with you briefly during the visit. I know you will understand that when the students are present, I will be attending to their needs.

If you would like to join us for a visit of 30 minutes to an hour, please circle the best days of the week and time for you:

Day   M   T   W   Th   F

Are there any specific dates you know will not be good for you?
_____

Time (Please circle all that would be okay for you)
- 9:00 - 9:30
- 9:30 - 10:00
- 10:00 - 10:30
- 10:30 - 11:00
- 12:00 - 1:00
- 9:00 - 11:30 (anytime)

Our lunch time is _____. Would you like to have lunch with the class? Yes __ No__

I'll get back to you to schedule your visit. We look forward to seeing you.

Sincerely,

Teacher's name

Student's name

A Visitor to Learner-Centered Classrooms

Tool 7.1.2

Will See...

Students working independently, with a partner, in teams, in small groups, as a whole group, or with adult volunteers, at their own desks, in the floor, at learning centers, at a computer, curled up in a bathtub or a loft with a good book, in the hall with a parent or learning partner (even from another grade)

Students who are curious, asking questions, learning to work with others from different backgrounds and characteristics, not afraid to make mistakes in order to learn, taking responsibility for their own learning, making decisions or choices about what to learn and how to learn, being inventive and creative thinkers, excitedly sharing what they are learning with others

Students who are engaged in completing independent assignments, memorizing important information, researching on their own, designing projects, thinking critically and solving problems, identifying behaviors are important in helping them be successful, monitoring their own learning, developing plans and gathering resources, setting goals, using knowledge in ways that are meaningful and relevant, quizzing each other, tutoring others, and occasionally appearing to be frustrated as they push the limits of their ability

Teachers who are facilitating student learning, coaching, monitoring students' progress, providing feedback for improvement, reinforcing with praise and encouragement, answering students' questions with probing questions to guide their learning, modeling thinking processes to help students think on their own, coordinating several activities

A classroom that has a democratic atmosphere, many activities occurring at the same time, students moving about without having to ask for permission, flexible and movable furniture arrangements, walls decorated with student work and works in progress (not always perfect)

Will Hear...

students interacting with peers, the language of thinking, comments that indicate that students are taking charge of their own learning, respectful interactions, a can do attitude, less than correct answers being acknowledged as starting points for better understanding, laughter, students discussing how what they are learning related to "real life"

May Not See or Hear...

All the preparation time and effort the teacher has put into planning and developing lessons and materials

---

> Don't be surprised at the students' eagerness to share what they are doing and learning as you visit.

The Value of Cooperative Learning

Cooperative learning differs from group work in several ways.

Students are given a group goal that requires all members to work together. The group is only successful when all members are learning. No one is allowed to "ride the coat tails" of other team members.

Each student is first responsible for his or her own learning and then for the learning of all team members. Every one is held "individually accountable."

Students are given roles to ensure the group's progress. These roles, such as "encourager," "checker," "runner," "timekeeper," etc. all contribute to the team's effectiveness and success.

Students are often given part of the information to complete a task and must share what they have learned with their team mates. This requires that each student participates. Teachers are aware of differences in students' abilities and assign material accordingly.

Cooperative learning groups are carefully designated and rotate throughout the year to give students a chance to work with many classmates. They do stay as a team long enough to learn how to work well together. Group membership is not the hit or miss approach of traditional group work where students are randomly assigned.

Students' grades are not totally dependent on the group's performance. In many cases, students receive bonus points when all team members score well on a test, produce an outstanding project, or show significant improvement. Students still receive grades for their individual achievement.

Cooperative learning prepares students for the world of work.

The SCANS Report, U.S. Secretary of Labor's Commission on Achieving Necessary Skills (1991), was published to alert schools to desirable workplace skills and traits. Among the most critical to success in the workplace are decision making, team work, problem solving and other outcomes of cooperative learning.

Companies are as interested in potential employees' ability to work as a contributing, supportive team member as they are in formal training.

Cooperative learning develops students' capacities to help one another. In the process, students also realize that they have something important to contribute, which enhances self-esteem.

Cooperative learning develops students' interpersonal skills. Many "gifted" people lack the ability to work with others. As a result, they do not make the progress in their work lives that their "IQ" might have indicated. Cooperative learning provides valuable training for students who might not develop effective interpersonal skills on their own.

Cooperative learning trains students to assess their ability to work as an effective team. By self-assessing their strengths and weaknesses, they learn a process that is critical to personal as well as professional growth and success.

Cooperative learning teaches social skills that are critical for productive citizenship.

Teachers make sure that students develop and use appropriate social skills. They teach students how to communicate effectively, make decisions, work as a team, and resolve conflicts. When groups are working, teachers monitor to assure that students are applying what they have learned.

Cooperative learning helps students develop more positive relationships with their peers. They learn to communicate with others who are different from themselves. Students practice working with people from diverse backgrounds. Since cooperative groups mix students of different races, ethnic origins, genders, intellectual abilities, and physical abilities, students learn to overcome barriers and differences by working together and getting to know each other as individuals.

Students learn to make shared decisions. They learn to listen to others' points of view and to discuss alternative approaches for making a decision. In doing so, they often improve their own methods of decision making.

Students have more opportunities to assume leadership roles. One student in three or four will lead their teams through a cooperative activity. Leadership roles are rotated among team members so that each student has leadership responsibilities on a regular basis.

Students learn to trust in others by working closely with them. They support each other's learning, share ideas, needs, successes, and failures. In the process, they learn to rely on others and to be relied upon by their team members.

Students of all ability levels achieve more through cooperative learning.

Although cooperative learning was initially designed to promote acceptance among students of diverse backgrounds, researchers have documented that academic gains are as significant as social gains. When activities are structured correctly, all students benefit.

Students learn more because they are actively processing the content as they discuss it or teach it to others. Higher level thinking is promoted through social interaction.

Cooperative learning also has a positive impact on self-esteem and psychological adjustment. Students perceive themselves as valuable members of a group with even the least academically talented making contributions to the group. Success breeds success as the groups continue to work and grow together.

Strategies for Involving Individuals and Groups in the Private or Public Sector

Tool 7.1.4

Request overstocks, seconds, to be recycled furniture and office equipment, materials that could be used for projects. Letting the businesses know how the donated materials, etc. were used could encourage further contributions. One local television station (WBIR in Knoxville, Tennessee) in cooperation with several other local sponsors coordinates *Our School Needs.* They publicize the identified needs of schools in the Channel 10 viewing area (books, landscaping materials, computers, art paper, etc.). They also conduct a telethon to connect individuals or businesses with items to donate with educators or schools that need them. The response has been very satisfying for all.

Request items, gift certificates, or coupons that could be used for **rewards and incentives.** Local grocery stores often provide food items to be used for school events.

Develop **Adopt A School** relationships with good adopters--and be a good adoptee in return. See Tools 4.3.3 and 4.3.4 for additional strategies to consider.

Encourage employers to **allow employees time away from work** to spend with child at school. Parents could have opportunities to have lunch with their children or to volunteer in some capacity.

Encourage employers to **recognize employees who contribute their time and talents** as mentors, guest speakers, etc. Educators should also provide formal and informal recognition. An appreciative comment can make a difference.

Educators can ask local businesses to suggest **real-world problems for students to solve.** The tasks then become more authentic and meaningful for students. It also helps them see that learning to solve problems has relevance in the real world.

Work with employers to provide **on site educational opportunities.** Employers could flex work schedules for employees who do not have their GED or are not literate. Educators could take learning opportunities to them.

Ask business and manufacturing leaders to provide **renewal experiences** for teachers during the summers. While these opportunities can provide temporary employment, they will more importantly allow teachers to gain new perspectives and skills. Students benefit when teachers share what they learned.

Business persons, professionals, and others can provide placements for **interns.** The interns could be high school-aged students. The internship could be for a designated period during the junior or senior years. Providing early experiences for students helps them gain a greater awareness of real world demands.

Tool 7.1.4

Business, industry, medicine, government, education, and other work settings could provide **opportunities for middle school-aged students to shadow professionals in their workplaces.** Collaborating with willing professionals could provide highly educational experiences for students who are interested in their particular field. Even if students are not sure what they might want to pursue as a career, these experiences could help them gain some understanding of the workplace and its requirements.

Chamber of Commerce programs in larger metropolitan areas often support a **Leadership Program** that includes educators, civic leaders, and business representatives. The Chamber provides opportunities for dialogue, guest speakers, and field trips to enhance the groups' experiences. One enjoyable activity commonly included is the swap for a day. Educators go to work with a non-educator professional one day and that person helps teach another day.

Work with community members to identify work settings that would be appropriate sites for **field trips** for students.

Many schools are requiring students to volunteer in community service activities for specified periods of time. Educators are collaborating with businesses and government agencies in identifying the most appropriate and beneficial **service learning experiences** for students. Service learning experiences require students to complete volunteer assignments (in hospitals, nursing homes, community centers, housing projects, etc.) and also to attend seminars focused on what they have learned from these situations.

One specific example of service learning was a **Neighborhood Vol Corp.** Students worked with community leaders to first identify mutual problems in the community and then to provide needed services (e.g., maintaining recreation areas, meals on wheels to local shut-ins, shopping for elderly or those unable to drive). Students were the ones responsible for planning, coordinating, and carry out the services. One major positive outcome was that students began to feel connected to the community (something that has been lost in modern times) and were taking ownership in its well being. Both the students and the adults began to see the students as part of the solution instead of part of the problem.

Educators can work with local employers of high school students to develop some sensible policies regarding their employment. For example, guidance counselors could help develop **hiring guidelines** to assure that employers hire the most promising candidates--those without discipline, attendance, or academic problems. Employers could also be advised about potentially good applicants. The guidelines may also stipulate that the employer will monitor a student's hours and progress in school if he or she does not have at least a C average at the time of employment.

Educators and employers could develop better **two-way communication.** School newsletters and other information can be distributed to community businesses and work settings and vice versa.

Plan 7.2
Supporting Learning at Home

Whether the partnerships are focusing on parents supporting teachers' academic expectations at home or educators supporting parents' desires for their child at school, it is critical to work together to support learning. Homework and academic problem solving are two areas that often initiate discussion and dialogue that promote educator and parent partnerships. In fact, these issues prompt more parent-teacher conferences than any other.

Homework is a controversial issue for educators and parents alike. While parent and educator views about homework often differ, they are both generally very strong. Homework can generate positive feelings for all involved or become a major source of frustration. For many parents, it is through monitoring homework assignments that they know what is going on in school. In these homes, homework-related discussions are an almost nightly event. Teachers observe the benefits that this type of support provide for the student's achievement. They know that monitoring homework is one way that parents can make a major contribution to their child's success. They also realize that many parents are either unaware or unwilling to provide the necessary support for learning at home. Many educators view clarifying expectations about homework and ways parents can be involved as another vehicle in developing their partnerships with parents.

When students are not succeeding in school, it poses additional challenges for educators and parents as well as for the child. If the child is not achieving or making grades that reflect his or her real academic potential, parents often feel as if they have failed and are at a loss as to what to do. Educators may have the answers they need, but may lack sufficient information about the causes of the problem. When educators and parents develop a relationship that promotes collaborative problem solving, they are more likely to exchange information that will benefit the child. By working together they can agree upon the most productive course of action and can monitor progress at home and at school to assure their desired results.

- The most productive first step is for the faculty to "explore" issues related to homework. Homework is intended to extend or enhance learning opportunities for students. When implemented properly, it can improve student achievement and attitude towards learning while developing independence, self-discipline, and responsibility. It can also be a source for creativity--some of the excuses given for not doing it are priceless. On the other hand, homework can also decrease student interest, take time away from leisure or recreational activities, encourage parental interference, or be counterproductive when there is limited home support or an inappropriate environment. For homework to be beneficial, it is important that teachers design meaningful assignments and parents provide appropriate home conditions and support.

- Educators should decide about a homework policy individually and collectively. It is helpful to work together to establish a homework policy for the school. Having consistent procedures across classes and grade levels benefits students as well as educators. Tool 7.2.1 is a discussion guide for developing a schoolwide or grade level homework policy.

- Helping parents understand expectations for homework is critical to securing their support for it at home. Decisions should be made about how and what to communicate to parents. Tool 7.2.2 is a sample educator communication to parents about homework.

- When students' grades are not what they should or could be, when they do not attempt or complete homework assignments, or when their diligence at studying does not result in good test scores, some investigation into the problem may prove to be very helpful to all--the student, teachers, and parents. See Tool 7.2.3 for a student self-assessment of his or her study habits. The questionnaire could also be used to gather parents' perceptions of their child's study habits. The assessment can provide important information for discussing the problem and providing direction for improvement. With good practice, effective study skills can become habits for successful learning. Starting early is recommended, but it's never too late to begin developing productive habits for lifelong learning.

- Learning extends beyond the school walls. Many educators are exploring strategies for engaging parents and community members in supporting learning at home and in the community. Some suggestions are presented in Tool 7.2.4. Review the list to identify those that may be appropriate and helpful for your school.

- Helping students develop attitudes and skills of lifelong learning is a focus throughout this book. Educators and parents can discuss lifelong learning skills and make decisions about the ones that are important to teach and reinforce with their students--at home and at school. See Tool 7.2.5 for one school's example, called MegaLife Skills, which were collaboratively identified as essential skills for their students to acquire. They are taught and consistently reinforced by all school personnel. By attempting mastery of these MegaLife skills, the students are becoming self-regulated and self-directed learners who possess the organizational and time management skills necessary for success in school and life.

- Parents seem to appreciate attempts by educators to provide helpful hints to improve their child's academic success and behavior. See Tool 7.2.6 for a list of sample topics that could be presented in written form as "Parenting Tips" or used for individual focus sessions with parents. Educators need to supply relevant, age-appropriate examples to extend and to help explain each tip. They can be included in newsletters and learning calendars. For example, they could be thoughts for the day. This list only provides a starting point. Ask the faculty or parents for additional suggestions. Again, a great deal of valuable information is readily available from other sources.

Discussion Guide for Developing a Schoolwide Homework Policy

Tool 7.2.1

As with all collaborative sessions, review the Rules We Live By (Tool 1.2.5) before engaging in the discussion about homework. It is a challenging area for educators to discuss since they have such varying opinions and use so many different approaches.

Discussion Participants: School faculty and support staff are the primary participants. Representative parents and older students could also be included in the discussions. They have important perspectives to share and could contribute to the quality of the product.

Necessary Materials and Information: Current research on the criteria for and effects of homework should be acquired, distributed, read, and discussed by participants prior to making decisions about homework. This is a critical step. Participants will find that the research is not conclusive about the benefits of homework, but does provide important information about when homework is most effective and when it may be counterproductive.

Major Components of Homework Policy:
- rationale for homework (e.g., reasons why it is important, it's potential benefits, the faculty's philosophy)
- the estimated amount of homework that should be required per day and week
- ways to ensure that students are not overloaded due to conflicting demands
- ways it will be graded
- percentage of the student's grade
- consequences for noncompletion (or not attempting)
- ways to require or encourage completion
- communication to parents

Discussion Questions: Before beginning the discussion, emphasize that it is to be an "exploration of the issue" and *not* a binding agreement for everyone. Perhaps the major question is, "Should we have a schoolwide homework policy?" The following questions are important for faculty consideration, but it takes time for study and discussion before any decisions are made.

- What is our rationale for homework? Why it is important? What are the potential benefits?

- What is the "right" amount of homework for our students? Be sure to consider the needs of low ability students as well as higher ability students,* those with home support and those without, those who have easy access to computers and those who do not, those who have outside school obligations, etc.
    * There is some research to suggest that for low ability students, the best approach may be to meet the students' needs with classwork rather than homework.

Tool 7.2.1

- How can the faculty schedule major tests and due dates so that students will not be overloaded?

- What types of homework seem to work best for our students?

- How will homework be graded? Will it be by the teacher or an assistant, volunteer, or other student? Will it be graded for correctness or for completion? Will comments or feedback be provided?

- What percentage of the student's grade should homework represent?

- What are some constructive ways to require and ensure that it will be completed? How can we encourage students to complete their homework? One good example is the use of cooperative homework teams. The few minutes at the beginning of class are allotted to ensuring that all team members have completed their homework and have no unanswered questions about it.

- What should be the consequences for noncompletion (or not attempting)? Should teachers insist that the child make up the work?

- How can teachers ensure that the student is the one doing the homework? Generally students have difficulty doing the complicated assignments alone and everyone knows who gets involved in doing them!

- How should we communicate our homework policy to parents?

Homework

Tool 7.2.2

Homework is . . . an extension of classwork, preparation for classwork, an additional opportunity for needed practice or extended exploration, and a way for students to show their creativity as well as their understanding.

Homework should be . . . interesting to students with a meaningful purpose, clear directions, and a goal of successful completion.

Homework should require . . . no more than 20 minutes each day for children in first through third grades, 20 to 40 minutes each day for students from fourth to sixth grades, and up to 2 hours per day for 7th to 9th graders.

Homework can . . . extend or increase learning opportunities for students; improve student achievement and attitude towards learning; develop independence, self-discipline, and responsibility; and provide an outlet for creativity.

Homework can also . . . decrease student interest; take time away from leisure or recreational activities; create parental interference and frustration; and be counterproductive when there is limited support or an inappropriate environment.

As your child's teacher, I will . . .

▼ Make every attempt to provide homework that is interesting, meaningful, and relevant.

▼ Help students see the value of homework. It will be collected and graded or checked quickly and given back to students with comments and an opportunity to correct errors. I will insist that it be done and will show students the effect of homework on their progress and performance.

▼ Not give homework as a punishment. I will make every attempt to not have homework be perceived as a negative experience.

▼ Ensure that students can be successful in completing homework without major adult assistance.

▼ Individualize assignments and provide options and choices when possible.

▼ Help students accept responsibility for homework completion (assignments books, agendas).

Tool 7.2.2

▼ Provide assistance options for students (Dial a teacher; homework buddies; Homework study teams; before and after school tutoring; peer tutors).

▼ Collaborate with my colleagues to schedule major homework commitments so that we can avoid overloading students.

▼ Work with the student in making up missed homework assignments.

Here's what parents can do . . .

▼ Provide time and appropriate conditions (desk or study area, materials, supplies, necessary resources).

▼ Help your child manage time and obligations so that they are rested and have enough energy to focus on the assignments.

▼ Provide emotional support and understanding rather than added pressure, stress, and nagging. Remember, it's your child's homework, not yours. Support, but don't do it.

▼ Reinforce your child's effective study habits and organizational skills.

▼ Encourage your child to take advantage of the extra time teachers provide for additional assistance. Arrange for tutorial help when needed.

▼ Talk with the teacher or counselor if the child is having problems with homework. Also let the teacher know if the assignments cause undue frustration because they are too difficult or perceived as boring. Work with them to determine specific problems and to develop some reasonable expectations and strategies.

▼ Show your child that you value homework: ask about it, discuss what they are learning, and check to see that they have completed it (or attempted it to the best of their ability).

Thanks for your help and support. Let me know how it is going as the year progresses. Please feel free to share your comments or questions with me at any time.

Additional comments could address:
- the estimated amount of homework that will be required on a weekly basis or the reasons why it is not given.
- any future special assignments.
- any particular considerations or emphasis given to homework assignments.
- your (or the school's) homework policy, if not supplied in another communication.

Student Study Habits Assessment

Tool 7.2.3

	Almost Always	Most of the Time	About Half of the Time	Not Very Often	Almost Never
1. I write down my assignments in a place I can keep track of them.	○	○	○	○	○
2. I set aside enough time each day for studying and reading.	○	○	○	○	○
3. I allow enough time for each subject.	○	○	○	○	○
4. I don't have to "cram" for tests and "hurry" on assignments because I allow enough time to do it right.	○	○	○	○	○
5. If given a long term assignment or project, I schedule particular dates as midpoints to check my progress so I don't have to throw it together at the last minute.	○	○	○	○	○
6. I have a special place I like to study that has a large enough desk or work area, that is well lighted, and is "quiet" and free of distractions. (Remember music at a reasonable level may not be a distraction!).	○	○	○	○	○
7. I have the equipment (computer, modem), materials (paper, pencil, toner), and resources (books, programs) I need.	○	○	○	○	○
8. I have a good "study buddy" for times when I want to study with someone.	○	○	○	○	○
9. When I sit down to study, I do not have difficulty getting settled and focused.	○	○	○	○	○
10. I find ways to make "boring" subjects or topics more interesting or relevant.	○	○	○	○	○
11. I take notes, draw pictures, doodle, or use symbols to help remember important information.	○	○	○	○	○
12. If I have a reading assignment, I use particular strategies or techniques that help me understand what I am reading (e.g., previewing the whole chapter before reading; referring to the teacher's study guide; asking myself questions and looking for the answers; summarizing main points periodically).	○	○	○	○	○

Tool 7.2.3

Student Study Habits Assessment

	Almost Always	Most of the Time	About Half of the Time	Not Very Often	Almost Never
13. I am able to "make sense" of my class notes when I review them.	○	○	○	○	○
14. I review (and reorganize) my class notes when studying for tests.	○	○	○	○	○
15. I use memory techniques to help me remember important information (e.g., mnemonics, stories, flash cards, setting up a practice schedule).	○	○	○	○	○
16. I look for additional help from the teacher, a friend, or books when I do not understand material I'm supposed to know or when I'm stuck on an assignment.	○	○	○	○	○
17. I keep notebooks and returned papers in some organized way (folders, files) in case I want to refer to them later.	○	○	○	○	○
18. I discuss what I'm learning with others (parents, friends).	○	○	○	○	○
19. When studying for a big test, I organize my information from all sources (test, notes, reports, study guides) into an outline or some other way that helps me remember it.	○	○	○	○	○
20. When I think it will help, I ask others to ask me questions to review the material.	○	○	○	○	○
21. I am fairly accurate at predicting the questions that will be on the test.	○	○	○	○	○
22. On school nights, I get enough sleep.	○	○	○	○	○
23. I try to eat well and get a good night's sleep before tests.	○	○	○	○	○
24. I set some reasonable goals for developing good study habits and make every attempt to achieve them.	○	○	○	○	○
25. I feel good about what I do to prepare for school.	○	○	○	○	○

Additional Learning Support

Academic Guidance Tips
Educators can provide age-appropriate tips to parents about how to help students become self-regulated learners. They can help in developing good study and organizational habits and time management skills--one small tip at a time!

Parent-Child Homework Assignments
Educators can provide learning activities parents can supervise at home or do with the children. Some teachers have ingeniously devised science fair projects with an adult component. Know that the adults are going to be involved, why not do it overtly?

Interview Projects
Guide the child in asking questions or interviewing a knowledgeable adult (parent, neighbor, grandparent), sibling, or peer about particular topics or experiences.

Interactive Journal
The teacher provides the prompt or sentence stem and students respond individually in their journals. The parent or care giver must also provide a response either to what the child has written or to the teacher-provided prompt. If this strategy is selected, be sure that all children have the home support required or that accommodations have been made for those who do not.

Student Folders or Portfolios
Sending folders and portfolios home is another way to engage the parent or care giver. They can be involved in deciding about the most interesting piece of work included, the progress shown since the last time, any appropriate goals for growth, or other important topics of mutual interest.

Student K-12 Portfolio
As students move through the grades, a portfolio could be constructed. It would be a "work in progress" until graduation. It could document academic progress, but also recreational and artistic experiences, athletic participation and accomplishments, extracurricular activities, leadership positions, community service activities, honors, and so on. The portfolio is an important way to reinforce progress and accomplishments and to set goals for future growth. Another advantage of K-12 portfolios is that students have this important information readily accessible when students apply for jobs or college admission.

Vacation Activity Packets or Booklets
Lists of suggested books, games, software, family television viewing, local plays or performances could be provided to parents during holidays (December Holidays, Winter Break, Spring Break, Summer Vacation). Creating an awareness of accessible educational opportunities may be all it takes to encourage parents to take advantage of them.

Tool 7.2.4

Book Bags With Recorded Readings and Books
Volunteers and older students can construct tote bags with donated materials and record books on cassette tapes. The tape, book and bag can then be checked out to go home with the student. Tape players should also be available for check out for those who do not have one at home.

Laptop Computer Checkout
Donated or school purchased laptop computers could be available for checkout to responsible students who do not have access to one at home.

Test Reminders
Educators can communicate with parents about important testing dates. They can designate test days on a monthly calendar and send reminders home several days in advance.

Homework Club
Parents can arrange and monitor a homework club at students' homes or at the local community center. A less adventurous approach would be to arrange study buddies.

Tutors
Parents can provide additional assistance by hiring tutors or trading for the services of tutors.

Reading
The research is overwhelmingly clear. Children who are read to in their early years have a much easier time learning to read and a experience far greater enjoyment from reading. Parents who continue to read with and to their children find that the benefits do not end when the child enters school. Modeling a love of reading is also an important parental contribution.

Agendas
Agendas are commercially prepared student assignment folders used to help students develop organizational skills and to communicate with parents. In one middle school, teachers mark the agenda each time a student asks to be excused from class. By using this system, several teachers and parents have begun to notice some interesting patterns.

George Washington Elementary School's   Tool 7.2.5

MEGA LIFESKILLS

INTEGRITY: To act according to what's right or wrong

INITIATIVE: To do something because it needs to be done

FLEXIBILITY: The ability to alter plans when necessary

PERSEVERANCE: To continue in spite of difficulties

ORGANIZATION: To plan, arrange and implement in an orderly way

SENSE OF HUMOR: To laugh and be playful without hurting others

EFFORT: To do your best

COMMON SENSE: To think it through

PROBLEM SOLVING: To seek solutions in difficult situations

RESPONSIBILITY: To be accountable for your actions

PATIENCE: To wait calmly for someone or something

FRIENDSHIP: To make and keep a friend through mutual trust and caring

CURIOSITY: To investigate and seek understanding

COOPERATION: To work together toward a common goal (purpose)

CARING: To feel and show concern

COURAGE: To act according to one's belief

FITNESS: To be involved in a physical activity daily

By permission of Kingsport City Schools, Kingsport Tennessee

Tool 7.2.6

Developing Lifelong Learners

Praising and Encouraging Your Child

▼ Link praise with the child's action, behavior, or accomplishment.

▼ Identify the action or behavior specifically. Rather than saying, "good job," say "good job because you _____."

▼ Tell the child why the accomplishment is important. Recognize the difficulty of the task for *this* child.

▼ Help the child learn from experiences. Failures or disappointments can convey important lessons and stimulate motivation.

▼ Use a variety of reinforcers (100 ways to praise a child) and be spontaneous.

▼ Help the child see the value of his or her own task-related behavior. This attributes success and accomplishment to behaviors within the child's control--effort, paying attention, following directions, and being persistent rather than luck or ease of the task or ability.

▼ Emphasize the importance of teamwork and cooperation rather than the competitive aspects of winning and losing.

▼ When giving feedback to children, be sure to communicate their current level of competence and what they need to do to improve.

▼ Compare the child's level of competence or accomplishment with his or her previous behaviors rather than other children. Keeping the focus on improvements and "personal bests" is a key to motivating the child to want to improve.

▼ Promote enjoyment of any educational activity.

▼ Foster intrinsic motivation toward the experience. Let the child know that the accomplishment is for his or her own benefit, not just to please others or achieve a reward.

▼ Monitor the effect of tangible incentives and rewards. They can have a counterproductive effect when the child perceives that his or her behavior is being controlled by the hope of a reward. Being excessive in giving rewards can also send the wrong message. When children receive a reward in spite of minimal effort or accuracy, it sends the message that there really are no standards to achieve. Focusing too much attention on incentives and rewards can also reduce a child's intrinsic motivation to achieve for the sake of achieving.

Tool 7.2.6

Building Self-esteem

▼ Model positive self-talk. Help the child change a negative into a positive. Rephrase "I'm so stupid!" into "I can't do that yet. I haven't learned to . . . ."

▼ Never belittle, ridicule or negatively label a child or allow others to do it. Emphasize the positives, the accomplishments.

▼ Listen (uninterrupted and focused) to your child.

▼ Use non judgmental language in talking with your child.

▼ Hold family meetings. Allow children input into important family issues and decisions. In some families, children take turns with adults in organizing the meetings (e.g., time, topics for discussion, refreshments). What a tremendous way to provide opportunities for leadership at home.

▼ Be sure to find an appropriate place to display the child's work so that it can be enjoyed and shared with others.

Modeling Lifelong Learning

▼ Turn off the television and READ. Everyone reads or is read to. Inquire about what the child is reading or watching. Promote discussion.

▼ Set goals and monitor progress.

▼ Make decisions and solve problems as a family with children having input and equal "voting rights" when appropriate.

▼ Emphasize the steps of effective decision making and problem solving. Children soon learn the right words and processes to use on their own.

Developing Self-regulated Behaviors

▼ Help children develop time management and organizational skills. Let them be responsible for setting clocks, making sure they are on time, and organizing their toys, rooms, and school materials. Teach them strategies for getting prepared for each day.

▼ Help children learn to reflect on their own actions or behaviors. When they have succeeded at something important, talk about what they did to accomplish it. When they have failed at a task or have been involved in a confrontation with someone, discuss what behaviors caused the problem and what actions might have produced a different outcome. Develop strategies for avoiding similar problems in the future.

Plan 7.3
Promoting Lifelong Learning--"You're never too old to learn!"

> **Individuals generally only use 10% of their learning potential.**
> William James, Educational Psychologist

The information explosion, technological advances, changing working conditions, and difficulties in raising children in today's society are current trends that will continue into the 21st century. The almost overwhelming amount of new information and new opportunities and demands spawned by technology make the ability to be a lifelong learner a required "basic skill." As new information becomes available, important change is encountered and perplexing situations arise.

Educators and families find themselves searching for the most productive ways to gain knowledge, acquire new skills, and find possible solutions for problems created by these trends. As a result of the growing need for information and skills, adult learning has become an integral component of many school programs. Successful programs capitalize on the diversity of their participants who often represent various age groups, races, socio-economic levels, and cultures. They also build upon the wide range of previous life experiences, beliefs and philosophies, interests, and ways of learning. Learning opportunities are structured to acknowledge adults learners' need for relevant, pragmatic information provided in an emotionally safe and secure learning environment. Instructors realize that adults want to increase their feelings of confidence and competence and design activities to encourage sharing of relevant experiences and interaction with others to process new information. At the same time, they also recognize and capitalize on adults' desire to use the newly acquired knowledge or skill to meet some important personal goals or needs.

There are many challenges and anxieties inherent in facilitating adult learning, but several important considerations can make lifelong learning very appealing. Keeping the unique characteristics of adult learners in mind, adult learning facilitators can develop workshops, presentations, or focus sessions with parents or colleagues that can be highly satisfying to all involved. One of the significant rewards in working with adults is that there are learning opportunities for all involved--the instructors as well as the "students." This is so true that it is often difficult to tell who learned more.

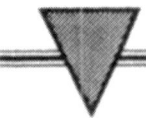

- Identify general and specific needs of the learners. Several informal and/or formal options could be used to assess needs. Tool 7.3.1 provides a list of topics that are of general interest to parenting adults. Tool 7.3.2 presents some strategies for identifying learner needs and interests.

- Decide how to best address the needs. A planning team made up of educators and parents could have the responsibility for the final decisions about how adult learning sessions will be structured. They could be single sessions on one topic or a series of sessions on a topic or combination of related topics. Remember that one shot experiences may be effective for informational purposes, but continued contact and opportunities for practice, feedback, and reflection may be necessary if application or transfer are involved. The planning team would also focus on designing and titling the sessions to be the most appealing to the parents and community members they are trying to attract. The group could also decide on an appropriate title for the sessions. Parent Academies or Parent Institutes have been used successfully by some schools. Others have instituted Saturday Schools with options available for both adult-aged and younger learners. Consider the appropriateness of videotaping sessions for distribution to interested parents who are unable to attend.

- Decide how to generate the greatest participation. Flyers, notes, radio spots, and public service announcements have all been used successfully. In some communities, schools work with local churches, social service agencies, and public housing authorities to advertise the sessions. Some schools send reminder post cards to those who have expressed an interest in attending.

- Make arrangements for the learning session(s) that accommodate the needs of adult learners. For psychological comfort, the learning environment should be as non-threatening as possible. For this reason, some educators offer sessions away from school buildings in such places as community centers, churches, and parents' homes. They have found that if families are not willing or able to come to the schools, the schools must go to them. In setting the time frame for the session(s) remain sensitive to the demanding schedules and needs of the adult students. The number of sessions to offer would also need to be decided. An option is to offer the same session for three consecutive days to expand the possibilities for attendance.

- Arrange for child care so that the learners can stay focused on the task at hand. Arrange for refreshments. School personnel know that the likelihood of participation increases when food is offered. Remember name tags or name tents to help identify participants by name. It is very important to know and use names. Tool 7.3.3 is a lesson plan outline with important reminders to make the sessions go smoothly.

- Consistently maintain the agreed upon schedule for the session. Begin and end on time and remember to include ample breaks. A common guideline for breaks is every 20-40 minutes, depending on the activity level of the session.

- Arrange the room so that it is the most appropriate for the anticipated activities. Arrangements that are the most conducive to learning are those that encourage interactive opportunities.

- Plan for a positive beginning. Then maintain attention and involvement throughout the session by attending to the pace, varying the activities, and incorporating opportunities for interaction and fun (if appropriate). Important keys to facilitating adult learning are maintaining a sense of humor and an enthusiastic approach. Enthusiasm has a way of becoming contagious.

- Consider the need for ice breaker activities. They can help reduce anxiety and allow participants and instructors to find out more about the particular characteristics and interests of others they may not know well.

- Provide high quality instruction. Using "best practices" is a requirement for the most productive adult learning. Tool 7.3.4 provides instructional suggestions to facilitate adult learning.

- Remain sensitive to the public nature of any classroom setting. Having to perform or even ask questions in front of others can involve significant risk taking. Instructors need to remain sensitive to the level of anxiety and make every attempt to lessen it by providing safe practice opportunities or experiences. Emphasizing that the only stupid question is the one not asked is one way to create an environment where taking risks is the norm. For some participants, the experience may be so intimidating that they will not ask a question no matter how diligently the instructor works to encourage them. In these cases, it may be helpful to use a question poster that allows participants to write questions without being identified in front of the group.

- Incorporate opportunities for questions and ways to get feedback about the learners' level of understanding. Although the session is focused and structured, there is a need to be flexible enough to accommodate the learners' needs, interests, and misunderstandings. It is important to involve the participants in setting the specific agenda for the session. Some type of preassessment can be helpful to ensure that participant questions and concerns are specifically addressed. Tool 7.3.5 presents some useful preassessment strategies.

- Handle questions with care. The way adult learning instructors deal with questions and the learner's dignity either establish or destroy their credibility. Listen attentively, clarify as needed, and address the questions as straightforwardly as possible. If they are beyond the instructor's level of expertise or experience, the most appropriate response is "I don't know." It may also be helpful to direct the question to participants for possible responses.

- Remember that adults are extremely perceptive about how their contributions are received. Be appropriately supportive and reinforcing of the adult learners' efforts. Neutral approaches are more effective than those that involve excessive praise, which may or may not be perceived as sincere.

- Instructors of adult learning sessions will generally say that the purposes are to give information and/or to teach new skills or techniques. But often, an important underlying purpose is to change attitudes, which is eminently more difficult. Some experts say that it is nine times more difficult. Be patient. Adults have had many years to form and solidify their beliefs and attitudes. Changes will be slow and will initially focus on actions. If the actions are successful, attitudes and beliefs will follow.

- To help ensure transfer of the knowledge or skill, have each participant identify one or two goals for applying what they have learned. These goals could include the specific ways they intend to use their new learning. Personal goal setting promotes a commitment to change, allows adults to take charge of their own learning, encourages pursuing directions of their own choosing, and involves them in assessing their own progress.

- Evaluate the sessions so that participant feedback can be used to improve future ones. Both informal and formal activities are appropriate for determining the effectiveness of each session or a series of sessions. Remember that how participants respond at the close of a session may not be the most helpful in assessing the real effect. Checking with them two or three weeks later to identify how they have been able to use or apply what they learned may provide more useful information. An important consideration in evaluating adult learning sessions is to gather meaningful information about how to improve. For these reasons, the suggested evaluation strategies are not ratings (excellent-average-poor), but narratives requiring more helpful information. Tool 7.3.6 provides options for easy to use, but informative, post assessment evaluation strategies.

In reflecting upon the evaluations, remember that all teachers who have had the responsibility of attempting to teach their colleagues know the anxieties of adult learning situations! It seems that most educators are very comfortable as teachers of children, but it is a very different story when facing a group of adults, especially those with whom they are closely associated. The best advice is to follow the adult learning guidelines, be as well prepared as possible, and remember that everyone faces difficult groups or participants once in a while. Do not feel that you have failed if some participants are negative during the session or on their evaluation. You won't reach them all! Use their feedback as an opportunity to improve as an educator of adults.

Other Possibilities . . .

Topics of Interest to Parenting Adults

Tool 7.3.1

As a beginning point, here are some topics that are generally of high interest...

- Knowing what to expect of children at specific ages or developmental stages
- Communicating with your child
- Building character
- Dealing with special needs children (e.g., ADHD, learning disabled)
- Disciplining children (e.g., setting limits and sticking to them--contracts, rewarding appropriate behavior, punishing inappropriate behavior)
- Helping with homework
- Home activities to help children learn
- How to motivate children to want to learn
- Help children set realistic goals/self-management
- Ways to build positive self-esteem
- Peer pressure and how to deal with it
- Influences on curriculum and instruction (e.g., cooperative learning, technology, sex education, AIDS awareness)
- Using computer technology
- Where to get additional resources and assistance
- Building character and encouraging responsible behavior
- Helping children cope with divorce
- Helping parents recognize signs of drug, alcohol, and substance abuse
- Helping students understand the negatives of drugs, alcohol, and substance abuse
- Helping students and parents understand "tough issues" such as AIDS, teen suicide, sex
- Using the media to our advantage
- Childhood and parent stressors
- In home safety
- Conflict resolution for parents
- Multiple Intelligence
- Reinforcing organizational skills
- Single parenting
- Recognizing signs of gang activity

Some additional high interest topics might include . . .

Options for Identifying Adult Learner Needs and Interests

Tool 7.3.2

No work required option
Needs of adult learners could be inferred from the information gathered during a recent formal needs assessment (See Plan 5.1). The information should be fairly current if the assessment had taken place in the last two or three years.

Informal option
A list of needs could be generated by having a representative group of educators reflect on:
- comments or concerns volunteered by parents and colleagues;
- needs that are evident from observations of the students (performance and behavior);
- new trends, demands, approaches, or emphases that are impacting curriculum and instruction.

A complete list could be generated through brainstorming (See Tool 1.2.6). Major themes could be identified and then prioritized and a resulting list could be used in the questionnaire described below.

Research required option
A discrepancy process could be applied to the topic under consideration (e.g., parenting skills, computer literacy, effective communication). Review available literature or research to determine the characteristics of the "peak performers." Then compare the identified characteristics with general assessments of the current parent population, areas of need can be identified.

Gathering input options
Option A: A brief, open-ended questionnaire could be distributed to appropriate groups to solicit topics of interest or concern. This could also be accomplished by telephone canvassing a sampling of parents.

Introductory statement: "The principal and teachers at _____ school are planning some workshop sessions for parents/educators. They want to address high-interest topics and issues of importance and concern to parents. Would you mind taking a few minutes to respond to the following questions? Please think about these questions as they relate to our school and to your child(ren)."

- In order to help my child be a better student, I have questions about . . .
- As a parent of an elementary/middle/high school student, I am concerned about . . .
- One topic or area I wish I knew more about is . . .
- I feel that I would be a better parent (or educator) if I knew . . .
- One particular area of interest to me is . . .

Tool 7.3.2

In order to plan our sessions to be most convenient for our parents and community members, would you please answer the following questions?

- If sessions on topics you are interested in are planned,
  would you be interested in attending?   Yes   No
- What day and time would be the best for you?   Yes   No
- Would you need child care?   Yes   No
  If so, what aged children? _____
- Would you need transportation?   Yes   No
- Would you require a translator*?   Yes   No
  (*The presentation will be in English and Spanish.)
- Would you require assistance with a physical disability
  that might limit your ability to participate?   Yes   No

Option B: A brief, more structured questionnaire could be distributed to appropriate representatives of the target group to gain their opinions about certain suggested topics.

This is a topic I would like to know more about...

	Very much	Some	Not at all
- Building character _____	___	___	___
- Dealing with ADHD children _____	___	___	___
- Encouraging responsible behavior _____	___	___	___
- Helping with homework _____	___	___	___
- Helping children cope with divorce _____	___	___	___
- Building positive self-esteem _____	___	___	___
- etc. _____	___	___	___

Could you suggest any additional topics?

What time and day of the week would be the best for you?

Monday	AM or PM	Thursday	AM or PM
Tuesday	AM or PM	Friday	AM or PM
Wednesday	AM or PM	Saturday	AM

Would you need...
- Child care?   Yes   No
  If so, what aged children? _____
- Transportation?   Yes   No
  If so, how many? _____
- A translator*?   Yes   No
  (*The presentation will be in English and Spanish.)
- Assistance with a physical disability
  that might limit your ability to participate?   Yes   No

Suggestions for Facilitating Adult Learning
(Applies to Sessions with Parents, Community Members, and Educators)

Tool 7.3.3

The purpose or objectives for the session must be clearly communicated as well as expectations for participant involvement.

The mode of delivery needs to be appropriate to the content, but also geared to the learners' needs and styles of learning. Each adult processes information in different ways.

Written materials and visuals should be clear and consistent with the needs of the learners.

Educational jargon or highly technical language should be avoided or used sparingly. Unfamiliar terms need to be defined.

Authentic examples or stories to which adults can relate are essential in making the learning meaningful. Participant examples can also help the adults connect with the new content.

Affirming the adult's knowledge and experiences is one of the most powerful teaching techniques. Building upon what they know capitalizes on their wealth of experience. They are often an untapped resource for learning.

Time for reflection should to be provided during the session or between sessions for the learners to integrate the new learning into their knowledge base and to assimilate it into their way of doing things.

Provide sample situations showing the range of ways the information or skill can be used. Participants can be helpful in identifying examples.

Be sure the learners know what to do, how to do it, why do it, and how to practice it.

Use strategies that promote self-directed learning, active engagement, and interaction such as:
- Personal inventories or self-assessments
- Role-play, simulations, or videos
- Group problem solving or case studies
- Poster exhibitions
- Mind-maps portraying the major themes, ideas, and connections (individual or group)
- Cooperative learning structures (informal and formal) especially *Think-Pair-Share, One Minute Summaries, Jig-Saw, Talk Walks, Fishbowl Sharing.*
- Practicing the technique to be learned in a triad or pair with one participant designated as the coach. Receiving specific feedback about performance is critical.
- Flow charts portraying the sequence of events if the learning is procedural.
- Reinforcement and emphasis on what has been learned or the progress that has been made. Instructor's direct observations can give some concrete examples.

Tool 7.3.4

Lesson Plan for Adult Learning Sessions
(Parents and/or Educators)

Instructor(s): _____

General topic: _____

Date: _____

Beginning and ending times: _____

Location: _____ Room #: _____

Child care requirements (and responsibility):

Refreshment requirements (and responsibility):

Transportation requirements (and responsibility):

Notable characteristics of the learners (general attributes of the total group or of particular individuals, any special learning needs or requirements):

Tool 7.3.4

Objectives of the session/Needs addressed:

Opening activities (Ice Breaker/Team Building):

Preassessment activities:

Major activities with anticipated timeframes:

Anticipated questions or concerns:

Closure and follow-up activities/reminders:

Handouts and other materials:

Room arrangement(s):

Equipment needs:

Participants' evaluation of the session:

> **Don't forget name tags or name tents!**

Meeting Learner Needs
Preassessment and Postassessment
(at the start of the session)

Tool 7.3.5

Gathering Participant Input

Near the beginning of the session, ask the participants the following question: "If this were to be a successful workshop for you, what would you hope to gain?" Provide a few minutes for thinking and then develop a collective list on a chalkboard, easel, or paper that will remain posted until the conclusion of the session. The post assessment could then be accomplished by reviewing their desired outcomes and determining the extent to which they were addressed.

KWL

Another informal approach is to use the K-W-L, a strategy that is familiar to many teachers. Define three columns on a sheet of butcher paper or an a board: K (What I know about the topic-or-think I know), W (What I want to know), L (What I learned). The K and W are used as a preassessment and the L as the post assessment (Marzano, et al., 1992).

K	W	L

Participants' Questions

Another option is to have participants use index cards or pieces of recycled paper to identify questions they hope to have answered during the session. Using those questions throughout the session can affirm the planners' purpose for the session, provide direction for the particular group, and serve an evaluative purpose at the end of the session.

Participant Evaluations of Learning Session
(Three Options for Workshops, Academies, or Institutes)

Tool 7.3.6

The most important things I learned from this workshop are . . .
"What are the two or three most important ideas or new information you gained from this workshop?" or "I now know about. . ."

I am now more confident in my ability to . . .
"What new information or new skill do you now have that you didn't previously know?" or "I now am able to . . ."

Because of this workshop, I am going to . . .

The most helpful part of the workshop was . . .

The only suggestion I have to improve the workshop is to . . .
"What part(s), if any, were the least helpful to you?" or "The only thing I would change about this workshop is . . ."

Provide participants with three index cards or small pieces of paper and ask them to write 3 words, phrases, or pictures that best represent their feelings about the session.

As a result of this workshop, here is one thing I am going to--

KEEP doing-----

START doing-----

STOP doing-----

Additional comments:

Bibliography

Ames, C., Khoju, M., & Watkins, T. (1993). *Parent involvement: The relationship between school to home communication and parents' perceptions and beliefs.* Boston, MA: Center on Families, Communities, Schools & Children's Learning.

Anderson, R.C., Heibert, E.H., Scott, J.A., & Wilkinson, I.A.G. (1985). *Becoming a nation of readers: The report of the commission on reading.* Washington, DC: National Academy of Education.

Argyris, C. (1990). *Overcoming organizational defenses.* Needham, MS: Allyn & Bacon.

Armstrong, T. (1994). *Multiple intelligences in the classroom.* Alexandria, VA: Association for Supervision and Curriculum Development.

Atkin, J., & Bastiani, J. (with Goode, J.). (1988). *Listening to parents.* New York, NY: Croom Helm in association with Methuen, Inc.

Bandura, A. (1977). Self-efficacy: Toward a unifying theory of behavioral change. *Psychological Review,* 84, 191-215.

Barickman, J. E. (1992). *Schoolwise.* Portsmouth, N.H.: Boynton/Cook Publishers.

Bartell, J. F. (1992). Starting from scratch. *Principal,* 72(2), 13-14.

Bellon, J.J., & Bellon, E.C. (1993). *Shared vision.* A document presented by The University of Tennessee Center for Government Training, The Tennessee State Board of Education, and The Tennessee Department of Education. Nashville, TN: Tennessee Department of Education.

Bellon, J. J., Bellon, E.C., & Blank, M.A. (1992). *Teaching from a research knowledge base: A development and renewal process.* New York: Merrill/Macmillan Publishing Company.

Bellon, J. J., Bellon, E.C., Blank, M.A., Brian, D.J.G., Kershaw, C.A., Perkins, M.T., Rose, T., & Veal, J.M. (1990). *Needs assessment guide* (2nd ed.). Knoxville, TN: The University of Tennessee and Tennessee Department of Education.

Bellon, J. J., Blank, M.A., Kershaw, C.A., Lambert, A., Perkins, M.T., Sun, J., & Wells, E. (1991). *Guide for long range educational planning.* Knoxville, TN: The University of Tennessee and the Tennessee Department of Education.

Bellon, J.J., Bellon, E.C., Blank, M.A., & Kershaw, C.A. (1992). *Observing, evaluating, and improving instruction: A professional development process*. Knoxville, TN: Authors.

Bellon, J.J., & Handler, J.R. (1982). Curriculum development and evaluation: A design for improvement. Dubuque, IA: Kendall/Hunt Publishing Company.

Berger, E. H. (1991). *Parents as partners in education: The school and home working together* (3rd ed.). New York: Macmillan Publishing Company.

Berla, N. (1992). Involving families in middle schools: Middle grade school state policy initiative. *Principal*, 71(4), 49-50.

Belton, L. (1996). What our teachers should know and be able to do: A student's view. *Educational Leadership*, 54(1), 66-69.

Bogdan, R. C., & Biklen, S. K. (1982). *Qualitative research for education: An introduction to theory and methods*. Boston: Allyn & Bacon, Inc.

Borg, W. R., & Gall, M. D. (1983). *Educational research: An introduction* (4th ed.). New York: Longman.

Bradley, D. F., King-Sears, M. E., & Tessier-Switlick, D. M. (1997). *Teaching students in inclusive settings: From theory to practice*. Boston, MA: Allyn and Bacon.

Brooks, J.G., & Brooks, M. G. (1993). *The case for constructivist classrooms*. Alexandria, VA: Association of Supervision and Curriculum Development.

Brown, D. (October, 1994). Youth violence: Causes and solutions. *Thrust for Educational Leadership*, 10-14.

Buffington, P.W. (November, 1988). A mater of trust. *SKY*, 79-84.

Casanova, U. (1996). Parent involvement: A call for prudence. *Educational Researcher*, 25 (8), 30-32, 46.

Chavkin, N.F., & Williams, D.L.Jr. (1989). Low-income parents' attitudes toward parent involvement in education. *Journal of Sociology and Social Welfare*.

Claremont Graduate School. (1993). *Voices from the inside: A report on schooling from inside the classroom*. Claremont, CA: Authors.

Clarridge, P.B., & Whitaker, E.M. (1994). Implementing a new elementary progress report. *Educational Leadership*, 52(2), 7-9.

Cody, W. S. (1988). *A handbook for parent involvement*. Baton Rouge, LA: Louisiana Department of Education.

Coleman, J. S. (1994). Family involvement in education. In C. L. Fagnano & B.Z. Werber (Eds.) *School, family, and community interaction: A view from the firing lines* (pp. 23-37). Boulder: Westview Press.

Coleman, M. (1991). Planning for the changing nature of family life in schools for young children. *Young Children*, 46(4), 15-20.

Comer, J. P. (1986). Parent participation in the schools. *Phi Delta Kappan*, 67, 442-446.

Comer, J. P. (1988). Educating poor and minority children. *Scientific American*, 25(5), 42-48.

Cotton, K., & Wikelund, K.R. (1989). *Parent involvement in education* (School Improvement Research Series, Close-up #6). Portland, OR: Northwest Regional Educational Laboratory.

Countryman, L.L., & Schroeder, M. (1996). When students lead parent-teacher conferences. *Educational Leadership*, 53(7), 64-68.

Covey, S. (1989). *The seven habits of highly effective people*. New York, NY: Fireside.

Cutright, M. J. (1990). Parents make a difference. *School Safety*, 13-15.

Daher, J. (1994). School-parent partnerships: A guide. In C. L. Fagnano & B.Z. Werber (Eds.) *School, family, and community interaction: A view from the firing lines* (pp. 111-130). Boulder: Westview Press.

deCharms, R. (1976). *Enhancing motivation*. New York: Halsted Press.

Delgado-Gaitan, C. (1994). Spanish-speaking families' involvement in schools. In C. L. Fagnano & B.Z. Werber (Eds.) *School, family, and community interaction: A view from the firing lines* (pp. 85-96). Boulder: Westview Press.

Department of Labor. (1991). *U.S. Secretary of Labor's Commission on Achieving Necessary Skills* (SCANS Report). Washington, DC: Author.

DiBenedetto, R., & Wilson, A. P. (1982). *The small school principal and school-community relations: Small school fact sheet*. Las Cruces, NM: ERIC Clearinghouse on Rural Education and Small Schools.

Dornseif, A. (1996). *A pocket guide to school-based management. Number 2: Improving council meetings*. Alexandria, VA: Association for Supervision and Curriculum Development.

Dornseif, A. (1996). *A pocket guide to school-based management. Number 3: Honing communication skills*. Alexandria, VA: Association for Supervision and Curriculum Development.

Dornseif, A. (1996). *A pocket guide to school-based management. Number 7: Succeeding at teamwork*. Alexandria, VA: Association for Supervision and Curriculum Development.

Dornseif, A. (1996). *A pocket guide to school-based management. Number 8: Planning for quality*. Alexandria, VA: Association for Supervision and Curriculum Development.

Education Update. (1995). *Teachers as researchers*, 37(3). Alexandria, VA: Association for Supervision and Curriculum Development.

Epstein, J. (1986). Parents' reactions to teacher practices of parent involvement. *The Elementary School Journal*, 86(3), 277-293.

Epstein, J. (1987). Parent involvement: What research says to administrators. *Education & Urban Society*, 2, 119-136.

Epstein, J. (1991). Pathways to partnerships: What we can learn from federal, state, district, and school initiatives. *Phi Delta Kappan*, 72(5), 344-349.

Epstein, J. L. (1994). Theory to practice: School and family partnerships lead to school improvement and student success. In C. L. Fagnano & B.Z. Werber (Eds.) *School, family, and community interaction: A view from the firing lines* (pp. 39-52). Boulder: Westview Press.

Epstein, J. (1995). School/family/community partnerships: Caring for the children we share. *Phi Delta Kappan*, 76(9), 701-712.

Fagnano, C. L., & Werber, B.Z. (Eds.) (1994). *School, family, and community interaction: A view from the firing lines*. Boulder: Westview Press.

Fantini, M. (1975). *The people and their schools: Community participation*. Fastback 62. Bloomington, IN.: Phi Delta Kappa Educational Foundation.

Finder, M. (1992). Looking at lives through ethnography. *Educational Leadership*, 50(1), 60-65.

Finney, P. (1993). The PTA/Newsweek national education survey. *Newsweek*. May 17.

Fredericks, A.D., & Rasinski, T.V. (1990). Working with parents: Involving the uninvolved. *The Reading Teacher*, 43(6), 424-425.

Fullan, M.G. (1991). *The new meaning of educational change*. New York, NY: Teachers College Press.

Garbarino, J., Dubrow, N., Kostelny, K., & Pardo, C. (1992). *Children in danger: Coping with the consequences of community violence*. San Francisco: Jossey-Bass Publishers.

Garcia, P. (October, 1994). Creating a safe school climate. *Thrust for Educational Leadership*, 22-24.

Gardner, J. W. (Fall, 1989). Building Community. *The Kettering Review*, Robert J. Kingston, Ed.

Garfield, C. (1986). *Peak performers: The new heroes of American business*. New York, NY: Avon Books.

Garmston, R.J. (1994) The listening presenter. *Journal of Staff Development*, 15(3), 61-62.

Glasser, W. (1986). *Control theory in the classroom*. New York: Harper and Row.

Good, T. L., & Brophy, J. E. (1987). *Looking in classrooms* (4th ed.). New York: Harper and Row.

Gotts, E. E., & Purnell, R. F. (1985). *Improving home-school communications*. Fastback 230. Bloomington, IN.: Phi Delta Kappa Educational Foundation.

Grolnick, W.S., & Ryan, R. (1992). Parental resources and the developing child in school. In M. Procidano & C. Fisher (Eds.) *Contemporary families: A handbook for school professionals*. New York, NY: Teachers College Press.

Guskey, T.R. (1996). *Communicating student learning*. Alexandria, VA: Association for Supervision and Curriculum Development.

Guthrie, L.F. (1995). *How to coordinate services for students and families*. Alexandria, VA: Association of Supervision and Curriculum Development.

Hammond, W. R., & Yung, B. (1993). Psychology's role in public health response to assultive violence among young African-American men. *American Psychologist*, 48, 142- 4.

Huang, G. (1993). *Beyond culture: Communicating with Asian American children*. New York, NY: ERIC Clearinghouse of Unban Education.

Hean, L.L., & Tin, L.Q. (1996). Winning students back from McDonald's. *Educational Leadership*, 54(1), 70-72.

Henderson, A. T. (date unknown). *Unpublished materials for Building home-school partnerships for learning workshops for urban educators (pilot version)*. Washington, DC: U.S. Department of Education, Office of Educational Research and Improvement.

Henderson, A., & Berla, N. (1994). *A new generation of evidence: The family is critical to student achievement*. Flint, MI: Danforth Foundation.

Hinkle, J.S. (1992). *Family counseling in the schools*. Ann Arbor, MI: ERIC Clearinghouse on Counseling and Personnel Services.

Hughes, M., Wikeley, F., & Nash, T. (1994). *Parents and their children's schools*. Oxford, U.K.: Blackwell Publishers.

Jesse, D. (1996). Increasing parental involvement: A key to student achievement. Internet Download: McREL.

Johnson, D. W. (1993). Reaching out: *Interpersonal effectiveness and self-actualization*. Needham Heights, MA: Allyn & Bacon.

Johnson, D. W., & Johnson, R. (1995). *Reducing school violence through conflict resolution*. Alexandria, VA: Association for Supervision and Curriculum Development.

Johnson, D. W., Johnson, R.T., Holubec, E. J., & Roy, P. (1984). *Circles of learning: Cooperation in the classroom*. Alexandria, VA: Association of Supervision and Curriculum Development.

Jones, L. (1991). *Strategies for involving parents in their children's education*. Fastback 315. Bloomington, IN: Phi Delta Kappa Educational Foundation.

Jones, R. A. (1995). *The child-school interface*. London, U.K., New York, NY: Cassell.

Kaplan, L. (1992). *Education and the family*. Needham Heights: Allyn & Bacon.

Kelley, M. L. (1990). *School-home notes*. New York: The Guilford Press.

Kline, P., & Saunders, B. (1993). *Ten steps to a learning organization*. Arlington, VA: Great Ocean Publishers.

Knowles, M.S. (1978). *The adult learner: A neglected species*. Houston: Gould Publishing.

Kirby, G., & Goodpaster, J. R. (1995). Creative thinking. In *Thinking* (pp. 99-110). Englewood Cliffs, NJ: Prentice Hall.

Kohn, A. (1996). *Beyond discipline from compliance to community*. Alexandria, VA: Association for Supervision and Curriculum Development.

Lantieri, L., & Patti, J. (1996) The road to peace in our schools. *Educational Leadership*, 54(1), 28-31.

Liben, L. (Ed.). (1987). *Development & learning: Conflict or congruence*. Hillsdale, N J: Lawrence Erlbaum Associates, Publishers.

Lickona, T., Shaps, E. & Lewis, C. (date unknown). *Eleven principles of effective character education*. The Charter Education Partnership.

Lindle, J.C. (1989). What do parents want from principals and teachers? *Educational Leadership*, 47(2), 12-14.

Liontos, L. B. (1992). *At-risk families and schools: Becoming partners*. Eugene, OR: ERIC Clearinghouse on Educational Management, College of Education, University of Oregon.

Liontos, L. B. (1994). *How can I be involved in my child's education?* Eugene, OR: ERIC Clearinghouse on Educational Management. America Online Download.

Litke, C. (1996). When violence came to our rural school. *Educational Leadership*, 54(1), 77-80.

Louis Harris and Associates. (1987). *The Metropolitan Life survey of the American teacher: Strengthening links between home and school*. New York: Author.

Louis Harris and Associates. (1993). *The Metropolitan Life survey of the American teacher 1993: Violence in American Public schools*. New York: Author.

Lutz, F. W., & Merz, C. (1992). *The politics of school/community relations*. New York, NY: Teachers College Press.

Maeroff, G. I. (1993). *Team building for school change: Equipping teachers for new roles*. New York: Teachers College Press.

Marzano, R. J., Pickering, D.J., Arredondo, D.E., Blackburn, G.J., Brandt, R. S., & Moffett,

C.A. (1992). *Dimensions of learning: Teacher manual.* Alexandria, VA: Association for Supervision and Curriculum Development.

Mastors, C. (1975). *School volunteers: Who needs them?* Fastback 55. Bloomington, IN: Phi Delta Kappa Educational Foundation.

McAfee, O. (1984). *Improving school-home communications: A resource notebook for staff developers.* Charleston, WVA: Appalachia Educational Laboratory.

McAfee, O. (1993). The potential of communications technology. In R. C. Burns (Ed.) *Parents and schools: From visitors to partners.* Washington, DC: National Education Association.

McCarthy, C. (1992). Why we must teach peace. *Educational Leadership,* 50(1), 6-9.

McGee, K. (1996). One family at a time. *Educational Leadership,* 53(7), 30-33.

Moles, O. C. (1996). *Reaching all families: Creating family-friendly schools.* Washington, DC: Office of Educational Research and Improvement, U. S. Department of Education.

Molnar, A. (1992). Too many kids are getting killed. *Educational Leadership,* 50(1), 4-5.

Moore, E.K. (1991). Improving schools through parental involvement. *Principal,* 71(1), 17-20.

Morrison, R., Furlong, M., & Morrison, G. (October, 1994). Knocking the wheels off the school violence bandwagon. *Thrust for Educational Leadership,* 6-9.

Munn, P. (Ed.). (1993). *Parents and schools: Customers, managers or partners?* London, UK: Routledge.

National Association of Secondary School Principals. (1996). *Breaking ranks: Changing an American institution.* Reston, VA: National Association of Secondary School Principals.

National Commission on Children. (1991). *Speaking of kids: A national survey of children and parents.* Washington, DC: Author.

National Committee for Citizens in Education. (1995). *Parent Involvement at the Middle School Level.* ACCESS ERIC-funding from the Office of Educational Research and Improvement, U.S. Department of Education. Transmitted 5/15/95 America Online.

Nowak, S.J. (1994). New roles and challenges for staff development. *Journal of Staff Development,* 15(3), 10-12.

O'Callaghan. J. B. (1993). *School-based collaboration with families.* San Francisco, CA: Jossey-Bass Publishers.

Partnership for Family Involvement in Education. (date unknown). *Better education is everybody's business! How business can support family involvement in education.* Washington, DC: Department of Education.

Paulu, N. (1996). *Helping your child with homework.* Washington, DC: Office of Educational Research and Improvement, U.S. Department of Education.

Perry, N. (1993). School reform: Big pain, little gain. *Fortune.* 128, November 29, 130-138.

Rich, D. (1987). *Teachers and parents: An adult-to-adult approach.* Washington, DC: National Education Association.

Rigsby, L., Reynolds, M., & Wang, M. (1995). *School-community connections.* San Francisco: Jossey-Bass Publishers.

Rutherford, R. B., Jr., & Edgar, E. (1979). *Teachers and parents: A guide to interaction and cooperation.* Boston: Allyn & Bacon, Inc.

Sagor, R. (1996). Building resiliency in students. *Educational Leadership,* 54(1), 38-43.

Saldem, M. (1992). *Social climate in the classroom*. New York, NY: Waxmann Munster.

Sanders, M.G. (1996). Building family partnerships that last. *Educational Leadership*, 54(3), 61-66.

Sanders, T. (1990). Parent involvement: An imperative for the 90s. *School Safety*, 8-13.

Saphier, J., Bigda-Peyton, T., & Pierson, G. (1989). *How to make decisions that stay made*. Alexandria, VA: Association for Supervision and Curriculum Development.

Schein, E. (1993). On dialogue, culture, and organizational learning. *Organizational Dynamics*.

Schmuck, R. A., & Runkel, P. J. (1985). *The handbook of organization development in schools*. Prospect Heights, IL: Waveland Press, Inc.

Schmuck, R.A., & Schmuck, P. A. (1975) *Group processes in the classroom* (2nd Ed.). Dubuque, IA: Wm. C. Brown Company Publishers.

Schneider, B., & Coleman, J. (Eds). (1993). *Parents, their children, and schools*. Boulder, CO: Westview Press, Inc.

Schuur, S.L. (1992). Fine tuning your parent power: Increasing student achievement. *Schools in the Middle*, 2(2), 3-9.

Scott-Jones, D. (1994) African American families and schools: Toward mutually supportive relationships. In C. L. Fagnano & B.Z. Werber (Eds.) *School, family, and community interaction: A view from the firing lines* (pp. 75-83). Boulder: Westview Press.

Senge, P., Robert, C., Ross, R. , Smith, B., & Kleiner, A. (1994). *The fifth discipline fieldbook: Strategies and tools for building a learning organization*. New York: Currency, Doubleday.

Slavin, R. E. (1991). Synthesis of research on cooperative learning. *Educational Leadership*, 48(5), 71-83.

Stipek, D. J. (1986). Children's motivation to learn. In T. M. Tomlinson & H. J. Walberg (Eds.) *Academic work and educational excellence: Raising student productivity* (pp. 197-221). Berkeley, CA: McCutchan.

Strickland, C.S. (1995). Partnershp is essential: How the Whole Village Project is making a difference in five schools. *New Schools, New Comminities*, 11(2), 4-13.

Swap, S. (1993). *Developing home-school partnerships: From concepts to prac e*. New York: Teachers College Press.

Swick, K. (1984). *Inviting parents into the young child's world*. Champaign, IL: Stipes Publishing Company.

Thousand, J.S., Villa, R.A., & Nevin, A.I. (1994). *Creativity and collaborative learning: A practical guide to empowering students and teachers*. Baltimore, MD: Paul H. Brookes Publishing Company.

U.S. Department of Education. (1994). *Strong families, strong schools: Building community partnerships for learning* (ED Publication No. 1994-381-888). Washington, DC: U.S. Government Printing Office.

Vaden-Kiernan, N. (1996). *Parents' reports of school practices to involve families*. Washington, DC: U.S. Department of Education, Office of Educational Research and Improvement.

Vandergrift, J. A., & Greene, A. L. (1992). Rethinking parent involvement, *Educational Leadership*, 50(1) 57-59.

Vigil, J. (1988). *Barrio gangs: Street life and identity in Southern California.* Austin: University of Texas Press.

Vivros, V. (1995). Presentation of adult learning to Loudon County Schools. (Unpublished documents) Loudon County, TN.

Wang, M.C, Haertel, G.D., & Walberg, H.J. (1993). Toward a knowledge base for school learning. *Review of Educational Research,* 63,3.

Weber, B.J., & Omotani, L.M. (September, 1994). The power of believing. *The Executive Educator,* 35-38.

Weisz, E. (1990). Developing positive staff-parent partnerships in high schools. *American Secondary Education,* 19(1), 25-28.

White, G. P., & Matz, C. (Summer, 1992). Parents as true partners in middle level education. *Schools in the Middle.* Reston, VA: National Association of Secondary School Principals.

Wiggins, G. (1994). Toward better report cards. *Educational Leadership,* 52(2), 28-37.

Winter, M. (1994). Parent networks strengthen communities. *Children Today,* 23(1), 12-13.

Wolfendale, S. (1992). *Empowering parents and teachers: Working for children.* New York: Cassell.

Yao, E.L. (1988). Working effectively with Asian immigrant parents. *Phi Delta Kappan,* 70(3), 223-225.

Youngs, B.B. (November, 1989), *Keynote address.* National Council of the States for Inservice Education. San Antonio, TX.

Ziegler, E., & Styfco, S. (Eds.) (1993). *Head Start and beyond.* New Haven, CN: Yale University Press.

Index

Action research, 68, 307
   problem solving, 68
Adult learners, 402-413
Alternative report cards, 199-201
Answering devices, 168
Atmosphere, 71-73, 76-79
Automated dialing devices, 168

Barriers, 7-10, 146,147, 211, 212, 342, 343
Behavior management, 116,118-123
Beliefs, 292
Brainstorming, 40, 52,
Business partnerships, 5, 262-264

Calendars, 165
Can do attitudes, 311, 314-316
Challenge identification, 53
Character development, 110-115
Climate, 73, 76-82, 85 ,86, 89-92, 94, 96 ,98, 116-118, 132-133
Collaboration, 1, 2 5, 6, 11, 12, 14, 17 19, 21, 39-44, 47, 48, 90, 119-121
   guidelines, 49-51
   pitfalls, 47,48
Communication, 12, 13, 17, 24, 25, 28, 79-82, 111-113, 120, 141, 143-145, 296
   barriers, 146, 147
   checklist, 161, 162, 183, 184
   dialogue, 146-148, 154
   effective practices, 174-209
   forms, 167,172
   interpersonal, 146, 147, 155, 183, 184, 190, 191
   ladders of inference, 148, 151-153
   mental models, 147

   multicultural, 156, 157
   parent-teacher conference, 174-191
   perceptual filters, 147, 150
   public relations, 203-209
   questionnaire, 176-179
   reporting student progress, 192-202
   telephone, 164, 169-171
   web, 169-171
Community, 3, 6, 11-14, 16, 22
Conflict resolution, 18, 116, 117, 124-131
Contracts, 120, 122, 123, 352
Creative thinking, 18, 19, 21, 41, 64-67

Data analysis, 284,285
Data collection, 281-283
Data portrayal, 284
Decision making, 15, 17, 19, 21, 39 41, 56-60, 69, 298,299
Dialogue, 146-148, 154
Dimensions of learning, 57-59
Discipline, 116, 118-123
Discrepancy analysis, 40, 280
Diversity, 6, 13, 102-106, 156, 157

E-mail, 167
Educator reflection, 21, 75, 145, 214, 227, 331, 379, 380
Effective practices, 158-209
Effective schools, 1, 5
Efficacy, 7
Expectations, 10, 13, 14, 26, 29, 116, 119, 273-326

Facilitator guidelines, 40, 44-46
Family centered school, 73

Focus group, 17, 22, 23, 40, 196
Future trends, 286

Gathering perceptions, 11, 16, 17, 19, 21, 22
Goals, 306
Goal setting, 13, 126, 312, 317-322
Guidelines for
    adult learning, 402-405, 409
    business partnerships, 262, 263
    collaboration, 49-51
    crisis intervention, 267
    developing life long learners, 400, 401
    facilitators, 40, 44-46
    helping parents reinforce social behaviors, 114
    holiday celebration, 229
    home visits, 243, 244
    homework, policy, 391, 392
    involvement, 332, 333
    parent center, 248, 249
    participation, 40, 44
    productive meetings, 366, 367
    recognition, 268-271
    retreats, 245-247
    social agency contracts, 261
    social behaviors, 114
    team building, 370, 371
    teamwork, 360, 361
    transitions, 250, 251
    trust and respect, 107, 108
    volunteers, 339-341

Hard to reach parents, 30, 84, 225, 232, 332, 333
High expectations, 311
Holiday celebrations, 229
Home pages, 167
Home visits 241-244
Homework, 15, 389-394

Idea groups, 307
Instructional innovations, 15, 375-377, 379-386
Interpersonal communication, 146, 147, 155, 183, 184, 190, 191
Interview, 17, 22-24, 30
Involvement, 5-7, 14, 15, 27, 29, 327-329, 331-333

Ladder of inference, 148, 151-153
Leadership, 6, 19
Learning expectations, 311, 313
Learning organizations, 3
Lesson lines, 168
Lifelong learning, 16, 399-401
Long range planning, 300-310

Media support, 209
Mental models, 147
Mission, 287, 290, 291, 306
Multicultural, 6, 13, 102-106, 156, 157

Needs assessment, 278-286
Networking, 259, 260
Newsletters, 165
Nontraditional families, 7
Notes home, 164

Open house, 226, 227
Opportunities for parental involvement, 332, 333, 335-338
Opportunity identification, 53, 307
Outdoor signs, 166

Parent academy/parent training sessions, 120
Parent center, 248, 249
Parent handbook, 163
Parent information and interest inventory, 237-239
Parent involvement, 1, 3, 5-7, 14, 15, 27, 29, 174-191, 327-374
    contract, 337
    increasing opportunities, 332, 333, 335-338
    roles, 335, 336
    types, 334
Parent involvement barriers, 7, 8-10
Parent involvement research, 3, 4
Parent talent book, 340, 347
Parent-teacher conference, 174-191
    details, 182
    effectiveness, 176-179, 183, 184
    follow up, 187, 188
    schedule, 180, 181
    student-led, 189
    teacher worksheet, 185, 186
    worksheet, 190, 191
Parent visits, 240
Parenting skills, 16
Participation guidelines, 40-44
Partnership assumptions, 5-7
Partnership barriers, 7
Partnership components, 1, 11-16
Partnerships, 1-3, 15-17, 39
Peer pressure, 132-135
Perceptual filters, 147, 150
Performances, 228
Planning, 6, 22, 26, 39, 90, 116, 130
Planning guide, 308
Prioritizing, 40, 41, 53-55
Problem solving, 17, 19, 21, 39-41, 61-63, 65, 66, 69, 126
Public relations, 73, 78, 203-205

media support, 209
school pride, 206, 207
student ambassadors, 208

Quality of school life, 3
Questionnaire, 17, 22, 87, 88, 92, 94, 96, 98, 104, 109, 139, 161, 162, 176-179, 183, 184, 295, 309, 310, 323-326, 342, 396, 396

Recognition, 268-271, 358
Recruiting poster, 348
Reinforcing social skills guidelines, 114
Relationships, 3, 13, 26, 28, 30, 80-82, 85-88, 117, 127, 211-271
    barriers, 211, 212
    connecting strategies, 234-255
    developing and maintaining, 256-271
    effective practices 216-271
    evaluating current practices, 216-219, 233
    formal event strategies, 226-229
    getting acquainted strategies, 220-223
    hard to reach parents, 225, 232
    informal event strategies, 224, 225
    recognition strategies, 268-271
    school as hub of community, 265, 266
    school visits, 224
    shared responsibilities, 213
    traditions, 230, 231
Reporting progress, 192-202
    methods, 192
    purposes, 193
    redesigning, 193-202
Retreat, 245-247
Reverse/interactive report card, 202
Role models, 326

School environment, 7, 12, 25, 28, 71, 73, 75-78, 85-88, 116,-118, 128, 139, 140, 275
School improvement, 2, 3, 18, 22
School pride, 206, 207
School visits, 224
Scout groups, 307
Self esteem, 132, 134, 136, 325
Shared expectations, 273-326
    establishing vision, 287-299
    long range planning 300-310
    needs assessment, 278-286
Shared responsibilities, 2, 3, 6, 11, 19, 73, 143, 275, 297, 329, 377
Social skills, 91, 110-115
Student achievement, 4, 13-15, 72
Student ambassadors, 208
Student involvement, 338
Student needs, 278-282

Study groups, 307
Study habits, 395, 396
Suggestion box, 166
Survey, 1, 16, 17, 19, 22-30

Teaching and learning, 375-413
    additional support, 397, 398
    adult learners, 402-413
    evaluation, 413
    identifying needs and interests, 407, 408, 412
    lesson plan, 410, 411
    topics of interest, 406
    business support, 387, 388
    classroom visits, 383-386
    conditions to support, 375, 376
    generating support, 381, 382
    home support, 389, 390
    lifelong learners, 399-401
Teamwork, 359-374
    developing teams, 360, 361
    evaluation, 372-374
    productive meetings, 366, 367
    roles and responsibilities, 363, 365
    stages of teams, 368, 369
    team behaviors, 364
    team building strategies, 370, 371
    team membership, 362
Telephone communications, 164
    communications web, 169-171
Traditions, 230, 231
Transition strategies, 250-255
Trust and respect guidelines, 107, 108

Videos, 167
Violence prevention, 12, 71, 116, 117, 139
Vision, 3, 26, 273, 287-299, 306
Volunteer coordinator, 346
Volunteer programs, 327-329, 339-358
    barriers, 342, 343
    contract, 352
    formative evaluation forms, 354, 355
    forms, 349, 350
    orientation and training agenda, 351
    overcoming barriers, 342-355
    parent talent book, 340, 347
    quality control, 353
    recruiting poster, 348
    roles and responsibilities, 340, 351
    steps in developing, 339-341
    summative evaluation forms, 356, 357
    volunteer coordinator, 346
    ways to recognize, 358

Web, 169-171